THE GREAT
SCIENCE FICTION
PICTURES

by
JAMES ROBERT PARISH
and
MICHAEL R. PITTS

Research Associates:
Stephen Calvert, John Robert Cocchi,
Florence Solomon & Vincent Terrace

The Scarecrow Press, Inc.
Metuchen, N.J. 1977

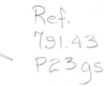

Library of Congress Cataloging in Publication Data

Parish, James Robert.
   The great science fiction pictures.

   Bibliography: p.
   1. Science fiction films--Catalogs.   I.   Pitts,
Michael R., joint author. II. Title.
PN1995.9.S26P37   016.79143'7   77-5426
ISBN 0-8108-1029-8

To the Memory of

RICHARD ARLEN

1898 - 1976

TABLE OF CONTENTS

Authors' Note and Acknowledgments   vii

The Great Science Fiction Pictures   1

Science Fiction Shows on Radio and Television,
    compiled by Vincent Terrace   367

A Select Bibliography of Science Fiction
    Bibliographies, Indexes and Checklists,
    by Stephen Calvert   377

About the Authors and Staff   381

AUTHORS NOTE and ACKNOWLEDGMENTS

More so than other film genre, science fiction pictures have concentrated on stimulating the viewer's imagination with new concepts. These futuristic theories usually deal with man's hopes and fears for the fate of civilization on Earth and what lies beyond in Outer Space. Often these hypotheses are founded in sound scientific documentation and socio-political studies. But it is the films' capacity to stress the unusual and unknown that provides the general appeal of the genre. On the filmmaker's part there is the creative challenge or escape (as the case may be) of providing a plot structure with no need for conformity--for who can rightfully argue with what is beyond man's actual present knowledge?

More so than with the other books in this series, the authors have realized the necessity of including not only the BEST science fiction pictures but some of the far lesser ones (the WORST by some critics' standards), in order to present a fair spectrum of the species. Then too, frequently sci-fi motion pictures blend into other cinema categories: the horror/monster realm and the world of the fantastic. We have attempted to avoid including those films which are not primarily science fiction.

Naturally the authors would appreciate communication from readers regarding their reactions to this volume.

Grateful acknowledgment of their helpfulness is given to Thomas Boren, King Donovan, Morris Everett, Jr., Film Favorites (Charles Smith), Filmfacts, Films in Review, Pierre Guinle, Ken D. Jones, William T. Leonard, Doug McClelland, Alvin H. Marill, Norman Miller, Movie Poster Service (Bob Smith), Screen Facts (Alan G. Barbour), Don Shay, Mrs. Peter Smith, T. Allan Taylor, and John S. Vasconi.

James Robert Parish   Michael R. Pitts
225 E. 70th Street No. 2F   2505 East 10th Street #E-31
New York City, N.Y.   10021   Anderson, Indiana   46012

"After all man could do had failed, the
Martians were destroyed by the littlest
things that God in his wisdom had put
on the Earth!"

--Cedric Hardwicke,
   in The War of the Worlds (1953)

THE GREAT SCIENCE FICTION PICTURES

A LA CONQUETE DU POLE (CONQUEST OF THE NORTH POLE)
(Star, 1912)   20 min.

Producer/director, Georges Méliès.

Toward the end of his prolific career in film production,
Frenchman Georges Méliés (1861-1936), the master of screen magic
and the father of the science fiction film, produced this fine little
twenty-minute epic. It may have been a rehash of some of his earlier celluloid work but it was, nevertheless, a well-made achievement in the art of screen fantasy.
     Like so many of Méliès' subjects, the film delved into an
area of public fascination, but one that was little known--the Arctic.
Air flight was still in its infancy at this time (as were the movies),
and the story revolved around Professor Maboul, an engineer who
has invented an aircraft called the Acrobus which takes the expedition
to the North Pole. The flight takes place through the stars and back
to Earth for the polar expedition. Along the way a giant snow monster devours one of the expedition's crew members. Such macabre
touches were quite uncommon in the fantasy films of Georges Méliès.
     Unfortunately, Méliès regarded the cinema as only a toy.
After his inventions had been displayed on camera, he was unable to
expand the scope of his work and he soon faded into obscurity. Perhaps it was not all his fault. Quickly changing times, and not the
artist, made his work passé. Denis Gifford says in Science Fiction
Film (1971), "The real war [World War I] brought rapid advances in
aviation, and flights of fancy became rare birds."

ABBOTT AND COSTELLO GO TO MARS   (Universal, 1953)   77 min.

Producer, Howard Christie; director, Charles Lamont; story,
Christie and D. D. Beauchamp; screenplay, John Grant and D. D.
Beauchamp; art directors, Alexander Golitzen and Robert Boyle; mu-
sic director, Joseph Gershenson; special camera effects, David S.
Horsley; camera, Clifford Stine; editor, Russell Schoengarth.
     Bud Abbott (Lester); Lou Costello (Orville); Robert Paige (Dr.
Wilson); Mari Blanchard (Allura); Martha Hyer (Janie); Horace Mc-
Mahon (Mugsy); Jack Tesler (Dr. Holtz); Hal Forrest (Dr. Nedring);
Harold Goodwin (Dr. Coleman); Joe Kirk (Dr. Orville); Jack Kru-
schen (Harry); Jean Willes (Captain); and the Miss Universe Beauties.

Even the title is misleading in these hastily-assembled shenanigans. Lester (Abbott) and Orville (Costello) find themselves locked in a space rocket which makes an unscheduled launching. The craft zooms through New York's Holland Tunnel and then off into space. Later, the boys think they have landed on Mars, but in actuality they have set down in New Orleans during Mardi Gras season. Thereafter they become involved with two escaped convicts (McMahon and Kruschen) who at gunpoint force the duo to relaunch the ship. This time they land on Venus where roly-poly Orville is made King--until he romances too many girls and annoys the ruler, Allura (Blanchard). Eventually they make their way back to Earth where they are proclaimed heroes.

Universal used the public enthusiasm for science fiction pictures (this was during the heavy craze of such features in the early Fifties) as a backdrop for yet another go-round of Abbott and Costello pratfalls, slapstick, and gags. The guffaws are rather minimal in this basic effort. Like many another film of this decade, it depicted outer space beings as very shapely females (especially Blanchard and Hyer).

THE ABSENT-MINDED PROFESSOR   (Buena Vista, 1961) 97 min.

Producer, Walt Disney; associate producer, Bill Walsh; director, Robert Stevenson; story, Samuel W. Taylor; screenplay, Walsh; art director, Carroll Clark; assistant director, Robert G. Shannon; music, George Bruns; sound, Dean Thomas; special camera effects, Peter Ellenshaw and Eustace Lycett; camera, Edward Colman; editor, Cotton Warburton.

Fred MacMurray (Professor Ned Brainard); Nancy Olson (Betsy Carlisle); Keenan Wynn (Alonzo Hawk); Tommy Kirk (Bill Hawk); Ed Wynn (Fire Chief); Leon Ames (President Rufus Daggett); Elliott Reid (Shelby Ashton); Edward Andrews (Defense Secretary); David Lewis (General Singer); Jack Mullaney (Air Force Captain); Belle Montrose (Mrs. Chatsworth); Wally Brown (Coach Elkins); Alan Carney (Referee); Raymond Bailey (Admiral Olmstead); Wendell Holmes (General Poynter); Wally Boag (TV Newsman); Forrest Lewis (Officer Kelly); Alan Hewitt (General Hotchkiss).

Fantasy has always played a large part in the works of Walt Disney. The Absent-Minded Professor presented a comical blend of sci-fi (a substance called "flubber" which caused things to float effortlessly) and lunacy which proved to be exceedingly popular at the box-office in the Sixties. Time labeled this "The season's kookiest science-fiction farce," and the picture grossed $11,110,000 in distributors' domestic rentals.

The film breathed new life into the movie career of Fred MacMurray who starred as Professor Ned Brainard, a rather goofy college science professor who accidentally concocts a formula for "flubber." Engrossed by his discovery, he misses his third scheduled wedding, to Betsy Carlisle (Nancy Olson), who now snubs him for rival Shelby Ashton (Elliott Reid), the latter taking her to the

big basketball game.   There the home team is being overwhelmed
until the prof attaches flubber to their shoes.   As a result they score
a resounding victory.   When Brainard "flies" home in his Model T,
which has been flubberized, corrupt Alonzo Hawk spots the machine
and later steals it, making Brainard look like a fool when government officials come to see his discovery and find a substituted Model
T that won't fly.   Betsy, however, now feels sorry for Ned and they
are re-united and work together to retrieve the real car from Hawk.
In it, they fly to Washington where they are regarded as an Unidentified Flying Object.   All works out in the end however; Ned is proclaimed a hero and he and Betsy marry.

In typical Disney fashion, The Absent-Minded Professor was
a well-constructed film geared to amuse the kiddies and not to offend adults.   Although slight of plot it was visually pleasing (especially for its live-action material on flying cars and floating basketball players).   It boasted professional performances from the leads
as well as pleasing cameos from the supporting cast, including Ed
Wynn (repeating his famous "The Fire Chief" role), Leon Ames,
Edward Andrews, and the once popular comedy team of Alan Carney
and Wally Brown.

The media also approved of the film.   The New York Times
noted, "it is remarkably bouncy entertainment.   What is more, it
is absolutely clean. "   Variety commented, "Deeply rooted within the
screenplay is a subtle protest against the detached, impersonal machinery of modern progress.   It is an underlying theme with which
an audience can identify. "

Two years after the film was issued most of the cast members repeated their assignments in the sequel, Son of Flubber, which
was not up to the original but grossed a hefty $9 million in U. S.
and Canadian distributors' rentals.

THE ADVENTURES OF CAPTAIN MARVEL   (Republic, 1941)   twelve
chapters

Associate producer, Hiram S. Brown, Jr. ; directors, William
Witney and John English; based on the character appearing in Whiz
comics; screenplay, Sol Short, Ronald Davidson, Norman S. Hall,
Joseph Poland, and Arch B. Heath; music, Cy Feuer; special effects,
Howard Lydecker; camera, William Nobles.

Tom Tyler (Captain Marvel); Frank Coghlan, Jr. (Billy Bat-
son); William Benedict (Murphy); Louise Currie (Betty Wallace); "?"
(The Scorpion); Robert Strange (John Malcolm); Harry Worth (Pro-
fessor Bentley); Bryant Washburn (Henry Carlyle); John Davidson (Tal
Chotali); George Pembroke (Dr. Stephen Lang); Peter George Lynn
(Dwight Fisher); Reed Hadley (Rahman Bar); Jack Mulhall (Howell);
Kenneth Duncan (Barnett); Nigel de Brulier (Shazam); John Bagni
(Cowan); Carleton Young (Martin); Leland Hodgson (Major Rawley);
Stanley Price (Owens); Ernest Sarracino (Akbar); Tetsu Komai (Chan
Lai).

Chapters: 1) Curse of the Scorpion; 2) The Guillotine;
3) Time Bomb; 4) Death Takes the Wheel; 5) The Scorpion Strikes;
6) Lens of Death; 7) Human Targets; 8) Boomerang; 9) Dead Man's

Trap; 10) Doom Ship; 11) Valley of Death; 12) Captain Marvel's Secret.

Superheroes were always good fodder for the Saturday matinee
trade, especially in serials, the one domain of the cinema where sci-
fi had always had a good foothold. It seemed anything was permis-
sible, no matter how "far out." In the early silent pictures, all
kinds of ray machines and robot monsters inhabited the plots; with
the coming of sound, various comic book heroes began to appear in
chapterplays. In 1941 Republic Pictures produced this cliffhanger
based on the character which had been introduced the year before in
Whiz comics.

Jim Harmon and Donald F. Glut noted in their book The Great
Movie Serials: Their Sound and Fury (1972), "This serial had time
for plot and characterization, as well as action. The result was what
may well be the world's mightiest movie serial."

The late Thirties and early Forties were the golden years of
Republic's serials and it was in this time period that the studio produced the finest chapterplays ever made in Hollywood. No doubt the
tandem directing team of William Witney and John English--astute
veterans at this genre--had a good deal to do with the quality of this
entry, as did its well written scenario (considering the competition)
and fine musical score (by Cy Feuer, later the Broadway producer).
An excellent cast, headed by virile Tom Tyler in the title role, added
greatly to the production's authenticity, as did the superior stunt work
by David Sharpe and the intriguing special effects conceived by Howard Lydecker.

The chapterplay opens in Siam where a scientific group
searches for knowledge of the ancient Scorpion Dynasty. While the
expedition is in a hidden cave, a young radio operator, Billy Batson
(Frank Coghlan, Jr.) is given the secret for becoming the mighty
Captain Marvel (Tom Tyler), by saying the word "Shazam." In the
holy temple, the scientists find a powerful golden weapon powered by
five lenses. Each takes a lens so as not to allow the weapon's power to be unleashed on an unsuspecting world. Meanwhile, the group's
secretary (Louise Currie) nearly meets her death when the expedition
is forced to battle hostile tribesmen, but she is saved by Captain
Marvel. Back in America, gangsters supervised in their scheme by
the "Scorpion," attempt to corral all the lenses. After various in-
cidents, which include the capture and rescue of Betty (Currie), the Scorpion captures both Betty and Billy Batson. Now having all the lenses,
he plans to set the weapon into operation. When the gang leader,
however, removes the gag from Billy's mouth in order to learn the
secret of Captain Marvel, the boy says "Shazam" and Marvel saves
the girl again. He turns the ray on the Scorpion, who is revealed as one
of the leaders of the expedition. With the Scorpion dead, peace
reigns again.

The serial would be re-issued in 1953 as Return of Captain
Marvel.

THE AIRSHIP, OR ONE HUNDRED YEARS HENCE see ONE HUN-
DRED YEARS AFTER

ALPHAVILLE: UNE ETRANGE AVENTURE DE LEMMY CAUTION
(Athos-Film, 1965) 100 min.

Producer, Andre Michelin; director/screenplay, Jean-Luc
Godard; assistant directors, Charles Bitsch, Jean-Paul Savignac, and
Hélène Kalouguine; music, Paul Misraki; sound, René Levert; cam-
era, Raoul Courard; editor, Agnes Guillemot.

Eddie Constantine (Lemmy Caution); Anna Karina (Natacha von
Braun); Akim Tamiroff (Henry Dickson); Howard Vernon (Professor
Leonard Nosferatu); Laszlo Szabo (Chief of Engineer); Michel Dela-
haye (Von Braun's Assistant); Jean-Louis Comolli (Professor Jeckell);
Alpha 60 (Itself).

Espionage and its mechanisms occurred thousands of years ago
and will undoubtedly be part of the human scene millenia hence. Secret agent Lemmy Caution (Eddie Constantine) journeys into the world
of tomorrow to the sterile, computerized metropolis of Alphaville.
His mission is to discover what happened to agent Henry Dickson
(Akim Tamiroff) and to Professor Leonard Nosferatu (Howard
Vernon). In his trek through the murky city controlled by the Alpha
60 computer he meets a beguiling young woman, Natacha von Braun
(Anna Karina), with whom he falls in love. Finally he short-circuits
the all-knowing computer and with Natacha at his side, "drives" out
of the destroyed Alphaville back to the "outer countries."
        Alphaville can be enjoyed on many levels. As a blend of a
George Raft-type underworld thriller and science fiction, the movie
offers engrossing contradictions, correlations, and observations. As
a celluloid exercise by New Wave leader Jean-Luc Godard it is a
sterling example of French filmmaking. The ultimate message of
this pre-2001: A Space Odyssey (q.v.) futuristic spy drama is that
mankind must continue to rule its own destiny, no matter how base
or banal the individual human being may be.

ALRAUNE (Luna-Film, 1918)

        Based on the novel by Hanns Heinz Ewers.

ALRAUNE (Phoenix, 1918)

        Directors, Mihály Kertész [Michael Curtiz] and Odon Fritz;
based on the novel by Hanns Heinz Ewers; screenplay, Richard Falk.
        With: Guyla Gál, Rózsi Szöllösi, Jenö Torzs, Margit Lux,
Kálman Körmendy, Géza Erdélyi, Andor Kardos, Violette Szlaténnyi,
Kâroly Arnyai, and Böske Malatinszky.

ALRAUNE (UNHOLY LOVE) (Ama Film, 1928) 122 min.

        Director, Henrik Galeen; based on the novel by Hanns Heinz
Ewers; screenplay, Galeen; sets, Walter Reimann and Max Heilbronner;
music, Willy Schmidt-Gentner; camera, Franz Planer.

With: Brigitte Helm (Alraune), Paul Wegener, Ivan Petrovich,
Mia Pankau, Glorg John, Valeska Gert, Wolfgang Lilzer, Louis
Ralph, Hans Trautner, John Loder, Heinrich Schroth, and Alexander
Sascha.

ALRAUNE (DAUGHTER OF EVIL) (UFA, 1930) 103 1/2 min.

Director, Richard Oswald; based on the novel by Hanns Heinz
Ewers; screenplay, Charles Roellinghoff and Richard Weisbach; art
directors, Otto Erdmann and Hans Sohnie; music, Bronislaw Kaper;
camera, Gunther Krampf.
With: Brigitte Helm (Alraune); Albert Bassermann (The Scientist), Agnes Straub, Käthe Haack, Martin Kosleck, Bernhard Goetzke,
E. A. Lichs, Ivan Koval-Samborski, Paul Westermeier, Henry Bender, Harold Paulsen, and Liselott Schaak.

ALRAUNE (UNNATURAL) (Styria/Carlton, 1952) 92 min.

Director, Arthur Maria Rabenalt; based on the novel by Hanns
Heinz Ewers; screenplay, Fritz Rotter; music, Werner Heymann; cam-
era, Friedl Behn-Grund.
With: Hildegard Kneff [Neff] (Alraune); Erich von Stroheim,
Karl Böhm, Julia Koschka, and Trude Hesterberg.

Hanns Heinz Ewers' novel has been brought to the screen no
less than five times, with varying quality.   The story, however, has
remained pretty much the same throughout the quintet of features.
Its basic plotline is that of a scientist who creates a female child
through artificial insemination, the product of a hanged criminal and
a prostitute.   The soulless child grows up to adulthood and eventually learns the secret of her being (by reading her creators' diary) and
realizes she is without feeling.   She meets a tragic demise.   "Alraune" refers to an ancient root which is supposed to have magical
powers.
Two versions of the tale allegedly appeared in 1918, one made
in Germany by Luna-Film and the other in Hungary by director Michael Curtiz.   In the latter's version the young girl was supposedly
fathered by a mandrake root.   The best-appreciated version of the
story was produced in 1928 in Germany and was written and directed
by Henrik Galeen.   Paul Wegener played the doctor and Brigitte Helm
was the young girl.   By today's standards, the film is slow and overly arty, with its creation sequences muddled beyond comprehension
and the plot motivation slowed by a lack of a character on the part
of the girl (despite Helm's fine performance).   According to Ivan
Butler in Horror in the Cinema (1970), Helm's performance conveyed
a "sort of pale menace which is quite formidable," while the film
itself contained sets which were "among the best of the German Goth-
ic period. "
Brigitte Helm repeated the role of Alraune two years later in
a sound version of the novel directed in Germany, with Albert Bassermann as the scientist.   When the feature was issued in the U. S.

in 1934 it was called Daughter of Evil. It was definitely not up to
the earlier Henrik Galeen version.

In 1952 the Germans again filmed the story under the direction of Albert Maria Rebenalt with Hildegard Kneff (Neff) as Alraune
and Erich von Stroheim as her creator. Despite the presence of the
two international stars, Ivan Butler, (Supra) found the film "another
victim of the descending series." When issued in the United States
in 1957 by DCA it was retitled Unnatural.

Predating Universal Pictures' teaming of monsters in Forties'
Hollywood entries, the German company Riestenbioskopfilm made Al-
rune und der Golem (Alraune and the Golem) in 1919. It combined
the Jewish legend of the man of clay and Ewers' story of the artificial girl.

ALRAUNE AND THE GOLEM   see   ALRAUNE

L'AMANTE DELLA CITTA SEOPOLTA   see   L'ATLANTIDE (1960)

THE AMAZING COLOSSAL MAN (American International, 1957)
80 min.

Producer/director, Bert I. Gordon; screenplay, Mark Hanna
and Gordon; music, Albert Glasser; assistant director, Nate D. Slott;
wardrobe, Bob Richards; camera, Joseph Birco; editor, Ronald Sinclair.

Glenn Langan (Lieutenant Colonel Glenn Manning); Cathy Downs
(Carol Forrest); William Hudson (Dr. Paul Lindstrom); James Seay
(Colonel Hallock); Larry Thor (Dr. Eric Coulter); Russ Bender (Rich-
ard Kingman); Lynn Osborn (Sergeant Taylor); Diana Darrin (Typist);
William Hughes (Control Officer); Hank Patterson (Henry); Scott
Peters (Sergeant Lee Carter); Myron Cook (Captain Thomas); and
Jack Kosslyn, Jean Moorehead, Frank Jenks; Bill Cassady, Edmund
Cobb, Paul Hahn, June Jocelyn, Stanley Lachman.

During the late Fifties some of the least inspired sci-fi films
produced in Hollywood were made by filmmaker Bert I. Gordon. The
Amazing Colossal Man is far above his usual standards, and was good
enough to provide two sequels, The Cyclops and War of the Colossal
Beast (both q. v.). The co-scripting by Mark Hanna helped salvage
the project, as did the lead performance by Glenn Langan in a role
that required more from the actor than the script dialogue provided.

Relying heavily on Gordon's sometimes mediocre special effects, the film has Langan as an Army officer who is caught accidentally in a plutonium explosion. As a result the military man begins to grow and develops into a virtual giant. Subsequently, his
enormous size causes him severe emotional problems; he becomes
a rampaging monster who must be eventually destroyed.

The script presented the title character as a decent human
being--a rarity for the species, which usually showcased cardboard
figures--who is driven to insanity and destruction because of the

Glenn Langan in The Amazing Colossal Man (1957).

effects of the explosion and the sudden size increase. However, the
minuscule budget and slipshod production values militated against the
film's success. Still, The Amazing Colossal Man appeared on the
scene at a time when the public was hungry for such fare and it provided a tidy box-office return for its releasing company, the fledgling
American International Pictures.

THE AMAZING TRANSPARENT MAN (American International, 1960)
60 min.

     Executive producers, John Miller and Robert L. Madden; pro-
ducer, Lester D. Guthrie; director, Edgar G. Ulmer; screenplay,
Jack Lewis; music composer/conductor, Darrel Calker; production
designer, Ernest Fegte; set decorator, Louise Caldwell; assistant
director, Leonard J. Shapiro; sound, Earl Snyder and Don Olson;
special effects, Roger George; camera, Meredith M. Nicholson; editor,
Jack Ruggiero.
     Marguerite Chapman (Laura); Douglas Kennedy (Joey Faust);
James Griffith (Krenner); Ivan Triesault (Dr. Ulof); Red Morgan (Julian); Carmel Daniel (Maria); Edward Erwin (Drake); Jonathan Ledford

John Wengraf in The Amazing Transparent Man (1960).

(Smith); Norman Smith and Patrick Cranshaw (Security Guards); Kevin
Kelly (Woman); Dennis Adams and Stacy Morgan (State Policemen.)

     In 1960, veteran director Edgar G. Ulmer helmed two features
for American International Pictures, this entry and Beyond the Time
Barrier (q. v.). Both films were accomplished on a shoestring budget but Ulmer invested them with interesting little touches.
     The Amazing Transparent Man combined the plotlines of sci-
fi and the gangster feature in unfolding the tale of a hoodlum (Douglas Kennedy) who is accidentally administered an invisibility serum
which he uses for gain, ending up at odds with rival crooks and the
police. After robbing a bank the transparent criminal continues his
criminal life until he is hunted to the finish. Shades of H. G. Well's
The Invisible Man (q. v.)!
     Sadly, the special effects, which should have been the highlight
of the production, were not convincing. Although the criminal was
supposed to be invisible, he was often easily seen. Mercifully, the
performances and the direction were brisk.

AMMUTINAMENTO NELLO SPAZIO   see   MUTINY IN OUTER SPACE

THE ANDROMEDA STRAIN (Universal, 1971) C-130 min.

Producer/director, Robert Wise; based on the novel by J. Michael Crichton; screenplay, Nelson Gidding; music, Gil Melle; production designer, Boris Leven; art director, William Tuntke; set decorator, Ruby Levitt; titles and optical effects, Attila DeLado; costumes, Helen Colvig; makeup, Bud Westmore; assistant director, Ridgeway Callow; sound, Waldon O. Watson, James Alexander, and Ronald Pierce; special camera effects, Douglas Trumbull and James Shourt; camera, Richard H. Kline; editors, Stuart Gilmore and John W. Holmes.

Arthur Hill (Dr. Jeremy Stone); David Wayne (Dr. Charles Dutton); James Olson (Dr. Mark Hall); Kate Reid (Dr. Ruth Leavitt); Paula Kelly (Karen Anson); George Mitchell (Jackson); Ramon Biere (Major Manchek); Kermit Murdock (Dr. Robertson); Richard O'Brien (Grimes); Peter Hobbs (General Sparks); Mark Jenkins (Lieutenant Shawn); Peter Helm (Sergeant Crane); Ken Swofford (Toby); Michael Pataki (Mic T); John Carter (Captain Morton); Carl Reindel (Lieutenant Comroe); Eric Christmas (Vermont Senator); Joe Di Reda (Burke); Richard Bull (Air Force Major); David McLean (New Mexico Senator); Susan Brown (Allison Stone); Bart La Rue (Medic Captain); Michael Bow (M. P. Sergeant); Walter Brooke (Secretary of Defense); Garry Walberg (Technician); Ivor Barry (Murray); Glenn Langan (Secretary of State); Paul Ballantyne (Hospital Director); Judy Farrell (Pam); Emory Parnell (Old Doughboy); Johnny Lee (Boy); William Dunbar (Air Force Sergeant); Joe Billings, Ray Harris, and Ted Lehmann (Scientists).

J. Michael Crichton, who later directed Westworld (q. v.), wrote the novel from which this expansive Robert Wise production was taken. Its basic plotline details the work of the Wildfire research team in isolating and destroying an alien micro-organism which has come to Earth attached to a falling satellite. The opening scenes, in an eerie arid town where all life, except for a baby and a drunk, has been destroyed by an unknown force, are the best in the film. Thereafter follows the action at the intricate Wildfire project lab where the erudite team battles the organism until the human body resistances to it are discovered and the force can thus be destroyed.

Obviously out to exceed (or at least match) 2001: A Space Odyssey (q. v.), Robert Wise devoted much of the $6.5 million budget to the technical/production details. But as the San Francisco Chronicle observed, "The mechanical complexity of the huge, computerized installation is fascinating for a while, but meanwhile no momentum is building." On the other hand, Judith Crist in New York magazine insisted, "Robert Wise's The Andromeda Strain is the 'purest' science fiction thriller to come to the screen in years, its purity based on its propinquity to fact rather than fantasy; its consistency of theme without the usual sex-schmaltz trappings that reduced Marooned [q. v.] to soap opera and The Forbin Project [q. v.] to B-level slickery; its high-class production values and its terrible significance in relation to the truths of germ warfare and militaristic purpose in space exploration.... That clinical microbiology, epidemiology, pathology and electrolyte chemistry are made the stuff of breath-stifling

James Olson and Arthur Hill in The Andromeda Strain (1971).

suspense while the film sustains its quasi-documentary stature is the
major tribute to all involved. "

For the general public, Castle of Frankenstein magazine was
most on base when it carped, "[It] Attempts to show what scientists
are 'really like' ... but why do it with a plot straight out of the
Fifties films?" Variety confirmed, "In the first half hour, the plot
puzzle and eerie mood are well established, and in the final half
hour, there is a dramatically exciting climax. The middle hour,
however, drags proceedings numbingly. The four scientists repeatedly get into long-winded discussions not unlike those of radio serials,
where audiences had to be taken step by step lest they be confused
by missing an episode's plot point. There are times in The Andromeda Strain when one wants to shout at the players to get on with it."

Perhaps the most impressive aspect of this well-mounted feature (which Variety labeled "science-fact") was its special photographic
effects by Douglas Trumbull (who worked on 2001: A Space Odyssey)
and James Shourt, along with Boris Levin's extremely effective,
sterilized production designs. A major force behind the plotline may
have been contemporary scientists' real fear that Moon astronauts
might bring back with them to Earth some long dormant and deadly
virus.

THE ANGRY RED PLANET (American International, 1960) C-94 min.

Producers, Sidney Pink and Norman Maurer; director, Ib Melchoir; story, Pink; screenplay, Pink and Melchoir; music, Paul Dunlap; assistant director, Robert Johannes; wardrobe, Marjorie Corso;
makeup, David Newall; sound, Vic Appel and Glen Glenn; special effects, Herman Townsley; camera, Stanley Cortez; editor, Ivan J.
Hoffman.

Gerald Mohr (O'Banion); Nora Hayden (Iris Ryan); Les Tre-
mayne (Professor Gettell); Jack Kruschen (Sergeant Jacobs); Paul
Hahn (General Treegar); J. Edward McKinley (Professor Weiner);
Tom Daly (Dr. Gordon); Edward Innes (General Prescott).
A. k. a. Invasion of Mars / Journey to Planet Four.

Contrary to some jokesters' comments, this entry has no relationship to Communist ideology. Its premise revolves about a
group of astronauts who land on Mars and find a hostile world containing giants, carnivorous plants, giant blobs of matter, monsters
that are a combination of bats/rats/spiders/crabs; and super-intelligent Martians who seem to be more insect than human and who are
definitely hostile. After a few of the crew members are massacred,
the space explorers return home.

The chief promotional gimmick of The Angry Red Planet was
"Cinemagic. " As Variety detailed it, "It is a kind of photographic
trick that produces the effect of a negative. Shown in pinkish-colored
tones, shadings are reverse; light's dark, dark's light. While it may
take considerable ingenuity to produce this effect, the result isn't
really worth it.... " Another side effect of the trick is that it makes
it difficult for the viewer to distinguish the action during the Mars
sequences.

Jack Kruschen, Nora Hayden, Gerald Mohr and Les Tremayne in
The Angry Red Planet (1960).

ANTINEA, L'AMANTE DELLA CITTA SEPOLTA   see   L'ATLANTIDE
(1961)

ASSIGNMENT TERROR   see   EL HOMBRE QUE VINE DEL UMMO

ASTOUNDING SHE MONSTER (American International, 1958) 59 min.

Producer/director, Ronnie Ashcroft; screenplay, Frank Hall;
music, Guenther Kauer; sound, Dale Knight; camera, William C.
Thompson.
Robert Clarke (Dick Cutler); Kenne Duncan (Nat Burdell);
Marilyn Harvey (Margaret Chaffee); Jeanne Tatum (Esther Malone);
Shirley Kilpatrick (Monster); Ewing Brown (Brad Conley).

Sometimes films are worth (re)viewing just to see how impov-
erished a genre entry can be and how it could have been improved.
Donald C. Willis, in his Horror and Science Fiction Films (1972),
says that this picture is "one of those that have to be seen to be believed, they're so bad. " The British Monthly Film Bulletin reported,
"The feminine monster shimmers and wobbles and oscillates on each
of her many sinister appearances--but, unfortunately, the rest of the
picture behaves accordingly, and it is only the absence of the monster that allows the image to remain static. The film is a feeble
and ridiculous contribution to the science fiction library, weakly
scripted and poorly acted. "
An heiress (Marilyn Harvey) and a geologist (Robert Clarke)

Shirley Kilpatrick in Astounding She Monster (1958)

are kidnapped and hustled to a remote Sierra Madre ski lodge where they are to be held for ransom.   Complications arise, however, when a flying saucer lands and out steps an eerie, but sexy, alien (Shirley Kilpatrick) who has a decidedly killing touch since she is surrounded by radioactivity.   In the course of the film's 59 minutes, the lovely she monster does in a bear and the three hoodlums (led by Kenne Duncan) before Clarke concocts a home-made acid bomb which eats through the girl's metallic suit and brings about her demise.   At the finale, however, it is learned she was actually a benign invader who had come to this planet to invite its leaders to join other heavenly bodies in a sort of "league of the planets. "

The film's working title was The Astounding She Creature (part of which was used by AIP for another of their films, The She Creature, the same year) and it was issued in Britain as The Mysterious Invader.

THE ASTRONOMER'S DREAM (Méliès, 1898) C-195'

Producer-director, Georges Méliès.

Color has played an integral role in the sci-fi film since the Fifties, giving graphic detail to any number of monster and alien invaders.   Actually the use of color goes back a long way in the history of the cinema.   Perhaps the first genre film to use this process was produced before the turn-of-the-century.   In 1898 French genius Georges Méliès produced this one-reel film and its frames were hand-colored.   Its brief and simple plot had an astronomer dreaming that he travels to the moon on a rope ladder.

While most critics insist that this early effort was hardly one
of Méliês best, the film certainly has an interesting history.   To
begin with, it has a flock of titles--Le Rêve d'un Astronome / La Lune
à un Mètre / L'Homme dans la Lune--for its French releases and in
the U. S. the situation got even more complicated.   Filmmaker Sigmund Lubin claims to have released a film in 1889 called A Trip to
the Moon (no relation to the later Méliês film which Lubin issued
here as A Trip to Mars) which was actually the 1898 Méliês entry.
     The finale of The Astronomer's Dream had the Moon following
the adventurer back to Earth as it came tumbling through his observatory window.

L'ATLANTIDE / DIE HERREN VON ATLANTIS / LOST ATLANTIS
(Nero-Film, 1932) 94 min.

     Producer, Seymour Nebenzal; director, G. W. Pabst; based
on the novel by Pierre Benoit; screenplay, Ladislaus Vajda and Hermann Oberlander; production designer, Erno Metzner; music, Wolfgang Zeller; sound, A. Jansen; camera, Eugen Schtffftan, Joseph
Barth, and Ernst Koerner; editor, Hans Oser.
     German version: Brigitte Helm (Antinea); Florelle Tela-Tchaï
(Tanit-Zerga); Odette Florelle (Clementine); Heinz Klingenberg (Captain St. Avit); Gustav Diesal (Captain Mochange); Georges Tourreil
(Lieutenant Ferrieres); Mathias Wiemann (The Norwegian); Vladimir
Sokoloff (Count Bielowsky / Jitomir Chieftain).
     French version: (adaptator, Alexandre Arnoux; French dia-
logue, Jacques Duval); Brigitte Helm (Antinea); Florelle Tela-Tchaï
(Tanit Zerga); Odette Florelle (Clementine); Pierre Blanchar (Captain
St. Avít); Jean Angelo (Captain Morchange); Georges Toureil (Lieu-
tenant Ferrieres); Mathias Wiemann (The Norwegian); Vladimir Soko-
loff (Count Bielowsky / Jitomir Chieftain); and Jacques Richet (Jean
Chataignier).
     English version: Brigitte Helm (Antinea); John Stuart, Gibb
McLaughlin, Gustav Diesal, Odette Florelle (Clementine), Vladimir
Sokoloff (Count Bielowsky / Jitomir Chieftain).

     The first film to deal with the fabled lost world of Atlantis
was probably made in 1913 in Denmark by the Nordisk Company from
Gerhardt Hauptmann's novel.   Directed by Ole Olsen, it starred Olaf
Fonss and Hauptmann adapted his work for the screen.   In 1930 former Belgian actor Jacques Feyder bought the film rights to Pierre
Benoit's 1919 novel and transported a crew to the Sahara where he
shot the 103-minute Atlantis for Gaumont Picture.   Staoia Napierkow-
ska starred as Antinea, the queen of Atlantis and the meandering
film was highly successful.
     The definitive version of the Benoit novel came in 1932 when
German director G. W. Pabst lensed the story in German / French /
English-language versions with Brigitte Helm playing Antinea in all
three editions.   Shot in Morocco, the picture traced the life history
of the royal person, shown here to be a cruel and evil woman intent
on destroying those who could not compete with her or who stood in her
path.   Like the earlier version, this production contained the fascinating

16 L'Atlantide

sequences of the queen's hall of mummified lovers. (A similar scene would be used in Universal's The Black Cat [1934], directed by Edgar G. Ulmer, the man who would later helm the third version of Benoit book, Journey Beneath the Desert, [q. v.].)

Writing in Science Fiction in the Cinema (1970), John Baxter stated, "Pabst's film is in every way a superior work, one of the finest romances from the golden age of the German cinema."

This picture is known under a variety of titles. All three language versions are often called Lost Atlantis, but the French version was also issued as L'Atlantide and Mistress of Atlantis while in Germany the production was also known as Die Herren von Atlantis.

L'ATLANTIDE (ANTINEA, L'AMANTE DELLA CITTA SEPOLTA) (C. C. M- Fides, 1961) C-100 min.

Executive producer, Nat Wachberger; directors, Edgar G. Ulmer, Giuseppi Masini, and (uncredited) Frank Borzage; based on the novel by Pierre Benoit; screenplay, Ugo Liberatore, Remigio del Grosso, Andre Tabet, and Amedeo Nazzari; production designer, Ulmer; music, Carlo Rustichelli; special effects, Giovanni Ventimiglia; camera, Enzo Serafin; editor, Renato Cinquini.

Haya Harareet (Antinea); Jean-Louis Trintignant (Pierre); Rad Fulton (Robert); Amedeo Nazzari (Tamal); Georges Riviere (John); Giulia Rubini (Zinah); Gabriele Tinti (Max); Giammaria Volonte (Tarath).

A. k. a.: The Lost Kingdom, Queen of Atlantis, Journey Beneath the Desert, City Beneath the Desert, Journey Under the Desert.

The oft-filmed legend of Atlantis received another rendering in this French-Italian co-production. The feature was heavily mutilated, although smartly dubbed when shown in the U. S. The storyline lags, but it is visually arresting and at times even stunning, especially in the display of the dark underground world leading to Atlantis.

Three oil prospectors (Jean-Louis Trintignant, Rad Fulton, and Georges Riviere) are forced to crash land in a mountainous area beyond the Sahara desert. They save the life of Tamal (Amedeo Nazzari) who claims to be a local chieftain. Later he takes them prisoner and escorts them to the lost world of Atlantis, ruled by the beautiful but cruel queen Antinea (Haya Harareet). One noteworthy sequence has the ruler apparently killed by snake strangulation, and then arising from death to be renewed by the sacred flame (reminscent of the various versions of She). Pierre (Trintignant) is the only one of the three prospectors to survive; he escapes with Zinah (Giulia Rubini), a slave woman with whom he has fallen in love. Atlantis is destroyed by a nuclear test in the desert, but Pierre and Zinah are spared.

Low-budget whiz director Edgar G. Ulmer seems to have met his match here, for the paltry finances expended on the project hindered any sense of credibility or magnificence. Trying to bring the Pierre Benoit novel of 1919 up-to-date by including nuclear testing did not bolster the story's premise.

ATLANTIS   see   L'ATLANTIDE; also SIREN OF ATLANTIS

ATLANTIS, THE LOST CONTINENT (MGM, 1961) C-90 min.

Producer/director, George Pal; based on the play by Sir Gerald Hargreaves; screenplay, Daniel Mainwaring; assistant director, Ridgeway Callow; music, Russell Garcia; art directors, George W. Davis and William Ferrari; set decorators, Henry Grace and Dick Pefferle; color consultant, Charles K. Hagedon; makeup, William Tuttle; recording supervisor, Franklin Milton; special effects, A. Arnold Gillespie, Lee LeBlanc, and Robert R. Hoag; camera, Harold E. Wellman; editor, Ben Lewis.

Anthony Hall (Demetrios); Joyce Taylor (Antillia); John Dall (Zaren); Bill Smith (Captain of the Guard); Edward Platt (Azor); Frank DeKova (Sonoy); Berry Kroeger (Surgeon); Edgar Stehli (King Kronas); Wolfe Barzell (Petros); Jay Novello (Xandros); Buck Maffei (Andes); Paul Frees (Narrator).

After the critical and financial success of The Time Machine (q. v.), producer/director George Pal revisited the sci-fi genre for this inexpensively-mounted offering.   It is one of the flimsiest pictures dealing with the legendary Atlantis--a big disappointment to fans of the films of George Pal.

Some 150 centuries ago, a young Greek fisherman named Demetrios (Anthony Hall) becomes lost in the land of Atlantis and while there falls in love with its Princess (Joyce Taylor).   It is not long before Demetrios joins the fight to stop the rise of dictator Zaren (John Dall).   But the fisherman is enslaved and tortured by corrupt

Scene from Atlantis, the Lost Continent (1961).

alchemist who turn many prisoners into men-beasts. Later the
hero regains his freedom by undergoing the Ordeal of Fire and water.
But he cannot stop two warring forces on the island who are fighting
over possession of a powerful death-ray machine. This invention
goes out of control and destroys much of the land, and then a volcano
erupts, causing the sinking of Atlantis, thus ending the advanced civilization.

It was Pal's purpose in this vehicle to provide entertainment
"with an element of wonder, stressing man's suppressed desire to
travel away from himself. " But the film failed in almost every department: the special effects were below par, too much stock footage from Quo Vadis cropped up, and the long-anticipated finale was
terribly flat. According to the New York Herald-Tribune, "I suppose
this picture was meant for the children, but it is too mushy and the
gadgetry too obviously makeshift to appeal to many children. "

Two years later MGM would release Beyond Atlantis, a shoddy
Eddie Romero-directed entry starring co-producer John Ashley and
Patrick Wayne, and featuring Leigh Christian as "Syrene. " (The ads
read, "SHE LEADS HER PEOPLE FROM THE SEA!" ... Their
Spawning Ground ... The Ocean Depths!") What next?

ATOM MAN VS. SUPERMAN (Columbia, 1950) fifteen chapters

Producer, Sam Katzman; director, Spencer Gordon Bennet;
based on the Superman adventure feature appearing in Superman and
Action magazines; adapted from the "Superman" radio program;
screenplay, George H. Plympton, Joseph F. Poland, and David Mathews; assistant director, R. M. Andrews; second unit director, Der-
win Abrahams; art director, Paul Palmentola; set decorator, Sidney
Clifford; music director, Mischa Bakaleinikoff; sound, Josh West-
moreland; camera, Ira H. Morgan; editor, Earl Turner.

Kirk Alyn (Clark Kent/Superman); Noel Neill (Lois Lane); Lyle
Talbot (Luthor); Tommy Bond (Jimmy Olson); Pierre Watkin (Perry
White); Jack Ingram (Foster); Don Harvey (Albert); Rusty Wescoatt
(Carl); Terry Frost (Beer); Wally West (Dorr); Paul Strader (Law-
son); George Robotham (Earl).

Chapters: 1) Superman Flies Again; 2) Atom Man Appears!;
3) Ablaze in the Sky!; 4) Superman Meets Atom Man!; 5) Atom Man
Tricks Superman; 6) Atom Man's Challenge; 7) At the Mercy of Atom
Man!; 8) Into the Empty Doom!; 9) Superman Crashes Through!; 10)
Atom Man's Heat Ray; 11) Luthor's Strategy; 12) Atom Man Strikes!;
13) Atom Man's Flying Saucer; 14) Rocket of Vengeance; 15) Superman Saves the Universe.

Following the gigantic success of the 1948 Superman serial,
Columbia and economy producer Sam Katzman turned out this sequel,
which utilized the leads from the previous effort. The project was
promoted as: "GREATER THAN EVER! The one and only SUPERMAN
in a Bigger ... Better ... Brand-New Super Serial Sensation!"

Here Superman (Kirk Alyn) is at odds with the arch-villain, Luthor (Lyle Talbot), alias the dome-headed, bald "Atom Man. " Luthor threatens to destroy Metropolis. Newspaper editor Perry White

(Pierre Watkin) dispatches his three ace reporters, Clark Kent (Alyn), Lois Lane (Noel Neill), and Jimmy Olson (Tommy Bond), to cover the momentous story.

Meanwhile, devious Luthor turns a number of deadly machines on the city and invents "synthetic Kryptonite," the only substance that can stop the Man of Steel. Luthor plants the Kryptonite aboard a ship about to be launched and Superman, there for the event, is badly weakened and is captured by the villains. Luthor then turns his henchmen loose on the defenseless city. Fortunately, the effects of the synthetic Kryptonite are brief and Superman quickly returns to his former powers, but not until after Luthor has plotted to destroy the city and to abduct Lois Lane in a space ship. Superman puts a stop to Luthor's mad plan to use the sonic vibrator, flies into the culprit's rocketship and rescues Lois, and sends the arch fiend to prison.

Not as solid as its predecessor, this cliffhanger was still entertaining fare and was directed at a fast clip by serial expert Spencer Gordon Bennet. Lyle Talbot enlivened the proceedings with his portrayal of the sinister genius Luthor, certainly one of the more fantastic villains ever to grace a serial. Kirk Alyn contributed his usual likable performance as the Man of Steel who flies "faster than a speeding locomotive," but production values were down from the prior entry. The use of gadgets and gimmicks was just no substitute for a substantial mounting; even the kiddie trade noticed the difference.

ATOMIC MONSTER: THE BEAST OF YUCCA FLATS see THE BEAST OF YUCCA FLATS

THE ATOMIC SUBMARINE (Allied Artists, 1960) 72 min.

Producer, Alex Gordon; associate producer, Henry Schrage, in association with Jack Rabin, Irving Block, and Orville H. Hampton; director, Spencer Gordon Bennet; screenplay, Hampton; music composer/conductor, Alexander Laszlo; art directors, Don Ament and Dan Heller; set decorator, Harry Reif; assistant director, Clark Paylow; wardrobe, Roger J. Weinberg and Norah Sharpe; makeup, Emile LaVigne; sound, Ralph Butler and Marty Greco; special effects, Rabin, Block, and Jack DeWitt; camera, Gilbert Warrenton; editor, William Austin.

Arthur Franz (Commodore "Reef" Holloway); Dick Foran (Captain Dan Wednover); Brett Halsey (Carl Nelson); Tom Conway (Sir Ian Hunt); Paul Dubov (Lieutenant David Milton); Bob Steele (Griff); Victor Varconi (Dr. Clifford Kent); Joi Lansing (Julie); Selmer Jackson (Admiral Terhune); Jack Mulhall (Murdock); Jean Moorhead (Helen); Richard Tyler (Carney); Sid Melton (Chester); Ken Becker (Powell).

Of all the features made in the Fifties and Sixties by producer Alex Gordon, this entertaining B thriller is probably the best. The film boasts solid direction (by Spencer Gordon Bennet), a literate script, good art direction (done in part by future director Daniel Heller), and a cast chock full of veterans--a trademark of Gordon's productions.

The plot has a new atomic powered submarine ordered to the North Pole on a test run. There it finds a flying saucer refueling beneath the Arctic waters. Upon exploring the craft, it is discovered that the alien missile is inhabited by an ugly eye-like creature which is anything but friendly. At the finale the monster is destroyed, thus saving the world from invasion.

The early scenes of the private lives of the ship's crew being interrupted for the voyage are amusing. Once aboard the craft, the experienced cast more than holds the script together, making it a most enjoyable double-bill entry.

Variety did point out, "There are, of course, newsreel clips (one is used at least twice) of present-day atomic subs and freighters, but one is supposed to believe them to be identical to future craft in design."

ATRAGON see KAITEI GUNKAN

ATTACK OF THE 50 FT. WOMAN (Allied Artists, 1958) 65 min.

Producer, Bernard Woolner; director, Nathan Hertz [Juran]; screenplay, Mark Hanna; music composer/conductor, Ronald Stein; assistant director, Ken Walters; makeup, Carlie Taylor; sound, Philip Mitchell; camera, Jacques R. Marquette; editor, Edward Mann.

Allison Hayes (Nancy Archer); William Hudson (Harry Archer); Roy Gordon (Dr. Cushing); Yvette Vickers (Honey Parker); George Douglas (Sheriff Dubbitt); Otto Waldis (Dr. Von Loeb); Frank Chase (Charlie); Eileene Stevens (Nurse); Dale Tate (Commentator); Tom

William Hudson and Allison Hayes in Attack of the 50 ft. Woman (1958).

Jackson (Prospector); Mike Ross (Tony).

Surely this entry deserves inclusion as one of the "camp" classics of the Fifties. It is so terrible that it even makes Astounding She Monster (q. v.) seem a genre classic. But it does boast the presence of Allison Hayes, one of the more frequent leading ladies of this film format.

Not long after being released from a mental asylum, Nancy Archer (Allison Hayes) sees a large satellite settle down on a California stretch of desert. She escapes, but neither her husband (William Hudson) nor the police will believe her. (A coy little twist has her spouse carrying on with another woman, Yvette Vickers, and using this UFO episode as a reason to have his wife recommitted.) Later Nancy is captured by the outer space monster and suffers ray burns which transform her into the title character. Before she meets her timely demise, she wreaks vengeance on her husband and his mistress.

The film was directed by Nathan Juran, who for this low calibre entry dropped his last name and was billed as Nathan Hertz. No wonder, this was the craftsman who accomplished such other genre items as The Deadly Mantis, Twenty Million Miles to Earth, and First Men in the Moon (all q. v.).

Although a "really rotten" film, the picture did make money, showing that one can fool some of the people sometimes. For several years, producers threatened a sequel, Return of the Fifty-Foot Woman, but mercifully it has not appeared to date.

AUTNAT NA PRANI   see   THE WISHING MACHINE

THE BAMBOO SAUCER (World Entertainment, 1960) C-100 min.

Producer, Jerry Fairbanks; associate producer, Charles E. Burns; director, Frank Telford; story, Rip Von Ronkel and John Fulton; screenplay, Telford; music, Edward Paul; art director, Theodore Holsopple; assistant director, Henry Gilbert; sound, Dean Gilmore; special effects, John Fulton and Glen Robinson; camera, Hal Mohr; editor, Richard Harris.

Dan Duryea (Hank Peters); John Ericson (Fred Norwood); Lois Nettleton (Anna Karachev); Bob Hastings (Garson); Vincent Beck (Zagorsky); Bernard Fox (Ephram); Robert Dane (Miller); Rico Cattani (Dubovsky); James Hong (Sam Archibald); Bartlett Robinson (Rhodes); Nick Katurich (Gadyakoff); Bill Mims (Joe Vetry); Nan Leslie (Dorothy Vetry); Andy Romano (Blanchard).

The premise that aliens have visited the Earth in recent decades has often been exploited in the cinema, but finding an abandoned alien space craft (without a foreign being around) is a plotline which has rarely been touched on the screen. (There has been a real-life counterpart; in the early Fifties, the shell of an alien craft was supposedly located on an island near Sweden.)

In Bamboo Saucer, a team of U.S. scientists, led by John

Vincent Beck, Lois Nettleton and Dan Duryea in The Bamboo Saucer (1960).

Ericson and Dan Duryea (in his final film role), clandestinely travel to Red China to investigate the rumor that a strange space craft has been found near a rural village. The rumor proves true and the Americans do locate an advanced vehicle that was abandoned. But trouble with the locals brings out the Red Guard, and in the skirmish Duryea and several in the party are killed. Up to this juncture, the film is a moderately interesting effort. In the incredible finale, Ericson and Lois Nettleton board the ship (which they have learned to control) and escape. They lose control of the UFO and head into outer space, then regain control and return to earth, vowing that their discovery will be the basis for world peace. Such a forced climax ruins whatever credibility the production might have had for its audience.

The Bamboo Saucer was lensed by Oscar-winning cinematographer Hal Mohr.

BARBARELLA (Paramount, 1968) C-98 min.

Producer, Dino De Laurentiis; director, Roger Vadim; based on the book by Jean-Claude Forest; screenplay, Terry Southern in collaboration with Vadim, Brian Degas, Claude Brule, Forest, Tudor Gates, Clement Biddle Wood, and Vittorio Bonicelli; music, Maurice Jarre; songs, Charles Fox and Bob Crewe; production designer, Mario Garbuglia; art director, Enrico Fea; set decorator, Giorgio Hermann; second unit director, Alberto Cardone; costumes, Jacques Fonteray; assistant director, Carlo Lastricati; sound, David Hildyard; special effects, Augie Lohman; camera, Claude Renoir; second unit camera, Vladimir Ivanov; editor, Victoria Mercanton.

Jane Fonda (Barbarella); John Phillip Law (Pygar); Anita Pallenberg (The Black Queen); Milo O'Shea (Durand-Durand [Concierge]); David Hemmings (Diladano); Marcel Marceau (Professor Ping); Ugo Tognazzi (Mark Hand); Claude Dauphin (President of Earth); Antonio Sabato (Jean-Paul); Talitha Pol (Pipe-Smoking Girl); Serge Marquand (Captain Sun); Veronique Vendell (Captain Moon); Maria Theresa Orsini (The Suicide Girls); Catherine and Marie Therese Chevalier (The Twins); Sergio Ferrero (The Black Queen's Messenger); Nino Musco (The Generale); Chantal Cachin (The Female Revolutionary).

Comic strips have always been a fine source of cinema fantasty with such strips as Flash Gordon, Buck Rogers, and Batman being turned into popular sci-fi serials. After the World War II years, however, comic strips became less and less prevalent as source material for the screen. In 1967 French producer/director Roger Vadim starred his then-wife Jane Fonda in this French/Italian co-production, which was based on the drawings of Jean-Claude Forest.

In the forty-first century, astronaut Barbarella (Fonda) lives at a time when sex is forgotten; that is until her desires are reawakened by the white blind angel (John Phillip Law). The strange duo are at odds with the beautiful, but evil, dark queen (Anita Pallenberg) of Sogo, a city where sin after sin is invented and delighted in by the populace. In this metropolis of the future are such items as the chamber where the queen (who engages Barbarella in a lesbian affair) can make her dreams come true. There is also an "excessive machine," a giant sex organ which blows its fuse trying to murder Barbarella with pleasure. Outside the orgiastic city are carnivorous dolls and tree-women. Eventually the evil queen is defeated (but saved from the destruction of Sogo) while Barbarella and her angel seek a future world more to their liking.

"Comic-strip buffs, science-fiction fans and admirers of the human mammae will get a run for their money in Barbarella," determined Time magazine. And Paramount exploited this project into one of the most awaited films in years. Mostly on the advance word-of-mouth and the titillating advertising campaign, the film grossed over $5.5 million in just United States and Canadian distributors' rentals. But, warned the New York Times, "All the gadgetry of science fiction--which is not really science fiction, since it has no poetry or logic--is turned to all kinds of jokes, which are not jokes, but hard-breathing, sadistic thrashings, mainly at the expense of Barbarella, and of women.... Throughout the movie, there is the

assumption that just mentioning a thing (sex, politics, religion) makes
it funny and that mentioning it in some offensive context makes it fun-
nier. For a while, the audience, catching all the pointless, witless
modernist allusions, feels in on something chic, and laughs. Then
it is clear that there is nothing whatever to be in on--except another
uninspired omnispoof...."

Somehow, in the emphasis on sex and quick laughs, much of
the inbred delight of the plotline (finding the Earth scientist who has
disappeared with the plans for the Positronic Ray; the plotting of the
underground revolutionaries on Lythion) is sidetracked.

It is ironic that this entry would be released in the same
year as the trend-shattering 2001: a Space Odyssey (q.v.), which
forced the viewer to think rather than chuckle, to delve visually, not
ogle, to relate event to event, not hunt for the oneliner.

THE BATMAN (Columbia, 1943) fifteen chapters

Producer, Rudolph C. Flothow; director, Lambert Hillyer;
based on the Batman Adventure feature appearing in Detective and
Batman comic magazines; screenplay, Victor McLeod, Leslie Wa-
backer, and Harry Fraser; assistant director, Gene Anderson; music,
Lee Zahler; camera, James S. Brown, Jr.; editors, Dwight Caldwell
and Earl Turner.

Lewis Wilson (Bruce Wayne/Batman); Douglas Croft (Dick
Grayson/Robin, the Boy Wonder); J. Carrol Naish (Dr. Daka); William Austin (Alfred); Shirley Patterson (Linda); Charles C. Wilson
(Captain Arnold); Charles Middleton (Ken Colton); Robert Fiske (Foster); Michael Vallon (Preston); Gus Glassmire (Martin Warren).

Chapters: 1) The Electric Brain; 2) The Bat's Cave; 3) The
Mark of the Zombies; 4) Slaves of the Rising Sun; 5) The Living
Corpse; 6) Poison Peril; 7) The Phoney Doctor; 8) Lured by Radium;
9) The Sign of the Sphinx; 10) Flying Spies; 11) A Nipponese Trap;
12) Embers of Evil; 13) Eight Steps Down; 14) The Executioner
Strikes; 15) The Doom of the Rising Sun.

Bob Kane's masked hero "Batman" first appeared in Detective
comics in 1939, and within four years Columbia Pictures had brought
Batman to the screen in a fifteen-chapter serial ("A Hundred Times
More Thrilling on the Screen!" proclaimed the ads.)

The Batman finds playboy Bruce Wayne, alias the Batman (Lewis Wilson) and his young comrade, Robin the Boy Wonder (Douglas
Croft), at odds with an enemy spy ring led by one Dr. Daka (J.
Carrol Naish) who has the power to transform victims into zombies
and use them at his will. In an attempt to aid the Axis, Daka tries
to steal a large amount of radium but Batman and Robin stop him.
In revenge, Daka abducts Wayne's girlfriend (Shirley Patterson) but
Batman rescues her and the mad doctor then tries to kill Batman
with his radium. Daka misses and still later falls into an alligator pit
where he is devoured. His spy ring is rounded up by the masked
crusader.

With the built-in popularity of the Batman property, this chapterplay could not miss. For added spice, it treated its World War II

Adam West (Bruce Wayne/Batman); Burt Ward (Dick Grayson/
Robin); Lee Meriwether (Catwoman/Kitka); Cesar Romero (The Joker);
Burgess Meredith (The Penguin); Frank Gorshin (The Riddler); Alan
Napier (Alfred); Neil Hamilton (Commissioner Gordon); Stafford Repp
(Chief O'Hara); Madge Blake (Aunt Harriet Cooper); Reginald Denny
(Commodore Schmidlapp); Milton Frome (Vice Admiral Fangschleis-
ter); Gil Perkins (Bluebeard); Dick Crockett (Morgan); George Sawaya
(Quetch).

On January 12, 1966, the ABC-TV series "Batman," based on
the cartoon strip and Columbia's movie serials of the Forties, made
its small-screen debut. The half-hour color show soon jumped to
the top of the ratings and remained there for more than a year. Before it ran its fad course, the program had chalked up 120 episodes,
and was as popular among youngsters (and some adults) as the Hopalong Cassidy and Davey Crockett crazes had been in the Fifties. A
& ' deal of viewer interest arose from the array of guest villains
and   o stars who "begged" to appear on the show. Among them
were M.   n Berle, Talullah Bankhead, Ida Lupino, Van Johnson,
Vincent P.   Otto Preminger (!), Edward G. Robinson, Art Carney,
Anne Baxter, nd a host of others.
    The show's producing company, Twentieth Century-Fox, was
quick to film a feature version, utilizing the program's cast of regu-
lars and bringing to the big screen four of the series' most delightful
arch villains: The Joker (Cesar Romero), The Penguin (Burgess
Meredith), The Riddler (Frank Gorshin), and The Catwoman (Lee
Meriwether). These devious rascals join forces to hijack the yacht
of the inventor of a "dehydrater," a gadget that turns humans
into dust. The evil quartet needs the invention to aid them in gaining control of the world. Needless to say, the intrepid heroes don
their costumes, jump into the Batmobile, and with(out) the aid of
Commissioner Gordon (Neil Hamilton) manage to foil the opponents.
    While the feature version of Batman was a visual joy to be-
hold, 105 minutes of unadulterated camp (played for outrageous jokes,
as was the teleseries) was more than the average filmgoer cared to
endure. Morever, as Judith Crist (TV Guide) noted "it proved at the
time that you shouldn't pay for what you get for free at home." The
movie, shot on a seven-week production schedule, grossed under $2
million in distributors domestic rentals.
    A good deal of the double entendre dialogue between Batman
(Adam West) and Catwoman, who fall in love despite between enemies,
was geared for adult minds. But the visuals were all aimed at the
juvenile market--e.g., Batman hoisting an oversized brandy snifter
filled with milk (!), or his gambit on the pier when he attempts to
divest himself of an activated bomb.

BATMAN AND ROBIN (Columbia, 1949) fifteen chapters

    Producer, Sam Katzman; director, Spencer Gordon Bennet;
based on the Batman comic feature appearing in Detective comics and
Batman magazine created by Bob Kane; screenplay, George H. Plympton, Joseph F. Poland, and Royal K. Cole; assistant director, R. M.

Andrews; music, Mischa Bakaleinikoff; camera, Ira H. Morgan; editors, Earl Turner and Dwight Caldwell.

Robert Lowery (Batman/Bruce Wayne); Johnny Duncan (Robin/Dick Grayson); Jane Adams (Vicki Vale); Lyle Talbot (Commissioner Gordon); Ralph Graves (Harrison); Don C. Harvey (Nolan); William Fawcett (Professor Hammil); Leonard Penn (Carter); Rick Vallin (Barry Brown); Michael Whalen (Dunne); Grey McClure (Evans); House Peters, Jr. (Earl); "?" (The Wizard); Jim Diehl (Jason); Eric Wilton (Alfred); Marshall Bradford (Roger Morton).

Chapters: 1) Batman Takes Over; 2) Tunnel of Terror; 3) Robin's Wild Ride; 4) Batman Trapped; 5) Robin Rescues Batman; 6) Target--Robin; 7) The Fatal Blast; 8) Robin Meets the Wizard; 9) The Wizard Strikes Back; 10) Batman's Last Chance; 11) Robin's Ruse; 12) Robin Rides the Wind; 13) The Wizard's Challenge; 14) Batman vs. Wizard; 15) Batman Victorious.

Sometimes called The New Adventures of Batman and Robin, this fifteen-chapter serial was Columbia's "sorry sequel" (Alan G. Barbour, Days of Thrills and Adventure, 1970) to its 1943 Batman cliffhanger. Here, capable actor Robert Lowery played Batman with Johnny Duncan as his ever-present comrade, Robin. Both players appeared lost in the sub-par production maze, hampered by ill-fitting costumes, ludicrous plot (and sub-plots), and a supporting cast that seemed over-anxious to get done with it all. But the matinee crowd was not to be denied, and this multi-part entry did bring in the young audience.

In Gotham City, the police commissioner (Lyle Talbot) asks Batman and Robin (really playboy Bruce Wayne and one-time circus performer Dick Grayson) to help his department find a remote-control ray machine which has been stolen from its inventor (William Fawcett) and his assistant (Leonard Penn). In their search, the dynamic duo are aided by a female journalist (Jane Adams). It is not long before the champions of law discover that the mysterious Wizard, a heinous underworld figure, is the culprit in the caper. After the Wizard's gang tries to heist the valuables from a jewelry store (they need the diamonds to make the machine operate), Batman and Robin begin a lengthy pursuit of the villains, eventually learning the Wizard's identity. At that time, they capture the fiend, destroy his gang, and return the machine to its rightful owner.

Over the years the serial has enjoyed occasional revivals. In the mid-Sixties, it and the 1943 serial version were sometimes shown in "four-hour marathons" at drive-in theatres.

BATTLE FOR THE PLANET OF THE APES (Twentieth Century-Fox, 1973) C-86 min.

Producer, Arthur P. Jacobs; associate producer, Frank Capra, Jr.; director, J. Lee Thompson; based on characters created by Pierre Boulle; screenplay, John William Corrington and Joyce Hooper Corrington; art director, Dale Hennesy; set decorator, Robert DeVestel; special mechanical effects, Gerald Endler; make-up design, John Chambers; music, Leonard Rosenman; sound, Herman

Scene from <u>Battle for the Planet of the Apes</u> (1973).

Lewis and Don Bassman; camera, Richard H. Kline; editors, Alan
L. Jaggs and John C. Horger.
        Roddy McDowall (Caesar); Claude Akins (Aldo); Natalie Trundy
(Lisa); Severn Darden (Kolp); Lew Ayres (Mandemus); Paul Williams
(Virgil); Austin Stoker (McDonald); Noah Keen (Teacher); Richard
Eastham (Mutant Captain); France Nuyen (Alma); Paul Stevens (Men-
dez); Heather Lowe (Doctor); Bobby Porter (Cornelius); Michael
Stearns (Jake); Cal Wilson (Soldier); Pat Cardi (Young Chimp); John
Landis (Jake's Friend); Andy Knight (Mutant on Motorcycle); and John
Huston (The Lawgiver).

        The fifth and final (to date) film in the <u>Planet of the Apes</u>
series had crisp direction, excellent photography and scoring, a good
premise and performances, but suffered from a rather weak script.
The latter aspect detracted from the overall effectiveness of the picture.   Also <u>Battle for ...</u> was issued as the popularity of the long-
running movie series was seriously waning.   By now the audience
for these "simian shenanigans" was mainly juvenile, as was proven
by the brief thirteen-week run of the TV series (in 1974) based on
the <u>Apes</u> films.   (TV rating companies determined that the program
appealed mainly to sub-teenagers.)
        The chronicle takes up where <u>Conquest of the Planet of the</u>
<u>Apes</u> (q. v.) leaves off.   Now the world has been ravaged by atomic
warfare, caused when intelligent apes were made slaves of humans.
In the ruins of civilization, it is the benevolent apes who are the

masters of the world and they are aided by a black human (Austin
Stoker) who hopes to bring about a world of equality in which simians and humans can exist in peace. When chimpanzee Caesar (Roddy McDowall) and colleagues go to the city of the mutants to see
film records of his long-dead parents and to find out the future of
the Earth, they encounter the mutant leader Kolp (Severn Darden)
who is allied with Aldo (Claude Akins) the leader of a plot by a band
of militant gorillas to destroy the apes' city. Eventually an all-out
war breaks out between the groups as "all three forces clash and
there is carnage aplenty for all concerned. Humanity, dignity and
escapist entertainment win out in the end" (Ed Naha, Horrors: From
Screen to Scream, 1975). The British Monthly Film Bulletin ques-
tioned the value of the film's political content: "Somewhere beneath
the routine action and adventure a small voice still appears to be
whispering something about present-day racial intolerance, although
the juxtaposition of black and white humans with good chimpanzees
and bad gorillas ensures that the message is confusingly muffled."
        What is most evident about this motion picture is that produ-
cer Arthur P. Jacobs and Twentieth Century-Fox retained high production values for the Apes series. In such format films it was/and
is quite common for each succeeding installment to deteriorate in
quality. But even if the Ape scripts began to sink, the productions
themselves never wanted for decent budgets, solid mountings, and
sufficient entertainment values.

BATTLE OF THE ASTROS   see KAIJU DAISENSO

THE BEAST FROM 20,000 FATHOMS (Warner Bros., 1953) 80 min.

        Producers, Hal Chester and Jack Dietz; director, Eugene
Lourie; based on the story "The Foghorn" by Ray Bradbury; screen-
play, Lou Morheim and Fred Freiberger; music, David Buttolph; art
director, Hal Waller; camera, Jack Russell; editor, Bernard W.
Burton.
        Paul Christian (Tom Nesbit); Paula Raymond (Lee Hunter);
Cecil Kellaway (Professor Elson); Kenneth Tobey (Colonel Evans);
Donald Woods (Captain Jackson); Jack Pennick (Jacob); Lee Van Cleef
(Corporal Stone); Steve Brodie (Sergeant Loomis); Ross Elliott (George
Ritchie); Ray Hyke (Sergeant Willistead); Mary Hill (Nesbitt's Secre-
tary); Michael Fox (Doctor); Alvin Greenman (Radar Man); Frank
Ferguson (Dr. Morton); King Donovan (Dr. Ingersoll).

        This film is the initial entry in the never-ending series of
motion pictures dealing with a prehistoric monster unearthed by some
atomic explosion and going on a destruction rampage before it is destroyed. The picture is taken from Ray Bradbury's haunting short
story "The Foghorn," but bears little resemblance to the original.
Overall, however, it is an effective sci-fi movie, certainly far better
than the cheap imitations it spawned.
        After a nuclear explosion in the Arctic, an elderly professor
(Cecil Kellaway) spots what appears to be a dinosaur in a blizzard.

Scene from The Beast from 20,000 Fathoms (1953).

However, he is convinced he is suffering from snow blindness. Later, the creature migrates south, causing tremendous havoc. Then it heads for New York City, which once was its spawning ground. Once there the monster not only devastates parts of Manhattan but also infects its human opponents with primevil germs. Eventually the dinosaur is cornered in the Manhattan Beach Amusement Park and a radioactive isotope is fired into a wound in its throat. The beast is vanquished!

The success of this entry (it was produced on a $250,000 budget and grossed over $5 million) is mainly due to Ray Harryhausen's fine special effects (this was his first major film) and to Eugene Lourie's direction, which effectively employed darkness, shadows, and moods to establish an ambiance for the film.

Those who witness The Beast from 20,000 Fathoms for the first time in the Seventies must bear in mind that when it was filmed, its structure was novel, including the use of the poetic-justice finale (the beast destroyed by radioactivity, the force that unleashed it).

THE BEAST OF YUCCA FLATS (Crown International, 1960) 60 min.

Producer, Anthony Cardoza; director/screenplay, Coleman Francis; music, I. Nafshun and Al Remington; camera, John Cagle; editor, Francis.

Tor Johnson (Joseph Javorsky); Barbara Francis (Marcia Knight); and Douglas Mellor, Larry Aten, Bing Stafford, Linda

Bielima, Anthony Cardoza, Bob Labansat, Jim Oliphant, George Prince, Alan and Ronald Francis, Eric Tomlin, and Conrad Brooke.

A noted Russian scientist (Tor Johnson) escapes from behind the Iron Curtain and comes to the U.S., carrying with him a number of important secrets concerning a Soviet moon shot. Knowing he is being trailed by Soviet agents, the scientist hurries to Yucca Flats, where nuclear experiments are being conducted. At the Flats he is captured by the operatives at the moment a nuclear bomb is exploded. The agents are killed and the scientist is transformed into a hulking monster. Later he kidnaps a girl and takes her to his mountain cave where he kills her. He also abducts two small boys; but they escape and warn the local residents of the fiend. Two policemen use an airplane to parachute onto the top of the mountain where the monster lives. In the ensuing fight the beast is killed.

This poverty row production (filmed at a cost of $34,000) received scant release when issued in 1960. It is mainly remembered as a starring vehicle for Tor Johnson, who had something of a vogue in sci-fi films. For years Johnson wrestled professionally under the name of the Super Swedish Angel and he had been in pictures since 1935. In the late-Fifties he found his niche playing a variety of monsters (often without makeup, as had Rondo Hatton in the Forties). Among his sci-fi genre appearances were Bride of the Monster (q.v.) and its unissued sequel Night of the Ghouls; The Unearthly, The Black Sleep, and Plan 9 from Outer Space (all q.v.).

In 1974 this feature was issued to TV as Atomic Monster: The Beast of Yucca Flats.

BEAUTIFUL WOMEN AND THE HYDROGEN-MAN see BIJYO TO EKITAININ-GEN

BEGINNING OF THE END (Republic, 1957) 73 min.

Producer/director, Bert I. Gordon; screenplay, Fred Freiberger and Lester Gorn; camera, Jack Marta; editor, Aaron Stell.

Peggie Castle (Audrey); Peter Graves (Ed); Morris Ankrum (General Hanson); Richard Benedict (Corporal Mathias); Thomas B. Henry (Colonel Sturgeon); Than Wyenn (Frank); and John Close, Don C. Harvey, Steve Warren, Pierre Watkin, Frank Wilcox, Alan Reynolds, Alan Wells, Eilene Jansen, Hylton Socher, Paul Grant, and Patricia Dean.

"A picture such as this fantasy thriller," said the New York Times, " ... always poses three questions. First, of course, is it truly frightening? Yes, for about twenty minutes. Are the technical boys on their toes? Same answer, until the grasshoppers and the low budget, both, get pretty transparent. Finally, is there any saving sensibility or bolstering factual approach? No." Some pundits insisted that a film with such a title deserved critical razzing. But after all, when a "giant" grasshopper is supposed to be climbing a Chicago skyscraper and it is painfully obvious that it is just an ordinary-

sized insect placed on a screen with the building being projected onto
it, what does the filmmaker (Bert I. Gordon) expect of the viewer?
Yet this was one of the canon of entries making up the education of
sci-fi enthusiasts in the Fifties and thereafter.
    Radioactive isotopes have been introduced in Texas to aid
crop reproduction. After initial successes, the experiment is transferred to Illinois; there, it not only produces giant-sized harvests
but a snafu in the workings exposes a swarm of grasshoppers to the
radioactivity, and they soon develop into giant insects. The destruc-
tive creatures then invade Chicago, causing more chaos than Al Ca-
pone and his bad boys did in the Roaring Twenties. Much to the
chagrin of hero Peter Graves and the ever-suffering heroine Beverly
Garland, the military decide to destroy the Windy City in an atomic
holocaust. It seems the only way to rid the world of the invaders.
But ever-inventive Graves, at the last minute, duplicates the mating
call of the grasshoppers and lures them into Lake Michigan. Chicago
is saved!

THE BEHEMOTH   see   THE GIANT BEHEMOTH

BENEATH THE PLANET OF THE APES (Twentieth Century-Fox,
1970) C-94 min.

    Producer, Arthur P. Jacobs; associate producer, Mort Abra-
hams; director, Ted Post; based on characters created by Pierre
Boulle; screenplay, Paul Dehn and Abrahams; second unit director,
Chuck Roberson; assistant director, Fred Simpson; art directors,
Jack Martin Smith and William Creber; set decorators, Walter M.
Scott and Sven Wickman; music, Leonard Rosenman; orchestrator,
Ralph Ferraro; costumes, Morton Haack; makeup design, John Cham-
bers; sound, Stephen Bass and David Dockendorf; special camera ef-
fects, L. B. Abbott and Art Cruickshank; camera, Milton Krasner;
editor, Marion Rothman.
    James Franciscus (Brent); Charlton Heston (Taylor); Kim Hun-
ter (Zira); Maurice Evans (Dr. Zaius); Linda Harrison (Nova); Paul
Richards (Mendez); Victor Buono (Fat Man); James Gregory (Ursus);
Jeff Corey (Caspay); Natalie Trundy (Albina); Thomas Gomez (Minister); David Watson (Cornelius); Don Pedro Colley (Black Man); Tod
Andrews (Skipper); Gregory Sierra (Verger); Elson Burke (Gorilla
Sergeant); Lou Wagner (Lucius).

    When Twentieth Century-Fox issued this sequel to the immen-
sely popular Planet of the Apes (q.v.) the studio quickly wrote off
the entry as a fast dollar follow-up. Instead this well-conceived production was almost on par with its predecessor and proved so popular that eventually three more spin-offs appeared in the series.
    The storyline commences where the initial film stopped.
Charlton Heston as astronaut Taylor and Linda Harrison as Nova ride
off into the "Forbidden Zone" after finding the fallen Statue of Liberty
and realizing that the planet of the apes is the Earth of the future.
Another astronaut, Brent (James Franciscus), also breaks through the

James Franciscus in <u>Beneath the Planet of the Apes</u> (1970).

time barrier and finds Taylor. Under the ruins of Manhattan they
locate the remains of the human race, a group of horribly scarred,
mask-wearing mutants led by Victor Buono. The survivors worship
a cobalt missile, the last weapon surviving from the nuclear holocaust which dethroned the human race and made simians the Earth's
rulers. Later, a war erupts between the mutants and the apes, with
the astronauts caught in the middle. Finally the mutants force Taylor and Brent into a struggle to the death; Nova is killed. The mutants explode their atomic bomb and the film ends with the ominous
words, "In one of the countless billion galaxies of the Universe, one
of its planets is now dead. "
        Frederick S. Clarke wrote in Cinefantastique, "All technical
departments are up to the standard of the previous film, and the
special effects are much more plentiful. Beneath the Planet of the
Apes is the finest film that could possibly be made given Planet of
the Apes as a premise. " On the other hand, the British Monthly
Film Bulletin carped, "Against the dazzlingly beautiful and ironic
ending of the first [POTA], in which man seemed to confront his own
destiny in the form of auto-destructive art, the climax of Beneath the
Planet of the Apes is simply sensational, providing an obviously
weighty pessimism which, in the light of the Film's closing minutes,
turns out to be pure melodrama. And the careful elucidation of ape
society and its orthodoxy here becomes a straightforward caricature
of militarism, with a few heavy-handed allusions to the Vietnam War."

BEWARE THE BLOB! see   THE BLOB

BEYOND THE MOON (International Television Corp. , 1964) 78 min.

        Producer, Roland Reed; directors, William Beaudine, Hollings-
worth Morse, et al. ; teleplays, Clark Hittleman, Warren Wilson, et al.
        With: Richard Crane (Rocky Jones); Sally Mansfield, James
Lydon, Maurice Cass, Paul Marion, Ian Keith, et al.

        In the 1953-54 TV season, producer Roland Reed was respon-
sible for a low-budget video series which was distributed on the syn-
dication route as "Rocky Jones, Space Ranger. " Richard Crane was
the program's main asset, as a believable futuristic space pioneer,
and the program co-starred Sally Mansfield, James Lydon, and later
Scott Beckett. Strictly juvenile in nature, the show had a few sea-
sons' run across the country and then disappeared from the small
screen.
        About 1964, International Television Corporation (ITC), a Lon-
don-based firm which is now producing the "Space: 1999" TV series,
launched itself onto the U. S. video scene by acquiring old segments
of various syndicated shows (e. g. , "Hawkeye, " "Ramar of the Jungle" and "Sir Francis Drake"), pasting various episodes together and
issuing them as feature films. In the case of "Rocky Jones, Space
Ranger, " no less than a dozen feature films evolved.
        Beyond the Moon was followed by such other entries in the
"series" as The Cold Sun, The Forbidden Moon, Blast Off, Crash

of Moons, The Magnetic Moon, Menace from Outer Space, The Renegade Satellite, The Robot of Regalio, Duel in Space, Gypsy Moon, and Manhunt in Space.

BEYOND ATLANTIS   see   ATLANTIS, THE LOST CONTINENT

BEYOND THE TIME BARRIER (American International, 1960) 75 min.

     Executive producers, John Miller and Robert L. Madden; producer, Robert Clarke; director, Edgar G. Ulmer; Story/screenplay, Arthur G. Pierce; music composer/conductor, Darrell Calker; art director, Ernst Fegte; makeup, Jack Pierce; assistant director, Leonard J. Shapiro; costumes, Jack Masters; sound, Earl Snyder and Don Olson; special effects, Roger George; camera effects, Howard A. Anderson; camera, Meredith M. Nicholson; editor, Jack Ruggiero.
     Robert Clarke (Major William Allison); Darlene Tompkins (Princess Trirene); Arianne Arden (Markova); Vladimir Sokoloff (The Supreme); Stephen Bekassy (Karl Kruse); John Van Dreelen (Dr. Bourman); Red Morgan (The Captain); Ken Knox (Colonel Martin); Don Flournoy and Tom Ravick (Mutants); Neil Fletcher (Air Force Chief of Staff); Jack Herman (Dr. Richman); William Shapard (General York); James Altgens (Secretary Patterson); John Loughney (General LaMont); Russell Marker (Colonel Curtis).

     A decade after their work on the sci-fi "sleeper" Man from Planet X (q.v.), director Edgar G. Ulmer and star Robert Clarke (also a co-producer on this project) teamed up again for this genre effort. It was shot simultaneously in an eleven-day period with The Amazing Transparent Man (q.v.). This picture, unfortunately, was many rungs below Man from Planet X. "The only ingredient that distinguishes this effort from its many predecessors is the presence of a timely political message.... This preach-peace aspect is put over with some impact via the absence of the expected happy ending, but it is preceded by too much quasi-scientific mumbo-jumbo and melodramatic absurdity to register with a degree of conviction" (Variety).
     While testing the just developed hypersonic X-80 aircraft, Major William Allison (Robert Clarke) is catapulted into the future, to the year 2024. He finds the Earth a desolate place, the surface laid barren by the cosmic-nuclear plague of 1971 (!). When he is captured by the soldiers of the Underground Citadel he meets their leader (Vladimir Sokoloff) and falls in love with the ruler's daughter (Darlene Tompkins). He also learns that the Underground people are at war with the Surface Mutants. The test pilot then finds himself as a real life Buck Rogers and agrees to aid the Underground cause. Having accomplished his goal, he escapes back to the world of 1960, warning global leaders that atomic tests MUST be discontinued.
     The biggest fault of Beyond the Time Barrier is its impoverished sets. The airfield on which Major Allison lands after coming through the time barrier looks like a ghetto after a riot; the supposedly ornate Underground throne room is about as regal as a corner grocery store.

BIGFOOT (Ellman Enterprises, 1971) C-94 min.

Executive producer, Herman Tomlin; producer, Anthony Cardoza; associate producer, Bill Reardon; director/story, Robert F. Slatzer; screenplay, Slatzer and James Gordon White; art director, Norman Houle; makeup, Louis Lane; titles, Ray Mercer; wardrobe, Jeanne Segal; "Bigfoot" Bodies created by Mercy Montello; music, Richard A. Podolar; sound, Bob Dietz; special effects, Harry Woolman; camera, Wilson S. Hong; editor, Hugo Grimaldi.

Chris Mitchum (Rick); John Carradine (Jasper B. Hawks); Joi Lansing (Joi Landis); Lindsay Crosby (Wheels); Judy Jordan (Chris); James Craig (Sheriff Cyrus); John Mitchum (Elmer Briggs); Joy Wilkerson (Peggy); James Stellar (Bigfoot); Ken Maynard (Mr. Bennett); Doodles Weaver (Forest Ranger); Dorothy Keller (Nellie); Noble "Kid" Chissell (Hardrock); Nick Raymond (Slim); Sonny West (Mike); Suzy Marlin Crosby (Suzy); Lois Red Elk (Falling Star); Walt Swanner (Henry); Carolyn Gilbert (Mrs. Cummings); Kim Cardoza (Kim); Bill Bonner (Lucky); Tony Cardoza (Fisherman); Gloria Hill, Nancy Hunter, and A'leshia Lea (Female Creatures); Nick Raymond (Evil Creature); Jerry Maren (Baby Creature).

In this century there has been much interest in the so-called "Yeti, " the Abominable Snowman of the Himalayas, a supposedly hairy man-like creature which infests the area at the base of these mountains and which may provide scientists with the long-sought "missing link. " Only in recent years has interest arisen in the U.S. - Canadian counterpart, known here as "The Bigfoot. " In the Seventies, both a British Broadcasting Corporation telecast and an American TV special have examined the legend of this creature, and a number of books on the subject have appeared (including John Napier's well-researched Big Foot, 1972.)

The first real commercial effort to exploit public interest in the creature occurred in Robert Slatzer's Bigfoot, a 1969 film made on a $325,000 budget and a 25-day shooting schedule in Northern California and in Los Angeles. By the time it was issued two years later, the Bigfoot craze was well underway and the picture did brisk box-office business.

The rather simplistic plotline has Joi Lansing's plane being forced down in the Northwest and the perennial starlet being abducted by a bigfoot creature, who takes her to his lair. A group of trail bike riders (led by Lindsay Crosby and Chris Mitchum) come upon the girl in distress and help her escape from the creature. They bring back word of the Bigfoot to Ken Maynard's country store, and there peddler John Carradine decides to market the beast, but his plans eventually come to naught.

Some critics were unduly harsh to Bigfoot. "An utterly unconvincing 'missing link' monster movie, Bigfoot is one of those low-budget affairs boasting a large cast of has-beens, never-weres and stars' untalented offspring. Bigfoot leaves a small imprint indeed ... " (Los Angeles Times). Others were just amused: "Bigfoot is usually shot from a camera angle between his toes, making him loom over the camera like King Kong, but when we see him straight-on he looks about 5 feet 10 or 11. He wears a shaggy costume stitched

together out of old brown shag rugs, and his fur is so dirty he
should dial C-A-R-P-E-T-S right away" (Chicago Sun-Times).
Even the most lenient filmgoer had to accept the film's dialogue with a big grain of salt.   Near the end, Joi Lansing asks "Do
you ... think it's dead?" Lindsay Crosby replies, "Nothing could
live through that. "   Then there's John Carradine's tag line at the
film's end, 'It was beauty that did him in. "   (The wordage is a direct borrowing from the more famous King Kong, q. v.)

BIJYO TO EKITAININ-GEN (BEAUTIFUL WOMEN AND THE HYDRO-
GEN-MAN) (Toho, 1958) C- 79 min.

   Producer, Tomoyuki Tanaka; director, Inoshiro Honda; story,
Hideo Kaijo; screenplay, Takeshi Kimura; music, Masaru Sato; art
director, Takeo Kita; sound, Choshichiro Mikami and Masanobu Mi-
gami; special effects, Eiji Tsuburaya; camera, Hajime Koizumi.
   Yumi Shirakawa (The Girl); Kenji Sahara (The Detective);
Akihiko Hirata (The Scientist); and: Eitaro Ozawa, Koreya Senda,
and Mitsuru Sato.

Scene from Bijyo To Ekitainin-Gen (1958).

This anemic thriller was a poor substitute for the studio's rash of monster films. Director Inoshiro Honda seemed to be at a loss when dealing with human mutants, rather than the likes of Godzilla, Rodan and Gigantis. But, argued the New York Herald-Tribune, it was "A good-natured poke at atom-bomb tests.... The picture is plainly making a case against the use of nuclear bombs. At the same time, there is a great deal of lively entertainment in the story involving the police, dope smugglers, scientists and some very pretty Japanese girls.... "

H-bomb explosions in Japan so contaminate the air that an almost-liquid like creature is formed. It oozes about through almost everything imaginable in order to absorb others and thus remain alive. Eventually it slithers its way to Tokyo and interrupts a strip show, absorbing those present. Later it takes refuge in a sewer and is destroyed there by an Army-set gasoline fire.

When released in the U.S. as The H-Man in 1958, Columbia issued the film on a double bill with The Woman Eater, 1957 British-made entry about a scientist (George Coulouris) who returns from the Amazon basin with a tree that diets on young girls. One can only wonder how such a combination program affected the theatre's food concession department.

THE BIRDS (Universal, 1963) C-120 min.

Producer/director, Alfred Hitchcock; based on the story by Daphne du Maurier; screenplay, Evan Hunter; art director, Robert Boule; set decorator, George Milo; pictorial designs, Albert Whitlock; trainer of the birds, Ray Berwick; Miss Hedren's costumes, Edith Head; wardrobe supervisor, Rita Riggs; makeup, Howard Smith; assistant director, James H. Brown; electronic sound production and composition, Remi Glassmann and Oskar Sala; sound consultant, Bernard Herrmann; sound, Waldon O. Watson and William Russell; special camera advisor, Ub Iwerks; special effects, Lawrence A. Hampton; camera, Robert Burks; editor, George Tomasini.

Rod Taylor (Mitch Brenner); Tippi Hedren (Melanie Daniels); Jessica Tandy (Mrs. Brenner); Suzanne Pleshette (Anne Hayworth); Veronica Cartwright (Cathy Brenner); Ethel Griffies (Mrs. Bundy); Charles McGraw (Sebastian Sholes); Ruth McDevitt (Mrs. MacGruder); Joe Mantell (Traveling Salesman); Doreen Lang (Hysterical Woman); Malcolm Atterbury (Deputy Al Malone); Karl Swenson (Drunk); Elizabeth Wilson (Helen Carter); Lonny Chapman (Deke Carter); Doodles Weaver (Fisherman); John McGovern (Postal Clerk); Richard Deacon (Man in Elevator).

Alfred Hitchcock's one big-screen foray into the realm of the science fiction film was The Birds. At the time of its release the film met with a mixed critical reception (and still does), but it was immensely popular, and has been issued and re-issued and today is a top TV viewing item. Perhaps next to Psycho, it is the picture most associated with thriller master Hitchcock.

Rich playgirl Melanie Daniels (Tippi Hedren) gives chase to the attorney (Rod Taylor) she loves, pursuing him to the small island

Tippi Hedren, Jessica Tandy and Rod Taylor in The Birds (1963).

of Bogeda Bay, on the California coast near San Francisco. He has
gone there to see his schoolteacher love (Suzanne Pleshette), his
mother (Jessica Tandy) and his young sister (Veronica Cartwright).
Once they are there swarms of birds begin to converge on the island
and eventually begin attacking and killing the inhabitants. One terrifying scene has a cloud of birds landing on a school playground and
waiting--waiting for the recess bell to ring in order to attack the
children. Another scene shows thousand of finches flying down a chim-
ney and into a house where they attack and kill the inhabitants.
    Time seized on the picture's weakness: "Why did the birds
go to war? Hitchcock does not tell, and the movie flaps to a plot-
less end. " At the finale of The Birds, all the living persons on Bo-
dega Bay have departed, and the birds have full control of the isle.
Was the master of the thrill and the scream suggesting that the fine-
feathered creatures have a capacity for thought, organization, control,
and revenge? (The master filmmaker did admit that in making The
Birds, "I made sure that the public would not be able to anticipate
from one scene to another. " This is perhaps a key to realizing that
the film is to be taken as entertainment rather than as a deep probe
of ornithology and its relevance to science fiction.)
    Daphne du Maurier's story had been the basis of assorted ra-
dio and TV productions (one especially gripping live half-show in the
mid-Fifties) before the big screen rendition. But it is the Hitchcock exercise that remains the memorable version.

THE BLACK SCORPION (Warner Bros. , 1957) 88 min.

Producers, Frank Melford and Jack Dietz; director, Edward Ludwig; story, Paul Yawitz; screenplay, David Duncan and Robert Blees; art director, Edward Fitzgerald; stop motion animation, Willis O'Brien; music, Paul Sawtell; sound, Rafael L. Esparza; camera, Lionel Lindon; editor, Richard Van Enger.

Richard Denning (Henry Scott); Mara Corday (Teresa); Carlos Rivas (Artur Ramos); Mario Navarro (Juanito); Carlos Muzquiz (Dr. Velazco); Pascual Peña (Jose de la Cruz); Fanny Schiller (Florentina); Pedro Galvan (Father Delgado); Arturo Martinez (Major Cosio).

In Mexico in a mysterious underground cavern a number of giant scorpions are discovered. They are mutations of atomic blasts. Also in the cave are huge prehistoric earthworms. These are devoured by the scorpions who then set about devouring each other. Finally only one scorpion remains and this armored giant comes above ground to wreak havoc in a populated area of the country. The Army is called in to stop its terroristic activities. A helicopter is used to thrust an electrified metal harpoon into the monster. The mission is successful.

Hoping to cut into some of the profits being made in the sci-fi genre at this time by Universal, Columbia, American International, and a host of independents, Warner Bros. made this hardly delectable item. It was a harsh, dark, brutal movie and one that did not overly appeal to moviegoers, even devout sci-fi fans. Its chief virtue was the excellent stop motion animation by Willis O'Brien; this was one of his last films.

THE BLACK SLEEP (United Artists, 1956) 81 min.

Executive producer, Aubrey Schenck; producer, Howard W. Koch; director, Reginald Le Borg; screenplay, John C. Higgins; music director, Les Baxter; camera, Gordon Avil; editor, John F. Schreyer.

Basil Rathbone (Sir Joel Cadman); Akim Tamiroff (Odo); Lon Chaney (Mungo); John Carradine (Borg); Bela Lugosi (Casimir); Herbert Rudley (Dr. Gordon Ramsey); Patricia Blake (Laurie); Phyllis Stanley (Daphne); Tor Johnson (Curry); Sally Yarnell (Nancy); George Sawaya (K-6); Claire Carleton (Miss Daly).

For a B entry, The Black Sleep had an elaborate budget (about $250,000), workmanlike direction by Reginald Le Borg, John C. Higgins' literate script, and a top-notch cast. It should have emerged a far more engrossing venture.

Basil Rathbone starred as Sir Joel Cadman, an 1872 British brain surgeon who uses an East Indian drug to induce a cataleptic state in order to perform his lobotomies. The doctor is anxious to find a cure for his wife's zombie-like existence. At Cadman's estate near London, a former student (Rudley) is made to help the physician. But the partnership comes to an end when he discovers the doctor has been experimenting unsuccessfully on the living and has

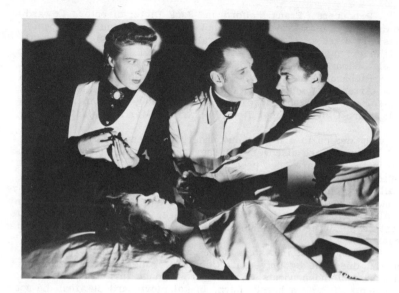

Phyllis Stanley, Patricia Blake, Basil Rathbone and Herbert Rudley
in The Black Sleep (1956).

produced a cellar full of freaks: mad killer Mongo (Lon Chaney),
imagined-Crusader Borg (John Carradine), gigantic imbecile (Tor
Johnson), and a scarred madman (George Sawaya). The student falls
in love with Mongo's pretty daughter (Patricia Blake) and after they
accidentally set the freaks free, they escape from the house. Dr.
Cadman is not so lucky--the human guinea pigs set upon him and kill
their tormentor.

      Due to its action house cast (with Bela Lugosi prominently
featured as Cadman's mute butler) the film did very good business.
In 1962 it was re-issued to theatres as Dr. Cadman's Secret.

      It is unfortunate that the filmmakers did not use the players
to better advantage in this sci fi/horror entry and try to explore the
intellectual and moral aspects of a man defying the laws of nature.

BLAST OFF   see   BEYOND THE MOON and FROM THE EARTH TO
THE MOON

THE BLOB (Paramount, 1958) C-85 min.

      Producer, Jack H. Harris; director, Irvin S. Yeaworth, Jr.;

screen idea, Irvine H. Millgate; screenplay, Theodore Simonson and Kate Phillips; music, Jean Yeaworth; title song, Bert Bacharach and Mack David; special effects, Barton Sloane; camera, Thomas Spalding; editor, Alfred Hillman.

Steve McQueen (Steve Andrews); Aneta Corseaut (Judy Martin); Earl Rowe (Dave, the Police Lieutenant); Olin Howlin (Old Man); Steven Chase (Dr. Hallen); John Benson (Burt); Vince Barbi (George, the Diner Owner); Audrey Metcalf (Mrs. Martin); Elinor Hammer (Mrs. Porter); Keith Almoney (Danny Martin); Julie Cousins (Sally the Waitress); Robert Fields (Tony Gressette); James Bonnet (Mooch Miller); Anthony Granke (Al).

Filmed in Valley Forge, Pennsylvania on a budget of $240,000 (and sold to Paramount Pictures for a profit) this modest entry has become a popular TV viewing item. Not only does it star a youthful Steve McQueen but the picture's title has gained a cult reputation. (During the mid-Sixties, the film's name, for some reason became synonymous among stand-up comics with really bad movies.)

The New York Herald-Tribune maintained in 1958, "A minor classic in its field," and explained, "Not only does it have a monster with propensities that will curdle the dreams, but it is made with a stress on naturalism of behavior by the human being.... Tension mounts to a suitably harrowing level [as] the parasitic monster oozes irresistibly and noiselessly through the evening." In contrast, Arthur Knight (Saturday Review) judged, "Not so much horror as horrid.... While it cannot be denied that there is a certain grim fascination in ... seeing the glowing, gelatinous 'blob' devour a human arm, such grisly moments invariably produce sensations of nastiness rather than of terror." Mr. Knight commented that pictures such as these are "sad enough as a commentary on our youth, but even more so on the standards of our motion-picture industry."

Like The Spider (q.v.), The Blob has teenagers in a battle of wits with a witless monster. Here the creature is a sponge-like substance which has dropped from outer space and begins to grow and grow. The law enforcers of the small town where it happens refuse to believe teenagers McQueen and Aneta Corseaut's tale of a monster which grows bigger than a house and attacks a movie theatre and a supermarket. Eventually the Blob engulfs the hero and heroine in an all-night diner. However, inventive McQueen attacks the monster with a foam fire extinguisher which causes it to freeze. At this juncture government forces arrive and cart the frozen Blob to a frigid grave in the Antarctic.

Abroad, this entry was entitled The Molten Meteor. American producers revived the creature in 1972 for a gooey sequel called Beware the Blob! (a.k.a. Son of Blob).

BLOOD BEAST FROM OUTER SPACE see THE NIGHT CALLER

BLOOD CREATURE see TERROR IS A MAN

BLOOD ON HIS LIPS   see   HIDEOUS SUN DEMON

THE BOOGIE MAN WILL GET YOU (Columbia, 1942) 66 min.

Director, Lew Landers; story, Hal Fimberg and Robert B.
Hunt; screenplay, Edwin Blum; camera, Henry Freulich; editor,
Richard Fantl.
Boris Karloff (Professor Nathaniel Billings); Peter Lorre (Dr.
Lorentz); Maxie Rosenbloom (Maxie); Jeff Donnell (Winnie Layden);
Larry Parks (Bill Layden); Maude Eburne (Amelia Jones); Don Beddoe
(J. Gilbert Brampton); George McKay (Ebenezer); Frank Puglia (Sil-
via Bacigalupi); Eddie Laughton (Johnson); Frank Sully (Officer Star-
rett); James Morton (Officer Quincy).

In an effort to capitalize on Boris Karloff's stage success in
Arsenic and Old Lace, Columbia Pictures starred him in this vehicle,
his last under a studio contract. Unfortunately, the crazy goings-on
failed to emulate the actor's stage hit and the little B entry was
quickly relegated to the bottom half of double bills.
Karloff portrayed a mad scientist, Professor Nathaniel Billings, who works in his laboratory-basement on a theory which will
transform ordinary men into supermen, all to aid the war effort.
Debts, however, force him to sell the house to lamebrained Winnie
Layden (Jeff Donnell) who wants to re-do the place and make it into a
hotel. Billings remains on the premises to continue his experiments,
aided by local sheriff-doctor, Dr. Lorentz (Peter Lorre). Bill Layden (Larry Parks), Winnie's divorced husband, arrives on the scene
hoping to divert her from her expensive scheme. When loony traveling salesman Maxie (Maxie Rosenbloom) shows up, Billings and Lorentz decide to experiment on him, hoping to make him their super
creation. The experiment fails. After Bill finds five bodies in the
basement the law is called into action. Just then a Fascist (Frank
Puglia) arrives, claiming to be a "human bomb." He attempts to
steal the professor's formula. When the five bodies are found to be
in a state of suspended animation, and the "human bomb" fizzles, all
concerned are escorted to the booby-hatch, an institution conveniently
run by the multi-talented Dr. Lorentz.
The British Kinematograph Weekly labeled the film a "screwy
comedy melodrama, a wild incursion into the macabre." Probably
the film's funniest scene had cook Maude Eburne dreaming/acting she
was a chicken. It is this picture that gave Peter Lorre the dubious
reputation of being the boogie man.
It is a shame that in the several decades of filmmaking in the
sci-fi genre, not more picturemakers have tried deliberately to blend
the comedic with the horrific. As demonstrated here, it makes for
an engaging contrast.

A BOY AND HIS DOG (LQJaf Films, 1975) C-89 min.

Producer, Alvy Moore; associate producer, Tom Conners;
director, L. Q. Jones; based on the novella by Harlan Ellison;

screenplay, Jones; music, Tim McIntire; "Topeka" music, Jaime
Mendoza-Nava; production designer, Ray Boyle; wardrobe, Carolyn
Moore and Steve McQueen; stunt co-ordinator, Bill Burton; titles,
Steve Smith; sound effects, Gilbert D. Marchant; special effects,
Frank Rowe; camera, John Arthur Morrill; editor, Scott Conrad.
Don Johnson (Vic); Susanne Benton (Quilla June); Tim McIntire
(Blood's Voice); Alvy Moore (Dr. Moore); Jason Robards (Lew); Helen Winston (Mez); Charles McGraw (The Preacher); Hal Baylor (Michael); Ron Feinberg (Fellini); Mike Rupert (Gary); Don Carter (Ken);
Michael Hershman (Richard); Tiger (Blood the Dog).

In the period after World War IV, some half-century into the
future, a malnutritioned and sex-starved young man named Vic (Don
Johnson), with Blood, his telepathic dog (who "talks"), searches for
food and females, not necessarily in that order. The world he knows
is a desolate one, filled by the scavenging survivors of two nuclear
holocausts. What little data Vic knows of the world's history has been
taught to him by the dog, the only living soul--so far--with whom he
can communicate.
Finally Blood sniffs out a female and the youth chases her to
an abandoned underground abode inhabited by "screamers"--war survivors contaminated by radioactive material. Quilla June (Susanne
Benton) convinces Vic to join her in the underground world. He finds
life as it must have been in the 1890s. He also discovers he is to
be used in a plan to repopulate the zombie-like underground and then
to be killed.
Eventually he escapes, deciding, "I want to get into a good
straight forward fight with some sonofabitch over a can of beans. I
gotta get back in the dirt, so I feel clean!" He and Quilla June return to the surface world, away from the savagery beneath, where
dissenters are sent to the "farm" to be exterminated. He locates
Blood and finds he is too hungry to make the trip to freedom. Vic,
who had been previously almost alienated from the dog by the girl,
kills the devious Quilla June and feeds her to the animal. Man and
intelligent beast set off then for the journey over the mountains to the
hoped-for nirvana.
A Boy and His Dog was shot during April-May, 1973 on a
27-day filming schedule. Location work was accomplished at the
since-torn-down Pacific Ocean Park in Venice, CA. with other filming at Barstow, CA.
Don Shay in Cinefantastique judged this independent feature
"funny, savage, uncompromising" and noted, "But what sets A Boy
and His Dog apart is that it is not merely a violent, cynical, action-
packed drama with a gimmick ending, but a personal story--a love
story ... between two beings as unlike in nearly every respect as
they were in appearance. "

THE BRAIN see VENGEANCE

THE BRAIN EATERS (American International, 1958) 60 min.

Producer, Ed Nelson; director, Bruno VeSota; story/screen-

play, Gordon Urquhart; assistant director, Mike Murphy; music, Tom
Jonson; title design, Robert Balser; art direction, Burt Shonberg;
wardrobe, Charles Smith; camera, Larry Raimond; editor, Carlo
Lodato.
  Ed Nelson (Dr. Kettering); Alan Frost (Glenn); Jack Hill (Sen-
ator Powers); Joanna Lee (Alice); Jody Fair (Elaine); David Hughes
(Dr. Wyler); Robert Ball (Dan Walker); Greigh Phillips (Sheriff); Or-
ville Sherman (Cameron); Leonard Nimoy (Protector); Doug Banks
(Doctor); Henry Randolph (Telegrapher).

  "Within its drawbacks, it is competently done.... This gimmick of outer space protoplasma which attach themselves to human
necks, has been used before. Since much of this fantasy-fiction material is the same in basis, it doesn't make too much difference, except that these pictures are supported by largely the same audiences
who notice such things... The cycle appears to have reached the
point of diminishing returns ..." (Variety).
  Parasites from deep in the earth emerge to the surface, attach themselves to human beings and devour their brains through
puncture holes in the neck. The government troops eventually destroy the subterranean invaders.
  The film's cast and technical staff hold special interest. Star
Ed (Edwin) Nelson, later of "Peyton Place" TV fame, is also the
picture's producer, and in the proceedings are Leonard Nimoy (later
the idol of "Star Trek") and Jack Hill (who would later produce and
direct a number of horror movies.)
  Abroad, the film was known under a variety of titles: The
Keepers/The Brain Snatchers/Keepers of the Earth.

THE BRAIN FROM PLANET AROUS (Howco International, 1958) 71 min.

  Producer, Jacques Marquette; director, Nathan Hertz [Juran];
screenplay, Ray Buffum; music, Walter Greene; camera, Marquette;
editor, Irving Schoenberg.
  John Agar (Steve); Joyce Meadows (Sally); and Robert Fuller,
Thomas B. Henry, and Ken Terrell.

  Within its modes limits intelligently and resourcefully produced ..." (Hollywood Reporter).
  The old story of a super intelligence from another planet
taking over the mind of a scientist was dusted off again. With its
minuscule budget, it no doubt turned a profit for the producers.
  Nathan Juran again used the credit ploy of Hertz in helming
this undernourished entry. The picture boasts one amusing, even if
rather ludicrous, twist for sci-fans, in the finale. After the evil
brain from Arous has overwhelmed John Agar's sensibilities, a
"good" brain called Vol, which has possessed the body of Agar's dog,
does battle with the wicked brain and destroys (!) it. Agar is liber-
ated and there is a happy ending.

THE BRAIN SNATCHER   see   THE MAN WHO CHANGED HIS MIND

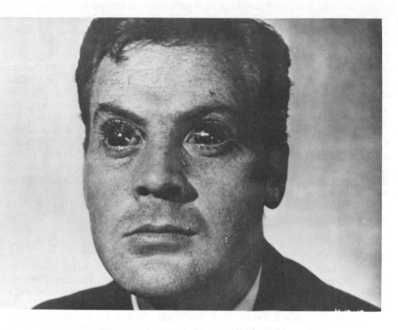

John Agar in The Brain from Planet Arous (1958).

THE BRAIN SNATCHERS   see   THE BRAIN EATERS

THE BRAIN THAT WOULDN'T DIE (American International, 1962)
81 min.

Producer, Rex Carlton; director, Joseph Green; story, Carlton
and Green; screenplay, Green; music, Abe Baker and Tony Restaino;
art director, Paul Fanning; assistant director, Tony La Marca; makeup, George Fiala; special effects, Byron Baer; camera, Stephen Haj-
nal; editors, Leonard Anderson and Marc Anderson.
Virginia Leith (Jan Compton); Herb [Jason] Evers (Dr. Bill
Cortner); Adele Lamont (Doris Powell); Bruce Brighton (Dr. Cortner);
Doris Brent (Nurse); Leslie Daniel (Kurt); Bonnie Shari (Stripper);
Paula Maurice (B-Girl); Lola Mason (Donna Williams); Audrey De-
vereau (Jeannie); Bruce Kerr (Announcer); Eddie Carmel (Monster).
A. k. a. The Head that Wouldn't Die.

The combination of sci-fi and horror does not always blend
well. The title of this effort seems to be the production's most imaginative ingredient.
Insane Dr. Bill Cortner (Herb Evers) is experimenting with

transplanting parts of the human anatomy. Despite pleadings from
his crippled assistant that he stop, the physician continues. He has
already made one serious mistake--locked behind the door in his
laboratory is a creature he created from dead bodies, a thing so
horrible even its creator cannot bear to look at it. One day while
out driving with his fiancée (Virginia Leith), the doctor and the young
lady have a terrible accident. Her head is decapitated. He takes
the severed head to the laboratory and keeps it alive, despite the
"girl's" protests. Later, the head begins to communicate via telepathy with the closeted monster and the lab assistant is killed. Still
later, the doctor locates a model (Adele Lamont) with a beautiful
body but a scarred face. He decides to operate and attach his fiancée's head to her body. He drugs the victim and takes her to his
lab. But the monster escapes and sets the place on fire. At the
finish, the monster departs with the unconscious girl, while the dead
doctor and the "head" are consumed in the lab fire.
    Obviously the storyline here owes a lot to the Frankenstein
(q. v.) and Donovan's Brain (q. v.) heritage.

BRICK BRADFORD (Columbia, 1947) fifteen chapters

    Producer, Sam Katzman; director, Spencer Gordon Bennet;
based upon the newspaper feature Brick Bradford, owned and copy-
righted by King Features syndicate; screenplay, George H. Plympton,
Arthur Hoerl, and Lewis Clay; assistant director, R. M. Andrews;
second unit director, Thomas Carr; music, Mischa Bakaleinikoff;
camera, Ira H. Morgan; editor, Earl Turner.
    Kane Richmond (Brick Bradford); Rick Vallin (Sandy Sander-
son); Linda Johnson (June Saunders); Pierre Watkin (Professor Salisbury); Charles Quigley (Laydron); Jack Ingram (Albers); Fred Graham
(Black); John Merton (Dr. Tymak); Leonard Penn (Byrus); Wheeler
Oakman (Walthar); Carol Forman (Queen Khana); Charles King
(Creed); John Hart (Dent); Helen Stanley (Carol Preston); Nelson
Leigh (Prescott); Robert Barron (Zuntar); George DeNormand (Meaker).
    Chapters: 1) Atomic Defense; 2) Flight to the Moon; 3) Pris-
oners of the Moon; 4) Into the Volcano; 5) Bradford at Bay; 6) Back
to Earth; 7) Into Another Century; 8) Buried Treasure; 9) Trapped in
the Time Top; 10) The Unseen Hand; 11) Poison Gas; 12) Door of
Disaster; 13) Sinister Rendezvous; 14) River of Revenge; 15) For the
Peace of the World.

    Action hero Kane Richmond is perhaps best remembered today as
the hero in Columbia's cliffhanger, Brick Bradford. Although it was a
shoddy affair, much of the serial--especially in the middle chapters--was
played with such delicious tongue-in-cheek that its self-kidding makes it
far more watchable today than most of its contemporary counterparts.
    The plot of Brick Bradford is a bit far out, even for the most
dyed-in-the-wool serial/sci-fi enthusiast. Brick (Richmond) is hired by
the United Nations to protect an interceptor ray, an early anti-missile
weapons device invented by Dr. Tymak (John Merton). The evil Laydron
(Charles Quigley) spies on Brick and friend Professor Salisbury (Pierre
Watkin), his daughter (Linda Johnson) and Brick's pal Sandy Sanderson

(Rick Vallin), because the sinister one wants to steal the powerful weapon. When cornered by Laydron, Dr. Tymak disappears through the "crystal door" and is transported to the Moon, where he is mining Lunarium, necessary for the working of the weapon.

On the moon, Lunarians capture him and Brick is forced to pass through the magical door to rescue the doctor. While in outer orbit, Brick helps the Lunarians overthrow evil forces which control them. When the duo returns to Earth, Laydron attempts to kidnap the experimenting doctor but again the latter is rescued by Brick. It then develops that Tymak requires a formula hidden in the eighteenth century in order to perfect the interceptor ray. Thus Brick and Sandy enter the "Time Top," a time-travel machine, and head back in centuries to obtain the formula. In accomplishing their mission, they are forced to battle a variety of adversaries, including hostile natives and pirates. Returning to the present, Brick again thwarts several attempts to kidnap the professor. Eventually Dr. Tymak perfects his machine and puts an end to the evil Laydron.

Not in the same league with the Buster Crabbe Flash Gordon (q. v.) or Buck Rogers (q. v.) serials, but a pleasant offering in itself.

BRIDE OF THE ATOM   see   BRIDE OF THE MONSTER

BRIDE OF THE MONSTER (DCA, 1956) 69 min.

Executive producer, Donald McCoy; associate producer, Tony

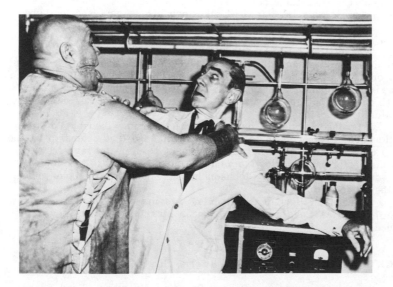

Tor Johnson and Bela Lugosi in Bride of the Monster (1956).

McCoy; producer/director, Edward D. Wood, Jr.; screenplay, Wood,
Jr. and Alex Gordon; music, Frank Worth; special effects, Pat Din-
gle; camera, William C. Thompson and Ted Allen; editor, Warren
Adams.

     Bela Lugosi (Dr. Eric Vornoff); Tor Johnson (Lobo); Tony
McCoy (Lieutenant Dick Cross); Loretta King (Janet Lawson); Harvey
B. Dunne (Captain Robbins); George Becwar (Professor Vladimir
Strowski); Don Nagel (Marty); Bud Osborne (Officer Melton); William
Benedict (Newsboy); Dolores Fuller (Marie); Ann Wilner (Millie); Ed-
die Parker (Double for Lugosi); and Paul Carco, John Warren, Ben
Frommer.

     A. k. a. Bride of the Atom.

     Bottom-rung productions sometimes have a special charm if
for no other reason than that they are incredibly bad. Such a picture
is Bride of the Monster, famous as Bela Lugosi's last starring film.
In it, he portrayed the epitome of the mad scientist, the "I will rule
the world!" type so often exemplified in the horror and science fiction genres.

     Past the age of seventy, Bela was engaged by writer/produc-
er/director Edward D. Wood, Jr. (who had previously directed him
in the little-known Glen or Glenda?) to star as Dr. Eric Vornoff, a
crazed (what else?) scientist. The latter's family has been murdered
by the Communists and he has fled to the swamps to carry out his
experiments. His theory is that the human race can be made into
a super race through the use of atomic power. First he turns an
octopus into a devouring monster and then he transforms his weak-
bodied assistant Lobo (Tor Johnson) into a brainless giant. When a
girl reporter (Loretta King) learns of mysterious murders in the
swamp she travels in search of the story and is captured by Lobo
and Vornoff. They decide to make her the bride of the title. Later,
a law enforcer (Tony McCoy) trails the girl, but is thwarted by Vornoff. Vornoff, in turn, is stopped by Lobo, who has fallen in love
with the young woman. Lobo turns the tables on the doctor, straps
him onto the experimental slab and fills him with radioactivity. The
superhuman Vornoff kills Lobo but is thereafter hunted by a sheriff's
posse. While battling the giant octopus in the swamp he is killed by
an atomic explosion.

     "Loathsome" is the description of the film given by Ed Naha
in Horrors: From Screen to Scream (1975), and that seems to be the
general consensus. But Lugosi is present in almost every frame,
and his performance varies from entertainingly hammy to touching. One
fun scene finds Lugosi and Johnson laughing as a victim is devoured
by the octopus.

     A sequel, Night of the Ghouls, was made by Wood in 1959,
with Johnson as Lobo and Kenne Duncan starring. It was never
issued.

BUCK ROGERS (Universal, 1939) twelve chapters

     Associate producer, Barney Sarecky; directors, Ford Beebe
and Saul A. Goodkind; based on novels by Philip Francis Nowland

and the syndicated comic strip by Phil Nowlan and drawn by Dick
Calkins; screenplay, Norman S. Hall and Ray Trampe; art directors,
Jack Otterson and Ralph De Lacy; camera, Jerry Ash.

Larry "Buster" Crabbe (Buck Rogers); Constance Moore (Wil-
ma Deering); Jackie Moran (Buddy Wade); Jack Mulhall (Captain Ran-
kin); Anthony Warde (Killer Kane); C. Montague Shaw (Dr. Huer);
Guy Usher (Aldar); William Gould (Marshall Kragg); Philson [Philip]
Ahn (Prince Tallen); Henry Brandon (Captain Lasca); Wheeler Oakman
(Patten); Kenneth Duncan (Lieutenant Lacy); Carleton Young (Scott);
Reed Howes (Roberts).

Chapters: 1) Tomorrow's World; 2) Tragedy on Saturn; 3)
The Enemy's Stronghold; 4) The Sky Patrol; 5) The Phantom Plane;
6) The Unknown Command; 7) Primitive Urge; 8) Revolt of the Zuggs;
9) Bodies without Minds; 10) Broken Barriers; 11) A Prince in Bon-
dage; 12) War of the Planets.

The comic strip character Buck Rogers had appeared in newspapers from the late Twenties onward. Early in the next decade the
property also made its way to radio where it lasted well into the
Forties. After the huge success of the Flash Gordon (q. v.) serial with
Buster Crabbe, it was only natural that Universal should cast stellar
serial champ Crabbe as Buck Rogers, the twentieth century American
who leads the battle against tyranny and evil in the twenty-fifth century. Although differing greatly from the plot of the comic strip,
the serial provides twelve chapters of almost heart-pounding action.
It is still quite popular today, mostly on TV revivals, although it in
no way matches its predecessor, Flash Gordon.

Opening in modern times, the serial reveals Buck Rogers
(Crabbe) and pal Buddy Wade (Jackie Moran) piloting a dirigible which
contains a new gas called Nirvano. When their craft crashes on an
Arctic mountain, they fall into a sleep which lasts for five centuries.
Eventually they are rescued and find out that the world is now under
the control of futuristic hoodlum Killer Kane (Anthony Warde). They
are transported to the Hidden City where they meet Kane's arch foes,
Dr. Huer (C. Montague Shaw) and Wilma Deering (Constance Moore).
In an attempt to drum up support for Kane's foes, Buck, Wilma and
Buddy take a spaceship to Saturn, hoping to solicit aid there. But
they are followed and captured by Kane's men. Both groups are
captured by the Saturnians, who rule in Kane's favor.

However, Buck, Buddy and Wilma escape in one of Kane's
ships and return to Earth. They later reappear on Saturn and bring
peace to the planet by quelling a rebellion led by the sub-human
Zuggs. Grateful for their aid, the Saturnian leader (Philip Ahn)
agrees to join in Buck's war against Kane. When the latter's henchman Lasca (Henry Brandon) demands that Saturn submit to Kane's
rule, Buck aids the people there in resisting Kane. Once back on
Earth, Rogers launches an attack on Kane's stronghold. With the
cooperation of the Saturnians, Kane is defeated and overthrown. Interplanetary peace is restored, and Buck, now the air marshal of
the earth, wins the love of Wilma.

With snappy direction by Ford Beebe and Saul A. Goodkind
and a myriad of futuristic inventions (e. g. , ray guns, degravity

belts, invisible rays, rocketships), along with cities of the future, space travels, the terrifying sub-human Zuggs, and the mind-controlling helmets of Kane (which turn his enemies into zombies), the film had more than enough excitement. It is one of the top serial efforts of the decade and certainly a shining light when compared with such later sci-fi cliffhangers as Captain Video and King of the Rocketmen (both q.v.).

    Edited feature film versions: Planet Outlaws (1953), Destination Saturn (1965).

CAGE OF DOOM   see   TERROR FROM THE YEAR 5000

CALTIKI, THE IMMORTAL MONSTER / CALTIKI, IL MOSTRO IM-
MORTALE (Allied Artists, 1959) 76 min.

    Directors, Robert Hampton [Ricardo Freda] and (English-dubbed version by) Lee Kresel and (uncredited) John Foam [Mario Bava]; based on an ancient Mexican legend; screenplay, Philip Just; sound, Maurice Rosenblum; camera, Foam [Bava]; editor, Salvatore Billiterri.

    John Merivale (Professor John Fielding); Didi Sullivan (Ellen); Daniela Rocca (Linda); Gerard Herter (Max); Daniele Pitani (Bob); Gay Pearl (Dancer).

    This respectable minor film was the precursor of the many horror/sci-fi pictures which later came from Europe. It was deliberately geared to seem like an American-made product, with its production credits using Americanized names for the Italian talent. In the U.S. the film was accepted as being of local origin, although its playdates were sparse and it soon passed into TV-land.

    A group of scientists unearths a Mayan tomb. In its subterranean pool lurks the long forgotten "god" Caltiki, a blob-like monster. The creature is vanquished after a battle with the investigators, but a small portion of it is taken to a laboratory for examination. There it begins to grow into a huge size and goes on a destructive rampage (much as in the earlier American film, The Blob, q.v.). In trying to combat this force, one of the scientists translate mysterious Mayan writing found in the tomb near the site of the monster. The words relate that the coming of a comet will give the creature immortal life, just as it enjoyed a thousand years ago. Fortunately, the old stand-by, fire, is used to exterimate the creature, almost at the moment that the tail of the comet enters the Earth's atmosphere.

    Carlos Clarens noted in An Illustrated History of the Horror Film (1967), "this modest effort seems a hybrid of The Quatermass Experiment and The Blob." In a recent interview with Photon magazine, the film's cinematographer Mario Bava (billed as John Foam in the credits admitted that the picture was "a take-off on Quatermass I." He added, "I directed most of Caltiki, the Immortal Monster. Ricardo Freda signed it 'Robert Hampton' but he left soon after the production had begun. The slime monster was just a ton of

plans to convert her into a mummy. The villain's plans are finally
thwarted by Captain America. Gail is saved and the Scarab and his
murderous mob are sentenced, jailed, and sent to the electric chair.
The well-made serial benefited from solid performances by
its lead players--both heroes and villains. As Jim Harmon and Donald F. Glut noted in The Great Movie Serials (1972), "Captain America represented the apex of the traditional action film fight, in the
opinion of many cliffhanger enthusiasts.... " And, of course, where
would the plotline be without those marvelous sci-fi weapons?
The serial was later re-issued as Return of Captain America.

CAPTAIN MIDNIGHT (Columbia, 1942) fifteen chapters

Producer, Larry Darmour; director, James W. Horne; based
upon the Mutual Network radio serial; screenplay, Basil Dickey,
George H. Plympton, Jack Stanley, and Wyndham Gittens; music, Lee
Zahler; assistant director, Carl Hiecke; camera, James S. Brown,
Jr.; editors, Dwight Caldwell and Earl Turner.
Dave O'Brien (Captain Midnight); Dorothy Short (Joyce); James
Craven (Ivan Shark); Sam Edwards (Chuck); Guy Wilkerson (Ichabod
Mudd); Bryant Washburn (Edwards); Luana Walters (Fury); Joe Girard
(Major Steel); Ray Teal (Borgman); George Pembroke (Dr. Jordan);
Charles Hamilton (Martel); Al Ferguson (Gardo).
Chapters: 1) Mysterious Pilot; 2) Stolen Range Finder; 3) The
Captured Plane; 4) Mistaken Identity; 5) Ambushed Ambulance; 6)
Weird Waters; 7) Menacing Fates; 8) Shells of Evil; 9) The Drop of
Doom; 10) The Hidden Bomb; 11) Sky Terror; 12) Burning Bomber;
13) Death in the Cockpit; 14) Scourge of Revenge; 15) The Fatal Hour.

The character of black-costumed "Captain Midnight" had been
a popular radio staple of the juvenile set for many years before Columbia purchased the screen rights for this actionful, if disappointing,
production. The chapterplay's two biggest assets are that it moves
fast and that stuntman/actor/writer Dave O'Brien plays the title role
with conviction.
The plot premise of this blend of patriotism, espionage, and
sci-fi, has U.S. Major Steel (Joe Girard) call in aviator Captain Al-
bright--alias Captain Midnight (O'Brien)--to investigate the harass-
ment of the nation by enemy bombing planes. The aerial raids are
being instigated by fifth-columnist Ivan Shark (James Craven), who
kidnaps a scientist (Bryant Washburn) in order to obtain his new
range-finder. The scientist, however, gives the model of his discovery to his daughter (Dorothy Short). She in turn goes to Captain Midnight. The captain tries to save the scientist, but he is
thwarted by Shark's henchman. Eventually, however, the inventor
makes good his own escape. Still later, Midnight corners Shark in
his mountain retreat but the villain again captures the scientist and
the girl. He imprisons them in an underground vault along with Major Steel. Shark plans to kill them with the range finder. Fortunately, Midnight and the police arrive on the scene. In the ensuing
donnybrook, Shark is electrocuted accidentally and his gang captured.
Captain Midnight had a heavy emphasis on flying and contained

Dave O'Brien in the cliffhanger, Captain Midnight (1942).

a number of flying stunts (especially plane crashes). Unfortunately the film was too weighted down with contemporary propaganda and did not live up to its potential.

CAPTAIN NEMO AND THE UNDERWATER CITY (MGM, 1969) C-106 min.

Executive producer, Steven Pallos; producer, Bertram Ostrer; director, James Hill; inspired by the character and created by Jules Verne; screenplay, Pip Baker, Jane Baker, R. Wright Campbell; art director, Bill Andrews; music, Walter Stott; costumes, Olga Lehmann; sound supervisor, A. W. Watkins; camera, Alan Hume; underwater camera, Egil S. Woxholt; editor, Bill Lewthwaite.

Robert Ryan (Captain Nemo); Chuck Connors (Senator Robert Fraser); Nanette Newman (Helena); John Turner (Joab); Luciana Paluzzi (Mala); Bill Fraser (Barnaby); Kenneth Connor (Swallow); Allan Cuthbertson (Lomax); Christopher Hartstone (Philip).

After good box-office response in 1956 (and in subsequent reissues) to 20,000 Leagues under the Sea (q. v.), Captain Nemo and his futuristic ship "Nautilus" returned in 1969 for this British-made, glossy MGM entry. Although not nearly as successful as the original, the film was a handsome and entertaining production. Jules Verne, the granddaddy of science fiction stories, would not have been offended. This spin-off of the Captain Nemo fantasy is far more satisfying than the 1972 excursion Mysterious Island, (q. v.) starring Omar Sharif.

Captain Nemo (Robert Ryan) is dwelling in an undersea city called Templemer where he has developed the process of making oxygen underwater. A byproduct of this invention is the ability to turn rocks into gold. Trouble quickly brews when ship-wrecked visitors come to the hidden city and note the abundance of the precious metal. Even more complications arise when a monster called Mobula--actually a giant manta ray mutated by radiation--threatens to destroy the city. The closing battle between the "Nautilus" and the giant fish results in the harpooning of the manta ray by a deadly spear attached to the craft.

If the viewer's interest in the "Nautilus" or "Templemer" lagged, there was always leading lady Luciana Paluzzi to observe, especially in her fetching brief underwater garb. The British Monthly Film Bulletin found some other points of interest: "The special effects explosions are satisfyingly spectacular, and the underwater photography (by Egil Woxholt) includes an examination of sea animals and plants that is worthy of [Jacques] Cousteau. Robert Ryan invests Nemo with a likable mixture of mystery and authority...."

CAPTAIN VIDEO (Columbia, 1951) fifteen chapters

Producer, Sam Katzman; directors, Spencer Gordon Bennet and Wallace A. Grissell; based on characters from the teleseries "Captain Video and His Video Rangers"; screen story, George H.

Plympton; screenplay, Royal K. Cole, Sherman L. Lowe, and Joseph
F. Poland; music, Mischa Bakaleinikoff; assistant director, Charles
S. Gould special effects, Jack Erickson; camera, Fayte Browne; edi-
tor, Earl Turner.

Judd Holdren (Captain Video); Larry Stewart (Ranger); George
Eldredge (Tobor); Gene Roth (Vultura); Don C. Harvey (Gallagher);
William Fawcett (Alpha); Jack Ingram (Aker); I. Stanford Jolley (Za-
rol); Skelton Knaggs (Retner); Jimmy Stark (Rogers); Rusty Westcoatt
(Beal); Zon Murray (Elko); George Robotham (Drock); Oliver Cross
(Professor Markham); Bill Bailey (Professor Dean).

Chapters: 1) Journey into Space; 2) Menace to Atoma; 3)
Captain Video's Peril; 4) Entombed in Ice; 5) Flames of Atoma; 6)
Astray in the Atmosphere; 7) Blasted by the Atomic Eye; 8) Invisible
Menace; 9) Video Springs a Trap; 10) Menace of the Mystery Metal;
11) Weapon of Destruction; 12) Robot Rocket; 13) Mystery of Station
X; 14) Vengeance of Vultura; 15) Video vs. Vultura.

Captain Video is the only theatrical release serial to be based
on a television program. The show began in 1948 on the Dumont
network as a weekday entry, with Richard Coogan (later replaced by
radio's "The Green Hornet," Al Hodge) in the title role and Don
Hastings as the Video Ranger. The popular juvenile program lasted
until the middle of the following decade.

Here Captain Video (Judd Holdren) and Ranger (Larry Stewart)
head for the planet Atoma, having blasted off from their underground
headquarters in their ship "The Galaxy." Their mission is to stop
the unholy alliance between the ruler of that planet, Vultura (Gene
Roth), and one Dr. Tobor (George Eldredge). When they land Vultura tries to kill the duo with a remote-control comet but fails, and
for the remainder of the chapters the team of justice is forced to
battle robots (reminiscent of The Phantom Empire, q.v.), all kinds
of ray devices and weapons, and assorted other perils. Eventually
there is a showdown with Vultura, who is killed with his own cannon
ray.

Coming at the end of the great cliffhanger era, Captain Video
did little to bolster the dying species. Rather, it was a testament
to the early days of TV when almost anything that moved on screen
found an audience.

CAT-WOMEN OF THE MOON (Astor, 1954) 64 min.

Producers, Jack Rabin and Al Zimbalist; director, Arthur
Hilton; story, Rabin and Zimbalist; screenplay, Roy Hamilton; art
director, William Glasgow; music, Elmer Bernstein; special effects,
Rabin and Zimbalist; camera, William F. Whitley; editor, John
Bushelman.

Sonny Tufts (Grainger); Victor Jory (Kip); Marie Windsor (Hel-
en); Bill Phipps (Doug); Douglas Fowley (Walter); Carol Brewster
(Alpha); Suzanne Alexander (Zeta); Susan Morrow (Lambda); the Hollywood Cover Girls (Cat Women of the Moon).

Astor released this picture in some areas in the 3-D process,

Some of the Cat-Women of the Moon (1954).

which gave the project novelty value.   More importantly, a good cast
was wasted in the quagmire of a bad story.
    A rocket ship from Earth lands on the dark side of the moon.
There, a group of feline-like females are discovered living in caves,
their leader being Alpha (Carol Brewster).   These super-intelligent
lovelies have hypnotic powers and can vanish at will into thin air.
Their mission is to seduce astronaut Grainger (Sonny Tufts), steal
the rocket ship and then land on Earth.   After an appropriate amount
of time in the catacombs under the moon and in the hidden city, the
girls' plans are thwarted and the earthlings return to their safer
world.
    Producers Jack Rabin and Al Zimbalist spared every expense
in packaging this effort.   It is so deliciously dismal, it must be
viewed to be verified.   Writing in Monsters of the Movies magazine,
Eric L. Hoffman noted, in his article "Bombs from Outer Space,"
"With Cat-Women quickie-filmmakers found that the female of the
species became a good draw at the box office whenever their heroes
landed on distant worlds--courtesy of the sound stages.   They were
very popular heavies for galactic quickies, whether on other planets
or visiting our worlds ... and they usually had less than honorable
intentions."
    Never a producing company to give up easily on a property,
Astor re-made the picture in 1958 as Missile to the Moon (q. v.).
Cat-Women of the Moon was also issued as Rocket to the Moon.

CESTA DO PRAVEKU see JOURNEY TO THE BEGINNING OF TIME

CHANDU, THE MAGICIAN (Fox, 1932) 75 min.

     Directors, Marcel Varnel and William Cameron Menzies;
based on the radio series by Harry A. Earnshaw, Vera M. Oldham,
and R. R. Morgan; screenplay, Barry Conners and Philip Klein;
camera, James Wong Howe; editor, Harold Schuster.
     Edmund Lowe (Chandu); Irene Ware (Princess Nadji); Bela Lu-
gosi (Roxor); Herbert Mundin (Albert Miggies); Henry B. Walthall
(Robert Regent); Weldon Heyburn (Abdullah); Virginia Hammond (Dorothy); June Viasek [Lang] (Betty Lou); Nestor Aber (Bobby).

     Frank Chandler--alias Chandu the Magician--a master of Yoga
with extraordinary powers which he used to fight crime, was a popular radio staple in the early Thirties and would remain so well into
the next decade. In the early years of the Depression, motion pictures began to capitalize on the popularity of radio programs and
personalities (like Amos 'n Andy and Rudy Vallee) and built vehicles
around the stars, transferring the audio programs to celluloid. In
most cases the switch was not very satisfactory. A case in point is
the Fox film, Chandu, the Magician.
     Chandu (Edmund Lowe) achieves the high order of Yogi in Tibet
and is told his mission is to rid the world of the evil Roxor (Bela
Lugosi), who plans to make himself the ruler of Earth. Roxor begins his mad scheme by kidnapping Chandu's brother-in-law, Robert
Regent (Henry B. Walthall), the inventor of a death-ray. In his plot,
Roxor seeks the aid of the beautiful Princess Naji (Irene Ware), the
girl Chandu loves. She rejects Roxor and Chandu saves her from

Irene Ware and Edmund Lowe in Chandu, the Magician (1932).

destruction by walking through fire. Next Roxor abducts Chandu's
sister (June Lang) and sells her in a slave auction. But it is Chandu, disguised as an old Arab, who buys her. Finally Roxor captures
Chandu and the Princess, puts the Magician in a sarcophagus and
drops him in the Nile. He then forces Regent to reveal his secret.
But before Roxor can use the perfected death ray, Chandu escapes
from the Nile. He hypnotizes the evil one, who is frozen to the
death ray and killed.

Seen today, Chandu, the Magician has a charm about it which
makes it good fun. At the time of its release, the critics were less
kindly. The New Yorker thought "none of the atrocities described
seems as fearful as the acting" and Variety labeled it "hoke." Perhaps one reason the picture was not liked by the fourth estate was
that Edmund Lowe underplayed the role of Chandu, while Bela Lugosi
did just the opposite as the arch enemy, Roxor. Yet, it is Lugosi's
performance which is remembered. By some twist of fate he would
later become associated with the role of Chandu, although he did not
play it in this film.

Two years later Principal Pictures would star Lugosi as Frank
Chandler in the serial Return of Chandu. Fox would turn out a sequel to Chandu, the Magician in 1933, entitled Trick for Trick, although it was not an official follow-up to the original. There a magician (Ralph Morgan) gathers several murder suspects at his eerie
mansion for a seance and then brings back the "spirit" of the murder victim.

CHARIOTS OF THE GODS? (Sun International, 1974) C-90 min.

Producer, Manfred Barthel; director, Dr. Harold Reinl; based
on the book by Erich von Daniken; music, Peter Thomas; camera,
Ernst Wild; editor, Herman Haller.
Commentary, Wilhelm Pogersdorff.

Somewhere in the region between science fiction and science
fact lies the area of science-maybe. Here numerous theories abound
on many subjects, some with allegedly solid evidence to support them,
despite continued nonrecognition by the scientific community. One
such theory is that in the distant past the Earth was visited by super-
intelligent beings who planted the seeds of civilization and that ever
since, mankind has worshipped these visitors as gods. Erich von
Daniken expounded this theory in four best-selling books: Chariots
of the Gods?, Gods from Outer Space, The Gold of the Gods, and
In Search of Ancient Gods.

Dr. Harold Reinl, best known for his thrillers and German
Westerns, directed this film which took a year to complete, using
locations all over the globe. The crew traveled to places where von
Daniken claims the "gods" left remnants of their stay on earth. The
resulting film is technically variable but intriguing in content. It is
a sensible visual representation of the author's views. Among the
sites shown are: the plain of Nazca in Peru where ancient aircraft
allegedly landed; huge monoliths in South America, which are not
natural structures although there is no known way to move them; the

pyramids of Peru and Egypt; various ancient drawings of beings in
what appears to be space garb and piloting flying machines; the huge
stone faces of Easter Island; and so forth.

This "documentary" was issued originally in Germany in 1970
as Erinnerungen an die Zukunft (Memories of the Future) and in England in the same year.   Some of its impact was lessened in the U. S.
because most of its footage was utilized to better advantage in the
1973 NBC-TV special, In Search of Ancient Astronauts, also based
on von Daniken's works and narrated by Rod Sterling.

Dale Wingura reported in Cinefantastique that the film "is
rather cold and dispassionate.   The offering makes an extremely
convincing case for the possibility of extraterrestrial beings visiting
earth many years ago, offering one startling bit of factual evidence
after another."

CHIKYU BOEIGUN (Toho, 1957) C-89 min.

Producer, Tomoyuki Tanaka; director, Inoshiro Honda; story,
Jojiro Okami; adaptor, S. Kayama; screenplay, Takeshi Kimura; art
director, Teruaki Abe; music, Akira Ifukube; special effects, Eiji
Tsuburaya; camera, Hajime Koizumi; editor, Hiroichi Iwashita.
With: Kenji Sahara, Yumi Shirakawa, Akihiko Hirata, Momo-
ko Kochi, and Takashi Shimura.
A. k. a. Earth Defense Force.

Japan's Toho Studios entered the alien-invasion race in 1957
with this fairly engrossing entry.   Again Inoshiro Honda helmed the
project and the film benefited from Eiji Tsuburaya's special effects.
The scenes in which the alien robot and flying saucers chase stam-
peding humans are well executed.

The Mysterians (the title for the English-language-dubbed version) are a group of pathfinders from another planet which has been
destroyed by an atomic explosion.   Their aim is to capture Earth
women and breed with them, while imprisoning all Earth men.   To
set their plan into motion, the invaders set loose their giant robot,
which is fifty times the size of a human.   This metal monster shoots
death rays from its eyes, and soon is destroying much of Japan.
Finally the Earthlings devise a plan whereby the robot will walk
across a bridge.   As it does so, dynamite is exploded, causing the
machine to tumble into the river below where it short-circuits.   The
alien invasion is ended.

Sadly, when shown on TV, the special effects lose much of
their visual power.

CHILDREN OF THE DAMNED   see   VILLAGE OF THE DAMNED

CITY BENEATH THE DESERT   see   L'ATLANTIDE

CITY BENEATH THE SEA (NBC-TV, 1971) C-120 min.

Producer, Irwin Allen; associate producers, George E. Swink and Sidney Marshall; director/story, Allen; screenplay, John Meredyth Lucas; art directors, Roger E. Maus and Stan Jolley; set decorator, James Cane; music/music director, Richard La Salle; costumes, Paul Zastupnevich; sound, Bob Post, Sr.; special camera effects, L. B. Abbott and John C. Caldwell; camera, Kenneth Peach; editor, James Baiotto.

Stuart Whitman (Admiral Michael Matthews); Robert Wagner (Brett Matthews); Rosemary Forsyth (Lia Holmes); Robert Colbert (Commodore Woodie Patterson); Burr De Benning (Dr. Aguila); Susan Miranda (Elena); Richard Basehart (The President); Joseph Cotten (Dr. Ziegler); James Darren (Dr. Talty); Sugar Ray Robinson (Captain Hunter); Paul Stewart (Barton); Whit Bissell (Professor Holmes); Larry Pennell (Bill Holmes); Sheila Mathews (Blonde Woman); Tom Drake (General Putnam); Charles Dierkop (Quinn); and Bill Bryant, Bob Dowdell, Edward G. Robinson, Jr.

This futuristic science fiction thriller (using the same title as a 1953 Universal skin-diving yarn) was produced on a $1.4-million budget by Irwin Allen. Made by Twentieth Century-Fox, the would-be series pilot was shown in the U.S. as a telefeature. Abroad it was issued theatrically by Motion Picture International, using the title One Hour to Doomsday. With an excellent cast and solid production values, City Beneath the Sea fared well in both media.

Set in the middle of the twenty-first century, the saga tells of the colonization of the world's first underwater city, Pacifica, and the troubles that occur when one of its creators (Stuart Whitman) returns to the city under presidential orders. Among the problems are: an attempted invasion, sea monsters, intrafighting among factions of the city, the possibility of the robbery of a shipment of gold from Fort Knox, the predicted use of a fissionable H-128 nuclear bomb, and a scare that the Earth might be hit by a planetoid.

Despite the classy mounting, the project failed to excite the critics. Judith Crist (TV Guide) insisted it was "as water-logged as its setting," while the British Monthly Film Bulletin commented, "Although the colour effects and sets are reasonably fetching, the overall stiffness of the production and the matching woodenness of the performances effectively kill any excitement from the start. Indeed, the film's only surprise is the momentary appearance of Joseph Cotten, who turns up in a tiny part as a marine scientist."

A CLOCKWORK ORANGE (Warner Bros., 1971) C-137 min.

Executive producers, Max L. Raab and Si Litvinoff; producer/director, Stanley Kubrick; based on the novel by Anthony Burgess; screenplay, Kubrick; production designer, John Barry; art directors, Russell Hagg and Peter Shields; paintings and sculpture, Herman Makkin, Cornelius Makking, Liz Moore, and Christiane Kubrick; stunt arranger, Roy Scammel; wardrobe supervisor, Ron Beck; costumes Milena Canonero; make-up, Fred Williamson, George

Partleton, and Barbara Daly; assistant directors, Derek Cracknell and Dusty Symonds; electronic music composed and realized by Walter Carlos; camera, John Alcott; editor, Bill Butler.

Malcolm McDowell (Alex); Patrick Magee (Mr. Alexander); Michael Bates (Chief Guard); Warren Clarke (Dim); John Clive (Stage Actor); Adrienne Corri (Mrs. Alexander); Carl Duering (Dr. Brodsky); Paul Farrell (Tramp); Clive Francis (Lodger); Michael Gover (Prison Governor); Miriam Karlin (Cat Lady); James Marcus (Georgie); Aubrey Morris (Deltoid); Godfrey Quigley (Prison Chaplain); Cheila Raymor (Mum); Madge Ryan (Dr. Branom); John Savident (Conspirator Dolin); Anthony Sharp (Minister of the Interior); Philip Stone (Dad); Pauline Taylor (Psychiatrist); Margaret Tyzack (Conspirator Rubinstein); Michael Tarn (Pete); John Carney (C.I.D. Man); Katya Wyeth (Girl in Ascot Fantasy); George Naught (Bootick Clerk); Cheryl Grunwald (Rape Girl); Jan Adair, Vivienne Chandler, and Prudence Drage (Handmaidens); Carol Drinkwater (Nurse Feeley).

Anthony Burgess would later say of his novel and the resultant film, "A Clockwork Orange was an attempt to make a very Christian point about the importance of free will. If we are going to love mankind, we will have to love Alex as a not unrepresentative member of it. If anyone sees the movie as a bible of violence, he's got the wrong point. Perhaps the ultimate act of evil is dehumanization, the killing of the soul. What my, and Kubrick's, parable tries to state is that it is preferable to have a world of violence undertaken in full awareness-violence chosen as an act of will--than a world conditioned to be good or harmless."

After the huge financial and critical success of his 2001: A Space Odyssey (q. v.), Stanley Kubrick again returned to the sci-fi field, but this time in a satirical examination of our violent society, projected into the not-too-distant future. The result was a grandly successful feature (it grossed $13.5 million in U.S. and Canadian distributors' rentals), with many interpretations, which solidified Kubrick's reputation as one of the finest filmmakers of the 1970s.

In the near future, gangs of young toughs terrorize the city. One evening, after drinking a beverage-stimulant called "milk plus," Alex (Malcolm McDowell) and his trio of "droogs" (Warren Clarke, James Marcus, and Michael Tarn) embark on another fun evening of violence. They beat up a drunk old tramp, pulverize a rival gang and, after a country ride, terrorize Mr. Alexander (Patrick Magee) and gang-rape his wife. The next night Alex and his droogs smash into the home of a rich artist. Later Alex pummels her to death with one of her own sculptures--a large plastic phallus. One of Alex's rebellious underlings prevents his escape from the police. Captured, Alex is sentenced to fourteen years in prison. When Alex learns that there is an experimental brainwashing treatment, known as the "Ludovico Technique," he volunteers for the program, being promised that he will be released from prison within two weeks. In the course of the "cure," Alex is subjected to watching hour after hour of film of brutality of all sorts. Only when he has been conditioned to abhor violence is he freed. Once on the outside world, Alex cannot cope with the rough way of life. By a quirk of fate, he finds himself a house guest of Mr. Alexander, who sets about

tormenting his former tormentor. Later, Mr. Alexander is imprisoned and the Minister of the Interior, who promulgated the brainwashing program, uses Alex as a wedge to win the next election.
At the finish, it is revealed that the real Alex, the corrupt, sadistic
soul, has emerged once again. "I was cured all right ... ," he
smirks at the Minister.

    "The only thing it seems possible to say about A Clockwork
Orange without fear of contradiction is that it has polarized the movie
public. Critics and audiences alike are divided into antipodal camps,
the one hailing the picture as a revelation and a cinematic landmark,
the other damning it as shallow and pernicious.... By making the
victims unsympathetic, Kubrick forces us to question the nature of
violence without the prop of simplistic diagrams, angels vs. devils.
You want to say that Kubrick is too brittle, too explicit and long-
winded in making his points, that much of his humor is leaden and
some of his imagery vulgar. I concur wholeheartedly. But this
seems to me a fair price to pay for a film so searing in its vision,
so dazzling in style and execution, so provocative in its confrontation
with a subject of cardinal concern to all of us" (Alan M. Kriegsman,
Washington Post).

    Regarding the film's maker, David Annan wrote in Movie Fan-
tastic (1975), "There is little question that Kubrick has pushed the
unsettling powers of the cinema beyond the limits probed by [Luis]
Buñuel. For savagery of image dredged from the depths of the sub-
conscious, Kubrick is the prince of darkness and the apostle of
light."

    With such recent events as Watergate a nauseating reality, one
might well question whether A Clockwork Orange is really science
fiction. The conceits of the genre have been utilized to provide one
of the landmark intellectual exercises of the cinema, told in (over-
stated) visual terms. In the hypothesis of the best format of the
species, A Clockwork Orange asks, "Is this the shape of things to
come?" Its plot twist at the finale provides a grim, sardonic bit of
hope for the free will of man.

THE COLD SUN   see   BEYOND THE MOON

COLOSSUS 1980   see   COLOSSUS: THE FORBIN PROJECT

COLOSSUS: THE FORBIN PROJECT (Universal, 1970) C-100 min.

    Producer, Stanley Chase; director, Joseph Sargent; based on
the novel Colossus by D. F. Jones; screenplay, James Bridge; art
directors, Alexander Golitzen and John J. Lloyd; assistant director,
Robin S. Clark; music, Michael Colombier; special effects, Albert
Whitlock; camera, Gene Polito; editor, Folmar Blangsted.
    Eric Braeden (Dr. Forbin); Susan Clark (Cleo); Gordon Pin-
sent (President); William Schallert (Grauber); Leonid Bostoff (First
Chairman); Georg Stanford Brown (Fisher); Willard Sage (Blake);
Alex Rodine (Kuprin); Martin Brooks (Johnson); Marion Ross (Angela);

Dolph Sweet (Missile Commander); Byron Morrow (Secretary of State);
Lew Brown (Peterson); Sid McCoy (Secretary of Defense); Rom Bas-
ham (Harrison); Robert Cornthwaite and James Hong (Scientits); Ser-
gei Tschernisch (Translator).
A. k. a. Colossus 1980/The Day the World Changed Hands.

This vastly underrated film was originally issued in 1970 as
The Forbin Project and obtained good reviews, but did poor business.
(Universal had no faith in the picture.) Retitled Colossus: the Forbin Project, the movie still did not experience good box-office though
it is a very well-made film and one that is well-liked. Its many admirers include science fiction author Richard Matheson and this
book's authors.
Set in the very near future, the narrative relates the strange
story of young Dr. Forbin (Eric Braeden) who develops an advance
computer which is housed in the Rocky Mountains. The President
of the United States (Gordon Pinsent) consents to allowing the computer to control the nation's defense system. Later it is announced
that the Russians have a similar computer called The Guardian.
Soon the two intricate systems are in contact and form an alliance
to control the world. They dictate that mankind must obey them or
it will be destroyed. Only Dr. Forbin appears to know the weaknesses of the computer. He develops a plan which eventually brings
about the demise of the computer's dictatorial activities.
This delightfully cerebral picture focuses on the fear that has
long plagued some people--that we will one day be ruled by the machines we have created to advance our civilization and ease the bur-
dens on mankind. (The example of HAL, the over-active computer
in Stanley Kubrick's 2001: A Space Odyssey [q. v.], is another such
excursion on this theme.)
The feature was produced in 1968 but was shelved for two
years, Universal being unsure how (or why) to market it. It benefits from a sturdy performance by Susan Clark as Cleo, Dr. Forbin's
assistant/girlfriend.

COMMANDO CODY, SKY MARSHAL OF THE UNIVERSE (Republic,
1953) twelve chapters

Associate producer, Franklin Adreon; directors, Fred C.
Brannon, Harry Keller, and Adreon; screenplay, Ronald Davidson and
Barry Shipman; art director, Frank Arrigo; special effects, Howard
and Theodore Lydecker; camera, Bud Thackery; editors, Cliff Bell
and Harold Minter.
With: Judd Holdren (Jeff King [Commando Cody]); Aline Towne
(Joan); Gregory Gay (Ruler); and: William Schallert and Lyle Talbot.

Commando Cody, Sky Marshal of the Universe, had already
been starred in two Republic serials, King of the Rocket Men (1951--
played by Tristram Coffin) and Radar Men from the Moon (1952--
played by George Wallace). In 1953 Judd Holdren assumed the role
of Jeff King, alias Commando Cody, in a twelve-part serial of the
same title. Actually it all originated from a TV series which

Republic issued theatrically as a chapterplay. (Each of the install-
ments was a complete story unto itself.) The series itself was eventually released to the small screen in 1955.

The pseudo chapterplay has Cody (Holdren) and his assistant
(Aline Towne) fighting and eventually destroying the evil ruler (Gregory Gay) of Mercury who has plans to dominate the universe. Like
other sci-fi entries, the serial boasts all kinds of futuristic gimmicks
including ray-guns and advanced means of transportation (Cody has a
portable propulsion system which enables him to fly). The production
is saddled with an overabundance of stock footage.

THE CONQUEST OF SPACE (Paramount, 1955) C-80 min.

Producer, George Pal; director, Byron Haskin; based on the
book The Mars Project by Wernher von Braun; screen story, Philip
Yordan, Barre Lyndon, and George Worthing Yates; screenplay,
James O'Hanlon; art directors, Hal Pereira and Joseph MacMillan
Johnson; music, Van Cleave; astronomical art, Chesley Bonestell;
special effects, John P. Fulton, Irmin Roberts, Paul Lerpse, Ivyl
Burks, and Jan Domela; process camera, Farciot Edouart; camera,
Lionel Lindon; editor, Everett Douglas.

Walter Brooke (Samuel Merritt); Eric Fleming (Barney Mer-
ritt); Mickey Shaughnessy (Mahoney); Phil Foster (Siegle); William
Redfield (Cooper); William Hopper (Fenton); Benson Fong (Imoto);
Ross Martin (Fodor); Vito Scotti (Sanella); John Dennis (Donkersgoed);
Michael Fox (Elsbach); Joan Shawlee (Rosie); Iphigenie Catiglioni
(Mrs. Fodor).

After such trend-setting sci-fi motion pictures as Destination
Moon, When Worlds Collide, and War of the Worlds (all q.v.), producer George Pal left the realm of space travel with Conquest of
Space. It was a project which seemed intriguing in its day, but which
is now very dated. Most of its content is either passé or else prov-
en incorrect.

The narrative tells of a group of rather comical men on a
space station who begin the first trip to Mars. The rudiments of
space travel are unveiled to the viewer as the astronauts are hurled
toward the Red Planet. The daily life of the crew and the workings
of the craft are explored ad nauseam. Along the way the space
travelers are faced with the usual meteor storms, the unknown and/
or experimental nature of their trip, and once they land on Mars they
are confronted with mechanical problems. (Mars is portrayed mis-
takenly as a young, lush planet.)

Conquest of Space does boast the usual fine visuals of George
Pal, including a well-modulated use of color to heighten the sci-fi
effect. There is also a good helping of unintentional humor; corny
at the time of its release, but today considered "camp."

The film was not well received by science fiction buffs. In
an article included in Focus on Science Fiction Cinema (1972) Richard Hodgens explains why: " ... there were some visually impressive shots, but unfortunately that was all. The script attempted to
'enliven' a subject that called for serious treatment; the result was

an inaccurate, misleading film ending with a miracle which, unlike
the 'miraculous' end of War [of the Worlds], was impossible and
pointless. It was an expensive production which could have contributed to the salvation of science fiction in motion pictures. But the
monsters had taken the field, and the facile Conquest of Space merely
seemed to prove that monsters are always necessary. "

CONQUEST OF THE NORTH POLE   see   A LA CONQUETE DU POLE

CONQUEST OF THE PLANET OF THE APES (Twentieth Century-Fox,
1972) C-86 min

        Producer, Arthur P. Jacobs; associate producer, Frank Capra,
Jr.; director, J. Lee Thompson; based on characters created by
Pierre Boulle; screenplay, Paul Dehn; art director, Philip Jefferies;
set decorator, Norman Rockett; titles, Don Record; makeup design,
John Chambers; makeup supervisor, Dan Striepeke; makeup, Joe Di
Bella and Jack Barron; assistant director, David "Buck" Hall; music,
Tom Scott; sound, Herman Lewis and Don Bassman; camera, Bruce
Surtees; editors, Marjorie Fowler and Allan Jaggs.
        Roddy McDowall (Caesar); Don Murray (Governor Breck); Na-
talie Trundy (Lisa); Hari Rhodes (MacDonald); Severn Darden (Police
Chief Kolp); Lou Wagner (Busboy); John Randolph (Commission Chair-
man); Asa Maynor (Mrs. Riley); H. M. Wynant (Hoskyns); David
Chow (Aldo); Bruce Kartalian (Frank the Gorilla); John Dennis and
Paul Comi (Policemen); Hector Soucy (Ape with Chain); Gordon Jump
(Auctioneer); Dick Spangler (Announcer); Joyce Haber (Zelda); and
Ricardo Montalban (Armando).

        With the first three in the Ape series having grossed over
$135 million in worldwide rentals, it was obvious that a fourth entry
would follow. By now the format and formula had began to wear
thin, but this installment still held a good entertainment quotient.
        In this segment, the relationship between chimpanzee Caesar
(Roddy McDowall), the son of Zira and Cornelius from the previous
three films, and circus owner Armando (Ricardo Montalban) is examined in a future world where intelligent simians are exploited by
humans. Armando is one of the few friendly humans in the tale.
Eventually the murder of an ape causes Caesar to lead a bloody rebellion against mankind, which results in apes controlling the world.
Victory for the simians holds no joy for Caesar, however, as he
learns that Armando has committed suicide. In the finale he turns
from activist to peacemaker, predicting that in the future, the human
race will annihilate itself in nuclear warfare and that the apes will
emerge the dominant force.
        As in the past entries (mostly scripted by Paul Dehn), the
filmmakers have utilized the ape gimmick to sugar-coat their philo-
sophical/political messages. As the Los Angeles Times summed it
up, it "is a self-contained allegory in which man's cruelty to beasts
becomes symbolic of man's inhumanity to man. It is a simple but
powerful premise, thoroughly developed with a good balance between

dialog and action. . . . " Ironically the picture makers filled the
screen with so much action and excitement (especially the violent,
bloody climax) that it is doubtful that the storyline preachings filtered
very deeply into the minds of most of the audience.

THE COSMIC MAN (Allied Artists, 1959) 72 min.

Producer, Robert A. Terry; asociate producer, Harry Marsh;
director, Herbert Greene; story/screenplay, Arthur C. Pierce; assistant director, Richard Del Ruth; music, Paul Sawtell and Bert
Sheftner; sound, Phillip Mitchell; special effects, Charles Duncan;
camera, John F. Warren; editors, Richard C. Currier and Helene
Turner.

Bruce Bennett (Dr. Karl Sorenson); John Carradine (The Cos-
mic Man); Angela Greene (Kathy Grant); Paul Langston (Colonel
Mathews); Scotty Morrow (Ken Grant); Lyn Osborn (Sergeant Gray);
Walter Maslow (Dr. Richie); Herbert Lytton (General Knowland).

The Cosmic Man was one of those B productions of the Fifties
which tried to add something more to the sci-fi field than just a giant
monster, frightened teenagers and a display of stock footage. Instead
it carried a message of peace and, as in the earlier The Day the
Earth Stood Still (q. v.), this pronouncement was brought to Earth by
an alien.

Produced at a time when flying saucers (and all UFOs) were
a major news topic, the film opens with a huge sphere from outer
space landing near an airbase. It causes an instant military alert.
Later, a darkly-garbed stranger (John Carradine) seeks rooms at a
nearby boarding house run by Angela Greene. Soon mysterious
sightings take place in the region and a physician (Bruce Bennett) deduces that the stranger (a "negative" creature with black skin and a
white shadow) is actually an alien. The populace and the military
then plot violence against the invader, but he cures a crippled child
and his message of interplanetary peace is finally believed.

Despite its good intentions, The Cosmic Man was pretty slow
going. It suffered from anemic production values and uninspired
special effects (e. g. , to show that Carradine was an unearthly alien,
he was filmed mostly in double exposure). Carradine and Bennett,
however, did bring professionalism to their roles.

COSMIC MONSTERS see STRANGE WORLD OF PLANET X

COSMONAUTS ON VENUS see PLANETA BURG

CRACK IN THE WORLD (Paramount, 1965) C-96 min.

Producers, Bernard Glasser and Lester A. Sansom; director
Andrew Marton; story, Jon Manchip White; screenplay, White and
Julian Halevy; art director, Eugene Lourié; costumes, Laure De

Dana Andrews, Janette Scott and Kieran Moore in Crack in the World
(1965).

Zarate; music, John Douglas; assistant director, Jose-Maria Ochoa;
sound, Kurt Hernfeld; special effects, Alec Weldon; camera, Manuel
Berenguer; editor, Derek Parsons.
      Dana Andrews (Dr. Stephen Sorensen); Janette Scott (Mrs.
Maggie Sorensen); Kieron Moore (Ted Rampion); Alexander Knox (Sir
Charles Eggerston); Peter Damon (Masefield); Gary Lasdon (Markov);
Mike Steen (Steele); Todd Martin (Simpson); Jim Gillen (Rand).

      Some scientists theorize that in the Earth's molten center there
are sufficient energy sources to supply mankind with power until the
end of time. Crack in the World was based on this assumption. Its
plotline concerned the efforts of Project Inner Space, an international-
ly-sponsored group in the near future, which was to design a scheme
to bring magma from deep in the globe's core to the surface for energy usage.
      Dr. Stephen Sorensen (Dana Andrews) the Nobel Prize-winning
chief of operations, theorizes that using a U. S. atomic missile to
penetrate the Earth's crust would be the quickest and easiest way to
bring up the magma.   But his geologist colleague (Kieron Moore)
fears that such an action might unleash unlimited energy, enough to
destroy the Earth.   Sorensen, despite protests from many associates,
clandestinely fires the missile into a fissure.   The result is a huge
crack in the Earth which causes mass destruction and threatens to
split the world in half.   The repentant scientist then works closely

with others to undo the harm he has wrought. Finally an atomic bomb is set off in the Krakamoa volcano, propelling the crack back along the Macedo Fault. When it meets itself it explodes, the debris is hurled into space, and the Earth has a new moon.

Since its plot premise was logical enough to have significance in our energy-starved times, Crack in the World took on topical interest. The picture benefited greatly from Dana Andrews' well-modulated performance as the slightly unethical American scientist who almost (accidentally) destroys the world.

Judith Crist (TV Guide) weighed that the film is "a harrowing glimpse at the way the world might end.... [It] is such a dandy bit of diversion that I suspect even the most stolid non-science-fiction addict will find himself caught up in this imagine-if-somebody-dunnit...." The British Monthly Film Bulletin added, " ... director Andrew Marton draws on his 40 years of second unit experience to make the most of the genuinely suspenseful sequence in which the bomb is lowered into the volcano, and his final shot, red filtered and apocalyptic, has an irrelevant but undeniable grandeur. "

CRASH OF MOONS see BEYOND THE MOON

THE CRAWLING EYE see THE TROLLENBERG TERROR

THE CRAWLING TERROR see STRANGE WORLD OF PLANET X

THE CREATURE FROM GALAXY 27 see NIGHT OF THE BLOOD BEAST

CREATURE FROM THE BLACK LAGOON (Universal, 1954) 79 min.

Producer, William Alland; director, Jack Arnold; story, Maurice Zimm; screenplay, Harry Essex and Arthur Ross; art directors, Bernard Herzbrun and Hilyard Brown; makeup, Bud Westmore and Jack Kevan; assistant directors, Fred Frank and Russ Maverick; music director, Joseph Gershenson; special camera effects, Charles S. Welbourne; camera, William E. Snyder; underwater camera, James C. Havens; editor, Ted J. Kent.

Richard Carlson (David Reed); Julia Adams (Kay Lawrence); Richard Denning (Mark Williams); Antonio Moreno (Carl Maia); Nestor Paiva (Lucas); Whit Bissell (Edwin Thompson); Ben Chapman (Gill-Man); Harry Escalante (Chico); Bernie Gozier (Zee); Sydney Mason (Dr. Matos); Julio Lopez (Tomas); Rodd Redwing (Louis); Ricou Browning (The Creature).

Jack Arnold's Creature from the Black Lagoon, shot in the 3-D process, is a landmark of the science fiction cinema. It presented a so-called monster, a throwback along the evolutionary trail, with qualities that were diversely human. For once, it is the

creature who is the real hero. Here science bullies its way into the
domain of the creature, a being who only seeks to be left alone. As
a result its world is destroyed and it is killed--all in the name of
scientific advancement!

Filmed in Florida, the picture is highlighted not only by Arnold's inspired direction but by beautiful underwater photography by
James C. Havens. The narrative tells of a group from a scientific
organization called SCUBA who go deep into the dense Amazon basin
in search of the remains of a creature who is supposed to be half-
man, half-fish. Near a solitary area, in a deep black lagoon, the
skeletal remains of such a creature are found. But a short time
later several of the expedition members are murdered mysteriously
by an unknown creature. It develops that it is a living specimen of
just what they are seeking. Later the creature abducts Kay Lawrence (Julia Adams), the lone female of the searchers. When Kay
is rescued, the creature is mortally wounded and falls into his la-
goon-home to die.

Although the black-and-white feature had a simple premise,
director Arnold gave the character of the creature (Ricou Browning)
such scope that it brought forth audience sympathy. The director
also smartly contrasted the dark, murky lagoon where the creature
existed and the bright world of sunlight where the scientists kept
busy. Finally Arnold more than hinted at the creature's sexual desire for the heroine. This is highlighted in the sequence in which
she swims in the lagoon, unaware that she is being watched by the
creature below, which is swimming around her in an almost mating-
like response.

John Baxter, in Science Fiction in the Cinema (1970), stated
that it was "a film that fulfills every promise Arnold made in It
Came from Outer Space [q. v.]. " He added, "Again our environment
acts as the stage for a confrontation between good and evil; again
Arnold's cool style involves us totally in an allegoric conflict wherein
man, puny and confused, struggles to subdue a creature deriving its
strength from wells descending perhaps to hell. For a brief moment
Lucifer is risen, and man is powerless to oppose him. "

Despite those who scoffed at the rubberized-suited monster,
the picture was a good financial investment for Universal. Two
follow-ups were produced in the succeeding few years: Revenge of
the Creature and The Creature Walks Among Us (both q. v.).

CREATURES OF THE RED PLANET see HORROR OF THE BLOOD
MONSTERS

THE CREATURE WALKS AMONG US (Universal, 1956) 78 min.

Producer, William Alland; director, John Sherwood; screen-
play, Arthur Ross; assistant directors, Joseph E. Kenny and Jimmy
Welch; music director, Joseph Gershenson; special camera effects,
Clifford Stine; camera, Maury Gertsman; editor, Edward Curtiss.

Jeff Morrow (Dr. William Barton); Rex Reason (Dr. Thomas
Morgan); Leigh Snowden (Jed Grant); Maurice Manson (Dr. Borg);

James Rawley (Dr. Johnson); Ricou Browning (Sea Creature); Don
Megowan (Land Creature); Paul Fierro (Morteno); Lillian Molieri
(Mrs. Morteno); David McMahon (Captain Stanley).

This is the third and final entry in the series about the Creature from the Black Lagoon (q. v.). Beginning where the second film,
Revenge of the Creature (q. v.), left off, the gill-man is located this
time off the coast of Florida by a group of scientists who give chase.
They track him to the Florida Everglades where he outwits them at
every turn and then becomes the attacker by jumping onto the scientists' motorboat. He is shot by a tranquilizer spear gun but it has
little effect on him as he terrorizes the crew. Finally one of the
scientists douses him with a kerosene lamp. The badly burned creature is taken to a laboratory where an emergency operation removes
his scorched scales. The operation transforms him from a fish-like
creature into a sub-human. Dressed in prison garb he is caged with
other animals in a zoo-like area where he looks longingly out to sea.
Eventually a gang of crooks commit a murder and blame the creature
who escapes and kills his tormentors. Chased by the military, he
is badly wounded. After causing minor havoc in the surrounding
countryside, the creature walks into the sea--the home he is no longer adapted to and which will bring about his final demise.
The arty finale to this feature saved it from the mundane and
certainly paved the way for another series entry. By this time, however, cheaply-made sci-fi films were glutting the market. Universal
had already cut to the quick its budgets on such fare and dropped the
series because of high overhead and dwindling profits.
Better than Revenge of the Creature, the film was still hardly
up to the initial entry, although the aura of dignity was still present.

CREATURES FROM ANOTHER WORLD   see   THE CRAWLING EYE

THE CREEPING EYE   see   THE TROLLENBERG TERROR

THE CREEPING UNKNOWN   see   THE QUATERMASS XPERIMENT

THE CURSE OF THE FLY (Twentieth Century-Fox, 1965) 86 min.

Producers, Robert L. Lippert and Jack Parsons; director,
Don Sharp; based on characters created by George Langelaan; screen-
play, Harry Spalding; art director, Harry White; music, Bert Shefter;
makeup, Eleanor Jones; special effects, Harold Fletcher; camera,
Basil Emmott; editor, Robert White.
Brian Donlevy (Henri Delambre); George Baker (Martin Delam-
bre); Carole Gray (Patricia Stanley); Yvette Rees (Wan); Michael
Graham (Albert Delambre); Rachel Kempson (Mme. Fournier); Bert
Kwouk (Tai); Jeremy Wilkins (Inspector Ranet); Charles Carson (In-
spector Charas); Stan Simmons (Creature).

Brian Donlevy and George Baker in The Curse of the Fly (1965).

        Filmed at Shepperton Studios in London, this was the last in
The Fly trilogy and the least satisfactory.   (The Fly and Return of
the Fly, both q. v. , were the others.)
        This entry focused again on the Delambre family and its ex-
periments into the fourth dimension and the process of electronic
teleportation throughout the world.   These experiments have continued
over the years in the family homes in Montreal and London.   As the
story begins, a girl (Carole Gray) has escaped from a mental institution and meets Martin Delambre (George Baker).   The couple go
to his father's home near Montreal and there the older Delambre
(Brian Donlevy) sees his son marry the young woman.   Soon the
bride learns that her spouse has an ex-wife who has been locked
away in the house with two other half-human creatures, all grave
mistakes in the family's teleportation experiments.   The police are
on the girl's trail and when the Delambres learn the truth, they decide to use their teleportation machine to escape to London.   But in
their haste to depart, the father is lost in the fourth dimension.   The
son ages badly as a result of the trip.   After his arrival in England
he is so shaken by the experience that he destroys the machine.
        The weakest link in Curse of the Fly is its thin plot motiva-
tion.   The production values and acting were satisfactory but the
overall effect of the picture was one of tedium.   At least the bored
viewer can divert himself a bit by studying the array of capsules,
consoles, glass tanks, fuses, wires, radar screens, and plotting
tables in the Delambre laboratories.
        Filmed in black-and-white CinemaScope.

Edward Franz and Michael Rennie in Cyborg 2087 (1966).

CYBORG 2087 (Feature Film Corp. of America, 1966) 86 min.

Executive producer, Fred Jordan; producer, Earle Lyon; director, Franklin Adreon; screenplay, Arthur C. Pierce; art director, Paul Sylos, Jr.; music, Paul Dunlap; camera (not available); editor, Frank P. Keller.

Michael Rennie (Garth); Karen Steele (Sharon); Wendell Corey (Sheriff); Warren Stevens (Dr. Zeller); Eduard Franz (Professor Marx); Harry Carey, Jr. (Jay).

For the record, a "cyborg" is a human being whose abilities have been drastically altered by surgically implanted devices. (This was in the days before the "bionic" craze became fashionable.)

In the year 2087 A.D. a cyborg, Garth (Michael Rennie), disgusted with his existence in a totalitarian state, steals a time machine and returns to the year 1966 in order to find the professor (Eduard Franz) who has invented, and is about to unveil, a device used in his era by governments to control an individual's mind. Garth hopes to persuade the experimenter to destroy this invention and thus reshape the future. Unfortunately, two agents from the future have followed Garth back in time in order to stop his mission.

He traces the inventor to a small town. There, the cyborg is opposed by the local sheriff (Wendell Corey) but is aided in his quest
by a biologist (Warren) and his comely assistant (Karen Steele).
The professor, now aware of the ramifications of his work, refuses
to demonstrate his machinery.   Thus Garth and the pursuing cyborgs
no longer exist.

Writing in Cinefantastique, Ted Issacs reported, "Cyborg 2087
is a colorful little science-fiction thriller which just fails to hit the
mark because of a threadbare script and too little plot to justify its
running time. " A disappointment to genre enthusiasts was the stiff
performance of Michael Rennie.   He had been much more effective
in The Day the Earth Stood Still (q. v.), back in 1951.

THE CYCLOPS (Allied Artists, 1957) 75 min.

     Producer, Bert I. Gordon; associate producer, Henry Schrage;
director /screenplay, Gordon; voice effects, Paul Frees; special effects, Gordon; camera, Ira Morgan; editor, Carolo Lodato.
     James Craig (Russ Bradford); Gloria Talbott (Susan); Lon
Chaney (Martin Melville); Tom Drake (Lee); The Cyclops (Duncan
Parkin).

Duncan Parkin as The Cyclops (1957).

    This is the second of three films in which multifaceted Bert
I. Gordon used the theme of a man mutated by science and thereafter becoming a rampaging giant. In The Amazing Colossal Man
(q. v.) the premise did have some poignancy despite the vapidity of
the mounting. War of the Colossal Beast (q. v.), like The Cyclops,
left a lot to be desired. The title creature is one of the uglier creations to populate a genre film.
    A young woman (Gloria Talbott) organizes an expedition with
a pilot (James Craig) and two fortune hunters (Lon Chaney and Tom
Drake). Her aim is to penetrate a remote region of Mexico to locate her missing fiancé. When they arrive the quartet discover
that the landscape had been exposed to high radiation which has ac-
celerated the growth of all living things in the vicinity. Eventually
the missing beau appears on the scene, but he is a twenty-five-foot
beast (Duncan Parkin) with a scarred face and one eye missing. In
trying to escape the creature, the group takes shelter in a nearby
cave, but one of their number (Chaney) is killed by the beast. Finally the others rig a spear apparatus, set it on fire, and shoot it into
the cyclops' one good eye (à la The Odyssey). The blinded creature
is left behind as the adventurers fly away. As they depart, the invaders barely miss the wildly swinging arms of the monster; the one
truly exciting scene in the film.
    The British Monthly Film Bulletin reported, "The Cyclops,
revoltingly ugly and emitting horrible noises, does not survive
searching close-ups, but despite this limitation he makes an unusual-
ly grim addition to the gallery of screen monsters." On the other
hand, the Los Angeles Mirror News carped, "Gimmick films fascin-
ate a lot of moviegoers like me. They can be preposterous, corny,
and unskillfully done. But they must never be dull, and that's what
The Cyclops is."

D-DAY ON MARS see THE PURPLE MONSTER STRIKES

DAIKAIJU BARAN (VARAN THE UNBELIEVABLE) (Toho, 1961)
87 min.

    Producer, Jerry A. Baerwitz; directors, Inoshiro Honda and
Baerwitz; story, Hajime Koizumi; screenplay, Shinichi Sekigawa and
Sid Harris; music, Akira Ifukubu; music editor, Peter Zinner; sound,
Glen Glenn; special effects, Eiji Tsuburaya and Howard Anderson;
camera, Koizumi and Jack Marquette; editors, Jack Ruggiero and
Ralph Cushman.
    Myron Healey (Commander James Bradley); Tsuruko Kobayashi
(Anna); Clifford Kawada (Captain Kishi); Derick Shimatsu (Matsu); and
Kozo Nomura, Aymi Sonoda, Koreya Senda, and Akihiko Hirata.

    On one of the smaller Japanese islands Commander James
Bradley (Mryon Healey), a scientist who resides there with his wife
(Tsuruko Kobayashi), is experimenting to change salt water into fresh
water. He is utilizing many untested chemicals, doing his experiments in the bay. Natives warn him to stop, insisting that legend

Kozo Nomura and Myron Healey in Daikaiju Baran (1961).

relates that a giant monster lies beneath the waters of the lagoon.
The scientist pays no heed and, sure enough, a huge prehistoric lizard, Varan, arises to wreak havoc on the island. After much chaos
the scientist reasons that a heavy concentration of the chemicals
which brought the monster out of the water might destroy it. His
theories prove correct.
    Toho made this paltry entry in 1958 as Daikaiju Baran but it
was not issued in the U.S. until 1962, when extra scenes with Myron
Healey were tacked on for box-office appeal. Some nineteen minutes
was chopped off in the translation version.

DAIKAIJU GAMMERA (Daiei Films, 1966) 88 min.

    Producer, Yonejiro Saito; director, Noriaki Yyasa [Yuasa];
screenplay, Fumi Takahashhi and Richard Kraft; art director (U.S.
sequences), Hank Aldrich; camera, Nobuo Nakashizu; editor, Tatsuji
Nakashizu.
    Brian Donlevy (General Terry Arnold); Albert Dekker (Secre-
tary of Defense); Diane Findlay (Sergeant Susan Embers); Eiji Funa-
koshi (Dr. Hidaka); Harumi Kiritachi (Kyoko); John Baragrey (Captain

Lovell); Dick O'Neill (General O'Neill); Junichiro Yamashiko (Aoyagi); Yoshiro Uchida (Toschio); Michiko Sugata (Nobuyo); Yoshiro Kitahara (Sakurai); Jun Hamamura (Dr. Maurase).

Another in the seemingly endless saga of resurrected prehistoric monsters, this Japanese special effects picnic was about one Gammera, a giant turtle with teeth, who lay dormant under the Arctic ice for several thousand years before being reawakened by an Atomic explosion. The creature immediately heads to a more temperate southern climate; along the way, it eats and destroys everything in its path (including Japan). Finally the roaming giant is brought under control and disposed of--no easy task since the big fellow thrived on fire and atomic energy.

For its American release entitled Gammera--the Invincible, the producers interpolated footage starring Brian Donlevy, Albert Dekker, and Diane Findlay as Americans working to oppose the giant beast. It is they who finally develop "Plan Z" which does in the creature.

As bad as this feature was in plotline and performance ("a monstrous yawn," claimed Variety), it was the only Gammera "epic" to be issued in American theatres. All the follow-ups, in which the creature's name was spelled "Gamera"--he learned to fly (with exhaust coming from his tail), and became friendly with children--have been distributed in America directly to TV by American International pictures.

The follow-ups to the original, with Gamera now the good guy, have been: Gamera vs. Barugon (1966), Gamera vs. Gyaos (1967), Gamera vs. the Outer-Space Virus (1968), Gamera vs. Guiron (1969) and Gamera vs. Jiger (1970).

DALEKS--INVASION EARTH 2150 A. D. (British Lion, 1966) C-84 min.

Executive producer, Joe Vegoda; producers, Max J. Rosenberg and Milton Subotsky; director, Gordon Flemyng; based ·on the BBC television serial by Terry Nation; screenplay, Subotsky; additional dialogue, David Whittaker; music composer/conductor, Bill McGiffie; electronic music, Barry Gray; art director, George Provis; set decorator, Maurice Pelling; wardrobe, Jackie Cummins; assistant director, Anthony Waye; makeup, Bunty Phillips; sound, John Cox and Buster Ambler; special effects, Ted Samuels; camera, John Wilcox; editor, Ann Chegwidden.

Peter Cushing (Dr. Who); Bernard Cribbins (Tom Campbell); Ray Brooks (David); Andrew Keir (Wyler); Roberta Tovey (Suand); Jill Curzon (Louise); Roger Avon (Wells); Keith Marsh (Conway); Geoffrey Cheshire (RoboMan); Steve Peters (Leader RoboMan); Philip Madoc (Brockley); Eddie Powell (Thompson); Godfrey Quigley (Dorfmun); Tony Reynolds (Man on Bicycle); Bernard Spear (Man with Carrier Bag); Robert Jewell (Leader Dalek Operator).

American TV title: Invasion Earth 2150 A. D.

Following the success of Dr. Who and the Daleks (q. v.), still another film version of the popular BBC series was issued. This

version was not nearly as good as the first; its production values
were scantier and there was an excess of comedy. Still the film was
thrilling enough for the juvenile trade and it proved popular. As
Variety observed, "it is the clever way in which the cone-like Daleks
are moved and juggled that gives the film its main kick. "

The brilliant Dr. Who (Peter Cushing) and his nieces (Jill
Curzon and Roberta Tovey) accidentally travel into the future in the
doctor's time machine. They arrive in the year 2150 and find the
earth is now a desolate planet under the domination of the Daleks.
It seems the evil aliens, who exist inside ferocious robots, have also
used a time tunnel to survive and have come to Earth to drain it of
of its magnetic core. The Earthly trio find some resistance among
scattered underground opponents of the Daleks, but the surviving
Earthlings are nearly helpless against the invaders. Finally Dr. Who
devises and carries out the plan which rids the planet of the fearful
Daleks: he reverses their mission by blasting the aliens to the center of the Earth, thus destroying them.

THE DAMNED (Columbia, 1963) 87 min.

Executive producer, Michael Carreras; producer, Anthony
Hinds; associate producer, Anthony Nelson-Keys; director, Joseph
Losey; based on the novel The Children of Light by H. L. Lawrence;
screenplay, Evan Jones; assistant director, John Peverall; production
designer, Bernard Robinson; art director, Don Mingaye; music,
James Bernard; music director, John Hollingsworth; sound, Jock

Alexander Knox and Viveca Lindfors in The Damned (1963).

May; camera, Arthur Grant; editors, James Needs and Reginald
Mills.
    Macdonald Carey (Simon Wells); Shirley Ann Field (Joan); Vi-
veca Lindfors (Freya); Alexander Knox (Bernard); Oliver Reed (King);
Walter Gotell (Major Holland); James Villiers (Captain Gregory);
Thomas Kempinski (Ted); Kenneth Cope (Sid); Brian Oulton (Mr. Din-
gle); Barbara Everest (Miss Lamont); Alan McClelland (Mr. Stuart);
James Maxwell (Mr. Talbot); Rachel Clay (Victoria); Rebecca Dignam
(Anne); Siobhan Taylor (Mary); Nicolas Clay (Richard); Kit Williams
(Henry); Christopher Witty (William); Caroline Sheldon (Elizabeth);
and John Thompson (Charles).

    Made in England in 1961, this film was not issued in the U.S.
until 1967, and then with ten minutes sheared from its running time
and a new title, These Are the Damned. Variety labeled it "a real
make-you-think-piece."
    At a seedy British seaside resort called Weymouth, which is
overrun by vicious Teddy boys, an American tourist named Simon
Wells (Macdonald Carey) is lured into a trap by pretty tart Joan
(Shirley Ann Field). The Teddy boys, led by her brother King (Oliver Reed) mug the man and confiscate his money. Later Joan is
repentant and agrees to go with Simon aboard his yacht. But the
couple is chased into the hills by the reckless gang. Also in these
hills is Freya (Viveca Lindfors), who believes her scientist lover
Bernard (Alexander Knox) has secreted a new mistress in the area.
    What Simon, Joan, and Freya discover in the vicinity is that
inside Bernard's barbed-wire enclosed compound, in a cave, exists
nine rather cold and strange children. It is brought out that these
youngsters were all subjected accidentally to radiation. Bernard's
plan is to rear and educate the brood to survive an atomic war and
to start a new civilization, if necessary. The group, which now includes King, gets involved in the matter. Bernard's men pursue
them and one by one they are killed: King tumbles over a cliff, Simon and Joan, who have been exposed to radiation, drift in their
small craft, knowing they will soon die. And Freya, who refuses to
forget what she has seen, is shot by Bernard.
    Films and Filming reported, "For all its faults, Losey's film
is in the highest class. Its social criticism cuts like a whip; and
yet it is full of haunting poetic images.... This is undoubtedly one
of the most important British films of the year, even, perhaps, of
the 60s." Time magazine noted, the film "is a small, harrowing
science-fiction thriller ... [which] exudes a mesmerizing air of in-
tangible menace."
    In 1964 the movie was voted the best picture at the Trieste
Science Fiction Film Festival. In Italy it was issued as Hallucination.

DAREDEVILS OF THE RED CIRCLE (Republic, 1939) twelve chapters

        Associate producer, Robert Beche; directors, William Witney
and John English; screenplay, Barry Shipman, Franklyn Adreon,

Herman Brix (Bruce Bennett), Charles Quigley, Harry Strang and
David Sharpe in Daredevils of the Red Circle (1939).

Ronald Davidson, Sol Shor, and Rex Taylor; music, William Lava;
camera, William Nobles.
          Charles Quigley (Gene); Herman Brix [Bruce Bennett] (Tiny);
David Sharpe (Burt); Carole Landis (Blanche); Miles Mander (Granville, the Prisoner); Charles Middleton (Granville, #39013); C. Montague Shaw (Dr. Malcolm); Ben Taggart (Dixon); William Pagan (Chief
Landon); Raymond Bailey (Klein); Snowflake (Himself); George Chese-
bro (Sheffield); Ray Miller (Jeff); Robert Winkler (Sammy); Tuffie
(The Dog).
          Chapters: 1) The Monstrous Plot; 2) The Mysterious Friend;
3) The Executioner; 4) Sabotage; 5) The Ray of Death; 6) Thirty Seconds to Live; 7) The Flooded Mine; 8) S. O. S. ; 9) Ladder of Peril;
10) The Infernal Machine; 11) The Red Circle Speaks; 12) Flight to
Doom.

          After fifteen years in prison, a convict (Charles Middleton)
escapes and kidnaps his former partner (Miles Mander), imprisons
the man and takes over his identity. He then promises to destroy

the partner's family and business, and he begins his revenge scheme
with an amusement pier the man owns.   His attempt to destroy the
pier is thwarted by three college athletes (Charles Quigley, Herman
Brix, David Sharpe) working on the pier, who call themselves The
Daredevils of the Red Circle.   When the small brother of one of the
Daredevils is killed in the attempt, the trio vows vengeance on the
arsonist.   They are joined in their fight by the granddaughter (Carole
Landis) of the kidnapped businessman.   Despite many attempts to
stop them, the Daredevils manage to thwart the villain at every chapter turn, even when he tries to kill the district attorney investigating
the case.   Finally it is learned that the kidnapped man is imprisoned
in the convict's basement.   But #39013 (Middleton) threatens to kill
him with a bomb.   Meanwhile, the villain equips the heroine's car
with a time bomb (set to detonate when the car reaches a speed of
70 mph), but the culprit is later injured when wrecking his own car.
One of his henchman places #39013 in the heroine's vehicle in order
to make their escape.   Unknowingly he accelerates the auto to a
speed of 70 mph and they are both killed.

Daredevils of the Red Circle was one of a number of excellent
Republic chapterplays from the late Thirties and holds a special level
of esteem among serial enthusiasts.   The proceedings are filled with
all kinds of futuristic gadgets and weapons devised and used by the
evil Charles Middleton (in one of his best villainous roles besides
that of Emperor Ming in the three Flash Gordon [q. v.] serials).   In
this entry, the idea of using three heroes in a cliffhanger was introduced, although the pattern had already been set some years before
in the B Western.

DAUGHTER OF EVIL   see   ALRAUNE (1930)

THE DAY MARS INVADED THE EARTH (Twentieth Century-Fox,
(1962) 70 min.

       Producer/director, Maury Dexter; screenplay, Harry Spalding;
art director, Harry Reif; music/music director, Richard LaSalle; assistant director, Clarence Eurist; sound, Carl Faulkner and Harry
M. Leonard; camera, John Nichkolaus, Jr.; editor, Jodie Copelan.
Kent Taylor (Dr. David Fielding); Marie Windsor (Claire
Fielding); William Mims (Dr. Web Spencer); Betty Beall (Judi Fielding); Lowell Brown (Frank); Gregg Shank (Rocky Fielding).

       In its title this low-budget entry appeared to be promising a
huge battle à la War of the Worlds (q. v.).   But it emerged a rather
tame psychological horror/science fiction film about entities from
Mars taking over the bodies of scientists who are exploring the Red
Planet.
       Dr. David Fielding (Kent Taylor) and Dr. Web Spencer (Wil-
liam Mims) are the heads of a Cape Canaveral project to explore
Mars.   But their project comes to a halt when a robot device which
has landed on the Martian surface is sucked into the desert sands.
Later, returning home to California to visit his almost-estranged

Lowell Brown, Betty Beall and Gregg Shank in <u>The Day Mars Invaded</u>
<u>the Earth</u> (1962).

family, Dr. Fielding becomes aware that an exact double of himself
(and later doubles of his family and Dr. Spencer) is roaming the estate where his family is housed.   Tracing the apparitions to a deserted mansion on the grounds, he is confronted by his double.   The
latter explains that the beings haunting his family are actually from
Mars and that they have come to Earth to prevent any future exploration of their planet.   Fielding tries to escape from the beings but,
like his family and Spencer, he is eventually assimilated by the Martians.
        The finale was especially hard-hitting; for once, the <u>invaders</u>
win the war.

THE DAY OF THE TRIFFIDS (Rank Film Distributors, 1963) C-93
min.

        Executive producer, Philip Yordan; producer, George Pitcher;
director, Steve Sekely; based on the novel by John Wyndham; screenplay, Yordan; music composer/conductor, Ron Goodwin; additional
music, Johnny Douglas; assistant director, Douglas Hermes; art

director, Cedric Dawe; wardrobe, Bridget Sellers; makeup, Paul Ra-
biger; sound, Matt McCarthy, Bert Ross, and Maurice Askew; special camera effects, Wally Veevers; camera, Ted Moore; editor,
Spencer Reeve.

Howard Keel (Bill Masen); Nicole Maurey (Christine Durrant);
Janette Scott (Karen Goodwin); Kieron Moore (Tom Goodwin); Mervyn
Johns (Professor Coker); Janina Faye (Susan); Alison Leggatt (Miss
Coker); Ewan Roberts (Dr. Soames); Colette Wilde (Nurse Jamieson);
Carole Ann Ford (Bettina); Geoffrey Matthews (Luis); Gilgi Hauser
(Terrsa); Katya Douglas (Mary); Thomas Gallagher (Burly Man); John
Simpson (Blind Man); Sidney Vivian (Ticket Agent).

The lack of a proper budget does not always ruin a solid property, as this production demonstrated ("A thriller of modest ambitions and generally exciting results," said the New York Times).
The Earth is drenched by a meteor shower, causing most of
the planet's population to lose their sight. Then alien spores land
and quickly grow into seven-foot-tall plants capable of fast movement.
These astounding plants attack and kill Earthlings in their mass effort to subdue the planet. Meanwhile, American naval officer Bill
Masen (Howard Keel) has been recuperating in a London hospital.
His eyes were bandaged following an operation and he is one of the
few whose sight was spared during the meteor shower. He meets
a sighted child (Janina Faye) and they travel to France where they
find another seeing survivor (Nicole Maurey). In the meantime, off
the Cornish Coast, a marine biologist (Kieron Moore) and his wife
(Janette Scott) work feverishly to discover a way to destroy the creatures. Finally, it is found that simple sea water dissolves the triffids. The world, once again, has been saved from doom.
Structurally, The Day of the Triffids has several shaky plot
lines. Part of this problem is due to the fact the film was not completed until a year after the major filming was finished. * The final
sequences with Moore and Scott in the lighthouse were tacked on, relying on a story twist that had been employed in Beginning of the
End (q. v.).
Variety termed this genre favorite, "A vegetarian's version
of The Birds. . . . [The triffids] look like a Walt Disney nightmare
and sound like a cauldron of broccoli cooking in Margaret Hamilton's
witchin' kitchen." Some critics were more biting. The New York
Herald-Tribune's Robert Salmaggi insisted, "The only logical thing
in this crawling bore is the means used to destroy the creature.
(No, it's not crab-grass killer.)"

THE DAY THE EARTH CAUGHT FIRE (Pax, 1961) 99 min.

Producer, Val Guest; associate producer, Frank Sherwin
Green; director, Guest; screenplay, Wolf Mankowitz and Guest; art

---

*Actor Howard Keel would later admit that the scenario was so talk-
less that he was forced to write much of his own dialogue in order
to have something to say in the film.

Janet Munro as Jeannie, being doused by beatniks, in The Day the
Earth Caught Fire (1961).

director, Tony Masters; set decorator, Scott Slimon; makeup, Tony
Sforzini; technical adviser, Arthur Christiansen; music director,
Stanley Black; costumes, Beatrice Dawson; assistant director, Philip
Shipway; sound, Buster Ambler; special effects, Les Bowie; camera,
Harry Waxman; editor, Bill Lenny.
        Edward Judd (Peter Stenning); Janet Munro (Jeannie Craig);
Leo McKern (Bill Maguire); Michael Goodliffe (Night Editor); Arthur
Christiansen (Editor); Bernard Braden (News Editor); Reginald Beck-
with (Harry); Gene Anderson (May); Renee Asherson (Angela); Austin
Trevor (Sir John Kelly); Peter Butterworth and John Barron (Sub Edi-
tors); Charles Morgan (Foreign Editor); Geoffrey Chater (Holyrod);
Ian Ellis (Michael); Jane Aird (Nanny); Robin Hawdon (Ronnie).

        Strange weather occurrences throughout the world baffle scien-
tists.   But Bill Maguire (Leo McKern), the science editor of the London Daily Express with the help of fellow reporter Peter Stenning
(Edward Judd), has an explanation; two simultaneous nuclear tests,
one at the North Pole and one at the South Pole, have led to a shift
in the earth's orbit.   Now the world is drifting straight to the sun.
International consultation determines that perhaps the detonation of
four major bombs might push the Earth back into its proper orbit.
The population goes underground on detonation day.   In the Express
composing room, two pre-set front-page headlines have been prepared.   One reads "World Saved," the other announces "World Doomed."

"Science fiction movies have threatened our world with extinction from a variety of causes; there have been things from outer
space, strange blobs, and magnetic monsters; but in the end the
earth has managed to survive. Less optimistic, though is The Day
the Earth Caught Fire. Its premise is, however, so close to prevalent and widespread fears and worries that it is not so much science
fiction as it is a dramatic and imaginative extension of the news. . . .
[It] is a model of expert moviemaking, continually and excruciatingly
suspenseful, with even a love story that is not too hard to take amid
the apocalyptic events, [and] it has hard good sense at its base. . . .
The movie achieves its impact because it was made not merely to
entertain, but out of a sense of outrage. It will be compared to On
the Beach [q. v.]. Good as that one was, The Day the Earth Caught
Fire is better" (Saturday Review).

Real-life newspaper man Arthur Christianson was cast in the
role of an editor, and the film itself is dedicated to British journa-
lists.

For the U. S. release, nine minutes of running time was chopped from the black-and-white, widescreen picture.

THE DAY THE EARTH STOOD STILL (Twentieth Century-Fox, 1951)
92 min.

Producer, Julian Blaustein; director, Robert Wise; based on
the story "Farewell to the Master" by Harry Bates; screenplay, Edmund H. North; art directors, Lyle Wheeler and Addison Hehr; music, Bernard Herrmann; special effects, Fred Sersen; camera, Leo
Tover; editor, William Reynolds.

Michael Rennic (Klaatu); Patricia Neal (Helen Benson); Hugh
Marlowe (Tom Stevens); Sam Jaffe (Dr. Barnhardt); Billy Gray (Bobby
Benson); Frances Bavier (Mrs. Barley); Lock Martin (Gort); Drew
Pearson (Himself); Frank Conroy (Harley); Carleton Young (Colonel);
Fay Roope (Major General); Edith Evanson (Mrs. Crockett); Robert
Osterloh (Major White); Tyler McVey (Brady); James Seay (Govern-
ment Man); John Brown (Mr. Barley); Marjorie Grossland (Hilda);
Glenn Hardy (Interviewer); House Peters, Jr. (M. P. Captain).

This adaptation of Harry Bates' Astounding magazine story,
"Farewell to the Master," is regarded as one of the classics of the
sci-fi world. Although the production has not withstood the test of
time in all areas, it still retains a passive charm, in sharp contrast
to the monsters, ray-guns, and rocketships which usually fill the
genre.

An alien, Klaatu (Michael Rennie), lands in Washington, D. C.
in a flying saucer, accompanied by a robot, Gort (Lock Martin).
This handsome and literate intruder informs the populace that atomic
tests must cease or the Earth will be demolished by other planets in
the galaxy to save them from certain destruction. The nations of the
world then convene to cope with the dilemma. Klaatu, under the
watchful eye of the F. B. I. , is permitted to associate with the earthlings and he wins many friends, including Helen Benson (Patricia
Neal) and her son Bobby (Billy Gray). Eventually the world's leaders

conclude that the alien must be a hoax. As he returns to his craft,
he is shot. Gort removes his body and plans to put in motion the
destruction of the Earth. But Helen repeats to Gort words said to
her by Klaatu. At the finale, Klaatu is resurrected and, before returning to the outer galaxy, he offers a final warning that peace must
come to the Earth--or else.

Obviously fashioned with many parallels to religious and political concepts, the film boasts a good script, tight direction, and a
stunning performance by Rennie as Klaatu. Unfortunately, the film
was hampered by inferior special effects.

"[It] remains not only a SF cinema classic, but one of the
few really intelligent science fiction films.... This film presented
visitors from space not as an excuse to indulge in a horror fest, but
to deliver a message and tell us something about ourselves as well"
(James Van Hise, Films Fantastique). In Science Fiction in the Cinema (1970), John Baxter noted, "The Washington backgrounds are
well used, especially in night sequences where stark side-lighting
gives a hard-edged intensity to the white flying saucer squatting in
the park. Klaatu's recipe for peace--a robot police force unsuscep-
tible to corruption or scientific tampering--sounds alarmingly Fascist but whatever its political pedigree, The Day the Earth Stood
Still remains one of the most entertaining excursions into sf attempted by Hollywood."

Michael Rennie would repeat his role for "Lux Radio Theatre"
in January, 1954, joined by Jean Peters.

In an interview with Rui Noqueira for Focus on Films (Spring,
1973), Wise would recall some of the "tricks" used in the making of
The Day the Earth Stood Still:

> For the robot, we had to have something of a giant size
> but still flexible and workable. There used to be a door-
> man at the Chinese Theatre on Hollywood Boulevard who
> was about seven feet tall and he was hired to be inside the
> suit. It was built in foam rubber to his proportions. In
> fact, we had to have two suits because he had to have a
> way to get into it, so we had one with a zipper up the back
> and another with a zipper up the front. If I had a shot of
> the man coming toward camera, he would be wearing the
> suit with the zipper up the back and if I wanted a shot in
> reverse we'd have to stop for an hour while he got into the
> other suit. He could only stay in there for an hour at a
> time because there wasn't enough ventilation and he was
> not a very strong man....
>
> The scenes where the lights go out in cities all over the
> world were all done by the trick department at Fox, getting
> actual newsreel shots and stop-framing and holding and then
> double printing. In some instances I think they had to paint
> some mattes to make it work but the basis was stock shots.

Wise also commented:

> The science-fiction type of film probably offers more
> opportunities for messages, for themes, for comments, for
> warnings about our own society now or about where it's
> going than any other type of film.

THE DAY THE WORLD CHANGED HANDS   see   COLOSSUS: THE
FORBIN PROJECT

THE DAY THE WORLD ENDED (American Releasing Corp. , 1956)
81 min.

   Executive producer, Alex Gordon; producer/director, Roger
Corman; screenplay, Lou Rusoff; music, Ronald Stein; special effects,
Paul Blaisdell; camera, Jock Feindel; editor, Ronald Sinclair.
   With: Richard Denning, Adele Jergens, Lori Nelson, Mike
Connors, Paul Birch, Jonathan Haze, and Paul Blaisdell (The Mutant).

   Roger Corman and Alex Gordon teamed for this early sci-fi
film from American Releasing Corporation (later American International Pictures).   Despite a minuscule budget, the project turned out
rather well.   It is one of the more enjoyable of the Grade B entries
that mushroomed in the mid-Fifties.   It proved that a little ingenuity
was worth more in entertainment value than just misplaced cash.
   The film opens with "The End" flashing on the screen.   The
viewer learns that the world (in the mid-Seventies) has just been
ravaged by an atomic war and that five survivors have made their
way to the mountains.   There, the scientist (Paul Birch) has built
an environment to withstand holocausts.   The scientist's daughter
(Lori Nelson) becomes romantically intrigued with one survivor (Richard Denning) but is at odds with his companions, a stripper (Adele
Jergens) and a hoodlum (Mike Connors).   The group soon learns that
they are not alone, as they are stalked by a radioactive mutant monster (designed and well played by Paul Blaisdell).   The survivors do
not stop their in-fighting, and find they are powerless against the
creature, who abducts and tries to rape the girl.   But a soft rain
begins and destroys the contaminated mutant.   The film ends with
"The Beginning" flashing on the screen as the hero and heroine walk
off together.
   There are obvious parallels between the film and religion: the
paradise world is an Eden where the survivors find sanctuary, the
mutant replaces the serpent, the squabbling between the survivors
represents the Cain and Abel conflict, and the ending finds Denning
and Nelson as the new Adam and Eve.
   The Day the World Ended would be remade in 1969 by AIP as
Year 2889.   This Larry Buchanan-produced/directed outing was so
lack-lustre that it was issued only to television.

THE DEADLY BEES (Paramount, 1967) C-85 min.

   Producers, Max J. Rosenberg and Milton Subotsky; director,
Freddie Francis; based on the novel A Taste for Honey by H. F.
Heard; screenplay, Robert Block and Anthony Marriott; art director,
Bill Constable; set decorator, Andrew Low; music, Wilfred Josephs;
assistant director, Anthony Waye; sound, Michael Pidcock; special
camera effects, John Mackie; special effects, Michael Collins; camera,
John Wilcox; editor, Oswald Hafenrickter.

Catherine Finn and Guy Doleman in The Deadly Bees (1967).

Suzanna Leigh (Vicki Robbins); Frank Finlay (Manfred); Guy Doleman (Ralph Hargrove); Catherine Finn (Mrs. Hargrove); John Harvey (Thompson); Michael Ripper (Hawkins); Anthony Bailey (Compere); Tim Barrett (Harcourt); James Cossins (Coroner); Frank Forsyth (Doctor); Katy Wild (Doris Hawkins); Greta Farrer (Sister); Gina Gianelli (Secretary); Michael Gwynn (Dr. Lang); Maurice Good (Agent); Alister Williamson (Inspector).
          A. k. a. Killer Bees.

        "Pic is not for the faint-hearted, but as a low-budgeted meller, should have appeal as an offbeat item" (Variety). TV Guide's Judith Crist was less kind, labeling it "a watered-down adaptation of H. F. Heard's classic thriller.... A real stinger, cinematically." The New York Times lamented, "Too bad Alfred Hitchcock [of The Birds, q. v.] wasn't around to pull this sloppy, raucously-framed little thriller into shape...."
        However, cinema enthusiasts of a less-demanding nature found this British-made picture deliciously macabre, with sufficient gore and suspense to make the eighty-five minutes worthwhile. The film's premise falls into the category of stories which examine what would happen if the balance of nature was disturbed.

Pop singer Vicky Robbins (Suzanna Leigh) comes to the country for a rest and meets two beekeepers. When a dog and its owner are killed by a lethal swarm of giant bees, the girl turns detective and attempts to track down the source of the killing, almost falling prey to the bees herself. Eventually she discovers that one of the beekeepers is actually mad and has trained the swarm of bees to kill (by dousing the intended victims with perfume). At the finale it is the mad scientist who is the final victim of his own trained bees, as he and his homicidal insects are consumed in a fire.

THE DEADLY MANTIS (Universal, 1957) 79 min.

Producer, William Alland; director, Nathan Juran; story, Alland; screenplay, Martin Berkeley; art directors, Alexander Golitzen and Robert Clatworthy; music, Joseph Gershenson; special camera effects, Clifford Stine; camera, Ellis W. Carter; editor, Chester Schaeffer.

Craig Stevens (Colonel Joe Parkman); Alix Tatton (Marge Blaine); William Hopper (Dr. Ned Jackson); Florenz Ames (Professor Anton Gunther); Donald Randolph (General Mark Ford); Pat Conway (Sergeant Pete Allen); Paul Smith (Corporal); Phil Harvey (Lou); Paul Campbell (Lieutenant Fred Pizar); Jack Mather (Officer); George Lynn (Bus Driver); Skipper McNally (Policeman); Harold Lee (Eskimo Chief).

"First quarter of the footage is extremely slow, taken up with tedious explanations and world map, so an audience is not immediately caught up in the plot" (Variety).

Universal-International was nearing the end of its Fifties' sci-fi cycle when it churned out The Deadly Mantis. It was yet another

The Deadly Mantis (1957).

in the run of the giant-insects-out-to-destroy-the-world formats. It
provided its action-hungry audience with an assortment of thrills, but
compared to such gems as Creature from the Black Lagoon, It Came
from Outer Space, and Them! (all q. v.), it was in the minor leagues.
     Produced by William Alland, who supervised most of the stu-
dio's monster movies in this period, the film "treats" the viewer to
a gigantic praying mantis which is migrating from Alaska down south,
causing a great deal of trouble along the way. For a time the oversized insect plagues the nation's capitol and then departs for Manhattan.   There, as did The Beast from 20,000 Fathoms (q. v.), it meets
its demise--in this case in the Holland Tunnel, where the heroes
(Craig Stevens and William Hopper) lead the Armed Forces in gassing
the mantis with cyanide bombs.
     The miniature work in this film is below par.

DEADLY RAY FROM MARS see FLASH GORDON'S TRIP TO MARS

DELUGE (RKO, 1933) 70 min.

     Producer, Samuel Bischoff; director, Felix E. Feist; based
on the novel by S. Fowler Wright; screenplay, John Goodrich and
Warren B. Duff; special effects, Ned Mann; special camera effects,
William B. Williams; camera, Norbert Brodine; editor, Rose Loew-
inger.
     Peggy Shannon (Claire Arlington); Sidney Blackmer (Martin
Webster); Lois Wilson (Helen Webster); Matt Moore (Tom); Fred Koh-
ler (Jephson); Ralf Harolde (Norwood); Edward Van Sloan (Professor
Carlysle); Samuel S. Hinds (Chief Forecaster).

     Alarmists have long predicted the destruction of modern cities
of "sin, " with New York as a favorite target. Capitalizing on this
concept, RKO, which would turn out the enormously popular King
Kong (q. v.) the same year, produced Deluge.
     Professor Carlysle (Edward Van Sloan) is alarmed at a plum-
meting barometer which he insists forecasts a disaster. Soon New
York City is destroyed by subterranean tremors. The earth opens
and swallows the city and Manhattan island is inundated in a giant
tidal wave. Martin Webster (Sidney Blackmer) survives the holocaust
but is convinced that his wife and children are dead. Thereafter he
meets a pretty young college graduate named Claire Arlington (Peggy
Shannon), with whom he falls in love. Together they combat the
dastardly Jephson (Fred Kohler) who has only no good on his mind.
Still later the young lovers encounter Webster's wife (Lois Wilson)
and their two children. Blonde Claire, a sturdy swimmer and a
sturdier soul, does the right thing. She leaves Webster to his family and swims off.
     Most of the post-deluge action is set about forty miles from
New York City, about the location where Martin Webster thought his
home once stood. For the most part, this science fiction soap opera
is pretty maudlin stuff. The only spectacular interest in the film
occurs at the beginning, with the scenes of destruction and the huge

tidal wave. (These sequences were later acquired by Republic Pictures who used them over and over again in quickies and serials, including S. O. S. Tidal Wave, q. v.)
     The critics were not that impressed with the special effects provided by Deluge and were less indulgent of the accompanying melodrama. "... [A] rambling and gurgling thriller.... The best moments in the film are those concerned with the excited weatherman and scientists. The destruction of skyscrapers is never particularly real and the rushing waters seem strangely out of focus at times. The dialogue never rises above the action of the story and the players deserve sympathy" (New York Times). Nevertheless, those who witnessed Deluge when it was first released still remember the film vividly.

THE DEMON PLANET see TERRORE NELLO SPAZIO

DESTINATION INNER SPACE (Magna Pictures, 1966) C-83 min.

     Producer, Earle Lyon; associate producer, Wendel E. Niles, Jr.; director, Francis D. Lyon; screenplay, Arthur C. Pierce; music, Paul Dunlap; art director, Paul Sylos, Jr.; set decorator, Harry Reif; assistant director, Joe Wonder; makeup, Bob Dawn; sound, John L. Bury, Joseph von Stroheim, and Douglas Grindstaff; special effects, Roger George; camera, Brick Marguard; editor, Robert S. Eisen.
     Scott Brady (Commander Wayne); Sheree North (Sandra); Gary Merrill (Dr. Le Satier); Mike Road (Hugh); and Wende Wagner, John Howard, William Thourly, Biff Elliot, Roy Barcroft, Ken Delo, and James Hong.

     Dr. Le Satier (Gary Merrill), photographer Sandra (Sheree North), and Hugh (Mike Road) are aboard an underwater sea lab. They request the help of Naval Commander Wayne (Scott Brady) to cope with an unidentified moving object beneath the seas. Later, Wayne determines the Thing is from outer space. Soon monsters are unleashed from the alien craft and the lab's air lines are disconnected. One of the monsters gains entrance to the enclosure and kills some crew members. But Hugh sacrifices his own life to save his lab co-workers.
     The New York Journal Tribune was not impressed: "Director Francis Lyon seems more interested in his underwater toys than in telling a coherent story." Variety was more sympathetic to the low-budget entry: "Suspense and surprise are neatly balanced and the underwater photography is at all times authentic and visually fascinating. "

DESTINATION MOON (Eagle-Lion, 1950) 91 min. (color sequences)

     Producer, George Pal; director, Irving Pichel; based on the novel Rocket Ship Galileo by Robert A. Heinlein; screenplay, Rip Van

Ronkel, Heinlein, and James O'Hanlon; astronomical art, Chesley
Bonnestell; animation sequences, Walter Lantz; music, Leigh Stevens;
special effects, Lee Zavitz; camera, Lionel Lindon; editor, Duke
Goldstone.
    John Archer (Barnes); Warner Anderson (Cargraves); Tom
Powers (General Thayer); Dick Wesson (Sweeney); Erin O'Brien
Moore (Mrs. Cargraves).

    Viewed today, Destination Moon seems old hat and very badly
dated.   In a quarter of a century, what this film regarded as science
fiction has become science fact.   Yet this feature (along with The
Thing, q.v.) was so popular when issued that it inauguarated an avalanche of space exploration films both in Hollywood and abroad.
Technically mediocre and never really very exciting, Destination Moon
nevertheless has carved for itself a solid niche in the hierarchy of
sci-fi classics.
    George Pal, who had previously helmed Puppetoon short sub-
jects, made this picture from Robert A. Heinlein's rather juvenile
novel Rocket Ship Galileo, which was greatly altered for the silver
screen.   The plotline has astronauts embarking on a moon trip, and
details their journey and their landing/exploration of the moon's surface (as well as their claiming the heavenly body for the U.S.).   A
rather sterile film, it did include the attempted sabotage of the mission by an unnamed foreign power, suggesting a fertile new field for

Scene from Destination Moon (1950).

cold war intrigue.
Produced for under $600,000 with a non-star cast, the movie had to rely on its catchy title and semi-documentary style for box-office appeal. Interestingly, when the U.S. astronauts made the first moon walk in 1970, Destination Moon was used by the TV networks as almost a blueprint for what was to come.

DESTINATION SATURN   see   BUCK ROGERS

DESTINAZIONE LUNA   see   ROCKETSHIP X-M

DEUX CENT MILLE LIEUES SOUS LES MERS (French, 1907) C-930'

Producer/director, Georges Méliès; based on the novel by Jules Verne; screenplay, Méliès.
See: 20,000 LEAGUES UNDER THE SEA

DEVIL GIRL FROM MARS (British Lion, 1954) 76 min.

Producers, Edward J. and Harry Lee Danziger; director, David MacDonald; based on the play by John C. Mather and James Eastwood; screenplay, Mather and Eastwood; music, Edwin Astley; special effects, Jack Whitehead; camera, Jack Cox; editor, Peter Taylor.

Joseph Tomelty, Patricia Laffan, Hazel Court, Adrienne Corri and Hugh McDermott in Devil Girl from Mars (1954).

Hugh McDermott (Michael Carter); Hazel Court (Eileen Prest-
wick); Patricia Laffan (Nyah); Peter Reynolds (Albert); Adrienne Corri (Doris); Joseph Tomelty (Professor Hennessey); Sophie Stewart
(Mrs. Jamieson); John Laurie (Mr. Jamieson); Anthony Richmond
(Tommy).

The title tells all in this fast-buck entry from Great Britain,
made by that country's answer to low-budget producer Sam Katzman,
the Danziger Brothers. It was an obvious carbon copy attempt of
The Day the Earth Stood Still (q.v.), with the alien this time being
a female. Like Klaatu in The Day film, she also comes equipped
with a large robot, here called Chani.
The devil girl (Patricia Laffan) and her robot land in a flying
saucer in the Scottish Highland. After at first seeming to be friendly she turns savage in her earnest quest for males to help repopulate
her planet. Eventually she is destroyed; but not until after she and
her (slapdash) robot have caused considerable trouble.
At least Adrienne Corri and Hazel Court graduated to much
better science fiction and horror films made in Great Britain later
in the decade.

THE DEVIL'S TRIANGLE (UFO/Cinema National, 1974) C-52 min.

Producer, Richard Winer; associate producer, Larry Kelsey;
director, screenplay, Winer; music, King Cremson; camera, Winer;
editor, Ron Sinclair.
Vincent Price (narrator)

The topicality and popularity of several books on the subject
of the still unexplained Bermuda Triangle, combined with the marquee
value of Vincent Price as narrator, gave box-office value to this 52-
minute documentary.
The celluloid study offers interesting color footage of the area
known as the Bermuda Triangle (in the Bahamas) where dozens of
crafts, planes, and people have suddenly and inexplicably disappeared
without a trace. The theories about these weird disappearances and
their histories are examined. (Thankfully, the presentation is both
informative and generally stimulating.)
The Devil's Triangle includes evidence of disappearances from
1880-1967 and assorted experts are interviewed to discuss the possible causes: these theories range from kidnappings by space aliens
to a change in dimension due to electromagnetic fields. Monster
Fantasy magazine judged the picture "An altogether fascinating treatment of one of life's real mysteries." On the other hand, the Hollywood Reporter commented, "Winer's unadventuresome textbook argument does not do justice to a thought-provoking situation. He fails
to evoke the fantasies that might give the phenomenon meaning."
In 1975 an ABC-TV telefeature entitled Satan's Triangle, with
Kim Novak, Doug McClure, and Michael Conrad, also dealt with the
topic, but in a fictional manner.
Portions of The Devil's Triangle, including Vincent Price's
narration, were used in the PBS TV program The Case of the

Bermuda Triangle on the "Nova" series. The program, which none too successfully tried to debunk the various Triangle theories, was originally made by the BBC in England and was telecast in the U.S. in 1976.

DICK BARTON--SPECIAL AGENT (Exclusive, 1948) 70 min.

Producer, Henry Halstead; director, Alfred Goulding; based on the radio serial by Edward J. Mason; screenplay, Alan Stranks and Goulding; camera, Stanley Clinton.
Don Stannard (Dick Barton); George Ford (Snowey White); Jack Shaw (Jock); Gillian Maude (Jean Hunter); Geoffrey Wincott (Dr. Caspar); Beatrice Kane (Miss Horrock); Ivor Danvers (Snub).

After World War II, Hammer Pictures, which had produced a few features before the war, returned to production with a steady series of films which would peak in the late Fifties and early Sixties with some of the best science fiction and horror movies made during that era. As if a hint of the sci-fi entries to come, Hammer's second post-war film was Dick Barton--Special Agent, based on the popular BBC radio series. The result was a deft combination of the detective and sci-fi genres.
In this outing Dick Barton (Don Stannard), a special operative for the British government, takes a holiday in a small fishing village. There he uncovers a plot by an enemy agent--a sinister and fanatical doctor--to pollute the water around England with "germ bombs" which would destroy the country's fishing trade and cripple its economy. Barton foils the plot and the evil doctor is eventually done in by his own invention.
This Hammer-Marylebone co-production was swift and entertaining. Through its veneer of juvenile plot action came more than a hint of the Cold War, as the enemy agent was obviously not from Western Europe. The motion picture proved so popular that two sequels followed: Dick Barton Strikes Back (1949) and Dick Barton at Bay (1950). There would probably have been more entries had not star Don Stannard been killed in an auto crash.

DICK TRACY (Republic, 1937) fifteen chapters

Associate producer, J. Laurence Wickland; directors, Ray Taylor and Alan James; based on the character created by Chester Gould; screen story, Morgan Cox and George Morgan; screenplay, Barry Shipman and Winston Miller; music, Harry Grey; camera, William Nobles and Edgar Lyons.
Ralph Byrd (Dick Tracy); Kay Hughes (Gwen); Smiley Burnette (Mike McGurk); Lee Van Atta (Junior); John Piccori (Moloch); Carleton Young (Gordon Tracy - After); Fred Hamilton (Steve); Francis X. Bushman (Anderson); John Dilson (Brewster); Richard Beach (Gordon Tracy - Before); Wedgewood Nowell (Clayton); Theodore Lorch (Paterno); Edwin Stanley (Odette); Harrison Greene (Cloggerstein); Herbert Weber (Martino); Buddy Roosevelt (Burke); George DuNormand

(Flynn); Byron Foulger (Korvitch); Oscar and Elmer (Themselves). Chapters: 1) The Spider Strikes; 2) The Bridge of Terror; 3) The Fur Pirates; 4) Death Rides the Sky; 5) Brother Against Brother; 6) Dangerous Waters; 7) The Ghost Town Mystery; 8) Battle in the Clouds; 9) The Stratosphere Adventure; 10) The Gold Ship; 11) Harbor Pursuit; 12) The Trail of the Spider; 13) The Fire Trap; 14) The Devil in White; 15) Brothers United.

Chester Gould's dynamic comic strip had been a popular newspaper item since its debut in 1931. Six years later Republic Pictures acquired the screen rights to the strip for an exciting fifteen-chapter serial which boasts an excellent cast (including silent screen favorite Francis X. Bushman), good production values and lots of action.

In this, the first of a quartet* of chapterplays about the fearless police investigator, Tracy (Ralph Byrd) is at odds with the evil Spider, who is aided by a hunchback named Moloch (John Piccori). The Spider abducts Tracy's brother and performs an operation on him, turning his victim into a zombie-like creature who will do his slightest bidding. This dastardly action puts the detective at a disadvantage and he is further hindered by the Spider's use of futuristic weapons and a multi-purpose plane called "The Flying Wing." But with the aid of girlfriend Gwen (Kay Hughes), partner Mike McGurk (Smiley Burnette), and buddy Junior (Lee Van Atta), the mighty detective succeeds in bringing an end to the Spider's amazing reign of terror.

Produced in the midst of Republic's Golden Age of serial-making, Dick Tracy was lucky to have Ralph Byrd in the title role; he seemed made for the part. He would play the role in the remainder of the studio's Tracy serials. Later, for RKO Pictures, he would replace Morgan Conway in a Dick Tracy series, and he would again play the police worker on TV in the early Fifties.

At a time when moviegoers (and perhaps people in general) were more naive than they are today, the nefarious, "unreal" inventions of the villainous Spider appeared far more amazing and futuristic than viewers of today might believe.

DIE, MONSTER, DIE (American International, 1965) C-81 min.

Executive producers, James H. Nicholson and Samuel Z. Arkoff; producer, Pat Green; director, Daniel Haller; based on the story "The Colour Out of Space" by H. P. Lovecraft; screenplay, Jerry Sohl; music, Don Banks; music director, Philip Martell; make-up, Jimmy Evans; art director, Colin Southcott; assistant director, Dennis Hall; sound, Ken Rawkins and Robert Jones; camera, Paul Beeson; editor, Alfred Cox.
Boris Karloff (Nahum Witley); Nick Adams (Stephen Reinhart); Suzan Farmer (Suzan Witley); Freda Jackson (Letitia Witley); Terence de Marney (Merwyn); Patrick Magee (Dr. Henderson); Paul

---

*The other chapterplays were: Dick Tracy Returns (1938), Dick Tracy's G-Men (1939), and Dick Tracy vs. Crime, Inc. (1941).

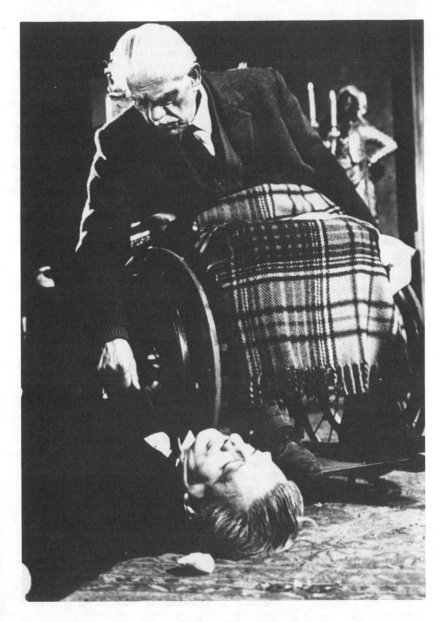

Boris Karloff and Terence de Marney in <u>Die, Monster, Die</u> (1965).

Farrell (Jason); Leslie Dwyer (Potter); Sheila Raynor (Miss Bailey); Harold Goodwin (Cab Driver); Sydney Bromley (Pierce); Billy Milton (Henry).

American International produced this thriller at the Elstree Studios of Associated British Pictures in London. The teaming of horror film superstar Boris Karloff and popular TV performer Nick Adams generated good box-office for this minor film on both sides of the Atlantic.

Adapted from H. P. Lovecraft's short story, the plot revolves around a young American named Stephen Reinhart (Adams) who comes to the remote country home of his fiancée (Suzan Farmer) only to be met with hostility from her invalid scientist-father (Karloff) and a complete rebuff from her hermit-like mother (Freda Jackson). Eventually the two young people discover that the energy from a meteor which landed on the estate years before is being harnassed. But the poison emanating from the meteor has caused both of the girl's parents to mutate, along with several "things" the father keeps secreted in the green house. When he tries to destroy the meteor he is turned into a glowing, mad mutant who attempts to kill the lovers. However, he falls from a flight of stairs to his death. Thereafter the house burns and the meteor explodes in the fire.

Die, Monster, Die is a visually eerie but slow-moving exercise, bolstered somewhat by good performances from Karloff and Adams. Still, the British Kinematograph Weekly disapproved: "This is somewhat obscure thriller stuff with hardly enough happening to keep the radioactive pot boiling."

The movie was issued in Britain as Monster of Terror and had been highly touted under its working title of The House at the End of the World.

DINOSAURUS! (Universal, 1960) C-85 min.

Producer, Jack H. Harris; co-producer/director, Irvin S. Yeaworth, Jr.; screenplay, Jean Yeaworth and Dan E. Weisburd; art director, Jack Senter; set decorator, Herman Schoenbrun; makeup, Don Cash; music, Ronald Stein; director of underwater sequence, Paul Stader; assistant director, Herbert Mendelson; sound, Jack Connall, Jack Wheeler, and Vic Appel; special camera effects, Tim Baar, Wah Chang, and Gene Warren; camera, Stanley Cortez; editor, John A. Bushelman.

Ward Ramsey (Bart Thompson); Kristina Hanson (Betty Piper); Paul Lukather (Chuck); Gregg Martell (Neanderthal Man); Alan Roberts (Julio); Fred Engelberg (Mike Hacker); Wayne C. Tredway (Dumpy); James Logan (O'Leary); Luci Blain (Chica); Jack Younger (Jasper); Howard Dayton (Mousey).

An amusing romp filmed in Scandinavia, boasting good use of color, excellent animation, and enough excitement to hold the audience's interest, Dinosaurus! makes little pretense at being a serious sci-fi entry.

It is set in the West Indies, where lightning revives a long

Scene from Dinosaurus! (1960).

dormant cave man and two dinosaurs, a benign brontosaurus and a
rampaging tyrannosaurus. A small boy named Julio (Alan Roberts)
becomes friends with a Neanderthal Man (Gregg Martell) and uses
the tame brontosaurus as a playmate. The police, however, enter
the scene and give chase to the cave man and his lizard friend. The
tyrannosaurus wounds the other oversized beast and pushes it into
quicksand to die. The police pursue the cave man, who manages to
save Julio but not himself. The boy tells the authorities of the tyrannosaurus and they set fire to a field to force the giant reptile onto a cliff. It does battle with a steam shovel before being pushed
into the sea to die.

Not only was Dinosaurus! well animated but it was also amusing. In one scene the cave man hurls pies at the lawmen as he
chases them. The relationship between the boy and his pet brontosaurus was adequately presented, and more sensibly handled than in
later Japanese films where children were often depicted as playmates
of various pre-historic reptiles.

The film was produced by Fairview Productions, which also
turned out The Blob (q. v.).

DOC SAVAGE--THE MAN OF BRONZE (Warner Bros. , 1975) C-100 min.

Producer, George Pal; director, Michael Anderson; based on
the novel by Kenneth Robeson [Lester Dent]; screenplay, Pal and Joe
Morhaim; music adaptor, Frank De Vol; songs, De Vol and Don Black;
costumes, Patrick Cummings; stunt co-ordinator, Toni Eppers; art
director, Fred Harpman; set decorator, Marvin March; sound, Harlan Riggs; special camera effects, Howard A. Anderson; camera,
Fred Koenekamp; editor, Thomas McCarthy.

Ron Ely (Doc Savage); Paul Gleason (Long Tom); Bill Lucking
(Renny); Michael Miller (monk); Eldon Quick (Johnny); Darrell Swerl-
ing (Ham); Paul Wexler (Captain Seas); Janice Heiden (Adriana); Robyn
Hilton (Karen); Pamela Hensley (Mona); Bob Corson (Don Rubio Gor-
ro); Carlos Rivas (Kulkan); Chuy Franco (Cheelok); Alberto Morin
(Jose); Victor Millan (Chief Chaac); Jorge Cervera, Jr. (Colonel Ra-
mirez); Frederico Roberto (El Presidente); Grace Stafford (Little
Lady); Dar Robinson (Native); Scott Walker (Borden).

The fictional "Doc Savage" superman had long enjoyed a cult
following. The Doc Savage magazine was in existence from 1933 to
1949, and over the years 181 stories about the characters have been
written--mostly by Lester Dent, under the name of Kenneth Robeson.
For many years there was industry talk of filming the many Doc
Savage books and comics; finally, in 1975, producer George Pal
turned out Doc Savage--Man of Bronze.

Ron Ely (who played "Tarzan" on TV and in two theatrical
films) made a physically perfect Doc Savage. His co-horts ("the
five greatest minds ever assembled in one group") were a motley
bunch: Johnny (Eldon Quick); Ham (Darrell Zwerling); Renny (Bill
Lucking); Monk (Michael Miller); and Long Tom (Paul Gleason). It
is 1936 and the conclave is at odds with Captain Seas (Paul Wexler),
a heinous villain who wants to control pools of gold discovered in a
remote region of South America. First, Seas tries to kill Doc on
his home ground, then he follows him to South America when Doc--
whose father died trying to protect the secret--goes there to unravel
a puzzle left to him by his late parent. The villain nearly eliminates
Doc, "the strongest and most intelligent man in the world," but the
hero saves the day and, of course, the secret of the golden pools.

Despite the solid production trappings, Doc Savage was an extremely inane telling of a potentially exciting story. British Monthly
Film Bulletin perceived the major fault: " ... [Pal] proceeded to
manufacture a film that never once looks back to its source, either
in substance or inspiration. ... Nothing in this unfortunate enterprise
is likely to please anyone: former Savage fans will be enraged, new-
comers bored, and children will probably feel far superior to the
whole mess. "

So inferior was this entry that the projected series concept
was dropped and the film quickly shunted to cable TV/home box-
office in America.

DR. CADMAN'S SECRET   see   THE BLACK SLEEP

Ron Ely in <u>Doc Savage--The Man of Bronze</u> (1975).

Janice Logan in Dr. Cyclops (1940).

DR. CYCLOPS (Paramount, 1940) C-75 min.

Producer, Dale Van Every; director, Ernest B. Schoedsack;
screenplay, Tom Kilpatrick; art directors, Hans Dreier and Earl
Hedricks; music, Ernest Toch, Gerard Carbonara, and Albert Hay
Malotte; special camera effects, Farciot Edouard and Wallace Kelly;
camera, Henry Sharp and Winton C. Hoch; editor, Ellsworth Hoag-
land.

Albert Dekker (Dr. Alexander Thorkel); Janice Logan (Dr.
Mary Mitchell); Thomas Coley (Bill Stockton); Charles Halton (Dr.
Bulfinch); Victor Kilian (Steve Baker); Frank Yaconelli (Pedro); Bill
Wilkerson (Silent Indian); Allen Fox (Cab Driver).

At the time of its theatrical release, Dr. Cyclops went largely unnoticed. It was not until television gave it much-deserved exposure that people really took notice. It is one of those fascinating
hybrid films that pops up occasionally to show moviegoers that the
sci-fi field can be quite imaginative in the hands of a creative craftsman. In this case the technical force was producer/director Ernest
B. Schoedsack. Not only is Dr. Cyclops a literate horror/sci-fi
film with good animation and special effects; it is also filmed in
Technicolor, something unheard of for such a low-budget film at that
time.

Albert Dekker created his most definitive screen portrayal as

the poor-sighted, bald-domed Dr. Alexander Thorkel, a man described by another character in the film as "the world's greatest living authority on organic molecular structure." Thorkel is conducting
clandestine experiments in size reduction in his laboratory located in
the upper head waters of the Amazon Jungle, near a radioactive deposit in Peru. A group of four scientists and a handyman arrive on
the scene, only to find themselves reduced by the doctor to the size
of small dolls. They then escape their captor but find horrors in
being tormented by a cat (which is scared away by a dog), a chicken,
an alligator, huge raindrops in a thunder storm, and by the doctor
himself, who is hunting his tiny prey. The little people devise a
plan to activate a gun via a rope, but this plan to shoot the doctor
fails. Then they try to break all of his eyeglasses. They succeed
except for one lens in one pair of spectacles. The doctor takes revenge by killing one of his victims, but then he slips and falls into
a well. He hangs onto the rope, grasping for life, but the life-line
is sliced by one of the doctors and the madman plunges to his death.
Ten days after undergoing the reduction treatment, the survivors regain their normal size as the rays' effects wear away.

The theme of human size reduction had been previously employed in MGM's The Devil Doll (1936) and would be used again in
the telling The Incredible Shrinking Man (q.v.), and in the vastly inferior Attack of the Puppet People (q.v.), among others.

DR. MANIAC see THE MAN WHO CHANGED HIS MIND

DR. WHO AND THE DALEKS (British Lion, 1965) 83 min.

Executive producer, Joe Vegoda; producers, Milton Subotsky
and Max J. Rosenberg; director, Gordon Flemyng; based on the BBC
television serial by Terry Nation; screenplay, Subotsky; assistant director, Anthony Waye; art director, Bill Constable; music/music director, Malcolm Lockyer; electronic music, Barry Gray; sound, Buster Ambler; camera, John Wilcox; editor, Oswald Hafenrichter.

Peter Cushing (Dr. Who); Roy Castle (Ian); Jennie Linden
(Barbara); Roberta Tovey (Susan); Barrie Ingham (Alydon); Michael
Coles (Gamatus); Geoffrey Toone (Temmosus); Mark Peterson (Elyon);
John Brown (Antodus); Yvonne Antrobus (Dyoni).

The rather absent-minded Dr. Who (Peter Cushing), his
granddaughters (Jennie Linden and Roberta Tovey) and the bumbling
assistant (Roy Castle) are accidentally thrust through space in the
doctor's machine "Tardis" (the time and relative dimension in space
transporter). They find themselves on another planet in another galaxy where they are soon captured by a group of robots which house
the Daleks--"a gelatinous mass of intensified brain power which is
a product of mutations after radiation fallout." The Daleks are a
murderous lot and have taken over the planet from its rightful inhabitants, the Thals. The Daleks trick Tovey into bringing the
Thals' leaders to their city on a mission of peace and they are captured. But Dr. Who discovers that the Daleks obtain their source

Roy Castle, Peter Cushing and Roberta Tovey in Dr. Who and the Daleks (1965).

of power from the metal floors of the city. He kills one of the creatures by cutting off his power. Later, the Daleks plan to destroy the planet with a time bomb. Meanwhile, the Tahls, with the aid of Dr. Who, attack the Daleks' city and destroy the monsters. The time bomb is deactivated and the planet saved. Dr. Who and his crew are able to return to Earth.

Jammed full of far-fetched gadgets, equipment, and scientific mumbo-jumbo, along with the horrible presence of the Daleks, the film proved popular in England and elsewhere. Not that it did not find its detractors: the British Monthly Film Bulletin criticized "some crude slapstick from Roy Castle, and absent-minded bumbling from Peter Cushing.... And the Thals, looking and sounding like ballet dancers with their golden hair-dos, heavy eye-shadow and camp speech, must be the wettest tribe on record."

The film spawned a sequel, Daleks--Invasion Earth 2150 A.D. (q.v.).

DONOVAN'S BRAIN (United Artists, 1953) 83 min.

Producer, Tom Gries; director, Felix Feist; based on the novel by Curt Siodmak; adaptor, Hugh Brooke; screenplay, Feist; production designer, Boris Leven; music, Eddie Dunstedter; special effects, Harry Redmond, Jr.; camera, Joseph Biroc; editor,

Herbert L. Strock.
    Lew Ayres (Dr. Patrick J. Cory); Gene Evans (Dr. Frank
Schratt); Nancy Davis (Janice Cory); Steve Brodie (Herbie Yocum);
Lisa K. Howard (Chloe Donovan); Tom Powers (Adviser); Michael
Colgan (Tom Donovan); Kyle James (Ranger Chief Tuttle); Peter
Adams (Mr. Webster); Stapleton Kent (W. J. Higgins); Victor Su-
therland (Nathaniel Fuller).

    This was the second of three theatrical film versions of the
Curt Siodmak novel: the other two are The Lady and the Monster
and Vengeance. More so than the other screen adaptations, this offering followed the original work rather closely. Unfortunately its
limpid production values detracted tremendously from audience interest. As for the actors, the New York Times noted, "They walk
through it all in stark confusion and speak such lines as 'Call me
when the brain quiets down,' as though they are undecided whether
a man in a white coat is stalking them. "
    A youngish doctor (Lew Ayres) residing in a remote region
of the desert comes upon the wreckage of a private plane and finds
a dead man whose brain still lives. He removes the pulsating organ
and keeps it alive, eventually beginning to mentally communicate with
it. Later the brain, whose body had belonged to a ruthless millionaire businessman, sends the physician to California to defend a man
in a murder trial. The brain wants the accused party released in
order to wreak vengeance on the associates who caused his plane accident. At the finale, of course, the doctor is able to break the
evil brain's spell and destroy it before it can do great harm.

DOPPELGANGER (Rank Film Distributors, 1969) C-101 min.

    Producers, Gerry Anderson and Sylvia Anderson; associate
producer, Ernest Holding; director, Robert Parrish; story, Gerry
Anderson and Sylvia Anderson; screenplay, Gerry Anderson, Sylvia
Anderson, and Donald James; music/music director, Barry Gray;
art director, Bob Bell; assistant director, John O'Connor; sound, Ken
Rawkins; visual effects director, Derek Meddings; special camera ef-
fects, Harry Oakes; camera, John Read; editor, Len Walter.
    Ian Hendry (John Kane); Roy Thinnes (Colonel Glenn Ross);
Patrick Wymark (Jason Webb); Lynn Loring (Sharon Ross); Loni von
Friedl (Lise); Herbert Lom (Dr. Hassler); George Sewell (Mark Neu-
man); Franco Derosa (Paulo Landi); Edward Bishop (David Poulson).

    For years many people believed the moon was but a reflection
of the Earth and this premise was developed for Doppelganger, in
which two astronauts in the 21st century are sent to explore a planet
on the opposite side of the Sun. The planet is in the same orbit as
the Earth and the two space travelers are forced to crash land on
it after an equipment malfunction. One of the astronauts dies and
the other, Colonel Glenn Ross (Roy Thinnes), awakens to find himself back on Earth, after only three weeks in space. He is later
accused of having sabotaged the mission. Thereafter, the survivor
and associate Jason Webb (Wymark) deduce that the new planet is a

Loni von Friedl and Roy Thinnes in Doppelganger (1969).

copy of Earth, but with everything reversed, and that Ross is actually his double from the new land. To validate the theory Ross charts
a second trip, with all the controls in his craft reversed. The ship
crashes and Webb, who survives, is transported to a recuperation
center where his bizarre tale is disbelieved.
      The faltering script and listless production values mitigated
against the film's success. Superior special effects were not enough
to endear this project to the public. In America, the film was retitled Journey to the Far Side of the Sun. As Judith Crist wrote in
TV Guide, it is "a nicely gadget-ridden sci-fier.... [It] comes up
with a fascinating premise but ultimately frustrates the true buff by
a final cop-out."
      The film was edited down from more than 120 minutes to its
present running time, which may account for some of its disjointed-
ness.

DRACULA JAGT FRANKENSTEIN   see   EL HOMBRE QUE VINE
DEL UMMO

DRACULA VS. FRANKENSTEIN   see   EL HOMBRE QUE VINE DEL
UMMO

THE DREAM MACHINE   see   ESCAPEMENT

DUEL IN SPACE   see   BEYOND THE MOON

EARTH DEFENSE FORCES   see   CHIKYU BOEIGUN

THE EARTH DIES SCREAMING (Twentieth Century-Fox, 1964) 62 min.

Producers, Robert I. Lippert and Jack Parsons; director,
Terence Fisher; screenplay, Henry Cross; assistant director, Gordon
Gilbert; art director, George Provis; music, Elizabeth Lutyens; mu-
sic director, Philip Martell; sound, Spencer Reeve; camera, Arthur
Lavis; editor, Robert Winter.
Willard Parker (Jeff Nolan); Virginia Field (Peggy); Dennis
Price (Quinn Taggett); Thorley Walters (Otis); Vanda Godsell (Violet);
David Spencer (Mel); Anna Falk (Lorna).

Still another in the series of invaders from outer space who
try to destroy civilization on Earth. Its premise provided a neat
packaging for the talent involved: a small group of humans attempt
survival after civilization has been almost wiped out by aliens.
Jeff Nolan (Willard Parker), an American experimental test
pilot, returns from a flight to discover that human life no longer
exists in London. Everyone in sight has been killed mysteriously.
In a small hotel he encounters two other survivors (Dennis Price and
Virginia Field), and in exploring the area they find two other people
(Thorley Walters and Vanda Godsell). Their trek is cut short by the
arrival of two huge robots which kill one of the survivors when she
(Godsell) tries to communicate with them. Retreating, the group
finds two others, a husband and wife (David Spencer and Anna Falk),
the woman being pregnant. Back at the hotel they are shocked to
find that the dead woman has been resurrected by the robots to ac-
complish their bidding. This leads the Earthlings to theorize that
the robots must be invaders from outer space and that they have a
control center which, if destroyed, would render them powerless.
The next day the pilot and Peggy (Field) set out to find the center,
Quinn Taggett (Price) having been killed too. While they are away
Lorna (Falk) gives birth to her child. Soon, two robots break into
their sanctuary but are stopped in the nick of time--the transmission
center has been found and destroyed. The group then decides to find
a plane and search for other survivors.
A low-keyed, effective, double-bill entry from England's creative director, Terence Fisher.

Hugh Marlowe and Joan Taylor in Earth vs. the Flying Saucers (1956).

EARTH VS. THE FLYING SAUCERS (Columbia, 1956) 83 min.

    Executive producer, Sam Katzman; producer, Charles H.
Schneer; director, Fred F. Sears; suggested by the book Flying Saucers from Outer Space by Donald E. Keyhoe; screen story, Curt
Siodmak; screenplay, George Worthing Tates and Raymond T. Marcus; art director, Paul Palmentola; music director, Mischa Bakaleinikoff; special effects, Ray Harryhausen and Russ Kelley; camera,
Fred Jackman, Jr.; editor, Danny B. Landres.
    Hugh Marlowe (Dr. Russell Marvin); Joan Taylor (Carol Mar-
vin); Donald Curtis (Major Huglin); Morris Ankrum (General Hanley);
John Zaremba (Professor Kanter); Tom Browne Henry (Admiral En-
right); Grandon Rhodes (General Edmunds); Larry Blake (Motorcycle
Officer).

    One of the best studies of the phenomenon of flying saucers
was Donald E. Keyhoe's Flying Saucers from Outer Space. With
fine direction by Fred F. Sears and top-notch special effects by Ray
Harryhausen and Russ Kelley, the film version is one of the best
flying saucer epics in the sci-fi genre.
    Flying saucers descend on the Earth. Their robot crews

soon begin shooting death rays from the ends of their metallic arms.
Ironically, it is through the aliens' warning that their weakness is
discovered. Later the Army employs a secret ultra high frequency
weapon to blast the saucers into oblivion. It is then that the true
secret is learned: the aliens are not the robots; the metal creatures
house beings who are infinitely old, too fragile to live outside a protective shell.

Audiences marveled at the realistic flying saucers employed
in this feature. In fact, the saucers have since become deeply embedded in many people's mind as the stereotype of flying saucers
(despite the "sightings" of many UFOs of varying size). "Most stop-
motion animation requires a willing suspension of disbelief in the
viewer, but with the saucers in ... [this film] it's more a matter of
making the effort to realize that they are animated, their movements
are so impeccably smooth" (Don B. Willis, A Checklist of Horror
and Science Fiction Films, 1972).

THE ELECTRONIC MONSTER   see   ESCAPEMENT

EMBRYO (Cine Artists, 1976) C-108 min.

Executive producer, Sandy Howard; producers, Arnold H. Or-
golini and Anita Doohan; director, Ralph Nelson; screenplay, Doohan
and Jack W. Thomas; music composer/conductor, Gil Melle; makeup
supervisors, Dan Striepeke and John Chambers; makeup, Mark Reedall; art director, Joe Alves; set decorator, Phil Abramson; assistant director, Michael S. Glick; stunt coordinator, Everett Creach;
sound, Bud Alper; special effects, Roy Arbogast; camera, Fred
Koenekamp; editor, John Martinelli.

Rock Hudson (Dr. Paul Holliston); Diane Ladd (Martha); Barbara Carrera (Victoria); Roddy McDowall (Riley); Ann Schedeen (Hel-
en); John Elerick (Gordon); Jack Colvin (Dr. Wiston); Vincent Baget-
ta (Collier); Joyce Spitz (Trainer); Dick Winslowe (Forbes); Lina
Raymond (Janet Novak); Dr. Joyce Brothers (Herself).

"Following a trend much in evidence today among makers of
sci-fi films, Embryo begins with a title stating that the story is 'not
all science fiction,' but is grounded in what current filmmakers
naively like to call 'science fact.' In the case of Embryo, the
change of emphasis isn't only semantics, because the film is unfortunately literal-minded and timid in dealing with its considerable fantasy potential" (Variety).

Shot well over a year before its May 1976 release, this tax-
shelter entry was a disservice to the sci-fi field and to the once
strong marquee name, Rock Hudson. Hudson is cast as a widowed
scientist who returns to the laboratory when he discovers that his
long-abandoned fetal acceleration experiments have viability. After
testing his genetic theories with unborn dogs he tries his skill with
a human embryo. The result is that within a few days the fetus
from a dying mother has grown into a mature woman (Carrera). At
this point the narrative degenerates into an embarrassing updated

variation of The Bride of Frankenstein. Hudson's Dr. Holliston falls
in love with the comely creation. He teaches the mentally superior
woman enough to cope with life in society, but then everything goes
awry. As with the experimental dogs, the artifically induced growth
procedures have instilled the woman with a mean, jealous streak.
She later murders her creator's sister-in-law (Ladd), daughter-in-
law (Schedeen), and son (Elerick). In the absurdly constructed finale,
before dying, a shriveled old woman (shades of She), she gives birth
to the scientist's baby.

The New York Post described the plot progress of Embryo:
"It becomes a melodramatic mishmash with nobody surviving in good
condition, except maybe the dog who was growling fiercely when last
seen as he was pushed into the cellar."

For the record, Embryo represents two cinema firsts for Mr.
Hudson: he has a nude scene and plays a grandfather-to-be. Watch
out for a shrill cameo by Roddy McDowall as a male chauvinist chess
whiz.

ENEMY FROM SPACE   see   QUATERMASS II

EQUINOX (VIP Distributors, 1971) C-80 min.

    Producer, Jack H. Harris; associate producer, Dennis Muren;
director, Jack Woods; story, Mark Thomas McGee; screenplay,
Woods; makeup, Robynne Hoover; matte paintings, Jim Danforth;
sound, Bradley Lane; special camera effects, Muren, David Allen,
Danforth; camera, Mike Hoover; editor, John Joyce.

    Edward Connell (Dave); Barbara Hewitt (Susan); Frank Boers,
Jr. (Jim); Robin Christopher (Vicki); Jack Woods (Asmodeus); Jim
Phillips (Reporter); Fritz Leiber (Dr. Waterman); Patrick Burke
(Branson); Jim Duron (Orderly).

    This amateur effort was shot in 16mm in 1967 in Pasadena, Ca-
lifornia. After years of re-editing, producer Jack H. Harris became in-
terested in the project, had new footage shot and released it in 1971.
    When Professor Waterman (Fritz Leiber) disappears and his
mountain abode is discovered demolished, four of his students (Edward Connell, Barbara Hewitt, Frank Boers, Jr., and Robin Christopher) request forest ranger Asmodeus (Jack Woods) to help them
undertake a search. The college youths, after being given a secret
book on devil worship by an incoherent old man, are thrust into a
macabre world of evil sorcerers, possession by demons, and
an assortment of monsters. At each turn, the young people are
threatened and frightened, and they soon turn on one another. It
proves that Asmodeus is a devil, and that Dave (Connell), the sole
sane survivor of the group, is destined for a grisly end.

ERINNERUNGEN AN DIE ZUKUNFT   see   CHARIOTS OF THE GODS?

ESCAPE FROM THE PLANET OF THE APES (Twentieth Century-
Fox, 1971) C-98 min.

Producer, Arthur P. Jacobs; associate producer, Frank Capra, Jr.; director, Don Taylor; based on characters created by Pierre
Boulle; screenplay, Paul Dehn; art directors, Jack Martin Smith and
William Creber; set decorators, Walter M. Scott and Stuart Reiss;
music, Jerry Goldsmith; orchestrator, Arthur Morton; creative makeup design, John Chambers; makeup, Dan Striepeke; assistant director,
Pepi Lenzi; sound, Dean Vernon and Theodore Soderberg; special
camera effects, Howard A. Anderson Company; camera, Joseph Bi-
roc; editor, Marion Rothman.
        Roddy McDowall (Cornelius); Kim Hunter (Zira); Bradford Dill-
man (Dr. Lewis Dixon); Natalie Trundy (Dr. Stephanie Branton); Eric
Braeden (Dr. Otto Hasslein); William Windom (The President); Sal
Mineo (Milo); Albert Salmi (E-1); Jason Evers (E-2); John Randolph
(Chairman); Steve Roberts (General Brody); M. Emmet Walsh (Aide-
Captain); Roy E. Glenn (Lawyer); William Woodson (Naval Officer);
Army Archerd (Referee); James Bacon (General Faulkner); John Al-
derman (Corporal); and Ricardo Montalban (Armando).

        This was third of the five-part series. Many critics and fans
alike consider it one of the best. "The film is an entertainment-al-
legory for our times, and it is gratifying that the usual sorry history
of sequels--more costly and/or less quality--has been smartly turned
around in this third Apes film" (Variety).
        Continuing where Beneath the Planet of the Apes (q.v.) ended, in-
telligent apes Zira (Kim Hunter), her husband Cornelius (Roddy Mc-
Dowall), and Milo (Sal Mineo) escape from the atomic blast instigated
by the human mutants of the future. They take the astronauts' spaceship back through the time warp and land in southern California of
1973. At first there is surprise at finding intelligent apes in place
of human astronauts, then the apes become the toast of society and
are beloved by the world. After Milo is accidentally killed (choked
by a gorilla), it is learned that Zira is pregnant. A presidential advisor (Eric Braeden) worries that this event may be the beginning of
the take-over of the world by intelligent simians. The government
then orders Zira sterilized. The "foreign" duo later escape and are
given refuge by a kindly circus owner, Armando (Ricardo Montalban).
Zira gives birth to young Milo. Still later the authorities track down
the apes and kill the two visitors. But in the meantime, unknown to
all, Zira had substituted a newly-born chimp for her son, leaving the
real young Milo to be tended by Armando. Having confused the authorities Armando says to the infant, "Intelligent creature ... but
then so were your mother and father." The little chimp slowly says,
"Mama ... mama...."
        Regarding the highly profitable Apes series, Frederick S.
Clarke wrote in Cinefantastique, "What we have here is not just three
separate films, but one great work that has the promise of being the
first epic of filmed science fiction."

Roddy McDowall and Kim Hunter in Escape from the Planet of the Apes (1971).

Scene from Escapement/The Electronic Monster (1957).

ESCAPEMENT (Anglo-Amalgamated, 1957) 76 min.

Producer, Alec C. Snowden; director, Montgomery Tully; based on the novel by Charles Eric Maine; screenplay, Maine and J. Maclaren-Ross; art director, Wilfred Arnold; makeup, Jack Craig; music, Richard Taylor; electronic music, Soundrama; wardrobe, Eileen Welch; camera, Bert Mason; dream sequence camera, Teddy Catford; editor, Geoffrey Muller.
Rod Cameron (Kennan); Mary Murphy (Ruth); Meredith Edwards (Dr. Maxwell); Peter Illing (Zakon); Carl Jaffe (Dr. Erich Hoff); Kay Callard (Laura Maxwell); Carl Duering (Blore); Larry Cross (Brad Somers).

"Since modern audiences seem intrigued with dramatic-clinical sorties into the mysteries of the human thought mechanism, the release generates a certain pseudo-scientific appeal" (Variety).
Long before 2001: A Space Odyssey (q.v.), this British-made feature delved into the idea of a man-made machine becoming an

uncontrolled monster. The theme of the computer taking over its creators' minds for its own ends has since become rather common place. Here, however, the theme of the masterful computer was short-circuited for a typical hero-bad guy premise. The end result was more tedium than enlightening sci-fi.

In London, a group of scientists is investigating the possible use of dream inducement for the cure of mental illness. A machine is developed to retain fantasies and then to project them back into the brain cell of mental patients under controlled situations. One of those involved in the project, Paul Zakon (Peter Illing), deduces this is a way to control the minds of others. He begins transmitting his own deranged fantasies into the minds of patients--with tragic results. Zakon's corrupt activities are halted eventually by American insurance investigator Jeff Keenan (Rod Cameron).

It was three years before Escapement was released in America; then it appeared under the title Zex, the Electronic Monster. Today on TV it is titled The Electronic Monster. It is also known as The Dream Machine / Zex, the Electronic Fiend / Zex.

THE EVIL FORCE see THE 4-D MAN

THE EXPLOITS OF ELAINE (Pathé, 1914) fourteen chapters

Directors, Louis Gasnier and George B. Seitz; based on the stories by Arthur B. Reeves and Basil Dickey; screenplay, Charles W. Goddard and Reeves.
With: Pearl White (Elaine Dodge); Creighton Hale (Craig Kennedy); Arnold Daly, Sheldon Lewis, Floyd Buckley.
Chapters: 1) The Clutching Hand; 2) The Twilight Sleep; 3) The Vanishing Jewels; 4) The Frozen Safe; 5) The Poisoned Room; 6) The Vampire; 7) The Double Trap; 8) The Hidden Voice; 9) The Death Ray; 10) The Life Current; 11) The Hour of Three; 12) The Blood Crystals; 13) The Devil Worshippers; 14) The Reckoning.

The science fiction motif in movie serials had its origins in The Exploits of Elaine, Pearl White's athletic follow-up to The Perils of Pauline. The chapterplay proved so popular that it developed into two continuations, The New Exploits of Elaine (1915) and The Romance of Elaine (1915), for a total of 36 chapters.
The cliffhanger has Elaine Dodge (Pearl White) on the trail of a sinister figure called "The Clutching Hand,"* who is the murderer of her father. She is aided by a very scientific detective (Creighton Hale) and at the finish she eventually catches up with the culprit who has nearly killed her in each of the serial's chapters.
The Exploits of Elaine grossed over $1 million for Pathé and solidified the popularity of serials in the pre-World War I years. This cliffhanger introduced many sci-fi elements into the plot, aspects

_____

*The villain was used again in 1936 by Stage and Screen for an inexpensive chapterplay called The Clutching Hand, with Jack Mulhall as Craig Kennedy, although Elaine was now nowhere to be seen.

Sheldon Lewis, Arnold Daly, Pearl White and Creighton Hale in "The Death Ray," chapter 9 of the serial, The Exploits of Elaine (1914).

that would become staples in the field. Among them are all types of futuristic gadgetry, as at the end of one chapter where Elaine is actually pronounced dead only to be revived by "science" at the beginning of the next installment. There is also the sinister, hooded villain, emphasizing the unknown, always a part of the mysterious "future."

Unfortunately at least one chapter of the serial is no longer intact, but the bulk of the episodes are still available for viewing.

THE EYE CREATURES (American International-TV, 1965) C-80 min.

Producer/director, Larry Buchanan; based (uncredited) on the book The Cosmic Frame by Paul W. Fairman; camera, Ralph K. Johnson.
With: John Ashley, Cynthia Hull, Warren Hammack, Chet David.

In the mid-Sixties, American International Pictures required several films to complete a package of features to be sold to TV. Therefore the studio dusted off the scripts to several of its mid-

Fifties' sci-fi thrillers and assigned director Larry Buchanan to
churn out the films for his Azalea Productions, this time using color.
The pictures were shot in the mid-West and at such a rapid pace
that no master shots were filmed to hold the action together; the resultant films seem like puzzles with many missing pieces.   The re-
makes were so inferior that by contrast the originals (mostly grade
B and C entries) seemed classic.
       The Eye Creatures was a revamping of Invasion of the Saucer
Men (q. v.) and followed the same plot: a group of teenagers foils
the attempts of aliens to land and conquer the Earth.   Star John Ashley was a rather mature teenager.

THE FABULOUS WORLD OF JULES VERNE   see   VYNALEZ ZKAZY

FAHRENHEIT 451 (Rank Film Distributors, 1966) C-111 min.

       Producer, Lewis M. Allen; associate producer, Michael Dela-
mar; director, François Truffaut; based on the novel by Ray Bradbury; screenplay, Truffaut and Jean-Louis Richard; additional dialogue, David Rudkin and Helen Scott; art director, Syd Cain; cos-
tumes/production designer, Tony Walton; assistant director, Bryan
Coates; makeup, Basil Newall; music, Bernard Herrmann; sound Norman Wanstall, Bob McPhee, and Gordon McCallum; special effects,
Charles Staffel; camera, Nicholas Roeg; editor, Thom Noble.
       Julie Christie (Linda/Clarisse); Oskar Werner (Montag); Cy-
ril Cusack (The Captain); Anton Diffring (Fabian); Jeremy Spenser
(Man with the Apple); Bee Duffell (The Book-Woman); Gilliam Lewis
(TV Announcer); Ann Bell (Doris); Caroline Hunt (Helen); Anna Falk

Oskar Werner and Julie Christie in Fahrenheit 451 (1966).

(Jackie); Rona Milne (Neighbor); Alex Scott (The Life of Henry Bru-
lard); Dennis Gilmore (Martian Chronicles); Fred Cox (Pride); Frank
Cox (Prejudice); Michael Balfour (Machiavelli's Prince); David Glover
(The Pickwick Papers); Yvonne Blake (The Jewish Question); Arthur
Cox and Eric Mason (Nurses); Noel David and Donald Pickering (TV
Announcers); Gillian Aldam and Edward Kaye (Gillian Couple); Joan
Francis (Bar Telephonist); Tom Watson (Sergeant Instructor).

The screen version of this Ray Bradbury novel (1953) has often
been compared to the motion picture made from George Orwell's 1984
(q. v.). Each was a warning to civilization concerning dictatorship
and its effect on freedom of thought and self-education. Both movies
did a poor job of translating their subject matter to celluloid and
neither was a satisfying film.

Director François Truffaut spent some five years writing the
script for Fahrenheit 451. He did so in French, and the resultant
scenario was translated into English for its London shooting. In a
society of the future, reading or possessing books of any sort is forbidden. Violators are hunted and punished. Montag (Oskar Werner)
is one of the firemen who tracks down books for public burning. He
is a regimented soul whose wife Linda (Julie Christie) also adheres
to the state's propaganda. Then Montag meets schoolteacher Clarisse
(Christie), who looks a good deal like Linda. One day Montag witnesses an old woman preferring to be burned alive with her treasured
books rather than be separated from them. The confused fireman
takes a book home with him and, in secret, begins to read it. As
his knowledge grows, he realizes he must leave the Fire Service.
But Linda denounces him and after confronting some of his colleagues--
whom he incinerates to escape--he and Clarisse join the Book People.
They are outcasts who save the World's great literature by commit-
ting it to memory. Montag's task is memorize the stories of Edgar
Allan Poe.

Critical reaction to this film varied greatly, from "Bloodless
and pompous" (New York Times) to "Vivid and imaginative" (Saturday
Review). As Judith Crist analyzed in New York World Journal Tribune, "Fahrenheit 451 is neither science nor fiction nor good red-
blooded movie.... Admittedly François Truffaut's primary interest
was not in the science-fiction aspects of the Bradbury story. But
even though the author's futuristic society of mindless robots has
gone by the board, the naiveté and simplistic didacticism of the genre
remain and dominate the work. We are left with the rather simple-
minded and late-in-the-day thesis that a society that burns books and
bans intellectual stimulation is a bad one.... "

Despite the presence of Oscar winner Miss Christie, the film
was a box-office disappointment. The public may not have been sure
if the offering was a satire or in deadly earnest, but it was perceptive enough to know it was a dull, misguided presentation.

THE FANTASTIC LITTLE GIRL   see   THE INCREDIBLE SHRINKING
MAN

FANTASTIC PLANET   see   LA PLANETE SAUVAGE

FANTASTIC VOYAGE (Twentieth Century-Fox, 1966) C-100 min.

Producer, Saul David; director, Richard Fleischer; based on
the story by Otto Klement and Jay Lewis Bixby; adaptor, David Duncan; screenplay, Harry Kleiner; music, Leonard Rosenman; technical
advisors, Fred Zendar and Peter Foy; titles, Richard Kuhn; art di-
rectors, Jack Martin Smith and Dale Hennesy; set decorators, Walter
M. Scott and Stuart A. Reiss; assistant director, Ad Schaumer; cre-
ative production research, Harper Goff; makeup, Ben Nye; sound,
Bernard Freericks and David Dockendorf; special camera effects, L.
B. Abbott, Art Cruickshank, and Emil Kosa, Jr.; camera, Ernest
Laszlo; editor, William B. Murphy.
Stephen Boyd (Grant); Raquel Welch (Cora Peterson); Edmond
O'Brien (General Carter); Donald Pleasence (Dr. Michaels); Arthur
O'Connell (Colonel Donald Reid); William Redfield (Captain Bill
Owens); Arthur Kennedy (Dr. Duval); Jean Del Val (Jan Benes); Bar-
ry Coe (Communications Aide); Ken Scott (Secret Service Man); Shel-
by Grant (Nurse); James Brolin (Technician); Brendan Fitzgerald
(Wireless Operator).
A. k. a. Microscopia / Strange Journey.

In the year 1995 a famous Czech scientist is smuggled out
from behind the Iron Curtain to the U.S. Enemy agents ambush him
and he requires a delicate brain operation or he will surely die.
Unfortunately the surgery cannot be performed from outside the body.
So, by a new scientific process, five doctors (four men and a woman)
are placed into an atomic submarine, it is all miniaturized, and the
vessel and crew are injected into the man's bloodstream. The quintet must travel to the brain area, conduct the surgery and eject themselves within an hour, the length of stable miniaturization. Along
the way it is discovered that one of their number, Dr. Michaels
(Donald Pleasence), is working for the other side. He and the submarine are later digested into the patient's white corpuscles; but the
others, having successfully completed the lasar beam operation, escape along the optic nerve and return to the outer world via a tear
duct.
Basically the film is a documentary of a bizarre voyage
through the human body, one as dangerous and hopefully exciting as
any trip devised by Jules Verne to outer or inner space. The visuals are stunningly handled by the special effects department, providing for colorful anatomical landmarks along the journey. (One of the
sights that most intrigued filmgoers was that of statuesque Raquel
Welch in a form-fitting skin diver's suit.) "But," warned the Saturday Review, "if the technical wizardry of this scientific adventure
is an altogether remarkable projection of things to come, the story
that motivates it is a rather humdrum recapitulation of things as
they are." Or, as Judith Crist pronounced on the NBC-TV Today
Show, 'It is a pity that the intellectual content never rises above
Raquel Welch's bustline or Stephen Boyd's histrionic talents but at the
very least physiology and trick photography provide some rip-roaring

good fun. "
Production costs for Fantastic Voyage included a 30,000 square
foot giant lab, while over $100,000 was expended on a four-ton fiber
glass vehicle, designed by Harper Goff, to serve as the tiny submarine. With much publicity from its sci-fi angle and the presence of
shapely Miss Welch, the feature grossed $5.5 million domestically.
There would be an animated cartoon ABC-TV series in 1968 based
on this show, with the voices of Marvin Miller and Jane Webb.

FIRE MAIDENS FROM OUTER SPACE (Eros, 1956) 80 min.

Producer, George Fowler; director/screenplay, Cy Roth; music, Borodin; art director, Scott MacGregor; makeup, Roy Ashton;
camera, Ian Struthers; editors, A. C. T. Clair and Lito Carruthers.
Anthony Dexter (Luther Blair); Susan Shaw (Hestia); Paul Carpenter (Larson); Harry Fowler (Sydney Stanhope); Jacqueline Curtis
(Duessa); Sydney Tafler (Dr. Higgins); Owen Berry (Prasus); Rodney
Diak (Anderson).

Hollywood and London teamed for this co-production, which
did little to enhance relations between the two countries. Outside of
bringing classical music to the sci-fi genre long before 2001: A
Space Odyssey (q.v.), the feature had little to offer, except a few
unintentional laughs.
Luther Blair (Anthony Dexter) is the leader of a group of astronauts which flies to the thirteenth moon of Jupiter in search of
life forms. When they enter the moon's atmosphere a strange voice
guides them to a landing space. Upon exploring the satellite (which
has a terrain and oxygen content similar to the Earth's), they discover the remnants of a city. Eventually they find the city is inhabited by beautiful girls, with only one man left, the high priest.
This old male tells the visitors that the inhabitants are the descen-
dants of the people of Atlantis who flew to and inhabited this moon
after the destruction of their continent thousands of years before.
Now, however, they have no way of reproduction and the city is,
moreover, constantly besieged by a monster. The creature (which
looks as though it has mange and sounds as if it suffers from gas
pains) gains entrance into the metropolis, kills the priest and abducts
one of the girls. Blair and his cohorts give chase and later corner
the creature, which falls into a fiery pit.
Eric L. Hoffman said, in Monsters of the Movies magazine,
(summer, 1975), "With a ridiculous monster, less than amateur rit-
ual dancing and even worse acting, it's easy to figure out the rest.
Receiving less than limited theatrical release, this turkey pops up
from time to time on the late-late-late show, promptly putting anybody with insomnia right to sleep. "
The good thing about this clinker was the use of Borodin's
score to Prince Ygor (later made into the popular song, "Stranger in
Paradise") as background music.

FIRST MAN INTO SPACE (Anglo-Amalgamated, 1959) 77 min.

Producers, John Croydon and Charles F. Vetter, Jr.; directors, Robert Day; story, Wyott Ordung; screenplay, John C. Cooper and Lance Z. Hargreaves; assistant director, Stanley Goulder; wardrobe, Charles Guerin; makeup, Michael Morris; art director, Denys Pavitt; music, Buxton Orr; sound, Terence Cotter; camera, Geoffrey Faithfull; editor, Peter Mayhew.

Marshall Thompson (Commodore Chuck E. Prescott); Marla Landi (Tia Francesca); Bill Edwards (Lieutenant Dan Prescott); Robert Ayres (Captain Ben Richards); Bill Nagy (Chief Wilson); Carl Jaffe (Dr. Paul Von Essen); Roger Delgado (Mexican Consul); John McLaren (State Department Official); Richard Shaw (Witney); Bill Nick (Clancy); Chuck Keyser (Control Room Official); Helen Forrest (Secretary); Sheree Winton (Nurse); Laurence Taylor (Shore Patrolman); Barry Shawzin (Mexican Farmer).

A. k. a. Satellite of Blood.

A decided rip-off of The Quatermass Xperiment (q. v.), this sci-fi thriller is as badly dated as its exploitation title. While testing the new Y-13 rocket plane, pilot Dan Prescott (Bill Edwards) pushes the craft beyond its limit. He becomes immersed in a cloud of meteorite dust. He then presses the ejector button, but later there is no trace of him or the craft (beyond the encrusted cone section of the plane). When several people are murdered and a blood bank is broken into, it develops that Dan has become a sort of monster, covered with an impervious dust. His scientist brother Chuck (Marshall Thompson) maneuvers the badly disfigured Dan into a decompression chamber where he survives long enough to detail his outer space experiences.

Variety was lenient on the film, "It is generally well-made and suffers only from a tendency to get cosmic in philosophy as well as geography.... Since these films are stories of effect rather than character or plot, there is little point in evaluating the performances."

THE FIRST MEN IN THE MOON (Gaumont, 1919) 5,175'

Director, Jack L. V. Leigh; based on the novel by H. G. Wells; screenplay, R. Byron Webber.

Bruce Gordon (Hogben); Heather Thatcher (Susan); Hector Abbas (Samson Cavor); Lionel d'Aragon (Rupert Bedford); Cecil Morton York (Grand Lunar).

FIRST MEN IN THE MOON (Columbia, 1964) C-103 min.

Producers, Charles H. Schneer and Ray Harryhausen; director, Nathan Juran; based on the novel by H. G. Wells; screenplay, Nigel Kneale and Jan Read; art director, John Blezard; music, Laurie Johnson; assistant director, George Pollard; sound, Buster Ambler; special effects director, Harryhausen; camera, Wilkie Cooper; editor, Maurice Rootes.

Edward Judd (Arnold Bedford); Martha Hyer (Kate Callender); Lionel Jeffries (Professor Cavor); Peter Finch (Bailiff); Erik Chitty (Gibbs); Betty McDowall (Maggie); Miles Malleson (Registrar); Gladys Henson (Matron); Lawrence Herder (Glushkov); Marne Maitland (Dr. Tok); Hugh McDermott (Challis); Paul Carpenter and Huw Thomas (Announcers).

H. G. Wells' visionary novel First Men in the Moon (1901) in- spired Georges Méliès to conceive the short film A Trip to the Moon, q. v. (sometimes called First Men in the Moon). An actual adapta- tion of Wells' novel came to the screen in 1919 when Gaumont filmed it under Jack Leigh's direction. This version had Professor Cavor (Hector Abbas) inventing a sphere which was coated with a helium alloy and which rose by repelling gravity. In two weeks the craft makes the journey to the moon and meets up with the rather fake- looking Selenites described in Wells' book.

The definitive film version of the novel came in 1964 when Columbia remade the British entry. Ray Harryhausen's fine special effects bolstered the picture's appeal. The color, widescreen movie opens with the first landing on the moon in modern times and the as- tronauts discovering a small British flag planted there. Back on Earth, Arnold Bedford (Edward Judd), whom everyone assumed was just a barmy old man, is finally believed as he recounts how he, his fiancée (Martha Hyer), and Professor Cavor (Lionel Jeffries) of Dym- church made the first lunar trip in the late nineteenth century, using the addled professor's anti-gravity space sphere. Once on the moon

Martha Hyer, Edward Judd and Lionel Jeffries in First Men on the Moon (1964).

the trio finds a civilization of ant-like Selenites who live beneath the
surface and who are ruled by a giant computer-like brain. They are
at odds with huge moon calfs, a strange type of fungus, and other
lunar wonders. Eventually the Selenites force the trio back to their
craft. But the professor decides to remain behind and try to become
friendly with the moon beings. The other two return home in their
craft, which is not capable of a second flight. The new astronauts
confirm Bedford's tale by finding the city of the Selenites, but it is
in shambles. Later it is learned that the professor had had a common cold when left on the moon and that the cold germs had destroyed the Selenites' civilization.

"For much of its length the humour, excitement and invention
of this quite ambitious SF film are on a level with Henry Levin's
Journey to the Centre of the Earth [q. v.].... The special effects
are variable (the moon monster, for instance, looks like nothing more
alarming than a jerkily magnified caterpillar) and the epilogue is too
scrambled and ambiguous. Otherwise director Nathan Juran has
risen to the occasion and the attractive talents at hand (including
Peter Finch in a heavily disguised guest appearance) to provide a
pleasantly entertaining fantasy."

FIRST SPACESHIP ON VENUS   see   DER SCHWEIGENDE STERN

FIVE (Columbia, 1951) 93 min.

          Producer/director/screenplay, Arch Oboler; camera, Louis
Clyde Stoumen and Sid Lubow; editor, John Hoffman.
          William Phipps (Michael); Susan Douglas (Roseanne); James
Anderson (Eric); Charles Lampkin (Charles); Earl Lee (Mr. Barn-
staple).

          Famous radio horror writer Arch Oboler, most associated
with the "Lights Out" program, produced and directed this talky,
moralistic play about the last five survivors of World War III.
Filmed at Oboler's desert home, which was designed by Frank Lloyd
Wright, the feature was one of the first celluloid warnings of the potential aftermath of atomic warfare. It was also a didactic indictment of mankind's prejudices and failure to exist in peace.
          Following the final atomic war, the last five survivors on
earth band together. They include a pregnant woman (Susan Douglas),
a terminally-ill bank cashier (Earl Lee), a black doorman (Charles
Lampkin), a frustrated idealist (William Phipps), and a murderer
(James Anderson). For a time the quintet lives in harmony but
eventually old prejudices break out again. After a visit to a ghost
city, fighting breaks out among the group and soon three are dead,
leaving only the hero and the heroine, she having lost her baby.
          With the real danger of atomic warfare in the daily headlines,
Five presented a prediction that science fiction could become tomorrow's science fact--only in this case there would be no tomorrow for
mankind. But, complained the New York Times (and rightly so), "It
takes Mr. Oboler a long time to get from here to there, so randomly

Susan Douglas and William Phipps in Five (1951).

does he let his camera wander over sea, sky, clouds and hills. And
he hasn't the slightest hesitation to take reckless liberties with physical facts and reason in his post-atomic world (which, on the face of
it, doesn't look much different from the physical world of right
now).... The consequence is that an idea which bears some imaginative thought is reduced to the level of banality and somewhat 'arty'
pretense."

FIVE MILLION YEARS TO EARTH   see   QUATERMASS AND THE
PIT

FLASH GORDON (Universal, 1936) thirteen chapters

        Director, Frederick Stephani; based on the cartoon strip by
Alex Raymond; screenplay, Stephani, George Plympton, Basil Dickey,
and Ella O'Neill; camera, Jerry Ash and Richard Fryer.
        Larry "Buster" Crabbe (Flash Gordon); Jean Rogers (Dale Ar-
den); Charles Middleton (Emperor Ming); Priscilla Lawson (Aura);
John Lipson (King Vultan); Richard Alexander (Prince Barin); Frank
Shannon (Dr. Zarkov); Duke York, Jr. (King Kala); Earle Askam
(Officer Torch); Theodore Lorch (High Priest); James Pierce (King
Thun); Muriel Goodspeed (Zona); Richard Tucker (Gordon, Sr.)
        Chapters: 1) The Planet of Peril; 2) The Tunnel of Terror;
3) Captured by Shark Men; 4) Battling the Sea Beast; 5) The

Priscilla Lawson, Jean Rogers, Buster Crabbe, John Lipson and
Charles Middleton in Flash Gordon (1936).

Destroying Ray; 6) Flaming Fortune; 7) Shattering Doom; 8) Tournament of Death; 9) Fighting the Fire Dragon; 10) The Unseen Peril;
11) In the Claws of the Tigron; 12) Trapped in the Turret; 13)
Rocketing to Earth.

    One of the best, most popular, enduring of sound era serials
this still enjoys a respectful acceptance in TV and theatrical revivals.
Through this chapterplay, Larry "Buster" Crabbe came to be known
as the "King of the Sound Serials." He reigns supreme even today,
as popular and as much thought of as Flash Gordon as he was four
decades ago.
    Alex Raymond's comic strip first appeared in 1934 and Uni-
versal bought the rights two years later. It spent $500,000 in pro-
ducing this thirteen-part cliffhanger.
    Seen today, the serial still holds up remarkably well, fun on
many different levels of entertainment. Of course Crabbe made the
perfect movie serial hero: intelligent, virile and courageous. In
contrast to the idealized heroics of Flash, there is virginal Jean
Rogers as Dale Arden, with her slightly-attired body giving more

than a hint of implied sexuality. In distinct contrast is Charles Middleton, representing the apex of serial villains as the slick, culpable, ruthless Ming the Merciless, the ruler of the gypsy planet Mongo. Even the supporting cast is endearing: Frank Shannon as the ever-alert Dr. Zarkov; bulky Richard Alexander as Prince Barin, the true ruler of Mongo and the secret admirer of Ming's captivating daughter Aura (Priscilla Lawson), who herself lusts after Flash; John Lipson as the pompous but good-hearted King Vultan, Ming's unsteady ally and eventual enemy; and James Pierce as the bearded King Thun, Ming's most natural adversary.

The story of Flash Gordon is a simple one. The planet Mongo comes hurtling toward the Earth, causing destruction. Flash, Dale, and Zarkov head to Mongo in the latter's new rocketship and there find a bizarre world ruled over by the calculating Ming. The Earthling trio is captured by Ming, who desires Dale and decides to use Zarkov to help him conquer the Earth. Later, King Thun and his Lion Men rescue the strangers, but thereafter they are cornered and taken to Ming's castle where Flash is saved from peril by Aura, who wishes to marry him. Still later Prince Barin rescues them and agrees to help in return for their aiding him in regaining his throne. Eventually Aura is drawn to Prince Barin, who saves her life. Flash and his hearty comrades, with the aid of Barin and Thun, attack Ming's palace. The deposed ruler rushes into his secret cave, intent on dying (or so it seems) at the hand of his fire-breathing dragon rather than face the ignominy of defeat.

Although the scripting of this serial was rather commonplace, the individual thrills in each chapter kept audiences coming back week after week. Not only were there futuristic rocket ships, ray guns and the like, but the hero encountered such terrors as dinosaurs, monkey-men, a "saceograph" TV device, shark-men, a floating city (the domain of King Vultan), the tortures of the horrible atom furnace, a tournament between Flash and assorted monsters, a memory-restoring ray, and the horrible Gocko, Ming's dragon, which had lobster claws and other unpleasant assets.

Perhaps it was the sheer fantasy which awed so many filmgoers at the time of its release. (Later audiences have appreciated the science fiction aspects but also enjoyed the inherent camp value of the presentation.) Flash Gordon not only spawned two sequels: Flash Gordon's Trip to Mars and Flash Gordon Conquers the Universe (both q. v.), but the chapterplay has been edited into three separate feature films: Rocket Ship and Spaceship to the Unknown were both given theatrical release while Space Soldiers was edited into a feature especially for television.

FLASH GORDON CONQUERS THE UNIVERSE (Universal, 1940)

Associate producer, Henry MacRae; directors, Ford Beebe and Ray Taylor; based on the comic strip by Alex Raymond; screenplay, George H. Plympton, Basil Dickey, and Barry Shipman.

Larry "Buster" Crabbe (Flash Gordon); Carol Hughes (Dale Arden); Charles Middleton (Emperor Ming); Frank Shannon (Dr. Zarkov); Anne Gwynne (Sonja); Roland Drew (Prince Barin); Shirley

Deane (Princess Aura); Victor Zimmerman (Thong); Don Rowan
(Torch); Michael Mark (Karm); Sigmund Nilssen (Korro); Lee Powell
(Roka); Edgar Edwards (Turan); Ben Taggart (Lupi); Harry C. Brad-
ley (Keedish).
      Chapters: 1) The Purple Death; 2) Freezing Torture; 3) Walk-
ing Bombs; 4) The Destroying Ray; 5) The Palace of Terror; 6)
Flaming Death; 7) The Land of the Dead; 8) The Fiery Abyss; 9) The
Pools of Peril; 10) The Death Mist; 11) Stark Treachery; 12) Doom
of the Dictator.

      With the ad lines, "NEW THRILLS! NEW MARVELS! NEW
WONDERS! in 12 NEW DYNAMIC EPISODES," Universal released its
third and final entry in the Flash Gordon series. This one was again
based on a book from the comic strip called Flash Gordon and the
Ice World of Mongo. By this time Carol Hughes had replaced Jean
Rogers as Dale Arden, but Charles Middleton (thankfully) was back
as Ming and Frank Shannon was again the ever-trusty Dr. Zarkov.
      This time around the Earth is being saturated by a deadly
epidemic called the Plague of the Purple Death. Flash, Dale and
Dr. Zarkov launch themselves into the stratosphere in Zarkov's craft,
only to find that Ming--still very much alive--is instigating the
spreading of the deadly dust. Allied with Prince Barin (Roland Drew),
who is now married to Ming's daughter Aura (Shirley Deane), Flash
and Zarkov invade Ming's city and partially wreck his equipment.
They then head to the dead world of Frigia to mine Plante, the only
known antidote for the Purple Death. Ming's allies (Anne Gwynne,
Don Rowan, Victor Zimmerman) later capture Dale and Dr. Zarkov
but Flash and Barin return and rescue them. Flash then sets the
controls of his ship, bails out, and the ship crashes into Ming's
city. The emperor is--once and for all--killed. Since Ming once
termed himself the Universe, Dr. Zarkov now announces that Flash
Gordon has conquered the Universe.
      A good deal of stock footage from a 1930 Universal feature,
White Hell of Pitz Palu, was employed to set the scene for the land
of Frigia and the production values on this entry were not up to par
with the two previous serials. Still, this cliffhanger was the most
graciously appointed of all serials, with a strong emphasis on pleasing costuming and set design.
      Like the previous two installments, this entry was also con-
densed into a feature version, Purple Death from Outer Space. A
specially edited version for television was called Space Soldiers Conquer the Universe.

FLASH GORDON'S TRIP TO MARS (Universal, 1938) fifteen chapters
(tinted)

      Associate producer, Barney Sarecky; directors, Ford Beebe
and Robert F. Hill; based on the comic strip Flash Gordon by Alex
Raymond; screenplay, Ray Trampe, Norman S. Hall, Wyndham Gittens, and Herbert Dolmas; art director, Ralph DeLacy; camera,
Jerome Ash; editor, Saul Goodkind.
      Larry "Buster" Crabbe (Flash Gordon); Jean Rogers (Dale

Arden); Frank Shannon (Dr. Zarkov); Charles Middleton (Emperor
Ming); Beatrice Roberts (Queen Azura); Richard Alexander (Prince
Barin); Montague Shaw (Clay King); Donald Kerr (Happy); Wheeler
Oakman (Tarnak); Earl Askam (Officer Torch); George Cleveland
(Professor Hensley); Fred Kohler, Jr., Lane Chandler, Al Ferguson,
and Glenn Strange (Soldiers); and Kane Richmond, Kenneth Duncan,
Eddie Parker, Anthony Warde, Jack Mulhall, Ben Lewis.
    Chapters: 1) New Worlds to Conquer; 2) The Living Dead;
3) Queen of Magic; 4) Ancient Enemies; 5) The Boomerang; 6) Tree-
Men of Mars; 7) The Prisoner of Mongo; 8) The Black Sapphire of
Kalu; 9) Symbol of Death; 10) Incense of Forgetfulness; 11) Human
Bait; 12) Ming the Merciless; 13) The Miracle of Magic; 14) A Beast
at Bay; 14) An Eye for an Eye.

    Flash Gordon had grossed millions for Universal and two
years after the release of that serial, the studio planned a sequel,
Flash Gordon and the Witch Queen of Mongo, a book version of the
newspaper serial. But that year Orson Welles made his historic War
of the Worlds radio broadcast and Mars was news. Universal
changed the locale of the chapterplay from Mongo to Mars and issued
Flash Gordon's Trip to Mars.
    The serial, which boasted tinted sequences, opens with Flash
Gordon (Larry "Buster" Crabbe), Dale Arden (Jean Rogers, now in
dark instead of blonde tresses and considerably more clothed), and
Dr. Zarkov (Frank Shannon) blast off for Mars. Their mission is

Frank Shannon, Buster Crabbe, Donald Kerr and Beatrice Roberts
in Flash Gordon's Trip to Mars (1938).

to locate the mysterious force which has been draining nitrogen from
the Earth's atmosphere. After landing, the trio is captured by the
Clay Men, humans turned to hardened slime by the evil Queen of
Magic, Azura (Beatrice Roberts), in order to do her bidding. Hoping to lift the yoke of Azura, the Clay People force Flash and Zarkov to try and steal the queen's White Sapphire, the source of her
power. Meanwhile, Prince Barin (Richard Alexander) arrives to convince the people of Mars not to ally themselves with Ming (Charles
Middleton) on Mongo. It seems that the evil emperor is using his
"great lamp" to strip the Earth of nitrogen. He is also promulgating
a war between the Clay and Tree peoples of Mars in order to take
over that planet. Later Ming allies himself with Azura, but her
White Sapphire is destroyed and she loses her powers. Meanwhile
Flash destroys Ming's great lamp and the emperor is thrown into a
"disintegration chamber" where he is apparently killed (or is he?).
     Although not up to the production values or heady pacing of
Flash Gordon, this cliffhanger holds up remarkably well today and
seems surprisingly modern (in contrast to the original) when viewed
in the Seventies.
     A feature version of the serial was issued in two parts,
Deadly Ray from Mars and Peril from the Planet Mongo. A con-
densed version was issued as Mars Attacks the World; there is also
a TV version called Space Soldiers' Trip to Mars.

THE FLESH CREATURES see HORROR OF THE BLOOD MONSTERS

FLESH CREATURES OF THE RED PLANET see HORROR OF THE
BLOOD MONSTERS

FLESH GORDON (Mammoth, 1973) C-78 min.

     Producers, Howard Ziehm and William Osco; associate pro-
ducer, Walter R. Cichy; directors, Michael Benveniste and Ziehm;
screenplay, Benveniste; art director, Donald Harris; music, Ralph
Ferraro; costumes, Ruth Glunt; camera, Ziehm; editor, Abbas Amin.
Jason Williams (Flesh Gordon); Suzanne Fields (Dale); Joseph
Hudgins (Dr. Felix Jerkoff); William Hunt (Emperor); John Hoyt (Pro-
fessor Gordon); and Mycle Brandy, Nora Wieternik, Candy Samples.
Steven Grummette, Lance Larsen, Judy Ziehm, Donald Harris, Li-
nus Gator, Susan Moore, Mark Fore, Maria Aranoff, Rick Lutze,
Sally Alt, Duane Paulsen, Leonard Goodman, Patricia Burns, Linda
Shepard, Mary Gavin, Dee Dee Dailes.

     Initially intended as a pornographic take-off on the Flash Gor-
don serials, this celluloid lark developed into a bigger project (16mm
film was enlarged to 35mm), more money was added for special effects, the porno scenes were softened through editing. The end result was a hinterland box-office success with class.
     Flesh Gordon follows closely the plotline of the original chap-
terplay although a good many sexual innuendoes have been added.

Scene from Flesh Gordon (1973).

For example, at the opening Emperor Wang (William Hunt) directs a
ray at Earth which turns human beings into copulating fiends.   This
is how Flesh Gordon (Jason Williams) meets lovely Dale Ardor (Suzanne Fields).   These two bail out of the plane and meet mad Dr.
Felix Jerkoff (Joseph Hudgins) and in his phallic-shaped capsule they
zoom to Wang's planet.   There they meet the Evil One, who captures Dale and plans to marry her.   For Flesh, Jerkoff vows death.
The hero escapes, however, and with the aid of Jerkoff puts an end
to Wang after the latter's monster, the great God Porno, is overcome.
        The overall production values of Flesh Gordon are quite inter-
esting, the special effects and animation are excellent, but the acting and
plotline are atrocious.   Only John Hoyt, in a brief role as Flesh's
father, gives an acceptable performance.   The film does provide a
few good laughs and some delights to those who appreciate the "in"
comments aimed at Flash Gordon fans.   To the filmmakers' credit,
the God Porno is probably the funniest and most ingratiating monster
in film history.
        This Graffiti Production was accomplished over a two-year
period at a reputed cost of $2 million plus.   When initially distri-
buted it was given an X rating but by 1975 it was re-issued with an
R certificate.   William Rotsler wrote in Contemporary Erotic Cinema
(1973), "Almost every figure model in Hollywood is in this one, along
with superb costuming and sets, excellent special effects, great gags,
fast pacing.   Super camp!"

THE FLIGHT THAT DISAPPEARED (United Artists, 1961) 71 min.

Producer, Robert E. Kent; director, Reginald Le Borg; screenplay, Ralph and Judith Hart, and Owen Harris; music, Richard La Salle; set decorator, Morris Hoffman; makeup, Harry Thomas; assistant director, Herbert S. Greene; sound, Harry Alphin and Ralph Butler; special effects, Barney Wolff; camera, Gilbert Warrenton; editor, Kenneth Crane.

Craig Hill (Tom Endicott); Paula Raymond (Marcia Paxton); Dayton Lummis (Dr. Morris); Gregory Morton (The Examiner); John Bryant (Hank Norton); Addison Richards (The Sage); Nancy Hale (Barbara Nielsen); Bernadette Hale (Joan Agnew); Harvey Stephens (Walter Cooper); Brad Trumbull (Jack Peters); Meg Wyllie (Helen Cooper); Carl Princi (Announcer); Francis De Sales (Manson); Roy Engle (Jamison); Jerry James (Ray Houser); Jack Mann (Garrett); Joe Haworth (Radio Operator).

A.k.a. The Flight That Vanished.

A Washington, D.C.-bound plane containing three U.S. bomb inventors is headed to meet with the President with plans for new demolition machinery. Suddenly it goes out of control. It elevates into the oxygen-starved stratosphere, and the passengers are rendered insensible. The plane passes through a dimension warp and its travelers are placed before three heavenly judges who have much to say to them about the current and future human race.

"Happily," reported the New York Herald-Tribune, "there are no grotesque, eighty-foot monsters looming across the horizon in the wake of nuclear explosions, no papier-mache skyscrapers toppling into Times Square, and no concentration on the B-film brand of sex and violence to contend with. This one poses its questions with admirable restraint.... Despite obvious budget restrictions, and some one-dimensional bits of acting in minor roles, the film manages to hold the attention throughout." Castle of Frankenstein magazine was less generous in its evaluation, "Solid plot idea suffers from hasty production."

THE FLIGHT THAT VANISHED   see   THE FLIGHT THAT DISAP-
PEARED

FLIGHT TO MARS (Monogram, 1951) C-72 min.

Producer, Walter Mirisch; director, Lesley Selander; screenplay, Arthur Strawn; music, Marlin Skiles; art director, David Milton; camera, Harry Neumann; editor, Richard Heermance.

Marguerite Chapman (Alita); Cameron Mitchell (Steve); Arthur Franz (Jim); Virginia Huston (Carol); John Litel (Dr. Lane); Morris Ankrum (Ikron); Robert Barrat (Tillamar); Edward Earle (Justin); William Forrest (General Acker); Lucille Balday (Terris).

Following the initial success of The Thing and Destination Moon (both q.v.), a raft of inexpensively mounted sci-fi thrillers

glutted the market.   One of the dullest and least adventuresome of
the lot was Flight to Mars.   The film contained all the by-now-known
aspects of space travel: the countdown, weightlessness in space,
pain during takeoff, a meteor storm, and assorted other clichés that
were a part of the specie of the time.

     The astronauts in this color outer space caper were a group
of scientists and a newsman (Cameron Mitchell) whose flight ends in
a crash landing on the Red Planet.   After initial exploration they
come across a civilized world under the planet's surface.   There the
reporter falls in love with Alita (Marguerite Chapman).   Trouble soon
develops between the Earthlings and the Martians.   The former plan
their escape, which is a success thanks to Alita's aid.

     "Just how the people of Mars, if any, feel if they know what
our pseudo-scientific films are saying about them cannot at present
be known.   But they might resent Flight to Mars, since it makes
them out a pretty mean lot" (Los Angeles Times).

FLOATING PLATFORM 1 DOES NOT ANSWER   see   F. P. 1 ANT-
WORTET NICHT

THE FLY (Twentieth Century-Fox, 1958) C-94 min.

     Producer/director, Kurt Neumann; based on the story by
George Langelaan; screenplay, James Clavell; art directors, Lyle R.
Wheeler and Theobold Holsopple; set decorators, Walter M. Scott and
Eli Benneche; wardrobe designer, Charles LeMaire; costumes, Adele
Balkan; makeup, Ben Nye; assistant director, Jack Gertsman; sound,

Advertisement for The Fly (1958).

Eugene Grossman and Harry M. Leonard; special camera effects, L. B. Abbott; camera, Karl Struss; editor, Merrill G. White.
    Al [David] Hedison (André); Patricia Owens (Hélène); Vincent Price (François); Herbert Marshall (Inspector Charas); Kathleen Freeman (Emma); Betty Lou Gerson (Nurse Andersone); Charles Herbert (Philippe); Eugene Borden (Dr. Ejoute); Torben Meyer (Gaston).

    This adaptation of George Langelaan's novelette began as just another exploitation monster picture with a fair budget ($325,000). But a top-notch cast and careful pacing/direction by Kurt Neumann transformed the CinemaScope, color feature into a pretty engaging thriller that proved both frightening and popular. It received critical endorsement: "The most originally suggestive hair-raiser since The Thing" (New York Times). "Unusual believability.... Has a compelling interest aside from its macabre effects ... " (Variety). "One of the more gruesome films in this genre.... Both the gory and the bizarre details are made extraordinarily explicit" (New York Herald-Tribune).
    Bright young scientist André (Al [David] Hedison) has developed a theory of transmitting matter from one location to another. In his basement laboratory he works with various animals and transmits them successfully. When the time comes, he decides to transfer a human body and uses himself as a guinea pig. Unfortunately a small fly also enters his machine and in the breakdown and transference of cells, a portion of his body becomes part of the fly and in return he obtains a huge fly's head and one claw (in place of an arm). Still retaining his human brain, although with some of the killer instincts of the fly, André asks his wife (Patricia Owens) to aid him in finding the fly and reversing the transference. Unfortunately the insect cannot be located. He begs his wife to crush his fly head in a huge vice before the creature's traits force him to kill her. She complies with his wishes. In the final plot-twisting scenes the fly (with André's head) is seen caught and screaming in a spider web. The experimentor's brother (Vincent Price) and the Inspector (Herbert Marshall) kill the fly, ending the results of the disastrous experiment.
    Despite the use of the large and horrible looking fly's head ("Trying to act in it was like playing a piano with boxing gloves," Hedison said), the film provided a certain amount of pathos. Especially touching were the scenes between the scientist and his son (Charles Herbert) and the climax when the wife kills her mutant husband.
    "The Fly stands out from the ordinary run of horror movies in nearly creating an authentic science-fiction monster and botching the job with an unscientific--and illogical--story-idea," insisted Carlos Clarens in An Illustrated History of the Horror Film (1967). But the film grossed over $3 million when issued. It did spawn, unfortunately, two shoddy sequels, Return of the Fly and Curse of The Fly (both q. v.).

FLYING DISC MAN FROM MARS (Republic, 1951) twelve chapters

    Associate producer, Franklin Adreon; director, Fred C. Brannon;

screenplay, Ronald Davidson; music, Stanley Wilson; special effects, Howard and Theodore Lydecker; camera, Walter Strange.

Walter Reed (Kent); Lois Collier (Helen); Gregory Gay (Mota); James Craven (Bryant); Harry Lauter (Drake); Richard Irving (Ryan); Sandy Sanders (Steve); Michael Carr (Trent); Dale Van Sickel (Watchman); Tom Steele (Taylor); George Sherwood (Gateman); Jimmy O'-Gatty (Gradey); John DeSimone (Curtis); Lester Dorr (Crane); Dick Cogan (Kirk).

Chapters: 1) Menace from Mars; 2) The Volcano's Secret; 3) Death Rides the Stratosphere; 4) Execution by Fire; 5) The Living Projectile; 6) Perilous Mission; 7) Descending Doom; 8) Suicidal Sacrifice 9) The Funeral Pyre; 10) Weapons of Hate; 11) Disaster on the Highway; 12) Volcanic Vengeance.

An eccentric scientist named Bryant (James Craven), who builds experimental planes, notices a strange craft hovering about his plant each night. He hires Kent (Walter Reed), a young aviator, to investigate. Kent shoots down the craft, which turns out to be from Mars and to be piloted by Mota (Gregory Gay). The Martian informs the scientist that Mars is centuries more advanced than the Earth. He offers to join Bryant in producing atomic-powered planes and bombs in exchange for taking control of the Earth and making it a satellite of Mars. Bryant agrees to this scheme and has his henchmen (Harry Lauter and Richard Irving) steal uranium from a nearby plant; but Kent stops them. Later Kent and his secretary Helen (Lois Collier) combat the gang, unaware of Mota and Bryant's mad plan. Eventually, however, Kent becomes apprised of the scientists' dirty work with the alien. At this point, Bryant and Mota decide that Kent must be destroyed. Meanwhile Bryant's task force drops atomic bombs on cities around the globe, trying to force the Earth to capitulate. Mota then captures Helen and secrets her in his hideout in a volcano. By accident, an atomic bomb falls into the volcano. Helen and the pursuing Kent escape just in time, before the bomb detonates, killing Mota and Bryant.

The Golden Age of Republic serials had long since passed and with the pressing competition of television, the studio made this chapterplay on a shoestring. It employed a good deal of stock footage from such previous Republic serials as The Purple Monster Strikes (q.v.), King of the Mounties (1942), G-Men vs. The Black Dragon (1943), Secret Service in Darkest Africa (1943), and King of the Rocket Men (1949). Here villain Gregory Gay as Mota even wore the same costume Roy Barcroft donned in The Purple Monster Strikes, in order to match up footage in the two serials. Cheapness in production diminished any entertainment value this chapterplay might have had for its action-oriented audience.

In 1958 Republic would issue a feature version of the serial entitled Missile Monsters.

THE FLYING EYE   see   THE TROLLENBERG TERROR

THE FORBIDDEN MOON   see   BEYOND THE MOON

Anne Francis and Robby the Robot in Forbidden Planet (1956).

FORBIDDEN PLANET (MGM, 1956) C-98 min.

Producer, Nicholas Nayfack; director, Fred M. Wilcox; story, Irving Block and Allen Adler; screenplay, Cyril Hume; art directors, Arthur Lonergan and Cedric Gibbons; electronic tonalities, Bebe and Louis Barron; special effects, A. Arnold Gillespie, Warren New-combe, Irving G. Ries, and Joshua Meador; camera, George Folsey; editor, Ferris Webster.

Walter Pidgeon (Dr. Moribus); Anne Francis (Altaira Moribus); Leslie Nielsen (Commander Adams); Warren Stevens (Lieutenant "Doc" Ostrow); Jack Kelly (Lieutenant Farman); Richard Anderson (Chief Quinn); Earl Holliman (Cook); George Wallace (Bosum); Bob Dix (Grey); Jimmy Thompson (Youngerford); James Drury (Strong); Harry

Harvey, Jr. (Randall); Roger McGee (Lindstrom); Peter Miller (Moran); Morgan Jones (Nichols); Richard Grant (Silvers).

Hardly the usual fare from MGM, this genre classic contains very impressive visuals, a sound story, and respectable acting. It is plotted and well-paced enough to delight most science fiction fans. It emerged during the mid-Fifties when monsters in sci-fi pictures were all the rage. Here the audience found an intelligent blending of the wild creature storyline and a retelling of Shakespeare's play, The Tempest.

In 2200 A.D. astronauts land on a small out-of-the-way planet called Altair. They are seeking evidence of the fate of the colony which settled there three years before. All they locate is a desolate world inhabited by Dr. Moribus (Walter Pidgeon), his daughter (Anne Francis), and their servant, Robby the Robot (who would be seen again the next year in MGM's The Invisible Boy).

For a time the planet seems an idyllic paradise but then a strange, invisible force begins to terrorize the astronauts. Later it sabotages their camp and ship. Finally Dr. Moribus takes them below the planet's surface where there exists a giant maze of computers, the product of the original civilization of the planet. Every aspect of life was fed into the computer complex, but the inhabitants did not realize the amount of evil in their own personalities and later were destroyed by the computer.

With the invisible creature accomplishing more devious deeds it is realized that the "monster" has been activated by the hatred of the visitors. As the space visitors fight the creature, the Doctor tries to kill it, but is himself annihilated as he activates a planetary destruction mechanism. After rescuing his daughter and the robot the astronauts view the destruction of Altair-4 and then chart their flight path homeward.

In its day, some reviewers took the project to be a comedy dressed in sci-fi trappings. ("It offers some of the most amusing creatures conceived since the Keystone cops," said the New York Times). But, explained John Baxter in Science Fiction in the Cinema (1970), "Elaborate beyond the dreams of sf fans, Forbidden Planet was and still is the most remarkable of sf films, the ultimate recreation of the future, a studio-bound extravaganza where every shot is taken under artificial light and on a sound stage. The system begun by George Pal had reached its logical conclusion; everything was false, everything controlled. Reality was not permitted to intrude on this totally manufactured, totally believable world."

THE FORBIN PROJECT see COLOSSUS: THE FORBIN PROJECT

THE 4-D MAN (Universal, 1959) C-85 min.

Producer, Jack H. Harris; director, Irwin Shortess Yeaworth, Jr.; screen idea, Harris; screenplay, Theodore Simonson and Cy Chermak; art director, William Jersey; set decorator, Don W.

Schmitt; makeup, Dean Newman; music composer/director, Ralph
Carmichael; sound, Carl Auel and Robert Spies; special effects, Bar-
ton Sloane; camera, Theodore J. Pahle; editor, William B. Murphy.
     Robert Lansing (Scott Nelson); Lee Meriwether (Linda Davis);
James Congdon (Tony Nelson); Robert Strauss (Roy Parker); Edgar
Stehli (Carson); Patty Duke (Marjorie); and Guy Raymond and Chic
James.

     Physicist Scott Nelson (Robert Lansing) and his brother Tony
(James Congdon) develop a method by which solid matters pass through
each other.   In the process Scott discovers that the procedure causes
him to age rapidly.   The only way to stop the enervating process is
to absorb other people's life forces.   Linda (Lee Meriwether), Scott's
fiancée, learns of his homicidal spree and determines to end his career.   She convinces him to temporarily abandon his power, and
while he is vulnerable she shoots him.   The closing credit on the
screen is "The End....?"
     "It is not offensively gruesome and has a fairly interesting
gimmick," reported Variety of this feature shot in Valley Forge,
Pennsylvania.   The cast was comprised mostly of New Yorkers, and
thus there is Patty Duke as the young girl, Marjorie.   A very trite
jazz soundtrack score mars viewer concentration.
     The film would be reissued in 1965 as Master of Terror and
would be known as The Evil Force (in England) and Four-Dimensional Man.

FOUR-DIMENSIONAL MAN   see   THE 4-D MAN

4, 3, 2, 1, MUERTE   see   ORBITA MORTAL

FOUR-SIDED TRIANGLE (Exclusive, 1952) 81 min.

     Producers, Michael Carreras and Alexander Paal; director,
Terence Fisher; based on the novel by William F. Temple; screen-
play, Fisher and Paul Tabori; art directors, J. Elder Wills; music,
Malcolm Arnold; camera, Reginald Wyer; editor, Maurice Rootes.
     Barbara Payton (Lena/Helen); James Hayter (Dr. Harvey);
Stephen Murray (Bill); John Van Eyssen (Robin); Percy Marmont (Sir
Walter); Jennifer Dearman (Lena - as a child); Glyn Dearman (Bill -
as a child); Sean Barrett (Robin - as a child); Kynaston Reeves (Lord
Grant); John Stuart (Solicitor).

     This early entry by Terence Fisher was a precursor of the
features which were to come from the Hammer film plant.
     In their youth two boys fall in love with the same girl and
their rivalry continues into adulthood, although they remain friends
and work together in an old barn on their pet project (the invention
of a machine that will duplicate anything).   After success with such
objects as watches, they decide to duplicate a human.   The matter

comes to a crux when Lena (Barbara Payton), the girl they both
adore, chooses Robin (John Van Eyssen) over Bill (Stephen Murray).
The latter then suggests they duplicate Lena, and they do, successfully. But her double (a clone-like creation) also loves Robin. Grief-
stricken, Robin goes mad and tries to operate on the double to take
away her love for him. A fire erupts and co-creator and clone are
destroyed. Robin and the real Lena are now able to pursue happiness.
    Critical reaction to Four-Sided Triangle has been mixed.
Denis Gifford in Science Fiction Film (1971) found it a "cheap and
dreary version of William F. Temple's novel," while the editors of
The House of Horror (1973) noted, "Four-Sided Triangle deserves
special comment as Hammer's first venture into fantasy and science-
fiction, although its idea of duplicating a woman to make up for the
loss of the original had already been tried in Stolen Face."

F. P. 1 ANTWORTET NICHT / FLOATING PLATFORM 1 DOES NOT
ANSWER (UFA/Gaumont/Fox, 1932) 90 min.

    Producer, Eric Pommer; director, Karl Hartl; based on the
novel by Curt Siodmak; screenplay, Walter Reisch and Siodmak (English dialogue, Robert Stevenson and Peter MacFarlane); set designer,
Erich Kettlehut; camera, Günther Rittau and Konstantin Tschet.
    German version: Hans Albers, Sybille Schmitz, Paul Hart-
mann, Peter Lorre, Hermann Speelmans, Rudolf Platte.
    English version: Conrad Veidt (Elissen); Leslie Fenton (Dro-
ste); Jill Esmond (Claire Lennartz); George Merritt (Lubin); Donald
Cathrop (Photographer); Nicholas Nannen (Matthais); William Fresh-
man (Conrad); Warwick Ward (Officer); Alexander Field and Francis
J. Sullivan (Sailors).
    French version: Charles Boyer, Danielle Parola, Jean Murat,
Pierre Brasseur, Marcel Vallée, Pierre Pierade, Ernest Ferny.

    The visuals are the most impressive facet of this thrice-
filmed story, a version being made by UFA in Germany, along with
English and French-language versions, all with different casts. The
mid-Atlantic aerodrome which is the film's setting was designed by
Erich Kettlehut and the photography of Günther Rittau (who had worked
on Metropolis, [q. v.] gave the production added lustre. Still the
overall film was not breathtaking. As William Johnson noted in an
essay included in Focus on the Science Fiction Film (1972), "Even
when spectacular technology did appear in films--such as F. P. 1
Does not Answer--its effects were limited in scope compared to the
moon flights of Die Frau im Mond and Things to Come [q. v.]."
    In Siodmak's story a chief engineer-pilot (Hans Albers) is
urged by a friend to construct Floating Platform One (F. P. 1) in the
middle of the Atlantic Ocean. As a result a futuristic city of steel
and glass is built. Foreign powers, however, do not want to have
such a city succeed and a saboteur gasses the maintenance crew there
and opens the compressed air tanks. But the attempt to destroy
F. P. 1 fails.
    Of this German entry, John Baxter noted in Science Fiction

in the Cinema (1970), "the UFA technical team created some exciting
scenes of the platform's construction ... [and] the scenes of huge
tri-motor airliners lumbering down on the metal surface of F. P. 1
are far more impressive than the routine thriller plot...."
      Denis Gifford in Science Fiction Cinema (1973) made a his-
torical observation about the British version: "In 1933 the mid-ocean
aerodrome seemed more immediately practical than long-range aircraft, a notion which made Karl Hartl's F. P. 1 rapidly obsolete."

THE FRANKENSTEIN series

      The films in this variant series are generally thought of as a
part of the horror film genre. Yet the concept of a scientist creating a living being from the tissues of the dead and imbuing it with
life is the purest form of science fiction. Add to this the crackle-
pop of the flashing machines created by Kenneth Strickfaden for Universal's Frankenstein pictures and the result is as much sci-fi as
horror: i. e. , the creation of a super-human monster is in the realm
of sci-fi; the terrible doings of the monster itself are in the sphere
of horror.
      To delve minutely into all the entries in the Frankenstein se-
ries would be to cover ground already well trodden on many occasions
in movie monster magazines and in many books (the best being The
Frankenstein Legend by Donald F. Glut, 1973).
      Charles Ogle made a nightmarish monster in the initial filmed
Frankenstein, produced by Thomas Edison in 1910. Life without a
Soul (1915) was also based on Mary Shelley's 1817 novel. The German films dealing with The Golem also had many trademarks of her
original book. It was the 1931 Universal classic, Frankenstein (originally intended to star Lon Chaney and later Bela Lugosi) which really launched the cinema career of Boris Karloff. He gave pathos and
menace to the role of the creature created by a crazed scientist.
Karloff continued the portrayal (aided by dialogue) in the best film of
the Universal series, Bride of Frankenstein (1935), and in the most
literate of the property, Son of Frankenstein (1939). Lon Chaney
took over the role and gave it the superhuman strength described in
the novel in The Ghost of Frankenstein (1942). Bela Lugosi finally
played a very sick monster, one who is only given his full power at
the finale, in Frankenstein Meets the Wolfman (1943). It was the
most atmospheric of the later Universal Frankenstein films. Glenn
Strange provided little more than cameos as the monster in House of
Frankenstein (1945) and House of Dracula (1945), but he was back in
a bigger role in Abbott and Costello Meet Frankenstein (1948), where
the poor creature met the ultimate of threats--having Lou Costello's
brain put in his head. This comedy marked the last of the Universal
movie series.
      In the Fifties Boris Karloff portrayed a descendant of Dr.
Frankenstein in the inferior Frankenstein--1970 (1958). The year
before, Christopher Lee played a most gruesome looking creation in
Hammer Films' British-made Curse of Frankenstein (1957). It was
Peter Cushing, however, as the mad inventive doctor who remained
with the series up to the present time. Of the Frankenstein films

since then, except for a few solid TV versions in the Seventies, the
less said the better. The monster ran the gamut from guest appearances to quickie productions to porno flicks to meeting all kinds of
monsters in Mexican and Japanese productions. Few of these offshot
entries could qualify as sci-fi entries.
    Two films of the period do deserve brief mention here.
Frankenstein Meets the Space Monster, released by Allied Artists in
1965, had nothing to do with the Mary Shelley original, but had an
artificial man (a precursor of "The Six Million Dollar Man") forced
to fight a group of aliens and their ghastly monster (called Mull) in
Puerto Rico. A worse film cannot be imagined and it does not even
have the grace to offer a few (un)intended laughs.
    Dracula vs. Frankenstein, made by Independent-International
in 1969 as The Blood Seekers and also known as Blood of Frankenstein, Frankenstein's Bloody Terror and Satan's Blood Freaks, had
Dracula (Zandor Vorkov) exhume the dormant monster (John Bloom)
and then force Dr. Frankenstein (J. Carrol Naish) to revive the creature. Then the duo, along with the doctor's mad assistant (Lon
Chaney), goes in search of the blood of young girls, needed to main-
tain their special powers. It was all a far cry from the early days
of the Universal series.

DIE FRAU IM MOND (UFA, 1929) 150 min.

        Producer/director, Fritz Lang; based on the novel by Thea
von Harbou; screenplay, von Harbou; art directors, Emil Hasler,
Otto Hunte, and Karl Vollbrecht; camera, Curt Courant, Oskar Fis-
chinger, Otto Kantrek, and Konstantin Tschet [Tschetwerikoff].
        Klaus Pohl (Professor Georg Manfeldt); Willy Fritsch (Wolf
Helius); Gustav von Wangenheim (Engineer Hans Windegger); Gerda
Maurus (Friede Velten); Gustl Stark-Gstettenbauer (Gustav); Fritz
Rasp (Walt Turner); Tilla Durieux, Hermann Vellentin, Max Zilzer,
Mahmud Terja Bey, and Borwin Walt (Five "Brains" and "Cheque
Books"), Karl Platen (Man at the Microphone); Josephine (The Mouse);
Margaret Kupfer (Mrs. Hippolt); Max Maximilian (Grotjan); Alexa von
Porembska (The Flower Girl); Gerhard Dammann (Chief of the Helius
Hangers); and Heinrich Gotho.

        Director Fritz Lang followed his successful Metropolis (q. v.)
with Die Frau im Mond (Girl in the Moon), an imaginative treat for
sci-lovers of that period. It is a film that quickly dated and is regarded today as little more than a curiosity. Still, the feature was
a precursor of such movies as Destination Moon (q. v.), which appeared two decades later. Die Frau im Mond based many of its
space travel conceptions on the works of Hermann Oberth, a writer
who approved of the Lang movie.
        Reportedly, a complete print of Die Frau im Mond no longer
exists. Prints that do survive are especially choppy in the first
portion, complicating the plotline flow.
        The story/screenplay by Thea von Harbou (then the wife of
Fritz Lang) told of a professor (Klaus Pohl) who developed a method
of space travel in order to reach the Moon, which he is convinced

has a rich deposit of gold. He dreams of this conquest for some
thirty years, eventually becoming a near madman. Finally, through
a wealthy young assistant (Willy Fritsch) he is able to obtain backers
for the trip. (The venture is bolstered a good deal when an un-
manned flight proves that gold is in abundance on the satellite.)
These wealthy men, however, demand that one of their number, Walt
Turner (Fritz Rasp), accompany the expedition to protect the gold
shipment. Also aboard the craft are an engineer (Gustav von Wagenheim) and two stowaways: the engineer's fiancée (Gerda Maurus)
and a young boy (Gustl Stark-Gstettenbauer).

The trip to the faraway moon is an uneventful one except
for the shock of acceleration and weightlessness, and the professor's
further drifting into insanity. Upon landing, he explores the lunar
landscape (which has oxygen) and finds the gold. But the wealthy
men's representative follows him, causing his death--the madman
falls into a crater. The engineer and the youth have witnessed this
crime. Back at the ship, a fight ensues, with Turner being killed--
but not before destroying half the ship's air supply, making it necessary for at least one of the crew to remain on the moon, so that the
remainder can return to Earth. At first the assistant volunteers,
but the engineer then drugs him, and puts the craft on automatic control. He remains behind on the lunar surface, as does the girl, hoping that someday a rescue ship will come to take them home.

The primary importance of Die Frau im Mond, shot and released as a silent feature, was that it was the real beginning of outer
space movie travels--not like the fantasies of Georges Méliès, but
in some part a scientific study of outer atmosphere travel. Producer-director Lang perhaps made one mistake in the film's execution,
refusing to at least use sound effects (which were readily available
when the film was produced in late 1928). The incorporation of these
audio effects would have enhanced the over-all impact of the picture
and given it (for its day) a futuristic quality it seemed to lack except
in plotline.

Paul M. Jensen in The Cinema of Fritz Lang (1969) points
out, "A knowledge of science was not needed to understand the actual
journey, since the charts and diagrams shown to the financiers informed the viewers as well. This was felt by most critics to be an
advantage, since it was 'educational'...." Yet, when released in an
abbreviated 97-minute version in the U.S., the New York Times would
criticize it on the grounds that the scientific sequences possessed "a
tantalizing incompleteness, an unfortunate genuflection to popular ig-
norance," and Variety reported that the movie contained too much
"mugging.... Performers are always 'acting' and camera conscious
in some of the story's highlights."

Many historians agree that Lang's feature had a real effect,
helping to spark the imagination of real scientists to make the fan-
tasy--moon travel--to come true.

FROM THE EARTH TO THE MOON (Warner Bros., 1958) C-100 min.

Producer, Benedict Bogeaus; director, Byron Haskin; based
on the story by Jules Verne; screenplay, Robert Blees and James

George Sanders and Joseph Cotten in From the Earth to the Moon
(1958).

Leicester; assistant director, Nacio Real; music, Louis Forbes;
wardrobe, Georgette; production designer, Hal Wilson Cox; sound,
Weldon Coe; special camera effects, Albert M. Simpson; camera,
Edwin B. DuPar; editor, Leicester.

     Joseph Cotten (Victor Barbicane); George Sanders (Stuyvesant
Nicholls); Debra Paget (Virginia Nicholl); Don Dubbins (Ben Sharpe);
Patric Knowles (Cartier); Melville Cooper (Bancroft); Carl Esmond
(J. V.); Henry Daniell (Morgana); Ludwig Stossel (Von Metz); Mor-
ris Ankrum (President U. S. Grant).

     This was one of those cinéma projects which never should have
gotten off the ground. It was produced in the dying days of RKO (and
sold to Warner Bros. for distribution), with location photography in
Mexico. It was lensed in the giantscope process which offered a 3-D
optical effect without the need for special viewer glasses.

     "Production design is interesting, often more fascinating than
the story in front of it" (Variety). Other critics were less kind.
Bosley Crowther (New York Times) weighed it "Pretty much of a
dud," explaining that the scriptwriters "made one disastrous miscal-
culation. They failed to compute how far this sort of fanciful nonsense required that they intrude their tongues into their cheeks. And
the director failed to correct their mistake."

In the post-Civil War period, a millionaire named Barbicane (Joseph Cotten) creates Power X, which can be used as both a fuel and an explosive. He informs the press that a ship with passengers can be shot from a cannon into space, even reaching the moon. He then raises the necessary $50 million for the experiment. The inventor also convinces a skeptical metallurgist named Stuyvesant Nicholls (George Sanders) to join in on the flight. After being propelled into the skies, Styvesant's daughter Virginia (Debra Paget) is discovered to be a stowaway aboard ship, having risked the trip to be near her lover (Don Dubbins), one of the ship's crew. Later Nicholls tries to reverse the course of the ship, causing the vessel to tear in half; the section with the lovers returns to Earth while the other part, in which Nicholls and Barbicane are clinging, heads for the Moon.

With good reason, this misfire did not have British distribution until the early Sixties. In 1967, the British did a comedy remake of the film called Those Fantastic Flying Fools (a. k. a. Blast-Off).

GAMERA   see DAIKAIJU GAMERA

THE GAMMA PEOPLE (Columbia, 1956) 79 min.

Producer, John Gossage; director, John Gilling; story, Louis Pollock; screenplay, Gilling and Gossage; art director, John Box; music, George Melachrino; special camera effects, Tom Howard; camera, Ted Moore; editors, Jack Slade and Alan Osbliston.

Paul Douglas (Mike Wilson); Eva Bartok (Paul Wendt); Leslie Phillips (Howard Meade); Walter Rilla (Boronski); Philip Leaver (Koerner); Martin Miller (Lochner); Michael Caridia (Hugo); Pauline Drewett (Hedda); Jackie Lane (Anna); Rosalie Crutchley (Frau Bikstein); St. John Stuart (Goon).

This overlooked thriller is a good example of how the Cold War affected the sci-fi genre. Far more political than entertaining, the feature attempted to depict how government intervention into education could have harmful, George Orwell-type results. Surprisingly the movie starred American comedy character lead Paul Douglas.

In a mythical (Communist) European country two Western reporters (Paul Douglas and Leslie Phillips) uncover a secret new educational theory being tried out on schoolchildren and old people. The subjects are exposed to intense gamma radiation treatments. The end result of these experiments is that persons become either near-geniuses or morons. After a large number of people have been subjected to the system, they band together, thus creating a problem to the state. Government leaders try to retain some control over their experimental mistakes, but with little success.

Because of the cast presence of Paul Douglas, this British-made film saw U.S. release. However, it was soon relegated to TV showings.

GAMMERA--THE INVINCIBLE see DAIKAIJU GAMERA

GAS-S-S-S! (GAS, or IT BECAME NECESSARY TO DESTROY THE
WORLD IN ORDER TO SAVE IT (American International, 1970) C-79
min.

Producer/director, Roger Corman; screenplay, George Armitage; music, Country Joe and the Fish; additional music, Barry Melton; art director, David Nichols; set decorator, Stephen Graham;
makeup, Dean Cundy; sound, James Tannenbaum; camera, Ron Dexter; editor, George Van Noy.

Robert Corff (Coel); Elaine Giftos (Cilla); Bud Cort (Hooper);
Talia Coppola (Coralie); Ben Vereen (Carlos); Cindy Williams (Ma-
rissa); Alex Wilson (Jason); Lou Procopio (Marshall McLuhan); Phil
Borneo (Quant); Jackie Farley (Ginny); George Armitage (Billy the
Kid); Pat Patterson (Demeter); Alan Braunstein (Dr. Drake); Country
Joe [McDonald] and the Fish (Themselves).

Shot in 1968, with location work in New Mexico, this minor
feature received some playdates in 1970 and 1971 before being tossed
to television. This is one of only two features (the other is The Intruder, 1962) with which Roger Corman has been associated that has
not turned a profit.

The plotline is highly derivative of Corman's Wild in the
Streets (1968). It tells of a mysterious gas being released from an
Alaskan defense plant which kills everyone on Earth over the age of
twenty-five. The power of the world is thus thrust into the hands of
young people. Their desperate and often comedic struggles are the
focus of attention. At the offbeat finale, the ground opens up and
world leaders like the Kennedys, Che Guevera, and Martin Luther
King are returned to life.

Seen today on TV, Gas-s-s-s! is mainly of interest for the
inclusion of two future TV stars in its cast: Cindy Williams and Ben
Vereen. One of the major characters in the feature was to have been
God. But American International excised this portion of the picture
after Corman had gone on to another project. Despite the film's
positive reception at the Edinburgh Film Festival, Corman wanted it
returned to its original form. But he found the original negative had
been destroyed. Allegedly because of the way AIP re-edited and distributed the film, Corman left the studio and formed his own outfit,
New World Pictures.

The occasional American critic who saw the film found it of
interest. Among them was Judith Crist (New York): "There's a cool
overlay and a serious undertone to the fun and games that give one
an insight into the youth level that has long been Corman's forte.
It's worth seeing for this alone...." Nearer the majority view was
the Village Voice's opinion: "For all its apocalyptic implications,
Gas-s-s-s! seems more likely to induce a nap than a nightmare."

GENE AUTRY AND THE PHANTOM EMPIRE see THE PHANTOM
EMPIRE

GENESIS II (CBS-TV, 1973) C-97 min.

Producer, Gene Roddenberry; director, John Llewellyn Moxey; teleplay, Roddenberry; art director, Hilyard Brown; camera, Gerald Perry Finnerman.

Alex Cord (Dylan Hunt); Mariette Hartley (Lyra-a); Ted Cassidy (Isiah); Percy Rodriguez (Isaac Kimbridge); Harvey Jason (Singh); Tito Vandis (Yuloff); Bill Striglos (Dr. Kellum); Lynne Marta (Harper-Smythe); Harry Raybould (Slan-u); Beulah Quo (Lu-Chan); Ray Young (Second Tyranian Teacher).

Gene Roddenberry, the producer of TV's famous "Star Trek" series, wrote and produced this sci-fi telefeature for Warner Bros. It proved to be a most literate rending (closely related to H.G. Wells' work, When the Sleeper Wakes) of the Flash Gordon-Buck Rogers type of futuristic drama.

Alex Cord stars as twentieth-century space scientist Dylan Hunt, who is buried alive in a natural disaster. Two centuries later he is discovered by other scientists. Preserved and living, Hunt finds he is a pawn sought after by the two forces competing for control of the Earth--one group being warlike, the other peaceful. At first Hunt joins the anti-war group, but then he becomes enamored of Lyra-a (Mariette Hartley), an agent of the aggressors, who has been sent to seduce him. Much to the chagrin of the doves, Hunt switches his allegiance and joins the hawks, causing many complications.

Judith Crist (TV Guide) approved: "[It] is superior TV SF with good production design and imaginative plotting...." The adult theme, with plot parallels to contemporary political situations, helped boost the show's import.

GHIDORAH, SANDAI KAIJU CHIKYU SAIDAI NO KESSAN (GHIDRAH, THE THREE-HEADED MONSTER) (Toho, 1965) C-85 min.

Executive producer, Tomoyuki Tanaka; director, Inoshiro Honda; screenplay, Sinichi Sekizawa; music, Akira Ifukube; special effects, Eiji Tsuburaya; camera, Hajime Koizumi; editor, Ryohei Fujii.

With: Yosuke Natsuki, Yuriko Hoshi, Hiroshi Koizumi, Takashi Shimura, Emi Ito, Yumi Ito, Eiji Okada.

Ghidrah, the three-headed monster born from the explosion of a fireball in outer space, is definitely the nastiest of Japan's many celluloid monsters. For Ghidrah is practically the only one of the creatures on camera which did not eventually turn to the good side of the fence. Ghidrah the nasty was continually at odds with the likes of Godzilla, Mothra, Rodan, and others.

The wicked creature first burst onto the movie scene in 1965, shooting death rays from each of its three ugly heads. With its great speed in flight it is able to destroy cities in a matter of minutes. Mankind is at a loss to stop the aggressor until Mothra, the flying giant moth, convinces Godzilla and Rodan to stop their "silly" fighting and to join him in destroying the invader. (The legendary

Scene from Ghidorah, Sandai Kaiju Chikyu Saidai No Kessan (1965).

battle between the four monsters, on Mount Fuji, was the turning
point in Godzilla's career. Thereafter he became a cinema hero and
the "idol" of almost every filmgoing child in Japan.) The quartet of
creatures engages in a horrendous battle which concludes with Ghidrah being spun into a web by Mothra and then being flung by Rodan
and Godzilla into the sea. And that is that.

The visuals for this color, widescreen feature were especially well executed, with the climactic battle of the giant monsters especially effective. In fact, in some distribution areas the film was
retitled The Greatest Battle on Earth.

Never a studio to keep a good monster down, Toho soon revived Ghidrah to do battle with Godzilla and Rodan again in Kaijii
Daiseno (Monster Zero, q.v.), and yet a further time in the all-star
creature extravaganza, Destroy All Monsters (1968).

THE GIANT BEHEMOTH (Allied Artists, 1959) 79 min.

Producer, Ted Lloyd; director, Eugene Lourie; story, Robert
Abel and Allen Adler; screenplay, Lourie; art director, Harry White;
music composer/conductor, Edwin Astley; assistant director, Kim
Mills; makeup, Jimmy Evans; sound, Sid Wiles; special effects, Jack
Rabin, Irving Block, Louis DeWitt, Willis O'Brien, and Pete Petter-
son; camera, Ken Hodges; editor, Lee Doing.

Leigh Madison, Henry Vidon (on ground) and John Turner in The
Giant Behemoth (1959).

        Gene Evans (Steven Karnes); Andre Morell (Professor Bick-
ford); John Turner (Ian Duncan); Leigh Madison (Jean MacDougall);
Jack MacGowran (Dr. Sampson); Maurice Kaufmann (Submarine Commander); Henry Vidon (Thomas MacDougall); Leonard Sachs (Interrupt-
ing Scientist).
        A.k.a. The Behemoth / Sea Monster.

        In many ways this British-made entry appears to be a follow-
up to the silent The Lost World (q.v.) and Beast from 20,000 Fathoms (q.v.).   In fact, Eugene Lourie, who directed the latter feature, also helmed and scripted this entry. ("Lourie has successfully piled one chill on another, a proposition that the cast goes along
with ..."--Variety.)
        Here a giant prehistoric dinosaur is resurrected by an atomic
explosion and it embarks on a furious onslaught of destruction, also
spreading dangerous radioactivity.   The oversized beast plows into
London and destroys a substantial part of the city.   But American
scientist Steven Karnes (Gene Evans) and his crew combat the creature with a radium-loaded submarine torpedo.   In its death throe,
the behemoth tumbles into London Bridge, collapses into the Thames

and dies.
Variety, ever alert to the basis of an adequate genre entry,
pointed out, "As is the case in so many monster films, the true terror is in the reaction of the people, the fear of the victims and the
effect of the unseen monster, rather than in the ugly sight of the
creature itself."

GIRL IN THE MOON see DIE FRAU IN MOND

GLEN AND RANDA (UMC Pictures, 1971) C-94 min.

Executive producer, Sidney Glazier; associate producer, Wat-
son James; director, Jim McBride; screenplay, Lorenzo Mans, Ru-
dolph Wurlitzer, and McBride; assistant director, Jack Baran; art
director, Gary West; sound, David Neuman and Jeffrey Lesser; cam-
era, Alan Raymond; editors, Mike Levine and Jack Baran.
Steven Curry (Glen); Shelley Plimpton (Randa); Woodrow
Chambliss (Sidney Miller); Garry Goodrow (Magician); and Roy Fox,
William Fratis, Richard Frazier, Martha Furey, Laura Hawbecker,
Mary Henry, Alice Huffman, Charles Huffman, Leonard Johnson,
Lucille Johnson, Ortega Sangster, Barbara Spiegel, Dwight Tate, and
David Woeller.

Like Flesh Gordon (q.v.), this California and Oregon-shot
feature was originally lensed in 16mm. and was blown up to 35mm.
for theatrical release. It was saddled with an X-rating, a cast of
unknowns, and a plotline not really likely to be satisfying to X-view-
ing audiences. Glen and Randa earned only spotty distribution, but
it was quite impressive to many of those who did see it. Today it
is regarded by some as a minor classic of the sci-fi film genre.
The time is 25 years after the nuclear holocaust of World War
III. A wandering young man named Glen (Steven Curry) meets and
falls in love with an equally lost girl, Randa (Shelley Plimpton).
Wandering through the desolation, they find a book, Metropolis by
Thea von Harbou, and soon long to locate the wondrous city described
therein. On their quest they encounter an old man (Woodrow Chambliss) who provides them with shelter in his dilapidated trailer. (It
is filled with such objects as a broken TV set and other decayed
remnants of the past.) During their stay with the elderly man, Randa dies in childbirth. Thereafter, Glen, the man, the infant, and
a goat set out on a raft, hoping to cross the sea and locate their
dream world of Metropolis.
The usually jaded Time magazine was impressed by the results of 29-year old filmmaker Jim McBride in his third film effort.
"Neither moralizing sci-fi nor melodrama, despite its fanciful premise, the film is rather like a cinema verité doomsday documentary--
a parable in newsreel form.... Using a rigorously unadorned style
... [it] conveys a sense of primitive desolation, transforming contemporary landscapes into primeval heaths. Although the film is un-
sparing in its apocalyptic vision, its dour brutality is frequently al-
leviated by a cool eye for satire...." On the other hand, some

sources, such as the San Francisco Chronicle, insisted, "[It] is a
catastrophe. For at least its first hour, it is the most tedious picture I can remember seeing. "

GODZILLA (Toho, 1954) 98 min.

Producer, Tomoyuki Tanaka; directors, Inoshiro Honda and
(English-language scenes) Terry O. Morse; story, Shigeru Kayama;
screenplay, Takeo Murato and I. Honda; art director, Satoshi Chuko;
music, Akira Ifukubu; special effects, Eiji Tsuburaya, Akira Watan-
abe, and Hiroshi Mukouyama; camera, Maseo Tamai and (English
language-scenes) Guy Roe; editor, Morse.
Raymond Burr (Steve Martin); Takashi Shimura (Professor Yamane); Momoko Kochi (Emiko Yamane); Akira Takarada (Ogata); and
Akohiko Hirata.

Godzilla is Japan's greatest and most popular screen monster:
a 400-foot tall prehistorical reptile. He has become a legend in his
time. In thirteen film appearances to date he has grossed over $130
million outside Japan; the Japanese domestic grosses swell that sum
vastly. He is the idol of Japanese schoolchildren and his likeness
is emblazened on playground models, monster kits, candy, comic
books, dolls, and clothing.
All of this major industry had a rather inauspicious beginning
in 1954 when Toho Studios, with Inoshiro Honda as director and
special effects man Eiji Tsuburaya joining forces, made Gojira, the
story of a giant prehistoric dinosaur (played by Tomoyuki Tanaka in
a rubber suit; vulcanized foam rubber in later films). The premise
finds the monster awakened by a giant atomic blast. The fire-
breathing creature rises from the ocean depths to wreak havoc on
Japan, nearly destroying Tokyo. Eventually a young scientist devises a means of extracting oxygen from water and when the amphibious
beast returns to the ocean, the life-giving oxygen is drained from the
water and the monster dies (or so it appears).
Godzilla did not remain dormant long, however. Joseph E.
Levine's Embassy Pictures bought the film for U.S. release. He had
director Terry O. Morse shoot new footage, with Raymond Burr
starring and interpolated it into the 81-minute Godzilla, King of the
Monsters, which was issued in 1956 to fantastic box-office results.
After this initial success Godzilla would return in a slightly
altered form in Gigantis, The Fire Monster (1959). Inactive until
1962, he was then revived for the greatest battle among monsters,
King Kong vs. Godzilla. In this film the giant beast is still a villain
and he remained so in Godzilla vs. the Thing (1964), in which he
does battle with the giant moth, Mothra. In Monster Zero (q.v.),
however, he switched to the side of "right" and joined Rodan and
Mothra to battle Ghidrah, the Three Headed Monster. In 1966 he
found Ebirah, the "Horror of the Deep" in Godzilla vs. the Sea Monster. Next came the very juvenile-oriented Son of Godzilla (1968),
followed by the greatest battle royal of them all, Destroy All Monsters (1969). In 1969 he was back in the realm of childish fantasy,
Godzilla's Revenge. In 1971 the reptile met and overcame one of his

Japan's most popular screen monster, Godzilla (1954).

greatest celluloid tests in Godzilla vs. the Smog Monster. That year
also had him in Godzilla vs. Gigan. The beast's most recent screen ap-
pearance--this time in a speaking role--was in Godzilla vs. Megalon
(1973) in which he and a man-made robot defeat Megalon and its ally,
Gigan.

GOG (United Artists, 1954) C-85 min.

Producer, Ivan Tors; director, Herbert L. Strock; story,
Tors; screenplay, Tom Taggart; art director, William Ferrari; mu-
sic, Harry Sukman; special effects, Harry Redmond, Jr.; camera,
Lathrop B. Worth; editor, Strock.
Richard Egan (David Sheppard); Constance Dowling (Joanna
Merritt); Herbert Marshall (Dr. Van Ness); John Wengraf (Dr. Zeit-
man); Philip Van Zandt (Dr. Elzevir); Valerie Vernon (Mme. Elze-
vir); Steve Roberts (Major Howard); Byron Kane (Dr. Carter); David
Alpert (Peter Burden); Michael Fox (Dr. Hubertus); William Schallert
(Engle); Marian Richman (Bit).
A.k.a. GOG, the Killer.

Since the Twenties, robots have been used in the cinema to
occasion fright. Many a Saturday matinee serial chapter had a rampaging metal monster under the control of some mad genius bent on
controlling the world, or some small fragment of it. The use of
mechanical beings designed to do the benign bidding of mankind, do
not appear on the cinema scene until the Fifties and the advent of
the early space age. In later films such as the Russian Storm Planet (q. v.) the robot would become a hero-type. But at this stage--
the early Fifties--no matter how passive and tame the robot might
seem, he was still regarded with suspicion and fear.
GOG was the name of a robot computer at a space station project located in New Mexico. A giant computer, Novac, runs the station's operation, with GOG designed and trained to follow orders.
When an enemy plane attempts to sabotage the operation by beaming
an ultra-high frequency ray to Novac, the machine re-directs the orders to GOG, who in turn goes haywire and tries to wreck the installation. Eventually the heroes (Richard Egan and Herbert Marshall) are forced to destroy the rampaging robot in order to save
their work and themselves.
Producer Ivan Tors had GOG filmed in the gimmicky third-
dimensional process and took care that the product was a visually
handsome affair. The superior cast provided more than adequate
performances. Yet, insisted the New York Times, it "is utter nonsense, on the whole."

GRAVE ROBBERS FROM OUTER SPACE see PLAN 9 FROM OUT-
ER SPACE

THE GREAT ALASKAN MYSTERY (Universal, 1944) thirteen chapters

Associate producer, Henry MacRae; directors, Ray Taylor and Lewis D. Collins; story, Jack Foley; screenplay, Maurice Tombragel and George H. Plympton; camera, William Sickner.
Milburn Stone (Jim Hudson); Marjorie Weaver (Ruth Miller); Edgar Kennedy (Bosun); Samuel S. Hinds (Herman Brock); Martin Kosleck (Dr. Hauss); Ralph Morgan (Dr. Miller); Joseph Crehan (Bill Hudson); Fuzzy Knight ("Grit" Hartman); Harry Cording (Captain Greeder); Anthony Warde (Brandon); Jack Clifford (Dunn); William Ruhl (Grey); Perc Launders (Haegle); Edward Gargan (Kurtz); Jay Novello (Eskimo Chief); Richard Powers (Burger).
Chapters: 1) Shipwrecked among Icebergs; 2) Thundering Doom; 3) Battle in the Clouds; 4) Masked Murder; 5) The Bridge of Diaster; 6) Shattering Doom; 7) Crashing Timbers; 8) In a Flaming Plane; 9) Hurtling through Space; 10) Tricked by a Booby Trap; 11) The Tunnel of Terror; 12) Electrocuted; 13) The Boomerang.

The Great Alaskan Mystery is a plausible, if minor, serial because it combines adequately several cinéma genres. Firstly, it is an adventure film, a North woods type of melodrama combined with a mystery motif. The plotline also contains many points of reference to both sci-fi and spy drama, each element playing a major role in the course of its action.
During World War II, scientist Dr. Miller (Ralph Morgan), his daughter Ruth (Marjorie Weaver), her fiancé Jim Hudson (Milburn Stone), and pal Bosun (Edgar Kennedy) depart for Alaska to find a mine discovered earlier by Dr. Miller's brother (Joseph Crehan). Miller wants to use the mine ore to perfect his new invention, a Peragron (deadly ray gun). Also joining in the Northern trek is Miller's assistant, Dr. Hauss (Martin Kosleck)--actually a Fascist in cahoots with Captain Greeder (Harry Cording) and a businessman named Herman Brock (Samuel S. Hinds). The group is later shipwrecked and caught in a plane crash, but they do manage to reach Alaska and find the mine. Another Axis henchman, Brandon (Anthony Warde), makes several attempts to steal the ray machine and Captain Greeder is actually killed by it. When all else fails, Brandon has the mine attacked by his gang. In the ensuing skirmish he is killed. Dr. Hauss, meanwhile, steals the Peragron and takes it to Brock's office. But the two argue and Hauss kills Brock. As a result Dr. Hauss is arrested, the ray gun is recovered and Helen and Jim are able to settle down to a life of happiness.
The serial was issued abroad as The Great Northern Mystery.

THE GREAT NORTHERN MYSTERY   see   THE GREAT ALASKAN MYSTERY

THE GREATEST BATTLE ON EARTH   see   GHIDORAH, SANDAI KAIJU CHIKYU SAIDAI NO KESSAN

GYPSY MOON see BEYOND THE MOON

THE H-MAN see BIJYO TO EKITAININ-GEN

HALLUCINATION see THE DAMNED

HAUNTED PLANET see TERRORE NELLO SPAZIO

HAUNTED WORLD see TERRORE NELLO SPAZIO

HAVE ROCKET, WILL TRAVEL (Columbia, 1959) 76 min.

    Producer, Harry Romm; director, David Lowell Rich; screen-play, Raphael Hayes; assistant director, Floyd Joyer; music conductor, Mischa Bakaleinikoff; title song, George Duning and Stanley Styne; art director, John T. McCormack; set decorator, Darrell Silvera; sound, John Livadary and Harold Lewis; camera, Ray Cory; editor, Danny B. Landres.
    Moe Howard (Moe); Larry Fine (Larry); Joe De Rita (Curley Joe); Jerome Cowan (J. P. Morse); Anna-Lisa (Dr. Ingrid Naaveg); Bob Colbert (Dr. Ted Benson); Don Lamond (Narrator).

    If everyone else seemed to be taking pot-shots at the science fiction genre, why not the Three Stooges, the slapstick trio who gained movie fame in the Thirties and Forties? This inexpensively mounted picture proved a delight to children's audiences, made a bundle at the box-office, and launched the veteran comedy team on a feature film career which would last until the late Sixties.
    The Three Stooges work as handymen at a missile installation. Cleaning a rocket ship, they accidentally launch it and find themselves zooming to Venus. On the new world they discover such things as unicorns, vicious villains, giant flame-throwing tarantulas, and a super computer. Eventually the dim-witted boys outmaneuver their opponents and return home as heroes. Especially joyous is a party scene which ends up, as per usual for the Stooges, in a terrific pie fight.
    The critics, naturally, did not respond to Have Rocket, Will Travel. Variety observed, "Strictly for the juve market.... It's a silly hash of sight gags and sound effects loosely organized around a funny enough theme...." The boys continued to make features for Columbia, some of which were in the sci-fi motif: The Three Stooges in Orbit (1962) and The Three Stooges Go around the World in a Daze (1963). Moe Howard had taken a part in Space Master X-7 (1958) and a few of the trio's final short subjects (circa 1957) had science fiction themes: Space Ship Sappy, Outer Space Jitters, and Flying Saucer Daffy.

HELL CREATURES see INVASION OF THE SAUCER MEN

THE HELLSTROM CHRONICLE (Cinema V, 1971) C-90 min.

Executive producer, David L. Wolper; producer, Walon Green;
associate producer, Sascha Schneider; director, Green; screenplay,
David Seltzer; music, Lalo Schifrin; music supervisor, Jack Tillar;
sound, David Ronne; sound effects, Charles L. Campbell; camera,
Helmut Barth, Green, Ken Middleham, and Gerald Thompson; addi-
tional camera, Fernando Armati, Heinz Seilmann, Tony Coggans, J.
M. Boufle, and James Fonesca; editor, John Soh.
Lawrence Pressman (Nils Hellstrom).

The Hellstrom Chronicle is a unique sci-fi film. It tells a
story in a documentary format, but the entire film is fiction. Nevertheless its premise could be fact. Supposedly based on the life work
and theories of Dr. Nils Hellstrom (Lawrence Pressman), the narrative claims to depict why mankind is doomed to extinction by insects.
The film delves into the life patterns of a variety of insects (locusts,
moths, flies, etc.) and show how they are equipped to withstand the
worst warfare with mankind and how they will eventually rule the
Earth.
Visually, the film is brilliant. Producer/director/cinemato-
grapher Walon Green has offered us a beautifully conceived picture
of the world under our feet--the small world of the bug. The movie
shows us in graphic terms that while we may be giants to them, the
insects have survived prehistoric reptiles and will survive us. They
can endure the effects of nuclear blasts and radiation and are most
likely to be the last living inhabitants of Earth.
Dale Winogura explained in Cinefantastique, "Science-fact is
is the basis here, but its presentation is a cross-breed of official
cinema verité, factual exposition, and beautiful, terrifying and amazing imagery that takes on a science fiction mystique.... [The] film
is visually dazzling and disturbing in its myriad implications; it's a
cold, sterile masterpiece." Countering, a bit, the seriousness provided by the film, Arthur Knight (Saturday Review) added in his cri-
tique, "I can only add that since I saw the film, no insect can cross
my path with impunity. If it's kill or be killed, I'm starting my
side of the fight right now."
The film won the Grand Prix de Technique at the 1971 Cannes
Film Festival and in its U.S.-Canadian release grossed a very respectable $1.5 million. It won an Academy Award for its superior
technical work.

DIE HERREN VON ATLANTIS see L'ATLANTIDE (1932)

HIDEOUS SUN DEMON (Pacific International, 1959) 74 min.

Producer/director, Robert Clarke; co-director, Thomas Boutross; story, Clarke and Phil Hiner; screenplay, E. S. Seeley, Jr.

and Doane Hoag; monster sequence, Gianbiatista Cassarino; music,
John Seeley; song, Marilyn King; sound, Doug Menville; camera,
John Morrill, Vilis Lapenicks, Jr., and Stan Follis; editor, Boutross.
    Robert Clarke (Dr. Gilbert McKenna); Patricia Manning (Ann
Russell); Nan Peterson (Trudy Osborne); Patrick Whyte (Dr. Freder-
ick Buckell); Fred La Porta (Dr. Jacob Hoffman); Bill Hampton (Po-
lice Lieutenant); Donna Conkling (Mother); Xandra Conklin (Little
Girl); Del Courtney (Radio Announcer).

    Robert Clarke had been a film actor since the Forties and he
later starred in such sci-fi features as Man from Planet X and Captive Women (both q. v.) before turning producer in the late Fifties
with such entries as Beyond the Time Barrier (q. v.). Since he usually had to work within a minuscule budget, the actor also starred
in his own productions, and he provided some reliable performances.
    More deadly than an oversized praying mantis--at least to
unsuspecting filmgoers--was The Hideous Sun Demon. Clarke was
seen as Dr. Gilbert McKenna who is exposed to a huge dosage of
radiation and is promptly converted into a lizardy creature. Hospital
tests confirm that if he ever goes into the sun, he will become the
scaly horror again. Quicker than one can say "Flash Gordon" Mc-
Kenna finds himself forced into the bright sunlight. Now a rampaging demon, he kills several people before being trapped on the roof
of a huge gas tank hundreds of feet in the air. In his effort to escape the law, he topples to his death.
    In England the film was entitled Blood on His Lips. It is also
known as Terror from the Sun / The Sun Demon.

EL HOMBRE QUE VINE DEL UMMO / DRACULA JAGT FRANKEN-
STEIN / LOS MONSTRUOUS DEL TERROR (Spanish/West German/
Italian, 1970) C-87 min.

    Producer, Jaime Prades; director, Tulio Demicheli; screen-
play, Jacinto Molina [Jacinto Molina Alvarez]; art director, Adolfo
Cofiho; makeup, Francisco R. Ferrer; music Rafael Ferrer; camera,
Godofredo Pacheco; editor, Emilio Rodriguez.
    Michael Rennie (Dr. Odo Warnoff); and Karen Dor, Craig Hill,
Patty Shepard, Angel del Pozo, Paul Naschy (Monster/werewolf).

    In the Forties, Universal attempted to bolster its box-office
take from horror films by featuring a number of monsters in the
same film (e. g., House of Frankenstein, Frankenstein Meets the
Wolfman) and promising a slug fest between the creatures. Over
the years this gimmick has been adopted by various producers throughout the world. This outing combined several world-famous monsters
with an alien from outer space. The results were tepid, a thriller
that promised a lot more than it delivered.
    Michael Rennie starred as Dr. Odo Warnoff, an alien from
the planet Ummo who has come to Earth with a beautiful assistant
(Karen Dor) in order to conquer the planet. To aid in this nefarious
scheme, the duo resurrects the famous monsters of the past: the
Frankenstein monster, Dracula, the Wolfman, the Mummy, and the

Robert Clarke in Hideous Sun Demon (1959).

Reptile.   The plan seems infallible until the creatures have a falling
out among themselves and duel to the death.   The Wolfman is the
winner, but only temporarily.   The aliens also meet a disastrous end:
the assistant abandons Dr. Warnoff, and he, in turn, kills her and
then liquidates himself.

In Britain the film was issued as Dracula vs. Frankenstein;
its American TV title is Assignment Terror.

L'HOMME DANS LA LUNE   see   THE ASTRONOMER'S DREAM

HORROR IN THE MIDNIGHT SUN   see   INVASION OF THE ANIMAL
PEOPLE

HORROR OF THE BLOOD MONSTERS (Independent International, 1971)
C-85 min.

Executive producers, Charles McMullen and Zoe Phillips; associate producer, Ewing Brown; producer/director, Al Adamson;
screenplay, Sue McNair; music, Mike Velarde; orchestrator, Restie
Umali; second unit director, George Joseph; production consultant,
Samuel M. Sherman; special effects, David L. Hewitt; camera, William Zsigmond and William G. Troiano; editors, Brown and Peter
Perry.

John Carradine (Dr. Rynning); Robert Dix (Colonel Manning);
Vicki Volante (Valerie); Joey Benson (Willy); Jennifer Bishop (Lian

Vicki Volante, Robert Dix and John Carradine in Horror of the Blood
Monsters (1971).

Malian); Bruce Powers (Bryce); Fred Meyers (Bob Scott); Britt Se-
mand (Linda).

The Earth is invaded by a vampire colony from outer space
and soon a wave of killings sweeps the world. It almost causes the
destruction of the human race. Meanwhile, scientist Dr. Rynning
(John Carradine) and his crew (Robert Dix and Vicki Volante) blast
off in a rocket to the "Spectrum" galaxy, where they hope to find
the origin of the vampire cult and learn how to destroy it. On a prehistoric planet they find an atmosphere of poisonous "chromatic radiation" and a world infested with such oddities as snake people, bat-
men, claw demons, animalistic cave dwellers, and more of the vampires who have invaded the Earth. After doing battle with these
overwhelming forces, the scientists discover a way to combat the
blood-suckers. The group returns to Earth and the vampires are
promptly exterminated.

Movies like this were definitely not meant to be seen by elit-
ists. The New York Times was repulsed by the entry and warned its
readers, "Horror of the Blood Monsters is a dull, excruciating and
unfrightening little science-fiction flapjack that looks and smells like
a piece of green cheese." A more appropriate response was offered
by Robert L. Jerome in Cinefantastique: "What is actually interesting about a very minor motion picture like this one is the amount of
effort exhibited by those who pasted it together out of bits and pieces
of other horror and outer-space films." Among the stock footage
employed were bits from One Million B.C. (1940) and Unknown Island
(1948).

Scenes of the prehistoric planet were lensed (in the Philippines
and Hollywood) in various pastel shades as in The Angry Red Planet.
The movie had more release titles than plot. It is also known as
Creatures of the Red Planet / Flesh Creatures of the Red Planet /
The Flesh Creatures. TV title: Vampire Men of the Lost Planet.

For the record, John Carradine gave an uncontrolled, zombie-
like performance as the chief scientist/explorer.

THE HOUSE AT THE END OF THE WORLD see DIE, MONSTER,
DIE

THE HUMAN DUPLICATORS (Allied Artists, 1965) C-82 min.

Executive producer, Lawrence Woolner; producers, Hugo Grimaldi and Arthur C. Pierce; director, Grimaldi; screenplay, Pierce;
music director, Gordon Zahler; art director, Paul Sylos; camera,
Monroe Askins; editor, Donald Wolf.

George Nader (Glenn Martin); Barbara Nichols (Gale Wilson);
George Macready (Professor Dornheimer); Dolores Faith (Lisa); Rich-
ard Kiel (Kolos); Richard Arlen (Intelligence Agency Head); Hugh
Beaumont (Austin Welles); and Tommy Leonetti and Lonnie Sattin.

Kolos (Richard Kiel): a super-intelligent being from another
planet, arrives on earth. He plans to infiltrate and take over the

operation of Professor Dornheimer (George Macready), who has developed a production-line format for creating a race of androids (very
human-ish robots). Later, the National Intelligence Agency orders
agent Glenn Martin (George Nader) to investigate certain disappearances. He soon uncovers Kolos' plot and, using human technology
and resources, does away with the outer space invader.

The Human Duplicators was financed by both an American
company (Woolner Brothers) and an Italian firm (Independenti Region-
ali). Despite a low budget the feature showcases a sturdy cast of
players, most of whom had headlined many a genre B effort.
Regarding this production, William Johnson wrote in Focus on
the Science Fiction Film (1972), "There was now a readiness to use
concepts and situations which might baffle spectators not already familiar with SF; some films, indeed, such as The Human Duplicators
and The Time Travelers [q. v.] were crammed with so many
disparate ideas that even the filmmakers could not digest them."

This film was issued at the height of the James Bond spy picture craze. Since George Nader, the hero of many a European
cheapie espionage flick, was a special agent in The Human Duplicators, the spy motif was accented in the title of this entry when it
was shown in Europe. There it was known as Spaziale K 1 (Special
Agent K 1).

I MARRIED A MONSTER FROM OUTER SPACE (Paramount, 1958)
78 min.

Producer/director, Gene Fowler, Jr.; screenplay, Louis Vit-
tes; assistant director, William Mull; art directors, Hal Pereira and
Henry Bumstead; makeup, Charles Gemora; sound, Phil Wisdom; special camera effects, John P. Fulton; camera, Haskell Boggs; editor,
George Tomasini.

Tom Tryon (Bill Farrell); Gloria Talbott (Marge Farrell); Ken
Lynch (Dr. Wayne); John Eldredge (Collins); Valerie Allen (Francine
the B Girl); Maxie Rosenbloom (Grady the Bartender); Alan Dexter
(Sam Benson); Jean Carson (Helen); Peter Baldwin (Swanson); Robert
Ivers (Harry); Chuck Wassil (Ted); Ty Hungerford (Mac); James Anderson (Weldon); Jack Orrison (Schultz); Steve London (Charles Mason).

This motion picture is shackled with perhaps the ultimate in
exploitation titles. But it proved to be anything but a tacky dud. It
was (and is) a delightful combination of horror and science fiction,
and is very well made. It is almost in the same league as Invasion
of the Body Snatchers. As Variety confirmed, "Technical credits
all rate highly.... Imaginative sci-fi ... given class production."
On the night of his bachelor party, Bill Farrell (Tom Tryon)
spots a corpse in the roadway. He stops to investigate and the next
day he is late for his wedding to Marge (Gloria Talbott). When he
does arrive at the festivities, he is cold and distant. On their honeymoon Marge notices some peculiar difference in the man she
thought she knew. When they return home several strange events
occur which arouse her suspicions; animals are afraid of this man

who was formerly an animal lover, for example. One night Marge follows her husband into a wooded area and sees him change into a monstrous creature.
  She attempts to contact the F.B.I., the local police, one-time friends; but no one will help. She finally confronts Bill with what she knows. He calmly tells her he is from a planet where all women have died and that he and his ilk have come to Earth for the purpose of procreation. Horrified, Marge goes to Dr. Wayne (Ken Lynch) for help and he rounds up all the recent fathers in the area. Back at the space craft, Marge and Dr. Wayne discover that the real counterparts of the fascimile husbands are wired to transmitters. When the circuits are yanked apart, the monsters disintegrate into a jelly-ish substance. The real humans are revived and prove to be all right.
  In Science Fiction in the Cinema (1970) John Baxter judges this as "a work of more than usual brilliance."

IDO ZERO DIASAKUSEN (Toho, 1969) C-106 min.

  Director, Inoshiro Honda; story, Ted Sherdeman; screenplay, Sherdeman and Shinichi Sekizawa; art director, Takeo Kita; music, Akira Ifukube; special effects, Eliji Tsuburaya; camera, Taiichi Kankura.
  Joseph Cotten (Captain); Cesar Romero (Malic); Richard Jaeckel (Perry); Patricia Medina (Lucretia); Linda Haynes (Anne); Akira

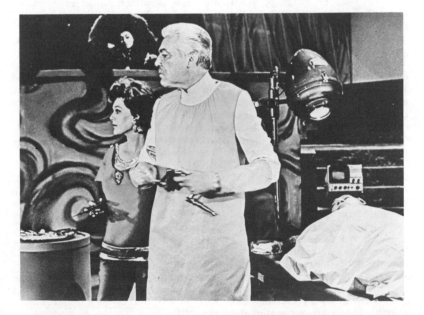

Patricia Medina and Cesar Romero in Ido Zero Diasakusen (1969).

Takarada (Ken); Masumi Okada (Mason); Hikaru Kuroki (Kroiga).

    After several years of dealing with Godzilla, Gamera, Mothra,
etc., Toho of Tokyo produced an adult-oriented sci-fi feature called
Ido Zero Diasakusen. (It was released in the U.S. as Latitude Zero.)
The combination of interesting special effects, a Jules Verne-type
plot, and a cast headed by "name" players gave the production an international appeal.
    The title referred to a scientific city located eleven miles be-
low the Pacific Ocean, where a group of world-renowned scientists
have gathered to work for the betterment of mankind. Malic (Cesar
Romero), however, is a madman who wants to destroy the futuristic
city in an effort to conquer the world. From his undersea craft he
creates a variety of problems for the citadel before he is finally
eliminated.
    Ted Sherdeman, the author of Them (q. v.), co-scripted this
Japanese-American co-production. The performances were rather
stilted but there was a host of visual stimulants for diversion (e. g.,
futuristic ships and machinery, death-rays, mutants, a flying lion-
vulture, and bat-like beasts). John R. Duvoli, in Cinefantastique,
summed up this programmer: "it's fun if taken as camp science fiction. "

IKARIA XB-1 (Czechoslovakian, 1963) C-81 min.

    Producer, Rudolph Wohl; director, Jindrich Polak; screenplay,
Pavel Juracek and Polak; art director, Jan Zazvorka; camera, Jan
Kalis; editor, Josef Dobricovsky.
    With: Zdenek Stepanek, Radovan Lakavsy, and Dana Medricka.

    In the twenty-fifth century, some forty people leave their plan-
et aboard an ultra-modern space craft, heading for the "green world. "
They are full of hope, but fearful of the unknown. The film presents
a log of that journey, a day-to-day space odyssey. Along the way the
travelers encounter a derelict ship. A team boards it to find the
corpses of its crew and learns that the passengers had died hundred
of years before and have been floating in space ever since. The in-
vestigators also find live atomic weapons and are accidentally killed
by them. Along the journey a baby is born and another crew member faces an excruciating death after radiation exposure. Finally the
ship reaches "the green world" but runs into further difficulties. The
crew is saved by the new world's inhabitants.
    Made in Czechoslovakia as Ikarie XB-1 the film was that coun-
try's entry at the 1963 Trieste Science Fiction Film Festival. In
1964, shorn to 65 minutes, the widescreen film was issued in the U.S.
by American International as Voyage to the End of the Universe. The
inanely dubbed version did have a rather neat ending added. In the
American edition, as the ship's passengers glimpse the "green planet, " they see the Statue of Liberty.
    In an essay included in Focus on the Science Fiction Film
(1972), Dario Mogno stated the Czech film was "... a noteworthy
achievement in its own right. By avoiding the clichés of space

travel--which, paradoxically, consist of extraordinary events--[direc-
tor] Polak creates a truly mature and accomplished film. "

L'ILE MYSTERIEUSE   see   THE MYSTERIOUS ISLAND

THE ILLUSTRATED MAN (Warner Bros.-Seven Arts, 1969) C-103
min.

Producers, Howard B. Kreitsek and Ted Mann; director, Jack
Smight; based on the book of the same title, including three short
stories: "The Veldt, " "The Long Rain" and "The Last Night of the
World" by Ray Bradbury; screenplay, Kreitsek; art director, Joel
Schiller; set decorator, Marvin March; visual arts consultant, Rich-
ard Sylbert; skin illustrations designer, James E. Reynolds; dog

Claire Bloom and Rod Steiger in The Illustrated Man (1969).

trainer, Frank Weatherwax; costumes, Anthea Sylbert; assistant director, Terry Nelson; sound, Francis E. Stahl; special effects, Ralph
Webb; camera, Philip Lathrop; editor, Archie Marshek.
     Rod Steiger (Carl); Claire Bloom (Felicia); Robert Drivas (Wil-
lie); Don Dubbins (Pickard); Jason Evers (Simmons); Tim Weldon
(John); Christie Matchett (Anna).

     During the height of Rod Steiger's macho period, he and his
distinguished then-wife co-starred in this well-mounted picture. Its
ambitions were too pretentious, its entertainment values too limited.
The box-office response was accordingly sparse.
     "Each person who tries to see beyond his own time must face
questions for which there are no absolute answers." Narrator Bloom
delivers this sermon at the film's finale, trying vainly to tie-up the
three-part "fantasy." Carl (Steiger) is the mysterious Illustrated Man,
a circus roustabout who has been seduced by a lovely tattoo artist
(Bloom). She has transformed his body into a mural, full of various
magical images, and has then disappeared. Any stranger who stares
for too long at the one blank spot on Carl's left shoulder is subjected
to bizarre glimpses into the future. Such is the premise which sets
the scene for young drifter Willie (Robert Drivas) who has set out in
1933 for California.
     Story number one focuses on a jungle playground for children;
it gains a life form of its own and devours the youngsters and, later,
their parents. Story number two tells of an endless, suffocating
downpour of rain from which Carl finds relief and sanctuary in the
Sun Dome. The third tale, set in the fortieth century, takes place
on the evening before doomsday, when all adults in the world vow to
poison their children to save them from the impending holocaust.
     The critical abuse tossed at this picture was justified. "The
Illustrated Man should have been a treat, but it was just a pretentious
comic strip with some interesting performances, and too much fancy
camera work and editing" (Newsday). Even more to the point was
Judith Crist in New York magazine, who noted: "it is only our curiosity and interest in Ray Bradbury that is being exploited ... [here]. ...
The fantasies are not only pointless but both muddled and maudlin."
William Wolf (Cue magazine) affirmed, "I can keep an open mind for
wild science fiction plots, but nobody can make me see the future by
gazing at Rod Steiger's tattooed rump, in fact, I don't see any future
at all for this pretentious mumbo-jumbo." Summing up the crux of
the film's many problems was Hollis Alpert (Saturday Review): "To
believe in the surreal, one must believe it is real."

THE IMMORTAL (ABC-TV, 1969) C-75 min.

     Producer, Lou Morheim; director, Joseph Sargent; based on
the novel The Immortals by James Gunn; teleplay, Robert Specht;
music, Dominic Frontiere; music supervisor, Leith Stevens; art directors, Bill Ross and William L. Campbell; camera, Howard
Schwartz; editor, David Wages.
     Christopher George (Ben Richards); Carol Lynley (Sylvia Cart-
wright), Barry Sullivan (Jordan Braddock); Jessica Walter (Janet

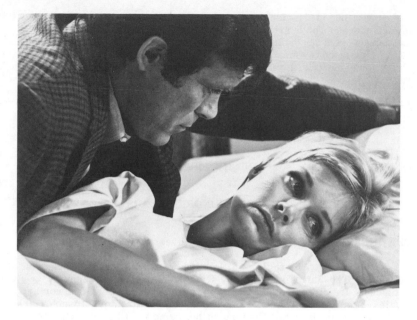

Christopher George and Carol Lynley in The Immortal (1969).

Braddock); Ralph Bellamy (Dr. Pearce); Vincent Beck (Locke); Marvin Silbersher (Doctor).

This telefeature was produced for "The ABC Movie of the Week" during the 1969-70 video season. It proved so agreeable that it became a series the following fall. Unfortunately the continuing program could not live up to the promise of the pilot and its "immortality" lasted only thirteen weeks.

This Paramount production starred Christopher George as an over-forty auto tester/race driver named Ben Richards who donates several pints of blood to his aged employer, Jordan Braddock (Barry Sullivan), in order to save his life. Not only does Braddock survive; he recovers fully and becomes more youthful. Ben's blood is tested and it proves to be immune to disease and the aging process. The millionaire boss immediately abducts the donor and keeps him in seclusion, rejuvenating himself from the victim's blood. This turn of events enrages the rich man's young wife (Jessica Walter), who wants him dead in order to obtain his fortune. Eventually the prisoner does escape, briefly visiting his mistress (Carol Lynley), whom he must leave in order to protect her life. He then goes in search of his long-lost brother, who may also have the same type of blood he has. All the while he is being pursued by the millionaire who must have his blood to remain alive.

Writing in Cinefantastique, Robert L. Jerome said that the
telefeature has "both artistic merit and pilot potential" and that it is
an "unusual and absorbing science fiction offering." TV Guide's
Judith Crist, however, thought differently: "It's the sort of stuff that
gives some mortals a vampire syndrome and some of us just a big
yawn."

When The Immortal became an ABC-TV series in the fall of
1970, Christopher George repeated the role of Ben Richards, but the
millionaire was now portrayed by David Brian. Carol Lynley returned for only one episode.

IN THE YEAR 2000 see ONE HUNDRED YEARS AFTER

IN THE YEAR 2014 see ONE HUNDRED YEARS AFTER

THE INCREDIBLE SHRINKING MAN (Universal, 1957) 81 min.

Producer, Albert Zugsmith; director, Jack Arnold; based on
the story "The Shrinking Man" by Richard Matheson; screenplay,
Matheson; art directors, Alexander Golitzen and Robert Clatworthy;
music, Fred Carling and E. Lawrence; music director, Joseph Ger-
shenson; special effects, Clifford Stine; camera, Ellis W. Carter;
editor, Al Joseph.
Grant Williams (Scott Carey); Randy Stuart (Louise Carey);
April Kent (Clarice); Paul Langton (Charlie Carey); Raymond Bailey
(Dr. Thomas Silver); Billy Curtis (Midget); and: Frank Scannell,
Diana Darrin, and William Schallert.

In the science fiction genre, motion pictures tend to be quite
good or very bad; there seems to be little middle ground. This is
especially true of the many entries issued in the Fifties. Even the
top directors and producers in the area had their professional ups
and downs, especially Jack Arnold who put out such polar contrasts
as It Came from Outer Space and Monster on Campus (both q.v.).
He also made the popular classic, The Incredible Shrinking Man, which
provided fans with a glimpse of what is perhaps mankind's worst
fear, that of eventual nothingness.
Grant Williams stars as Scott Carey, who is covered with
strange clinging particles from a cloud while sunbathing. Six months
later he begins to shrink. He becomes smaller, a little at first, until he is reduced to three feet in height. Soon he is a medical marvel and a public curiosity. Naturally, as he grows more compact he
becomes increasingly fearful. Finally, he is only a few inches tall.
When his cat breaks into the room where he is staying and tries to
devour him, he escapes. His wife (April Kent) thinks he has died.
Scott hides in the basement, a place which has taken on the trappings
of a jungle for him. He nearly drowns when his water heater springs
a leak, he is attacked by a spider (which is a giant to him), and he
nearly dies trying to loosen a bit of cheese from a mousetrap in order
to subsist. Finally he goes into the garden. There he becomes so

Grant Williams (and a pair of scissors) in The Incredible Shrinking Man (1957).

small that he merges with infinity. "To God there is no zero. I still exist," are his last words.

Clifford Stine's special effects and Jack Arnold's sensitive direction made this movie the well-rounded success it was. Universal hoped for a different ending, with the "hero" starting to grow again. But Arnold held fast to his original finale. The New York Times called it a "worthwhile, low-budget, science-fiction exercise." John Baxter, in Science Fiction in the Cinema (1970), observed that it is "a fantasy that for intelligence and sophistication has few equals ... this film is the finest Arnold made and arguably the peak of sf film in its long history."

A sequel, The Fantastic Little Girl, was planned but never made.

THE INCREDIBLE TWO-HEADED TRANSPLANT (American International, 1971) C-88 min.

Executive producer, Nicholas Wowchuk; producer, John Lawrence; co-producer, Wolodymyr Kowal; associate producers, Arthur N. Gilbert and Alvin L. Fast; director, Anthony Lanza; screenplay, James Gordon White and Lawrence; music composer/conductor, John Barber; orchestrator, William S. Baker; song, John Hill and Barnabus Hill; special makeup and head design, Barry Noble; sound, George Eddy; camera, Jack Steely, Glen Gano, and Paul Hipp; editor, Lanza.

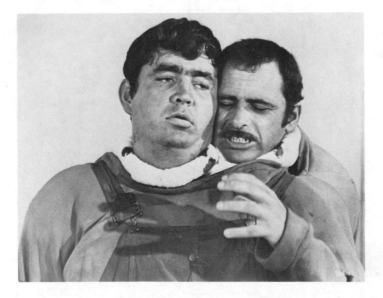

John Bloom and Albert Cole in The Incredible Two-Headed Transplant (1971).

Bruce Dern (Roger); Pat Priest (Linda); Casey Kasem (Ken); Albert Cole (Cass); John Bloom (Danny); Berry Kroeger (Max); Larry Vincent (Andrew); Jack Lester (Sheriff); Jerry Patterson (Deputy); Darlene Duralia (Miss Pierce); Ray Thorn, Donald Brody, and Mary Ellen Clawsen (Motorcyclists); Bill Collins and Jack English (Highway Patrolmen); Laura Lanza and Carolyn Gilbert (Nurses); Leslie Cole (Danny - as a Young Boy).

"Dreary," said Variety. " ... It gave me a headache," said the New York Daily News. These were some of the slurs leveled at this exploitation offering, made on a $300,000 budget by Mutual General Productions.

Bruce Dern plays Roger, an ever-twitching mad scientist who grafts the head of an escaped killer onto the body of a huge hulking idiot in the laboratory of his monkey compound/ranch. There is some poetic justice to the act, for the victim is the man who had abducted and raped Roger's wife (Pat Priest--in real life, daughter of one-time Secretary of the Treasury, Ivy Baker Priest). Naturally the creation escapes and, with its two ugly heads, horrifies the local residents. Eventually both the monster and the doctor meet their doom but not before the amateurish production has sickened its audience.

The plotline of two heads on a human body was employed to better advantage by American International in The Thing with Two Heads (q.v.). The Japanese also did better with The Manster (1960), in which a man grows another head and eventually splits in two.

THE INDESTRUCTIBLE MAN (Allied Artists, 1956) 70 min.

Producer/ director, Jack Pollexfen; screenplay, Sue Bradford and Vy Russell; art director, Ted Holsopple; music director, Albert Glasser; camera, John Russell, Jr.; editor, Fred Fettshan, Jr.

Lon Chaney (The Butcher); Marian Carr (Eva Martin); Robert Shayne (Professor Bradshaw); Ross Elliott (Paul Lowe); Kenneth Terrell (Joe Marcellia); Marvin Ellis (Squeamy Ellis); Stuart Randall (Police Captain); Casey Adams (Chasen).

Lon Chaney starred as The Butcher, the title character, which closely resembles his earlier feature, Man-Made Monster (1941). Here The Butcher is sent to the gas chamber at San Quentin Prison for several murders. Later, he is brought back to life, minus his vocal cords, by an unethical scientist (Robert Shayne). The revived killer soon escapes and goes on a murderous rampage, taking revenge on those who sent him to his death. In the standard crime-does-not-pay finale in Los Angeles, he is eventually killed by the law.

Had the film not opted for the obvious horror plotline formula, one used in several Boris Karloff features of the late Thirties and early Forties, it might have delved into new territory.

As a cinema footnote, in the "Spark of Life" segment of the terrible Dr. Terror's Gallery of Horror (1967), Chaney plays a scientist who brings an electrocuted killer back to life, only to become the man's next victim.

INTERNATIONAL HOUSE (Paramount, 1933) 70 min.

Director, Edward Sutherland; story, Neil Brent and Louis E.
Heifetz; screenplay, Francis Martin and Walter De Leon; songs,
Ralph Rainger and Leo Robin; camera, Ernest Haller.
Peggy Hopkins Joyce (Herself); W. C. Fields (Professor
Quail); Stuart Erwin (Tommy Nash); Sari Maritza (Carol Fortescue);
George Burns (Dr. Burns); Gracie Allen (Nurse Allen); Bela Lugosi
(General Petronovich); Edmund Breese (Dr. Wong); Lumsden Hare
(Sir Mortimer Fortescue); Franklin Pangborn (Hotel Manager); Har-
rison Greene (Herr von Baden); Sterling Holloway (Bit); Rudy Vallee,
Cab Calloway, Baby Rose Marie, Stoopnagle & Budd (Guest Artists).

Sci-fi was utilized in the madcap International House only in
the introduction of the television set, then a very advanced scientific
gimmick. To filmgoers of the day it seemed as farfetched a commercial possibility as Flash Gordon's space travels. The TV re-
ceiver was used as the main gimmick in the comedy.
The zany cast included Franklin Pangborn as a rather stiff
manager of the Chinese Hotel, George Burns as the house doctor, and
Gracie Allen as his addled assistant. On the way from Shanghai to
Wu-Wu (the hotel's location) a young American (Stuart Erwin) becomes
involved with society's darling, Peggy Hopkins Joyce. At the hotel
is Dr. Wong (Edmund Breese), the inventor of TV, who has his machine on display. The top bidder for the invention is a Russian (Bela
Lugosi), one of Joyce's ex-husbands. Onto the scene comes Professor Quail (W. C. Fields). He too wants to buy the TV and the scene
is set for intrigue and insanity.
A hilariously funny film, International House was a bit futuristic not only for the TV; the building itself was more than ultra-modern and the film had a breezy air of suspended reality.

INVADERS FROM MARS (Twentieth Century-Fox, 1953) C-78 min.

Producer, Edward L. Alperson; director, William Cameron
Menzies; screenplay, Richard Blake; art director, Boris Leven; pro-
duction designer, Menzies; music, Raoul Kraushaar; special effects,
Jack Cosgrove; makeup, Gene Hibbs and Anatole Robbins; camera,
John Seitz; editor, Arthur Roberts.
Helena Carter (Dr. Pat Blake); Arthur Franz (Dr. Stuart Kel-
ston); Jimmy Hunt (David MacLean); Leif Erickson (George MacLean);
Hillary Brooke (Mary MacLean); Morris Ankrum (Colonel Fielding);
Max Wagner (Sergeant Rinaldi); Janine Perreau (Kathy Wilson); and:
Bill Phipps, Milburn Stone, and John Eldridge.

Invaders from Mars is one of those tantalizing gems in the
sci-film film genre. When it surfaces occasionally on TV, the viewer ultimately wishes the film could be seen in its original version.
It was shot in 3-D and Cinecolor, but during its release the picture
was so spliced and re-edited that a compact original print probably
does not exist anymore. In Britain, the finale--the crux of the plot--
was deleted.

Morris Ankrum, William Phipps and Arthur Franz in <u>Invaders from</u>
<u>Mars</u> (1953).

In this, his final motion picture, director/production designer
William Cameron Menzies (who worked on <u>Chandu the Magician</u> and
<u>Things to Come</u>, both q.v.) allegedly co-authored the script. The
plot tells of David (Jimmy Hunt), a small boy who awakens one night
to observe a flying saucer land and bury itself in a hillside. The
next morning he tells everyone, from his parents (Leif Erickson and
Hillary Brooke) to the police, about the sighting, but no one believes
him. It is not long before David realizes that most people have been
taken over by the invaders (from Mars) and that control-crystals
have been implanted in their brains. Finally a doctor (Helena Carter) begins to believe David after other sightings have been confirmed.
Eventually the Martian lair is discovered, with the giant Martians
actually the slave of a glob-like brain head. When everything seems
at its worst in the battle with the Martians, David awakes. It has
all been a dream. Then he looks out the window and sees the Martian ship landing.
        Menzies constructed the film as a dream-like fantasy, with
everything a bit oversized, sterile, and out of focus with reality.
"... It stands as one of the most brilliantly conceived fantasy films
of the 1950s," decided Jim Wnoroski in <u>Photon</u> magazine.

INVASION EARTH 2150 A.D.   see   DALEKS--INVASION EARTH
2150 A.D.

INVASION FROM THE MOON   see   MUTINY IN OUTER SPACE

INVASION OF MARS   see   THE ANGRY RED PLANET

INVASION OF PLANET X   see   KAIJU DAISENSO

INVASION OF THE ANIMAL PEOPLE (Swedish/U.S. - Favorite
Films, 1962) 73 min.

Producer, Bertil Jernberg; art director, Nils Milsson; cam-
era, Hilding Bladh; English-language version: producer, Jerry War-
ren; director, Virgil Vogel and Warren; screenplay, Arthur C.
Pierce; music Allan Johannson and Harry Arnold.
With: Bengt Blomgren and Ake Grönberg.
English-language version: John Carradine (Dr. Frederick
Wilson); Barbara Wilson (Diane Wilson); Robert Burton (Eric Eng-
strom); and Stan Gester and Jack Haffner.
A. k. a. Space Invasion from Lapland / Horror in the Midnight
Sun / Terror in the Midnight Sun.

Shot in Lapland in 1960, this feature was re-edited in 1962
(down to 55 minutes) with new footage featuring John Carradine as
both a performer and narrator inserted.
Diane Wilson (Barbara Wilson) is discovered by the police;
she is in an unexplainable state of shock. She is sent to Sweden
with her geologist uncle (Carradine) to recuperate. While they are
there a large meteor falls on a nearby mountain and she joins her
uncle's expedition to the site. They find that the meteor was actually a space craft inhabited by aliens who control a stone-age giant.
The latter causes a lot of problems, destroying whole towns, until
the geologist puts a stop to it and the alien invasion.
Understandably this bottom-of-the-barrel offering had few U.S.
playdates.

INVASION OF THE BODY SNATCHERS (Allied Artists, 1956) 80 min.

Producer, Walter Wanger; director, Don Siegel; based on the
novel by Jack Finney; screenplay, Daniel Mainwaring and (uncredited)
Sam Peckinpah; art director, Edward Haworth; music, Carmen Drag-
on; special effects, Milt Rice; camera, Ellsworth Fredericks; editor,
Robert S. Eisen.
Kevin McCarthy (Dr. Miles Bennell); Dana Wynter (Becky
Driscoll); Larry Gates (Dr. Dan Kaufman); Carolyn Jones (Theodora
Velichec); King Donovan (Jack Velichec); Ralph Dumke (Nick Grivett);
Jean Willes (Sally); Virginia Christine (Wilma Lentz); Tom Fadden
(Ira Lentz); Beatrice Maude (Gradman Grimaldi); Bobby Clark (Jimmy
Grimaldi); Sam Peckinpah (Charlie Buckholtz); Richard Deacon (Dr.
Harvey Bassett); Whit Bissell (Dr. Hill).
One of the richest classics of the sci-fi film category is Don

Dana Wynter, King Donovan, Carolyn Jones and Kevin McCarthy in
Invasion of the Body Snatchers (1956).

Siegel's Invasion of the Body Snatchers. The picture was lensed in
very short order, after some ten days' rehearsal. The budget allowed
few re-takes. Siegel originally wanted the movie to have a humorous
quality but producer Walter Wanger believed this would lessen the
impact of the climax. Most of the very light humor that crept into
the storyline was deleted from the release print. Also the role of
the psychiatrist (Larry Gates) was greatly reduced; in the novel (first
appearing in Collier's magazine) the doctor had a much larger role
to play.
        A near hysterical doctor (Kevin McCarthy) begs authorities to
listen to his warning that his small California home town of Santa
Mira has been overwhelmed by aliens who have assumed the bodies of
the townpeople. His bizarre story is recounted through flashback.
        Returning home after a medical convention, his nurse (Jean
Willes) tells him that some kind of hysteria had briefly overtaken
the populace during his absence, but that everything now seemed to
have settled down. But Miles Bennell (McCarthy) does notice a
change in several people: they are too cool, too passive. Miles and
his one-time fiancée Becky Driscoll (Dana Wynter) visit friends (King
Donovan and Carolyn Jones) and in their greenhouse they find a pod-
shaped object which is turning into a likeness of Jack Velichec (Donovan). Eventually Miles and Becky realize that these pods have come
from outer space, and that they take on the form of a person, and

then take over the victim completely while he/she sleeps.   After all
their acquaintances have become pod-controlled, Miles and Becky
pretend to have been converted also.   But when she cries out as a
dog is killed, the restructured locals discover the charade and give
chase.   Becky makes the mistake of falling asleep and soon she is
lost to the pod-authority.   Miles, now hysterical, runs from her and
is taken into custody as a highway drunk.   In Los Angeles he again
relates his story, but no one believes him until a truckload of the
strange pods is found in a freeway wreck.   The F.B.I. is called in
and Miles can finally hope that the invasion may be stopped.   (Originally the film was to end earlier in the plotline, with the frightened
Miles screaming at passing cars--and ultimately into the camera's
eye, for direct audience identification--"You're in danger! ... They're
here already! ... You're next!   You're next...!")

     In Cinema of the Fantastic (1972), authors Chris Steinbrunner
and Burt Goldblatt comment, "... the film is an intensely realistic
drama of everyday people defending everyday values against inhuman
invasion, done with a great deal of human feeling.   Indeed it is the
humanity of the drama that is its greatest strength, and it is this,
too, that makes the story play so well."

INVASION OF THE SAUCER MEN (American International, 1957) 68
min.

     Executive producer, Samuel Z. Arkoff; producer, James H.

From Invasion of the Saucer Men (1957).

Nicholson and Robert Gurney, Jr.; director, Edward L. Cahn; based
on the story "The Cosmic Frame" by Paul W. Fairman; screenplay,
R. Gurney, Jr. and Al Martin; art director, Don Ament; makeup,
Carlie Taylor and Paul Blaisdell; music, Ronald Stein; special effects,
P. Blaisdell and Howard A. Anderson; camera, Frederick E. West;
editors, Ronald Sinclair and Charles Gross, Jr.

Steve Terrell (Johnny); Gloria Castillo (Joan); Frank Gorshin
(Joe); Raymond Hatton (Larkin); Lyn Osborn (Art); Russ Bender (Doc-
tor); Douglas Henderson (Lieutenant Wilkins); Sam Buffington (Colonel);
Jason Johnson (Detective); Bob Einer (Soda Jerk).

Made the year after Invasion of the Body Snatchers (q. v.),
this Roger Corman film not only borrowed a similar title, but also
employed the outer space invasion theme. This time, however, the
usurpers are nasty-looking little creatures with large cabbage heads
and eyes, and long, vein-covered fingers. These tiny invaders (three-
foot-high midgets) also appear in How to Make a Monster (1958).

The aliens make their Earth landing in the town of Hicksville
and disturb the teenagers in lovers' lane in the process. No one,
except two con artists (Frank Gorshin and Lyn Osborn) realizes that
there has been invasion. Later, two young lovers (Steve Terrell and
Gloria Castillo) drive home from their parking spot one night and accidentally hit one of the creatures. While the couple rush to find the
police, the interrupted invader disconnects his hand and has it crawl
over and slash the tires. A disgruntled old farmer (Raymond Hatton)
scares off the invaders with a pitchfork, thinking they are only more
bothersome youngsters. It is the teenagers who save the day. They
discover the aliens have no tolerance for light. They all crowd their
jalopies together and beam the headlights on the invaders, dissolving
them before they can return to the sanctuary of their space craft.

Director Edward L. Cahn gave this effort a tongue-in-cheek
quality. The horrors and scares are few and far between; but the
comedy, which does not always work, is always present. In essence,
this picture is a satire on all creature invasions from outer space,
a format that at one point threatened to engulf the trend-conscious
film industry.

In England the film was called Hell Creatures. Though no
classic, the movie is a joy when compared to its ghastly remake,
The Eye Creatures (q. v.).

INVISIBLE INVADERS (United Artists, 1959) 67 min.

Producer, Robert E. Kent; director, Edward L. Cahn; screen-
play, Samuel Newman; art director, William Glasgow; set decorator,
Morris Hoffman; makeup, Phil Scheer; assistant director, Herbert S.
Greene; costumes, Einar Bourman and Sabine Manella; sound, Al
Overton; camera, Maury Gertsman; editor, Grant Whytock.

John Agar (Major Bruce Jay); Jean Byron (Phyllis Penner);
Robert Hutton (Dr. John LaMont); Philip Tonge (Dr. Adam Penner);
John Carradine (Dr. Karol Noymann); Hal Torey (The Farmer); Eden
Hartford (WAAF Secretary); Jack Kenney (Cab Driver); Paul Langton
(General Stone); Don Kennedy (Pilot); Chuck Niles (Hockey Game
Announcer).

Nuclear physicist Dr. Karol Noymann (Carradine) is killed in a laboratory explosion. But soon thereafter his revitalized body reappears to his associate, Dr. Adam Penner (Philip Tonge). The once-dead scientist warns that invisible invaders from the Moon will take over the corpses of the recent dead and destroy mankind unless the Earth capitulates within twenty-four hours. Naturally the world refuses to surrender and terrible mass destruction begins around the globe. Finally, a group of isolated scientists headed by Major Bruce Jay (John Agar) devises a scheme to destroy the zombie-like corpses-- their method involved high-frequency sound waves.

A definite precursor of the later Night of the Living Dead, (q. v.), this low-keyed quickie employed a massive amount of stock footage and lost its credibility quotient rather promptly.

THE INVISIBLE RAY (Universal, 1936) 82 min.

Producer, Edmund Grainger; director, Lambert Hillyer; story, Howard Higgins and Douglas Hodges; screenplay, John Colton; art director, Albert D'Agostino; music director, Franz Waxman; special camera effects, John P. Fulton; camera, George Robinson; editor, Bernard Burton.

Boris Karloff (Dr. Janos Rukh); Bela Lugosi (Dr. Benet); Frances Drake (Diane Rukh); Frank Lawton (Ronald Drake); Walter Kingsford (Sir Francis Stevens); Beulah Bondi (Lady Arabella Stevens); Violet Kemble Cooper (Mother Rukh); Nydia Westman (Briggs);

Bela Lugosi and Boris Karloff in The Invisible Ray (1936).

Danell Haines (Headman).

Dr. Janos Rukh (Boris Karloff) develops a telescope which
proves that ages ago a meteorite landed in Africa, containing something far more powerful than radium. With his friend and colleague
Dr. Benet (Bela Lugosi), Rukh leads an expedition into the Mountains
of the Moon where he unearths "Radium X" in a volcano. Unfortunately he becomes contaminated by the substance, which causes anything he touches to die. Benet develops a temporary antidote for his
cohort. But Rukh later becomes consumed with jealousy, believing
his fellow scientists have turned his findings over to the Scientific
Congress. In revenge, he murders several of them, including Benet.
He also assumes his young wife (Frances Drake) is having an affair
with his assistant (Frank Lawton). After he attempts, unsuccessfully, to kill her, his mother (Violet Kemble Cooper) destroys the antidote. Dr. Rukh soon generates into a ball of fire and jumps to his
death from a window ledge.

This was still another teaming of Karloff and Lugosi, although
most claim Karloff enjoyed the better and larger role. But his portrayal of Rukh was a cold, dispassionate one in contrast to the re-
strained and human scientist played by Lugosi. John P. Fulton's
special effects were the film's highlight, especially his recreation of
the heavens (millions of years ago) and the scenes where Rukh discovers the super-radium in the volcano. (These sequences would be
lifted intact for The Phantom Creeps, a 1939 serial featuring Lugosi.)
A few standing sets from Flash Gordon (q. v.) were incorporated into
the picture, and the keen observer can spot stock footage of Kenneth
Strickfaden's creation machines from Frankenstein (q. v.).
"It isn't blood-curdling to the point achieved in some Hollywood efforts, but it is different and fairly entertaining," stated
Variety.

A printed prologue to the film announced on the screen, "That
which you are now to see is a theory whispered in the cloisters of
science. Tomorrow these theories may startle the universe as a
fact." The filmmakers were not far off; some of what is projected
as "fancy" in this film has become reality.

ISLAND OF LOST SOULS (Paramount, 1932) 72 min.

Director, Erle C. Kenton; based on the novel The Island of
Dr. Moreau by H. G. Wells; screenplay, Waldemar Young and Philip
Wylie; camera, Karl Struss.

Charles Laughton (Dr. Moreau); Richard Arlen (Edward Park-
er); Leila Hyams (Ruth Walker); Bela Lugosi (Sayer of the Law);
Kathleen Burke (Lota); Arthur Hohl (Montgomery); Stanley Fields
(Captain Davies); Robert Kortman (Hogan); Tetsu Komai (M'Ling);
Hans Steinke (Ouran); Harry Ekezian (Gola); Rosemary Grimes (Sa-
moan Girl); Paul Hurst (Captain Donahue); George Irving (American
Consul); Alan Ladd, Joe Bonomo, Randolph Scott, John George, Larry
"Buster" Crabbe, and Duke York (Ape-Men).

This weird account of speeded-up evolution derived from H.G.

Charles Laughton in Island of Lost Souls (1932).

Wells' novel. Here Charles Laughton as Dr. Moreau played the ultimate in mad scientists: a cool, calculating god-like figure who attempts to change animals into men and then corral them as his
slaves. The picture hinted at far more than it showed, especially in
Moreau's relationship to the panther girl Lota (Kathleen Burke), whom
he wants to mate with sailor Edward Parker (Richard Arlen).
     Shipwrecked gob Parker is left at Moreau's island, where he
notes a strange animal-type native. Moreau makes him welcome.
As Parker waits for the next freighter to take him home, he begins
to find out that the natives are actually animals which the doctor has
transformed into men through operations. He also learns that the
locals are fearful of Moreau and his "House of Pain" where the experiments take place. Into the strange situation comes Lota, a native girl. She is Moreau's only female creation. The panther girl
is attracted to Parker and Moreau hopes to mate them. But then
Parker's fiancée Ruth Walker (Leila Hyams) arrives. There is an
immediate rivalry between the two women and Lota has one of the
ape-men attack Ruth. Later Moreau has one of his beast-slaves kill
the captain who brought Ruth to the island. The ape-men, having
tasted blood, want more and rebel against their master. Parker and
Ruth escape to the safety of a boat, but the doctor stands up to the

insurgents, threatening them with the House of Pain. Their leader,
the sayer of the law (Bela Lugosi), attacks Moreau and the latter is
dragged to the House of Pain, where the creatures begin to perform
ghastly surgery on him. A fire breaks out and the island is soon
engulfed.
        The film was exceptionally well-made. An atmosphere of hor-
ror and degeneracy pervaded its every frame. It was not for all
tastes. Many Midwestern states banned it from release, as did Great
Britain and New Zealand.
        In late 1976 American International began shooting a new ver-
sion of The Island of Dr. Moreau, part of the craze to cash in on
the renewed popularity of H. G. Wells' subjects. Burt Lancaster and
Michael York are the stars of the fresh edition.

ISLAND OF TERROR (Planet, 1966) C-90 min.

        Executive producers, Richard Gordon and Gerald A. Fernback;
producer, Tom Blakeley; director, Terence Cooper; screenplay, Ed-
ward Andrew Mann and Alan Ramsen; music composer/conductor,
Malcolm Lockyer; art director and special effects, John St. John
Earl; assistant, Michael Aldrechtson; assistant director, Don Weeks;
sound, Bob McPhee; electronic effects, Barry Gray; camera, Red
Wyer; editor, Thelma Connell.
        Peter Cushing (Dr. Stanley); Edward Judd (Dr. David West);
Carole Gray (Toni Merrill); Eddie Byrne (Dr. Landers); Sam Kydd
(Constable Harris); Niall MacGinnis (Mr. Campbell); James Caffrey
(Argyle); Liam Caffney (Bellows); Roger Heathcote (Dumley); Keith
Bell (Halsey); Shay Gorman (Morton); Peter Forbes Robertson (Dr.
Phillips); Richard Bidlake (Carson); Joyce Hemson (Mrs. Bellows);
Edward Ogden (Helicopter Pilot).

        In the mid-Sixties, Hammer Films' top director, Terence
Fisher, helmed a few features for a British studio called Planet. Island of Terror is one of the best of these. A taut suspense item,
it proved to be a superior example of the monster-created-by-man-
through-science pictures turned out in that decade.
        Dr. Stanley (Peter Cushing), with two colleagues (Edward Judd
and Eddie Byrne), arrives at a small island off the Irish coast. They
have come to investigate a body which has washed ashore, a body
without bone marrow. The visitors are shown around the island by
Dr. West's (Judd) fiancée (Carole Gray). Their tour includes a stop-
over at the laboratories of a group of doctors working on a cancer
cure. There they find everyone dead. They also encounter large
tentacled creatures called silicates, which attach themselves to the
human body and drain it of bone marrow. Dr. Stanley learns that
these terrible predators cannot be destroyed through ordinary means.
Splitting them in any way causes them to mutate into still more creatures.
        The islanders try to destroy the beasts, but nothing works.
Finally, one of the silicates dies after devouring a dog infected with
a radioactive chemical called Strontium- 90. The doctor gathers the
natives into the town hall and surrounds the building with Strontium-
90-infected cattle. The silicates devour the cattle and then come for

the humans. They die before they can complete their mission. As
the film ends, a Japanese scientist is shown discovering the same
formula which resulted in the creation of the earlier silicates.

    "Scientific explanations are vague, but the situation is accept-
able because much that surrounds it is believable.... It is too often
true that the monsters in these films are not as convincing as the
rest of the cast. In this case, the silicates are adequate, but they
move awkwardly in a series of jerks and boast a food-grabbing ten-
tacle that no one ever tried to cut off" (Variety).

ISLAND OF THE BURNING DAMNED see NIGHT OF THE BIG HEAT

ISLAND OF THE BURNING DOOMED see NIGHT OF THE BIG HEAT

IT CAME FROM BENEATH THE SEA (Columbia, 1955) 77 min.

    Executive producer, Sam Katzman; producer, Charles H.
Schneer; director, Robert Gordon; story, George Worthing Yates;
screenplay, Yates and Hal Smith; art director, Paul Palmentola; music director, Mischa Bakaleinikoff; special effects, Ray Harryhausen
and Jack Erickson; camera, Henry Freuluich; editor, Jerome Thoms.
    Kenneth Tobey (Pete Mathews); Faith Domergue (Lesley Joyce);

Kenneth Tobey, Faith Domergue and Donald Curtis in It Came from
Beneath the Sea (1955).

Donald Curtis (John Carter); Ian Keith (Admiral Burns); Harry Lauter
(Bill Nash); Captain R. Peterson (Captain Stacy); Dean Maddox, Jr.
(Adam Norman); Del Courtney (Robert Chase); Tol Avery (Navy In-
terne); Ray Storey (Reporter); Ed Fisher (McLoed); Jules Irving (King).

Jules Verne first used a giant octopus in his novel 20,000
Leagues Under the Sea (1870), and John Wayne even fought such a
beast of the deep in Reap the Wild Wind (1942). It remained for It
Came from Beneath the Sea, however, to present the giant octopus
as the crux of its narrative. The combination of this horrific creature and the delightful special effects of Ray Harryhausen made this
feature popular with audiences. The only sour note in the proceedings was that, as with many sci-films of the Fifties, it took a long
time for the title monster to appear on the celluloid scene.
The creature was a huge mutation which is initially spotted
in the middle of the Pacific Ocean near Great Mindanao Deep. Two
scientists (Donald Curtis and Faith Domergue) and a Navy man (Kenneth Tobey) are called in to combat the monstrosity. They are unable
to cope with it and the oversized octopus heads for San Francisco,
dismantles the Golden Gate Bridge and destroys much of the city.
Finally the Navy overcomes the watery terror.
It Came from Beneath the Sea was photographed in a week's
time in and around San Francisco, with a few days' work at Columbia's home lot. As in most genre films of the period, there was
an implicit message behind the action storyline: a warning against
the uncontrolled use of atomic testing (it was an H-bomb test which
surfaced the restructured monster from the ocean floor).
The Los Angeles Times kiddingly remarked, "The movies just
can't let the poor homely old octopus alone very long." Variety gave
a slightly more serious review: "The early effect is towards the documentary, since some good sea footage has been obtained and there
are a number of natural cast contributions by actual naval personnel."

IT CAME FROM OUTER SPACE (Universal, 1953) 80 min.

Producer, William Alland; director, Jack Arnold; based on the
screen treatment "The Meteor" by Ray Bradbury; screenplay, Harry
Essex; art directors, Bernard Herzbrun and Robert Boyle; music,
Herman Stein; music director, Joseph Gershenson; makeup, Bud West-
more; special camera effects, David S. Horsley; camera, Clifford
Stine; editor, Paul Weatherwax.
Richard Carlson (John Putnam); Barbara Rush (Ellen Fields);
Charles Drake (Sheriff Matt Warren); Joe Sawyer (Frank Daylon);
Russell Johnson (George); Kathleen Hughes (Jane); Dave Willock (Pete
Davis); Alan Dexter (Dave Spring); George Eldredge (Dr. Snell); Brad
Jackson (Dr. Snell's Assistant); Warren MacGregor (Toby); George
Selk (Tom); Edgar Dearing (Sam).

Director Jack Arnold made his genre debut with this slight
adaptation of Ray Bradbury's story. Shot in 3-D, the picture is visually impressive. What is most remembered about the movie is
that the desert locale becomes a character unto itself, a focal part

Richard Carlson and Barbara Rush in It Came from Outer Space
(1953).

of the story. In a switch from the usual format, the film played down any appearances by horrible creatures and, instead, promulgated a message: tolerance, even if the aliens are from beyond. Near the small Arizona town of Sand Rock, amateur astronomer John Putnam (Richard Carlson) sees a huge spaceship land and burrow into the ground. He then tries for days to persuade others of what he has seen. No one listens, until two repairmen disappear and then return in an altered form (they seem to be cold and devoid of feeling). The same occurrence happens to Putnam's schoolteacher fiancée (Barbara Rush) and eventually Putnam arouses the townpeople to arm against the invaders. He later confronts the aliens and is told that they are Ectoplasmic Xenomorphs traveling through the galaxies, and that they have stopped here only to make repairs. When they leave, the humans who have been tampered with will be returned to their original form. Putnam, who is allowed to see the creatures only briefly (as Moses was allowed to see God's back in the Bible), seals off their hiding place so that they will not be found.

"One of the virtues of It Came from Outer Space is that It is here by accident, and wants to go home," says Richard Hodgens in Focus on the Science Fiction Film (1972). Ed Naha notes in Horrors: From Screen to Scream (1975), "Interesting in that most of the monster-townie confrontations are seen from the point of view of the creature."

IT CONQUERED THE WORLD (American International 1956) 71 min.

Executive producer, James Nicholson; producer/director, Roger Corman; screenplay, Lou Rusoff; music, Ronald Stein; special effects, Paul Blaisdell; camera, Frederic West; editor, Charles Gross.

Peter Graves (Paul Nelson); Beverly Garland (Elaine Anderson); Lee Van Cleef (Tom Anderson); Sally Fraser (Joan Nelson); Charles B. Griffith (Pete Sheldon); Russ Bender (General Patrick); Jonathan Haze (Private Manuel Ortiz); Richard Miller (Sergeant Neil); Karen Kadler (Ellen Peters); Paul Blaisdell (Visitor from Venus).

If one can accept light-hearted fare, this modest Roger Corman effort is quite enjoyable. Once again, the monster visiting the Earth is supposed to be so indescribably horrid that only It suffices as a term of referral.

It, a cone-shaped thing from Venus, travels in a flying saucer. Along the way to Earth it sets up communications with a scientist (Lee Van Cleef) in Beechwood, U.S.A., promising fame and fortune if he will help the alien overwhelm the world. Anderson agrees and the alien arrives, immediately cutting off all the world's power, except to the scientist's home and laboratory. The creature is based in a cave, but it dispatches bat-like things which bite victims and plant electrons in their necks, making them helpless servants of the alien. The scientist's wife (Beverly Garland) and their friend (Peter Graves) oppose the world domination scheme. Only when his spouse is attacked by the strange being does the scientist realize the error of his ways. He joins his pal in combatting the visitor. They are successful, but in the process the scientist is also destroyed.

Beverly Garland in It Conquered the World (1956).

The film was promoted with the catch line "EVERY MAN ITS PRISONER ... EVERY WOMAN ITS SLAVE." The film has its inner morality: "... [there can] be no gift of protection from outside of ourselves. Such dreams end only in death and destruction."

Variety was on target when it observed, "Producer Corman would have been wiser to merely suggest the creature, rather than construct the awesome-looking and mechanically clumsy rubberized horror. It inspires more titters than terror."

But It Conquered the World was light years better than its remake, Zontar: The Thing from Venus (1966). The latter featured John Agar as the leading man and the new version of the unearthly visitor seemed to be nothing more than a broken umbrella with a halloween face painted on it.

Since Lee Van Cleef's rise to stardom as the lead figure of Italian Westerns, this early acting credit, It Conquered the World, has found constant replay on TV.

IT! THE TERROR FROM BEYOND SPACE (United Artists, 1958) 68 min.

Producer, Robert E. Kent; director, Edward L. Cahn; screenplay, Jerome Bixby; assistant director, Ralph Black; art director, William Glasgow; set decorator, Herman Schoenbrun; music, Paul Sawtell and Bert Shefter; makeup, Lane Britton; sound, Al Overton; camera, Kenneth Peach, Sr.; editor, Grant Whytock.

Marshall Thompson (Colonel Carruthers); Shawn Smith (Ann Anderson); Kim Spalding (Colonel Van Heusen); Ann Doran (Mary Royce); Dabbs Greer (Eric Royce); Paul Langton (Calder); Robert Bice (Purdue); Richard Benedict (Bob Finelli); Richard Hervey (Gino Finelli); Thom Carney (Kienholz); Ray "Crash" Corrigan (It).

An American spaceship had landed on Mars in 1968 but has never returned. In 1972 another expedition, led by Colonel Van Heusen, reaches there and locates a survivor, Colonel Carruthers (Marshall Thompson). The latter relates that his crew was killed by an incredible monster. Van Heusen is convinced that Carruthers murdered his co-workers for their supplies. Once the explorers and prisoner have taken off for Earth, bizarre happenings occur. One of the technicians is found brutally murdered and soon It (Ray "Crash" Corrigan) is on the rampage within the ship. Even when they confine it in a cabin below deck, it breaks through the thick walls. Eventually the remaining crew members don space suits, turn off the oxygen in a section of the craft, and the monster suffocates to death. Once on Earth, Carruthers is found innocent of any charges and he and the others receive medals from the government.

The confrontation between the crew and It has quite a few scary moments. The low-keyed production demonstrates how a director can produce an entertaining film on a small budget.

Abroad, the film was titled It! The Vampire from Beyond Space.

It! The Terror from Beyond Space (1958).

IT! THE VAMPIRE FROM BEYOND SPACE   see   IT CONQUERED
THE WORLD

IT'S GREAT TO BE ALIVE   see   THE LAST MAN ON EARTH

JACK ARMSTRONG (Columbia, 1947) fifteen chapters

    Producer, Sam Katzman; associate producer, Mel Delay; di-
rector, Wallace Fox; based on the radio feature, "Jack Armstrong,
the All-American Boy"; screenplay, Arthur Hoerl, Lewis Clay, Royal
Cole, and Leslie Swabacker; assistant directors, Mike Eason and
Leonard Shapiro; music, Lee Zahler; camera, Ira H. Morgan; editor,
Earl Turner.
    John Hart (Jack Armstrong); Rosemary La Planche (Betty);

Joe Brown, Jr. (Billy); Claire James (Alura); Pierre Watkin (Uncle
Jim Fairfield); Wheeler Oakman (Professor Zorn); Jack Ingram
(Blair); Eddie Parker (Slade); Hugh Prosser (Vic Hardy); John Mer-
ton (Gregory); Frank Marlo (Naga); Charles Middleton (Jason Grood);
Russ Vincent (Umala); Gene Stutenroth (Dr. Albour).

    Chapters: 1) Mystery of the Cosmic Ray; 2) The Far World;
3) Island of Deception; 4) Into the Chasm; 5) The Space Ship; 6) Tunnels of Treachery; 7) Cavern of Chance; 8) The Secret Room; 9) Human Targets; 10) Battle of the Warriors; 11) Cosmic Annihilator; 12)
The Grotto of Greed; 13) Wheels of Fate; 14) Journey into Space;
15) Retribution.

    A. k. a. Jack Armstrong, the All-American Boy.

    Jack Armstrong (John Hart) learns from Jim Fairfield (Pierre
Watkin), the head of an aviation company, that cosmic radioactivity
is being used in experiments outside the U.S. With the man's niece
(Rosemary La Planche) and nephew (Joe Brown, Jr.), Jack decides
to investigate. Enemy agents then kidnap the industrialist's associate
Vic Hardy (Hugh Prosser) and the trio traces him to the mysterious
island of Grood. There a mad scientist (Wheeler Oakman) is making
plans to conquer the world. Eventually the group rescues Hardy.
When the madman escapes to a secret airfield Jack follows him and
kills him with a hand grenade. The world is saved from destruction.

    The Mutual Network radio program about "Jack Armstrong"
had been on the air since 1933. But this commercial quickie serial
from Columbia did not help to bring the show more popularity. In
fact, the show was still being aired long after this chapterplay was
nearly forgotten. Casting was a problem in this cliffhanger. Alan
G. Barbour noted in Days of Thrills and Adventure (1970), "John
Hart appeared too old to play the 'hero of Hudson High' ... although
Pierre Watkin was ideal as Uncle Jim Fairfield...." Moreover, the
serial made little attempt to infuse the plotline with sufficient fanciful
futuristic inventions and escapades, aspects which had endeared the
radio show to listeners.

LA JETEE (THE PIER) (Argos, 1962) 29 min.

    Director/screenplay, Chris Marker; music, Trevor Duncan
and Choirs of the Cathedral of St. Alexandre Newski; sound, Antoine
Bonfanti; special effects, C.S. Olaf; camera, Jean Chiabaud; editor,
Jean Ravel.
    With: Hélène Chatelain, Davos Hanich, Jacques Ledoux, Wil-
liam Klein, Ligia Borowczyk, André Heinrich, Jacques Branchu,
Philbert von Lifchitz, Pierre Joffroy, Etienne Becker, Janine Klein,
and Germano Facetti.

    Paris is destroyed in a nuclear war. The survivors exist in
underground vaults at Chaillot. To escape the disastrous present,
experiments are instigated to find some gap in the time continuum.
The person chosen for the test (Davos Henich) has a recurring memory: as a child he watched a beautiful girl standing on a jetty at
Orly Airport when a man came running nearby and was killed. The

subject is projected into the past to gain a foothold on time. On the
jetty he meets the girl of his dream and they fall in love. Given a
chance to go into the future he refuses and projects himself back to
the woman he adores. He runs to her on the jetty, but turns in time
to see that one of the underground scientists has followed him from
the future. He is killed.

This captivating short subject was depicted entirely in still
photographs with added narration. "In this film, visual images literally transcend time.... The commentary on its own stands up to
the most thorough examination in much the same way as a poem
does" (British Monthly Film Bulletin). John Baxter wrote, in Science
Fiction in the Cinema (1970), "[It] is in its way a perfect literary sf
piece, developed like a short story with a detached narration and bre-
vity of expression most writers would envy ... a unique combination
of literature and cinema."

Among the awards bestowed on this film were The Golden As-
teroid, the Trieste Science Film Festival Award, the International
Film Critics' Prize, Prix Jean Vigo, and the Ducat of Gold at the
Mannheim Festival.

JOURNEY BENEATH THE DESERT see L'ATLANTIDE (1960)

JOURNEY TO PLANET FOUR see THE ANGRY RED PLANET

JOURNEY TO THE BEGINNING OF TIME (New Trends Associates,
1966) C-87 min.

Producer, William Cayton; director, Karel Zeman; screenplay,
Zeman and Cayton; additional dialogue, Fred Ladd; technical advisor,
Dr. Edwin H. Colbert; music, E. F. Burian; camera, Anthony Huston.

James Lukas (Doc); Victor Betral (Joe); Peter Hermann (Tony);
Charles Goldsmith (Ben).

Eastern European films in the sci-fi genre have often sought
to combine education with entertainment. This production, issued in
its homeland in 1955 as Cesta Do Praveku, is one such example. A
decade later it was purchased by William Cayton who shot additional
sequences in New York with four American boys who looked a lot like
the youths in the Czech original. The Czech portion was then dubbed
into English. Prior to its theatrical showings, the film was serial-
ized and shown over National Educational Television (NET).

Jumping a time span in science fiction does not always mean
leaping forward. Here four boys are rowing in Central Park and discover a secret cave. They row into the dark cave and navigate along
a river that leads them back some 500 million years in time. They
witness a series of adventures that amaze their young minds, and
encounter a variety of prehistoric mammals, reptiles, and birds.
Later, the boys awaken in the American Museum of Natural History
and realize their trek was but a dream.

The New York Times printed, "It's a nice one for children ...

in a quietly winning way [it] is right up their alley as educational entertainment." The New York World Journal Tribune added, "The
trick photography ranges from effective to glaringly phony.... The
boys seem natural and unaffected." The highlight of the picture is
its fine stop-motion animation work, accomplished in such a way as
to keep the (small fry) audience on the edge of their seats. Czech
director Karel Zeman did an excellent job of presenting the oversized
animals via electronic puppets.

JOURNEY TO THE CENTER OF THE EARTH (Twentieth Century-
Fox, 1959) C-132 min.

Producer, Charles Brackett; director, Henry Levin; based on
the novel Voyage au Centre de la Terre by Jules Verne; screenplay,
Walter Reisch and Charles Brackett; music, Bernard Herrmann; music conductor, Lionel Newman; songs, Sammy Cahn and James Van
Heusen; Robert Burns and Van Heusen; art directors, Lyle R. Wheeler, Franz Bachelin, and Herman A. Blumenthal; set decorators,
Walter M. Scott and Joseph Kish; makeup, Ben Nye; assistant director, Hal Herman; technical advisors, Lincoln Barnett and Peter Ronson; costumes, David Folkes; sound, Bernard Freericks and Warren
B. Delaplain; special camera effects, L. B. Abbott, James B. Gor-
don, and Emil Kosa, Jr.; camera, Leo Tover; editors, Stuart Gil-
more and Jack W. Holmes.
Pat Boone (Alec McEwen); James Mason (Professor Oliver
Lindenbrook); Arlene Dahl (Carla); Diane Baker (Jenny); Thayer Da-
vid (Count Saknussemm); Peter Ronson (Hans); Robert Adler (Groom);
Alan Napier (Dean); Alex Finlayson (Professor Bayle); Ben Wright
(Paisley); Mary Brady (Kirsty); Frederick Halliday (Chancellor); Alan
Caillou (Rector).

Imaginative Jules Verne wrote Voyage au Centre de la Terre
in 1864 and it was first filmed as a one-reeler in France in 1909.
The definitive film version, though, came a half-century later when
Twentieth Century-Fox shot the work in CinemaScope and color as
a vehicle for their contract singer Pat Boone. Location scenes were
shot in Carlsbad Caverns, New Mexico and the finished product was
a well-photographed adventure story, a bit juvenile, but hale and
hearty. The one drawback was the use of blow-ups of live lizards
instead of expensive stop-motion photography to show giant reptiles.
As a gift to honor his being knighted, Professor Oliver Lindenbrook's (James Mason) students give him a paperweight. The gift
turns out to be a message from a man who had journeyed to the center of the earth. The Professor immediately launches an expedition,
including student Alex McEwen (Pat Boone), Carla (Arlene Dahl), the
widow of a scientist associate, Hans (Peter Ronson), an Icelandic
guide, and Gertrude, Hans' duck. Along their treacherous path they
are followed by the sinister Count Saknussemm (Thayer David) who
would like to claim the "discovery" for himself. Along the way the
expedition finds a garden of giant mushrooms, walls of self-illumin-
ation, and a variety of prehistoric monsters. In a magnetic storm
on the interglobal ocean, they are beached near the Lost City of

Pat Boone, Diane Baker, Arlene Dahl and James Mason in <u>Journey</u>
<u>to the Center of the Earth</u> (1959).

Atlantis. Still later the Count is killed and the survivors find themselves blown to the Earth's surface through the volcano Stromboli.
The film ends on a romantic note with the Professor and Carla about
to wed, and Alex reaffirming his love to Jenny (Diane Baker). Ironically the explorers have not one bit of evidence to prove their miraculous
journey.
          "Good, clean, gaudy fun without a brain or a message in its
pretty little head, which should be enough for anyone. But if we
must be serious, <u>Journey to the Center of the Earth</u> could be pointed
to as satire--really a great spoof of special-effects fantasies and
'science-fiction' weirdies" (<u>Films in Review</u>).

For the record, Pat Boone sings four songs in the film, including a version of "My Love Is Like a Red, Red Rose."

JOURNEY TO THE CENTER OF TIME (Borealis and Dorad, 1968) C-82 min.

Producers, David L. Hewitt and Ray Dorn; associate producer, J. Max Thornton; director, Hewitt; screenplay, David Prentiss; art director, Edward D. Engoron; sound, Arthur Names; special camera effects, Modern Film Effects; camera, Robert Caramico; editor, Bell Welburn.
Scott Brady (Stanton, Jr.); Anthony Eisley (Mark Manning); Gigi Perreau (Karen White); Abraham Sofaer (Dr. von Steiner); Austin Green (Mr. Denning); Poupee Gamin (Vina); Tracy Olsen (Susan); Andy Davis (Dave); and Lyle Waggoner, Larry Evans, and Jody Millhouse.

The well-executed special effects in The Time Travelers (q.v.) accomplished by David L. Hewitt led one to assume that he might produce other good projects in the sci-fi genre. Since that time he has directed several genre films, but they have been of very low calibre: Wizard of Mars (1965), Dr. Terror's Gallery of Horror (1968), The, Mighty Gorga (1970) and Journey to the Center of Time. Of the latter film, the British Monthly Film Bulletin reported, "its aspirations are ruthlessly outpaced by its minuscule budget.... The adventures of the stranded scientists ... are hardly original enough to stand up without a good deal of supporting gadgetry."
In an error of calculation, Dr. von Steiner (Abraham Sofaer) and his assistants Mark Manning (Anthony Eisley) and Karen White (Gigi Perreau), along with wealthy Stanton, Jr. (Scott Brady), are projected into the future to the year 6968 A.D., where they find the Earth being destroyed in a laser beam war. By another accident their time capsule leaps back in time to one million B.C. There the ruby, the basic power source for the capsule, is destroyed. In the search for a replacement von Steiner dies in molten lava and Stanton is later killed when he attempts to fly the time capsule himself (he is consumed when he meets himself being propelled in the opposite direction). Mark and Karen are then able to reboard the craft. But they reach their laboratory a day earlier than when they had first left it. Realizing they will endure Stanton's fate, they reboard the capsule for a journey into the unknown. Their counterparts are left in a continuous time trap, reliving their adventures over and over and over and....
Journey to the Center of Time is one of the most recent film appearances by ex-child star Gigi Perreau, the beloved moppet of a bygone era.

JOURNEY TO THE FAR SIDE OF THE SUN see DOPPELGANGER

JOURNEY TO THE SEVENTH PLANET (American International/Cinemagic/, 1961) 78 min.

Producer/director/story, Sidney Pink; screenplay, Ib Melchior and Pink; music, Ib Glindemann; assistant director, Szasza Zalabery; sound, Paul Nyrup; special effects, Bent Barford Films; camera, Age Wiltrup.
John Agar (Don); Greta Thyssen (Greta); Ann Smyrner (Ingrid); Mimi Heinrich (Ursula); Carl Ottosen (Eric); Ove Sprogoe (Barry); Louis Miche Renard (Svend); Peter Monch (Karl); Annie Birgit Garde (Ellen); Ulla Moritz (Lise); Bente Juel (Colleen).

A co-production of the U.S. and Sweden, this inexpensively-mounted effort was an offshoot of the premise used so strikingly in Forbidden Planet (q.v.): the concept of the alien brain confronting the thought patterns of Earth explorers in order to get rid of them.
In this dubbed feature an international team of explorers led by Don (John Agar) arrives in the year 2001 on Uranus. The United Nations team sets up bases on the green world and is promptly exposed to many unique experiences. One of the men, who is scared of rodents, is attacked by a giant rat. Another, a Swede, who is homesick, finds a reproduction of his own village. All of the men meet duplicates of their sweethearts or dream girls back home. They come to realize that their thought patterns are being controlled to produce these visual affects, and eventually learn that "The Brain," the ruler of Uranus wants them off the planet and is doing these morale-destructive things to conquer their minds. The evil brain finally appears--a monstrous looking glob--and is overcome by the Earth men's ingenuity. (The Brain is fearful of ultra-cold temperatures.)
"The opening scenes, once the party has landed on Uranus, are promisingly out-of-the-rut, even if the prettily coloured effects of the planet's own scenery are engaging rather than believable. With the second half of the story ... we are on familiar territory, which is merely a variation on conventional monster-fiction" (British Monthly Film Bulletin).

JOURNEY UNDER THE DESSERT   see   L'ATLANTIDE (1960)

JUST IMAGINE (Fox, 1930) 113 min.

Associate producers, B. G. De Sylva, Lew Brown, and Ray Henderson; director/continuity, David Butler; story/dialogue/songs, De Sylva, Brown, and Henderson; art directors, Stephen Goosson and Ralph Hammeras; music director, Arthur Kay; choreography, Seymour Felix; costumes, Sophie Wachner, Dorothy Tree, and Alice O'Neil; assistant director, Ad Schaumer; sound, Joseph E. Aiken; camera, Ernest Palmer; editor, Irene Morra.
El Brendel (Single O); Maureen O'Sullivan (LN-18); John Garrick (J-21); Marjorie White (D-6); Frank Albertson (RT-42); Hobart Bosworth (Z-4); Kenneth Thomson (MT-3); Wilfred Lucas (X-10); Mischa Auer (B-36); Joseph Girard (Commander); Sidney De Gray (AK-44);

New York City in 1980, from Just Imagine (1930).

Joyzelle (Loo Loo/Boo Boo); Ivan Linow (Loko/Bobo); Mary Lansing, Helen Mann, Mary Carr, Margaret La Marr, Janet De Vine, Kay Gordon, Marbeth Wright, Charles Alexander, Robert Keith, Clarence Simmons, Ed Rockwell, Don Prosser, Clarence Smith, and J. Harold Reeves (Chorus).

With a comical prologue set in 1880 to establish what styles and customs were in 1880 New York, the storyline jumps to 1980, a time when people have numbers but no name. In the overpopulated world of the future, food exists in the form of pills. If more than one man courts a woman, a marriage tribunal settles the matter based on qualifications.

A trans-Atlantic pilot, J-21 (John Garrick), loves a comely lass, LN-18 (Maureen O'Sullivan), but the courts award her pledge of love to a wealthy publisher (Kenneth Thomson). J-21 however, is granted a four-month probationary period by the court to prove his worthiness. Meanwhile the pilot's buddy, RT-42 (Frank Albertson), introduces J-21 to a scientist, MT-3 (Wilfred Lucas), who has just revived a man, Single O (El Brendel), who was supposedly killed by lightning in 1930. The two pals then proceed to show the "resurrected" fellow the sights of a new age. They meet a scientist, Z-4 (Hobart Bosworth), who has prepared a rocket for launching to the moon. J-21, hoping to win recognition for his love case, agrees to fly the rocket to outer space. RT-42 goes along on the journey, and so does Single O, as a stowaway. The group lands on Mars and they are met by the planet's queen (Joyzelle). They find out that all Martians have doubles: one good and one bad. The bad personality overthrows the Queen and the three Earth men are jailed. But Single O later overwhelms the guard (Ivan Linow) and they make it back to the ship and return to Earth. J-21 claims LN-18 as his own, and the court now rules in his favor. As proof that they have been to Mars, Single O has the Martian jailor in tow.

The songwriting team of De Sylva, Brown, and Henderson wrote the story and songs (this was the first science fiction musical) for this film in 1928 and sold it to Fox the next year; the trio remained as the associate producers of the feature. Dated (even for its period) regarding plot and story development, the picture did contain dazzling futuristic sets and backgrounds created by Ralph Hammeras. The New York City of 1980, as depicted in Just Imagine, cost nearly $250,000 to construct. Some of the projected ways of life included: airplanes (helicopters) for everyone, television, 200-story buildings, and nine-level cities.

Had the film not been devised so in keeping with the song and dance format of a musical, it might have had greater impact on its audience in 1930. Since then, the futuristic scenes have often been used as stock footage for other projects.

KAIJU DAISENSO (Toho, 1965) C-96 min.

    Producer, Tomoyuki Tanaka; director, Inoshiro Honda; screenplay, Sinichi Sekizawa; art director, Takeo Kita; music director, Akira Ifukube; special effects, Eliji Tsuburaya; camera, Hajime Koizumi; editor, Ryohei Fujii.

With: Nick Adams, Akira Takarada, Kumi Mizuno, Jun Tazaki, Akira Kubo, and Yoshio Tsuchiya.
A. k. a. Battle of the Astros / Invasion of Planet X.

In this chapter in the continuing Toho Studio tales of the giant
monsters, a new planet has come sailing into the Earth's solar system. It is learned that the heavenly body is inhabited by intelligent
beings. These aliens contact the Earth and request that Godzilla and
Rodan be given to them in order to defeat Ghidrah, who has taken
over that planet. The two Earth creatures are then drugged and
transported via flying saucer to Planet X. Once there, it is revealed
that the aliens actually plan to use the two monsters in alliance with
Ghidrah to enslave the Earth. A party of astronauts (led by Nick
Adams) comes to Planet X to aid the two giant reptiles, and they
eventually defeat Ghidrah. The astronauts and the two monsters return home, while the alien's civilization is torn apart by cosmic
forces.
        The film was released in the U. S. as Monster Zero. For
box-office appeal it boasted the presence of the late American actor,
Nick Adams.

KAITEI GUNKAN (ATRAGON)   (Toho, 1964) C-96 min.

        Executive producer, Yuko Tanaka; director, Inoshiro Honda;
screenplay, Shinichi Sekizawa; music, Akira Ifukube; special effects,
Eiji Tsuburaya; camera, Hajime Koizumi.
        Tadao Takashima (Photographer); Yoko Fujiyama (Commander's
Daughter); Yu Fujiki (Commander); and Kenjo Sawara, Tetsuko Kobayashi, Hiroshi Koizumi, Akemi Kita, Akihiko Hirata, Hun Tazaki,
and Ken Uehara.

        Destruction of cities by various prehistoric giant reptiles and
the invasion of Japan by hordes of aliens had been the usual formula
for pictures from Japan's Toho Studios and its busy director, Inoshiro
Honda. This outing drifted from that format in that the invaders, now
from the Earth's interior, were a super civilization with futuristic
machinery and weapons. It was a shame this film did not start a
more enduring trend for the Toho Company, for they were soon back
to producing the latest adventures of Godzilla, Ghidrah, and other
money-making monsters.
        Some 2000 years ago the Kingdom of Mu sank beneath an
ocean, but its civilization survived. Now the new Mu Queen determines to conquer the world, using the energy force from the earth's
center. When the United Nations' initial foray into Mu territory fails,
it is realized that the only hope for global peace is to use the Atragon, a submarine which flies, burrows through the Earth, and shoots
a deadly freeze-ray. The craft's inventor is a former Japanese naval
commander and it is his daughter who is captured by the Mu people.
Eventually the Atragon destroys the huge sea monsters which have been
sent against it by the Mu. The underworld civilization's plan to conquer the world is forestalled.
        The film was the Japanese entry at the 1964 Trieste Science

Fiction Film Festival. Castle of Frankenstein magazine noted that
it was "Moderately entertaining ... [with] enough gimmicks for several films." Variety added, "The special effects by Eiji Tsuburaya
are consistently excellent, including futuristic weapons, inevitable
monsters, underwater explosions and fine miniature work depicting
an earthquake which levels part of Tokyo." One of the more engrossing aspects of the picture is that the Mu society is depicted as being barbaric in its rites and customs, yet ultra-modern in its scientific achievements. Where have they gone wrong?
    Made as Kaitei Gunkan, the film received wide distribution in
an English-dubbed version called Atragon. (It is also known as Atra-
gon--Flying Supersub / Atragon the Flying Sub.)

THE KEEPERS see THE BRAIN EATERS

KEEPERS OF THE EARTH see THE BRAIN EATERS

KILLER BEES see THE DEADLY BEES

KILLERS FROM SPACE (RKO, 1954) 71 min.

        Producer/director, W. Lee Wilder; story, Myles Wilder;
screenplay, Bill Raynor; music, Manuel Compinsky; optical effects,
Consolidated Film Industries; camera, William Clotheri; editor, William Faris.
        With: Peter Graves, Barbara Bestar, James Seay, Frank
Gerstle, Shep Menken, John Merrick.

        Peter Graves stars as a scientist who is given a new heart
by a group of bug-eyed aliens who arrive on Earth aboard a flying
saucer directed from Astron Delta. In return for their favor, the
invaders demand atomic and nuclear information so they can establish
a laboratory in their (green-tinted) cave. There, they begin breeding
all types of giant insects to aid their scheme to dominate the Earth.
The scientist, however, saves his fellow humans by short-circuiting
the invaders' atomic equipment, thus killing the aliens.
        There were those who insisted this was a terribly inferior
item, even when compared with the rash of mediocre sci-fi junk being turned out by the studios at this time. The aliens here looked
like rejects from a Flash Gordon serial. As the Los Angeles Examiner's critic gibed, "[It] is out of this world, but not far enough."

KING DINOSAUR (Lippert, 1955) 63 min.

        Producers, Bert I. Gordon and Al Zimbalist; director, Gordon;
story, Gordon and Zimbalist; screenplay, Tom Gries; special effects,
Howard A. Anderson Company; camera, Gordon Avil; editors, John
Bushelman and Jack Cornwall.

Bill Bryant (Dr. Ralph Martin); Wanda Curtis (Dr. Patricia Bennett); Douglas Henderson (Richard Gordon); Patricia Gallagher (Nora Pierce).

While there may be dispute as to the best sci-fi features, there is little argument that King Dinosaur ranks among the worst. It was the first effort of Bert I. Gordon, who used a good deal of stock footage from One Million B.C. (1940). His biggest mistake was adding a silly "modern" plot to the borrowed celluloid.
When a new planet, Nova, is discovered in an orbit near the Earth, scientists prepare the first rocket flight to explore its surface. Landing on Nova, the astronauts find a world much like prehistoric Earth. It is inhabited by such notables as a giant stinging spider, a gila monster, and dinosaurs. After their scenic exploration and a climactic explosion, the astronauts return home.
"Absurdly implausible science fiction fantasy. It seems that the makers of the film have been dazzled by having such an explosion (accomplished by suitable cut-in shots) for the climax. Some of the trick work comes off, but much of it is unsatisfactory--an alligator, be it ever so large, remains recognizably an alligator" (British Monthly Film Bulletin).

KING KONG (RKO, 1933) 100 min.

Executive producer, David O. Selznick; directors/screen idea, Merian C. Cooper and Ernest B. Schoedsack; story, Edgar Wallace and Cooper; adaptors, James Creelman and Ruth Rose; chief technician, Willis O'Brien; technical staff, E. B. Gibson, Marcel Delgado, Fred Reefe, Orville Goldner, and Carol Shepphird; art directors, Carroll Clark and Al Herman; art technicians, Mario Larrinaga and Byron L. Crabbe; production assistants, Archie Marshek and Walter Daniels; music, Max Steiner; sound, E. A. Wolcott; sound effects, Murray Spivak; camera, Edward Linden, Verne Walker, and J. O. Taylor; editor, Ted Cheeseman.
Fay Wray (Ann Darrow); Robert Armstrong (Carl Denham); Bruce Cabot (John Driscoll); Frank Reicher (Captain Englehorn); Sam Hardy (Weston); Noble Johnson (Native Chief); James Flavin (Briggs, the Second Mate); Steve Clemento (Witch King); Victor Long (Lumpy); Ethan Laidlow (Mate); Dick Curtis and Charlie Sullivan (Sailors); Vera Lewis and LeRoy Mason (Theatre Patrons); Paul Porcasi (Apple Vendor); Lynton Brent and Frank Mills (Reporters); and King Kong, the Eighth Wonder of the World.

There are still controversies today whether this amazing feature properly belongs in the sci-fi, the horror, or the fantasy genre. In actuality, it is a bit of all three, demonstrating how superior imagination and craftsmanship can produce a masterpiece thriller/adventure yarn. It is perhaps the most cohesive film ever to combine the stop-motion animation and live performance process.
Much of King Kong is presented tongue-in-cheek. Robert Armstrong as Carl Denham is a take-off of "Bring 'Em Back Alive" Frank Buck, while Fay Wray, never lovelier, is the archetype of

KK and Fay Wray (in the tree trunk) in King Kong (1933).

the Thirties' virginal heroine.

   Many talents were employed to create King Kong, each vastly essential to the overall success of the feature. Merian C. Cooper first conceived the notion for the picture, which has obvious borrowings in plot motivation from The Lost World (q. v.). He co-directed the venture with Ernest B. Schoedsack, an old hand at action documentary type movies. Willis O'Brien (the genius who did the stop-motion animation work in The Lost World, among others) was hired to create the special effects. His presentation of Kong, and of various dinosaurs, has yet to be topped. Max Steiner wrote one of his most meaningful and powerful scores for this project, a creation so substantial that it is often presented in classic music recitals. The art direction of Carroll Clark and Al Herman aptly recreated the primeval world of Skull Island, that teaming world of dinosaurs and death. Finally, without the original story by Edgar Wallace (expanded

by Cooper), there could have been no film at all. Wallace, the master of thrillers, beautifully modernized the beauty and the beast story.
(In an earlier novel, The Hairy Arm, Wallace had dealt with an ape-
type creature and the British film industry.)

The early portions of King Kong find Carl Denham seeking to
leave New York City on the morning tide before authorities can stop
his latest expedition. The discussions of the pending voyage between
Denham and Captain Engelhorn (Frank Reicher) set up a good mystery
atmosphere for the balance of the picture. Having found the girl
(Fay Wray) to play the heroine in the filmed odyssey, the ship gets
underway. Eventually they come to Skull Island, where before long
there is the night kidnapping of the heroine by the natives and her intended sacrifice to the beast. Kong's appearance, heralded by the
loud stomping of his feet and the breaking of trees, is shown in a
frenetic close-up of his face. Thereafter Denham leads the crew in
a chase through the primeval jungle, hoping to recover the girl.
They do battle with assorted prehistoric beasts. Meanwhile, the audience is developing a sympathy for the oversized Kong, who obviously is quite smitten with the lovely lass. Later Kong is captured and
shipped back to the States, where he is put on display in a New York
theatre. But he escapes, nearly tears up the town, and abducts the
girl. With her in his paw, he climbs to the top of the Empire State
Building. There, in the film's most poignant moment, he bids his
love goodbye before he is shot off the building by aircraft. Truly
it was "beauty who killed the beast," eulogizes Denham at the finale.

When King Kong was initially released, about ten minutes of
intended footage was deleted, including Kong devouring a villager,
men fighting a giant spider, and Kong ripping off Mis Wray's dress
to better appreciate her body. Some of these scenes, plus a few
other cuts, have been re-inserted in some restored prints.

The phenomenal success of King Kong led Cooper, O'Brien,
and Schoedsack to turn out Son of Kong for RKO release in 1934, with
Robert Armstrong again in the lead. It could not match its predecessor. In 1949 Cooper and O'Brien would team yet again for Mighty
Joe Young, in which an African ranch owner's daughter (Terry Moore)
raises a huge black gorilla. Robert Armstrong was on hand as the
showman who sees a way to commercialize on the beast. The Japanese would revive the Kong legend for King Kong vs. Godzilla (1963)
and again in King Kong Escapes (1967). Both were very pale imitations of the original.

In 1976 Dino De Laurentiis produced a new remake of King
Kong for Paramount Pictures, amid much hoopla but equal cynicism
from devout fans of the 1933 version. The new $20 million pro-
duction met with success, and he intends to make a sequel, King Kong
Goes to Africa.

KING KONG ESCAPES   see   KING KONG

KING KONG VS; GODZILLA   see   KING KONG

James Craven and Tristram Coffin in <u>King of the Rocket Men</u> (1949).

KING OF THE ROCKET MEN (Republic, 1949) twelve chapters

    Associate producer, Franklin Adreon; director, Fred C. Brannon; screenplay, Roy Cole, William Lively and Sol Shor; music, Stanley Wilson; special effects, Howard and Theodore Lydecker; camera, Ellis W. Carter.
    Tristram Coffin (Jeff King); Mae Clarke (Glenda Thomas); Don Haggerty (Tony Dirken); House Peters, Jr. (Burt Winslow); James Craven (Professor Millard); I. Stanford Jolley (Professor Bryant); Douglas Evans (Chairman); Ted Adams (Martin Conway); Stanley Price (Gunther Von Strum); Dale Van Sickel (Martin); Tom Steele (Knox); David Sharpe (Blears); Eddie Parker (Rowan); Michael Ferro (Turk); Frank O'Connor (Guard); Buddy Roosevelt (Philliph).

Chapters: 1) Dr. Vulcan--Traitor); 2) Plunging Death; 3) Dangerous Evidence; 4) High Peril; 5) Fatal Dive; 6) Mystery of the Rocket Man; 7) Molten Menace; 8) Suicide Flight; 9) Ten Seconds to Live; 10) The Deadly Fog; 11) Secret of Dr. Vulcan; 12) Wave of Disaster.

For many, King of the Rocket Men was Hollywood's last decent serial.
The corrupt Dr. Vulcan is anxious to control the world. He begins his scheme by nearly killing a professor (James Craven) at a privately operated research center. Reporter Glenda Thomas (Mae Clarke) learns of the murder attempt and goes to the project, where she meets young research member Jeff King (Tristram Coffin). Two of Vulcan's men later attack Jeff but he defeats them and heads for the secret cave where he has hidden the professor from further murder attempts.
The two have developed a jet-propelled flying suit and Jeff tries out the equipment, dubbing himself The Rocket Man. Eventually Vulcan discovers that Jeff and The Rocket Man are one and the same. He has a henchman (Don Haggerty) capture Jeff, but the former is scared away by The Rocket Man (this time the professor is wearing the suit).
Meanwhile, Vulcan demands a billion dollars not to destroy New York City with a powerful decimator he has stolen from the professor. When the mayor of Manhattan refuses the blackmail scheme, Vulcan causes an earthquake and a tidal wave to devastate New York. (Stock footage from The Deluge [q.v.] had another airing.) Vulcan also plans to use the decimator to penetrate a fault in the ocean floor and thus cause further havoc. But Jeff arrives in time to stop the crazed villain. The hero manages to escape the island retreat before the Air Force drops bomb on the site, killing the Vulcan and his men.
Stock footage from this entry would be employed in three later Republic serial offerings: Flying Disc Man from Mars, Radar Men from the Moon, and Zombies of the Stratosphere (all q.v.).
It had been eighteen years since Mae Clarke co-starred with James Cagney in Public Enemy and received a grapefruit in the face. But she was still a game actress, as demonstrated by her heroine's role here.
This serial was later issued in a feature version entitled Lost Planet Airmen. Abbreviating the chapterplay to a compact 65 minutes was a storyline blessing.

KRONOS (Twentieth Century-Fox, 1957) 78 min.

Executive producer, E. J. Baumgarten; producer/director, Kurt Neumann; story, Irving Block; screenplay, Lawrence L. Goldman; music, Paul Sawtell; art director, Theobold Holsopple; special effects, Jack Rabin, Irving Block, and Louis DeWitt; camera, Karl Struss; editor, Jode Copelan.
Jeff Morrow (Les); Barbara Lawrence (Vera); John Emery (Eliot); George O'Hanlon (Culver); Morris Ankrum (Dr. Stern);

Kenneth Alton (McCrary); John Parrish (General Parry); Jose Gonzales Gonzales (Manuel); Richard Harrison (Pilot); Marjorie Stapp (Nurse).

Arriving in a huge fireball from space, Kronos, a giant machine-like robot, is deposited on a California beach. It rises up and hopes to begin a trek eastward across the United States. To provide itself with fuel energy, it absorbs enormous doses of electricity, getting bigger all the time. Needless to say, Kronos causes a good deal of destruction in the Los Angeles area and panics the population. Finally, jet planes dust it with atomic particles, causing its circuits to short. Kronos expires.

Producer/director Kurt Neumann had earlier done The Fly (q. v.), which was far more imaginative. Here the technical aspects were more than adequate but the title character was arid and after a few reels Kronos sank into boredom. There were some, however, including John Baxter (Science Fiction in the Cinema, 1970), who could find virtues to the production: "The sight of this strange machine, half creature, half construction, pounding across the hills of America is one worthy of modern 'underground' cinema."

THE LADY AND THE DOCTOR   see   THE LADY AND THE MONSTER

THE LADY AND THE MONSTER (Republic, 1944) 86 min.

Associate producer/director, George Sherman; based on the novel Donovan's Brain by Curt Siodmak; screenplay, Dane Lussier and Frederick Kohner; art director, Russell Kimball; set decorator, Otto Siegel; assistant director, Bud Springsteen; music, Walter Scharf; sound, Earl Crain, Sr.; camera, John Alton; editor, Arthur Roberts.
Erich von Stroheim (Professor Franz Mueller); Vera Hruba Ralston (Janice Farell); Richard Arlen (Patrick Cory); Mary Nash (Mrs. Fame); Sidney Blackmer (Eugene Fulton); Helen Vinson (Chloe Donovan); Charles Cane (Grimes); Bill Henry (Roger Collins); Juanita Quigley (Mary Lou); Josephine Dillon (Mary Lou's Grandmother); Tom London (Husky Man in Tails); Sam Flint (G. Phipps the Bank Manager); Lane Chandler (White the Ranger); Edward Keane (Manning); Antonio Triano and Lola Montes (Dance Team); Maxine Doyle (Receptionist); Harry Hayden (Dr. Martin); Wallis Clark (Warden); Billy Benedict (Bellhop); Herbert Clifton (Butler); Harry Depp (Bank Teller); Lee Phelps (Headwaiter); Frank Graham (Narrator); Janet Martin (Cafe Singer).

This initial screen version of Curt Siodmak's novel Donovan's Brain was designed as the first non-musical film for European skating star Vera Hruba Ralston. However, the future wife of Republic studio head, Herbert J. Yates, emerged in no more than a support role among mad scientist Erich von Stroheim, weak-willed boyfriend Richard Arlen and the dominating brain of deceased tycoon W. H. Donovan. George Sherman shot the feature on a middling budget. The direction and cinematography far outdistanced the loose adaptation of Siodmak's popular novel.

In the desert, a deranged doctor (von Stroheim) removes the brain of a dead man found in a plane crash. He keeps the organ alive in his laboratory. His assistant, Patrick Cory (Richard Arlen), and nurse, Janice Farell (Vera Hruba Ralston), who are lovers, watch over the brain, which slowly begins to renew itself and has a marked influence over the weak-willed Cory. The professor, who lusts for Janice, hopes to find a way of ridding himself of Cory's competition for Janice's affection. Thus he is delighted when the brain schemes to eliminate those business rivals who caused Donovan's accident and decides to use Cory as the assassin. Cory nearly commits a murder before the powerful brain is silenced. The unstable doctor suffers a like fate, and the lovers are finally left to find a way to happiness.

Outside of a few eerie moments, The Lady and the Monster was lightweight entertainment. Von Stroheim provided some scene-chewing moments in his intense characterization of Professor Franz Mueller, and the supporting cast was a versatile one: including such "names" as Sidney Blackmer and Helen Vinson. One of Clark Gable's ex-wives, Josephine Dillon, was also in the production. (The star trio would be reunited that year for Republic's espionage thriller, Storm Over Lisbon, also directed by George Sherman.)

The feature was shown in Britain as The Lady and the Doctor and Republic would later reissue it in America as The Tiger Man. Two other versions of the books have also been made as theatrical films: Donovan's Brain and Vengeance (The Brain) (both q. v.).

THE LAST CHILD (ABC-TV, 1971) C-75 min.

Producer, Aaron Spelling; director, John L. Moxey; teleplay, Peter S. Fischer; art director, Paul Sylos; music, Laurence Rosenthal; camera, Arch Dalzell.

With: Van Heflin, Michael Cole, Harry Guardino, Janet Margolin, Edward Asner, Kent Smith.

This was yet another telefeature entry for ABC-TV's "Movie of the Week." Set in the near future, it deals with oppressive government operations in 1994 when, due to overpopulation, couples are permitted to have only one child. Michael Cole and Janet Margolin were cast as young marrieds whose first child has died and who are told that the wife must abort their oncoming second baby since they have exceeded their quota. Rather than comply, the couple takes flight and ends up seeking sanctuary and help from a highly-respected retired senator (Van Heflin). The latter tries to aid them but his efforts are in vain. Eventually the young fugitives are tracked down by the state's secret police.

Director John Moxey imbued the project with an ominous vision of a possible future of oppression. It certainly was not in the same league as 1984 (q. v.), however; the storyline was too weak.

This was Van Heflin's last major film appearance.

THE LAST DAYS OF MAN ON EARTH (New World, 1975) C-81 min.

Executive producers, Ray Baird and David Putnam; producers, John Goldstone and Sandy Liebson; director, Robert Fuest; based on the novel The Finale Programme by Michael Moorcock; screenplay, Fuest; music, Paul Beaver, Bernard Krause, and Gerry Mulligan; art director, Philip Harrison; camera, Norman Warwick; editor, Barrie Vince.

Jon Finch (Jerry Cornelius); Jenny Runacre (Miss Brunner); Hugh Griffith (Professor Hira); Patric Magee (Dr. Baxter); Sterling Hayden (Major Wrongway Lindberg); and Harry Andrews, Graham Crowden, George Coulouris, Basil Henson, Derrick O'Connor, Gilles Milinaire, Ronald Lacey, Julie Ege, Sandy Ratcliff, Sarah Douglas, and Dolores Del Mar.

Thematically this tale lacks substance: a self-oriented intellectual embarks on an unpromising mission in the devastated world of the future, seeking a latter day Messiah. Variety passed off this visually engaging study (populated with a wide variety of seasoned character actors) as "a silly, pretentious potboiler...."

THE LAST MAN ON EARTH (Fox, 1924) 6, 637'

Presenter, William Fox; director, John G. Blystone; based on the story by John D. Swain; screenplay, Donald W. Lee; camera, Allan Davey.

The Prologue: Jean Johnson (Hattie at Age Six); Buck Black (Elmer at Age Eight); Maurice Murphy (Elmer's Pal); William Steele (Hattie's Father); Jean Dumas (Hattie's Mother); Harry Dunkinson (Elmer's Father); Fay Holderness (Elmer's Mother).

The Play: Earle Foxe (Elmer Smith); Grace Cunard (Gertie); Gladys Tennyson (Frisco Kate); Derelys Perdue (Hattie); Maryon Aye (Red Sal); Clarissa Selwynne (Dr. Prodwell); Pauline French (Furlong); Marie Astaire (Paula Prodwell).

The Fox drama of 1924, starring Earle Foxe and one-time serial star Grace Cunard, was a futuristic melodrama set in 1954, when a plague kills all males over fourteen, except one. Despite the serious setting the film verges into farce as the survivor (Foxe) is captured by a female ganster (Cunard) and sold to the government in Washington for $10 million. Two women senators battle it out with boxing gloves to determine who will have Elmer. But Elmer's former childhood sweetheart Hattie (Derelys Perdue) reappears and claims the man as her own. A year later, twins are born: the human race will continue. Photoplay was severe on this fantasy/comedy: "Stay away from this picture. It is the dullest show in many months. The title tells the story but not badly enough." Nine years later, Fox re-made the feature with sound as It's Great to Be Alive. Paul Roulien, Gloria Stuart, Edna May Oliver, Herbert Mundin, and Edward Van Sloan were the stars. Politics were injected in the plotline, with the League of Nations being asked to decide which country is to provide the female to mate with the last man alive on Earth.

A Spanish-language version of the film, El Ultimo Varon Sobre la Tierra was made at the same time by Fox; it was directed by James Tinling.

THE LAST MAN ON EARTH (1964)   see   ULTIMO UOMO DELLA TERRA

THE LAST WOMAN ON EARTH (Filmgroup, 1960) C-71 min.

Producer/director, Roger Corman; screenplay, Robert Towne; music, Ronald Stein; assistant director, Jack Bohrer; camera, Jack Marquette; editor, Anthony Carras.
Anthony Carbone (Harold); Betsy Jones-Moreland (Evelyn); Edward Wain (Martin).

The title might indicate that this is the women's liberation answer to the preceeding entries.   But no, it is a disappointing film from Roger Corman; a clichéd romantic triangle.
Three people, a fugitive from justice (Anthony Carbone), a lawyer (Edward Wain) and his wife (Betsy Jones-Moreland), are the last of the human race alive on Earth after an atomic war.   The trio

Anthony Carbone, Betsy Jones-Moreland and Edward Wain in The Last Woman on Earth (1960).

remains on a boat harbored near Puerto Rico. It is not too long before the two men argue over Evelyn and, at the old Spanish fortress
of El Morro, a fight to the finish ensues.   When it is over, two of
the three survive to face the grim future.

Filmed in VitaScope and color, with location lensing in Puerto
Rico, the picture could best be dubbed as three actors without a story.

LATITUDE ZERO   see   IDO ZERO DIASAKUSEN

LIFE IN THE NEXT CENTURY   see   ONE HUNDRED YEARS AFTER

LOGAN'S RUN (MGM/United Artists, 1976) C-118 min.

Producer, Saul David; associate producer, Hugh Benson; director, Michael Anderson; based on the novel by William F. Nolan
and George Clayton Johnson; screenplay, David Zelag Goodman; art
director, Dale Hennessy; set decorator, Robert De Vestel; music,
Jerry Goldsmith; costumes, Bill Thomas; assistant director, David
Silver; stunt coordinators, Glen Wilder and Bill Couch; sound, Jerry
Jost, Harry W. Tetrick, William McCaughey, and Aaron Rochin;

Michael York and Jenny Agutter in Logan's Run (1976).

special visual effects, L. B. Abbott; additional visuals, Frank Van
Der Veer; camera, Ernest Laszlo; editor, Bob Wyman.

Michael York (Logan); Richard Jordan (Francis); Jenny Agutter
(Jessica); Roscoe Lee Browne (Box); Farrah Fawcett-Majors (Holly);
Michael Anderson, Jr. (Doc); Peter Ustinov (Old Man); Randolph Ro-
berts (Sanctuary Man); Lara Lindsay (Woman Runner); Gary Morgan
(Billy); Michelle Stacy (Little Girl).

One of the most expensive science fiction entries in recent
years, Logan's Run promises much but delivers little, either visually
or intellectually. Nevertheless, within its first five days of release
in mid-1976 at some 340 theatres it grossed $2,518,008.

In the year 2274 the remaining segment of civilization (nuclear
destruction has ravaged the world) lives in relative luxury within a
domed city. In the orderly society, it is programmed that no one
over thirty is to remain alive. At precisely that age each individual
goes "willing into the Carousel" where they--and the spectators at the
city's arena--believe they have an opportunity for life renewal. But,
in reality, they are exterminated. Those who attempt to circumvent
this fate are labeled Runners. They become the prey of the Sandmen
who chase and kill them. One of these watchdogs is Logan (York),
who at age twenty-six is ordered by the computer leaders to become
a Runner, so that he can trace just where the Sanctuary is that the
Runners want to find. The key to the case is Jessica (Agutter), a
Runner who is associated with other underground rebels in helping
individuals escape on the path to Sanctuary.

As it develops, when Logan and Jessica do escape the city and
pass beyond the Cave of Ice, there is no Sanctuary. It is a fantasy
dreamed up to give the people hope. In their travels they encounter
a survivor in the ruins of Washington, D.C. The Old Man (Ustinov)
returns with them to the futuristic city and the computerized order is
overthrown. Now no one has to die at age thirty. Freedom of choice
has returned to Earth's survivors.

There are few subtleties within Logan's Run. You either accept the fantasy or you do not. The magnetic presence of York and
the very attractive Miss Agutter provide some relief and focus for the
storyline. Ustinov, in a rather modified performance (by his usually
hammy standards), does a Charlie Ruggles-like characterization of a
senile old man whose only companions in recent decades have been
cats.

LOOKING FORWARD   see   ONE HUNDRED YEARS AFTER

LOST ATLANTIS   see   L'ATLANTIDE (1932)

THE LOST KINGDOM   see   L'ATLANTIDE (1960)

THE LOST PLANET (Columbia, 1953) fifteen chapters

Producer, Sam Katzman; director, Spencer G. Bennet; screen-
play, George H. Plympton and Arthur Hoerl; assistant director,
Charles S. Gould; music, Mischa Bakaleinikoff; camera, William
Whitney; editor, Earl Turner.

Judd Holdren (Rex Barrow); Vivian Mason (Ella Dorn); Ted
Thorpe (Tim Johnson); Forrest Taylor (Professor Dorn); Michael Fox
(Dr. Grood); Gene Roth (Reckov); Karl Davis (Karlo); Leonard Penn
(Ken Wolper); John Cason (Hopper); Nick Stuart (Darl); Joseph Mell
(Lah); Jack George (Jarva); Frederic Berest (Alden); I. Stanford Jol-
ley (Robot # 9); Pierre Watkin (Ned Hilton).

Chapters: 1) The Mystery of the Guided Missile; 2) Trapped
by the Axial Propeller; 3) Blasted by the Thermic Disintegrator; 4)
The Mind Control Machine; 5) The Atomic Plane; 6) Disaster in the
Stratosphere; 7) Snared by the Pryamic Catapult; 8) Astray in Space;
9) The Hypnotic Ray Machine; 10) To Free the Planet People; 11) Dr.
Grood Defies Gravity; 12) Trapped in a Cosmic Jet; 13) The Invisible
Enemy; 14) In the Grip of the De-Thermo Ray; 15) Sentenced to
Space.

The Lost Planet was Hollywood's final sci-fi serial made for
theatrical release. This chapterplay was so futuristic-oriented that
it contained over fifty different machines and creations. Unfortunately
the production values of the project were so limited that it was an
unfitting swan song for the science fiction serial.

Reporter Rex Barrow (Judd Holdren) uncovers the devious
working of mad scientist Dr. Grood (Michael Fox). Barrow and his
pals (Vivian Mason and Ted Thorpe) are later captured by Grood's
henchmen and teleported to the lost planet of Ergo aboard the "Cosmojet." Once on Ergo, the trio learns that the girl's father, Professor Dorn (Forrest Taylor), has been kidnapped by the mastermind
criminal and his assistant (Gene Roth) and forced to aid them in their
world domination plot. Later, the professor and Barrow make plans
for their escape, including one which makes the newsman invisible.
Eventually friends from Earth locate Ergo and rescue the imprisoned
quartet.

At the conclusion Grood seeks to escape his fate. He boards
the "Cosmojet" and orders his robot to set the ship's course for outer
space. But the metal servant errs and sets the craft's direction for
infinity. Thus Dr. Grood must make an eternal, never-ending odyssey.

LOST PLANET AIRMEN see KING OF THE ROCKET MEN

THE LOST WORLD (First National, 1925) 9,7000'

By arrangement with Watterson R. Rothacker; supervisor, Earl
Hudson; director, Harry O. Hoyt; based on the novel by Arthur Conan
Doyle; adaptor/screenplay, Marion Fairfax; chief technician, Fred W.
Jackman; architecture, Milton Menasco; technical director/researcher,

Willis H. O'Brien; camera, Arthur Edeson; editorial director, Fairfax.
        Bessie Love (Paula White); Lloyd Hughes (Ed Malone); Lewis
Stone (Sir John Roxton); Wallace Beery (Professor Challenger); Arthur Hoyt (Professor Summerlee); Margaret McWade (Mrs. Challenger); Finch Smiles (Austin - Challenger's Butler); Jules Cowles (Zambo); Bull Montana (Apeman); George Bunny (Colin McArdle); Charles Wellesley (Major Hibbard); Alma Bennett (Gladys Hungerford).

THE LOST WORLD (Twentieth Century-Fox, 1960) C-97 min.

        Producer/director, Irwin Allen; based on the novel by Sir Arthur Conan Doyle; screenplay, Allen and Charles Bennett; music, Bert Shefter and Paul Sawtell; art directors, Duncan Cramer and Walter M. Simonds; set decorators, Walter M. Scott, Joseph Kish, and John Sturtevant; assistant director, Ad Schaumer; costumes, Paul Zastupnevich; makeup, Ben Nye; sound, E. Clayton Ward and Harry M. Leonard; special camera effects, L. B. Abbott, Emil Kosa, and James B. Gordon; camera, Winton Hoch; editor, Hugh S. Fowler.
        Claude Rains (George Edward Challenger); Michael Rennie (Lord Roxton); Jill St. John (Jennifer Holmes); David Hedison (Ed Malone); Fernando Lamas (Gomez); Richard Haydn (Professor Summerlee); Ray Stricklyn (David Holmes); Jay Novello (Costa); Vitina Marcus (Native Girl); Ian Wolfe (Burton White); John Graham (Stuart Holmes); Colin Campbell (Professor Waldron).

        Frequently film genres overlap, as here, where the worlds of sci-fi, fantasy, and monster blend for a fanciful whole. It demonstrated that the engaging storyline by Arthur Conan Doyle (more famous for his Sherlock Holmes characterization) had as much to offer as any futuristic story by Jules Verne. Here the juxtaposition of events led the characters back into another age, where giant beasts were rulers.
        Conan Doyle's novel was published in 1912; thirteen years later First National released its fine silent film version of the amazing tale. Thanks to sturdy acting, and especially to Willis O'Brien's ultra-fantastic use of stop-motion photography in the scenes involving dinosaurs, the picture was very popular when issued and is still enthusiastically received today. It set the stage for the best of such films, King Kong (q.v.), to which it still remains a very close second.
        Unlike King Kong, the storyline of The Lost World is overshadowed by the events and sights which transpire on the prehistoric plateau in South America. Here an expedition led by Professor Challenger (Wallace Beery) verifies his previous findings: an amazing lost world of prehistoric animals and ape-like men existing as if time had stood still millions of years prior. The subordinate love story involves lovely Paula White (Bessie Love), the daughter of Challenger's late explorer partner, and two rivals: Irish newsman Ed Malone (Lloyd Hughes) and dignified Sir John Roxton (Lewis Stone), a bee specialist.
        The real excitement of the silent The Lost World occurs when

the exploration party escapes from the Amazon country and returns
to London, with a captured-alive brontosaurus. The creature is to
be exhibited in England but it escapes (naturally) and causes havoc
in the city before tumbling through London Bridge and swimming down
the Thames River out to sea and, hopefully, back home. As an anti-
climactic note, Malone and Paul are thereafter wed.
        Photoplay called it a "spectacular production ... cleverly
done," and Joe Franklin in Classics of the Silent Screen (1959) noted
that it was "pleasantly off-beat and even revolutionary in its climax."

        Technological advances do not always make for creative im-
provements, as was amply demonstrated in the remake of The Lost
World. The addition of sound, color, and CinemaScope did nothing
to enhance the silent original. The new version does not include the
exploration team returning to London with the young Tyrannosaurus
Rex. More importantly, the film abandoned stop-motion animation
and reverted to the cheaper use of blow-ups of various reptiles in
the guise of dinosaurs, etc. Of the cast, only Claude Rains (as Professor Challenger) seemed to care what he was about. But the film,
observed the New York Herald Tribune, "Has much in common with
the recent Journey to the Center of the Earth [q. v.] in that it refuses
to take itself too seriously and maintains a consistent tone of easy
good nature. Even its so-called Jurassic reptiles stomping through
the camp site represent fright with a smile on its face." The New
York Times dismissed the tinseled effort as an "obvious, plodding
and often heavy-handed remake...."
        In the new edition, only the finale is intriguing. The party
escapes from the prehistoric plateau with only one reminder of their
unusual expedition (since the lost world is destroyed by a volcanic
eruption)--a dinosaur egg revealing a baby dinosaur, which Challenger plans to take to England. Only here is stop-motion animation
employed and this scene is the most convincing of the film.

THE LOVE WAR (ABC-TV, 1970) C-76 min.

        Producers, Danny Thomas and Aaron Spelling; director, George
McCowan; teleplay, Guerdon Trueblood and David Kidd; art director,
Tracy Bousman; assistant director, Wes Barry; music, Dominic Fron-
tiere; camera, Paul Uhl; editor, Bob Lewis.
        Lloyd Bridges (Kyle); Angie Dickinson (Sandy); Harry Basch
(Bal); Dan Tavantry (Ted); Bill McClean (Reed); Allen Jaffe (Hart);
and: Byron Foulger and Pepper Martin.

        Like the earlier The 10th Victim (q. v.), the futuristic premise
here is that eventually mankind will turn war into games, with repre-
sentatives fighting for each side, rather than millions of needless
deaths.
        Six aliens from two warring planets take human form and con-
tinue their battle on Earth. The numbers soon dwindle until there are

Opposite: Charging monsters in two versions of The Lost World.
Top, in the 1925 film; below, in the 1960 release.

only two survivors. Kyle (Lloyd Bridges), from Argon, does not know who his adversary from Zinan is. Besides he is weary of war and wants to live a peaceful life. On a bus he meets Sandy (Angie Dickinson) and they promptly fall in love. Still on the run from his unseen enemy, Kyle informs Sandy that he will remain with her once he has vanquished his foe. In a ghost town Kyle comes face to face with his enemy. It is Sandy. She kills him despite his pleadings that they should forget their planets' feud for the sake of love.

Location work was accomplished at Union (Train) Station in Los Angeles and at a deserted "ghost" town. It was a quickly-assembled thriller which Judith Crist rather hastily dismissed as "sappy sci-fi." It may not be deeply philosophical or expertly produced, but it offers intriguing speculation on the outcome of man's warlike nature, and Miss Dickinson is always interesting viewing.

LA LUNE A UN METRE   see   THE ASTRONOMER'S DREAM

THE MAGNETIC MONSTER (United Artists, 1953) 76 min.

Producer, Ivan Tors; director, Curt Siodmak; screenplay, Siodmak and Tors; music, Blaine Sanford; production designer, George

Leo Britt in The Magnetic Monster (1953).

Van Marter; special effects, Jack Glass; camera, Charles Van Enger.
Richard Carlson (Jeffrey Stewart); King Donovan (Dan Forbes);
Jean Bryon (Connie Stewart); Harry Ellerbe (Dr. Allard); Kathleen
Freeman and Strother Martin (Bits); Leo Britt (Benton); Byron Foul-
ger (Simon); Michael Fox (Dr. Serny); Leonard Mudie (Denker).

This Ivan Tors-Curt Siodmak project was created not only for
theatrical release, but also for a possible TV series (which never
materialized). In an essay included in Focus on the Science Fiction
Film (1972), Richard Hodgens judged, "... of all the earthly monsters, only The Magnetic Monster ... displayed much originality and
consistency."
The 76-minute feature proved to be largely an "educational"
study on the dangers of excess use of atomic energy; a magnetic isotope begins to grow and double its strength every 12 hours. The
substance takes root in a hardware store where everything becomes
magnetized by the radioactive source, which threatens to consume--
eventually--all the world's energy. But at the finish, the magnetic
substance is forced to destroy itself in a cyclotron by generating an
equal amount of counter-energy.
The final reel of the picture was actually footage from the
German-made Gold (1934), interpolated with new footage of The Magnetic Monster's hero (Richard Carlson).
Castle of Frankenstein magazine weighed it a "good, inventive
little atomic thriller," but Carlos Clarens claims, in An Illustrated
History of the Horror Film (1967), "Examples of this type [of film]
are few and unpopular, relying as they do on endless expository dialogue; and nuclear reactors and atomic piles are rather undramatic
in the long run."

THE MAGNETIC MOON see BEYOND THE MOON

THE MAN FROM 1997 (Warner Bros-TV, 1957) 56 min.

With: James Garner, Gloria Talbott, Jacques Sernas, Charles
Ruggles.

This TV feature was originally shown on the November 11,
1956 episode of ABC-TV's "Conflict" series and, like several other
such dramas, has been syndicated by NTA as a short feature to fill
compact movie time slots on local TV stations.
James Garner stars as a Polish immigrant who comes to pos-
sess a magical book which can foretell the future. With it he wins
riches and the good life. A man from the future (Charles Ruggles),
however, visits the man and reclaims the tome which was accidentally lost in a time vacuum.

THE MAN FROM PLANET X (United Artists, 1951) 70 min.

Producers, Aubrey Wisberg and Jack Pollexfen; director,

Margaret Field in The Man from Planet X (1951).

Edgar G. Ulmer; screenplay, Wisberg and Pollexfen; music, Charles
Koff; art director, Angelo Scibetti; special effects, Andy Anderson
and Howard Weeks; camera, John L. Russell; editor, Fred R. Feit-
shans, Jr.
        Robert Clarke (Lawrence); Margaret Field (Enid Elliott); Ray-
mond Bond (Professor Elliot); William Schallert (Mears); Roy Engel
(The Constable); George Davis (Geordie); Gilbert Fallman (Dr. Blane);
David Ormont (Inspector).

        In 1950 the release of The Thing (q.v.) coincided with a "fly-
ing saucer scare" which was gripping the country. The first intelligent (cinema) space invader, and the leader of a vanguard of such
celluloid aliens who would land on Earth with amazing frequency, was
a bullet-headed little man encased in a glass head-case in The Man
from Planet X. This trend-setting feature is one of the more neglected films of the genre. Thanks to Edgar G. Ulmer's ability to do
wonders with a small budget, the film is well-made and atmospheric.
It presented some Earthlings as being equally as vicious and heartless
as the invader.
        In fog-ridden Scotland a reporter named Lawrence (Robert
Clarke) has come from a big city newspaper to investigate UFO reports. Enid (Margaret Field) soon sees the invader and her father,
Professor Elliott (Raymond Bond), and his assistant, Mears (William
Schallert), attempt to capture the creature. They do so with Lawrence's help. They desire to communicate peacefully with the alien.

Mears develops a means of communication with the little "man" and
soon learns that he is from another world whose sun is dying, and
that he is the vanguard of an invasion to settle on Earth. Before
he escapes the lab, the outer space man has been tortured, in the
hope that he will reveal some information about space. Later, the
alien uses a hypnotic beam to control victims to help him repair the
damaged spacecraft. The British Army shows up and bombards the
alien and his craft with bazookas. The alien invasion is prevented.
At the finish, the Earthlings observe Planet X whizzing by in the
skies, its inhabitants doomed to be frozen to death.

MAN IN THE MOON (J. Arthur Rank, 1961) 98 min.

     Producer, Michael Relph; director, Basil Dearden; screenplay,
Relph and Dearden; production designer, Don Ashton; art director,
Jack Maxted; music, Philip Green; sound, Norman Savage, C. C.
Stevens, and Bill Daniels; camera, Harry Waxman; editor, John
Guthridge.
     Kenneth More (William Blood); Shirley Anne Field (Polly);
Norman Bird (Herbert); Michael Hordern (Dr. Davidson); John Glyn-
Jones (Dr. Wilmot); John Phillips (Professor Stephens); Charles Gray
(Leo); Bernard Horsfall (Rex); Bruce Boa (Roy); Noel Purcell (Pro-
secutor); Ed Devereaux (Storekeeper); Newton Blick (Dr. Hollis);
Richard Pearson and Lionel Gamlin (Doctors); Russell Waters

Kenneth More (center) and Michael Hordern (right) in Man in the
Moon (1961).

(Woomera Director); Danny Green (Lorry Driver); Jeremy Lloyd
(Jaguar Driver).

"By this time it is obvious that no area of human activity is
safe from the British humorists, who come very near having a mo-
nopoly these days on the business of satirizing the contemporary
scene" (New York Herald-Tribune). A more pointed evaluation came
from Variety: "It's an amiable spoof science fiction but is rarely
as funny as its original idea promises. It ambles along towards a
gimmick ending which is not strong enough to justify the word 'climax' ... The whole affair has the air of a serious film into which
comedy has been rather desperately dumped." And Time, that pur-
veyor of final judgments, decided, "A noodly British farce made by
a crew of subversives who have obviously heard more than they care
to hear about astronauts and rocket scientists."

William Blood (Kenneth More) is an uniquely healthy Britisher.
He is able to endure almost any discomfort and has a total immunity
to all diseases. He is selected to be part of a team of potential astronauts to be Britain's first men on the moon. After seemingly endless training, including athletics, refrigeration, heat endurance, rocket slides into centrifugal vehicles, Blood is chosen as the astronaut
and blasts off for his mission target from the Australian missile site.
But the flight is a failure and he returns to Earth. He returns to
England and his stripteaser girlfriend (Shirley Anne Field), telling
the scientists, "I'm sorry chaps. I guess it's back to the old draw-
ing board."

Mr. More offers a sterling performance in this offbeat entry,
one of the few spoofs to date of the sci-fi genre.

THE MAN WHO CHANGED HIS MIND (Gaumont, 1936) 68 min.

Director, Robert Stevenson; screenplay, L. du Garde Peach,
Sidney Gilliat, and John L. Balderston; makeup, Roy Ashton; camera,
Jack Cox; editor, R. E. Dearing.
Boris Karloff (Dr. Laurience); Anna Lee (Claire Wyatt); John
Loder (Dick Haslewood); Frank Cellier (Lord Haslewood); Donald Cal-
throp (Clayton); Cecil Parker (Dr. Gratton); Lyn Harding (Professor
Holloway).

In plot and production this British-made feature was little different from the series of "mad scientist" films in which Boris Karloff had been starring in Hollywood.
Here Karloff plays Dr. Laurience, a kindly scientist who, in
his lonely manor on the outskirts of London, invents a strange machine which transfers a person's mind from his body to another.
His assistant, Clayton (Donald Calthrop), is gravely ill, but is mysteriously kept alive by the doctor. When a rich publisher (Frank
Cellier) finds out about the experiments, he finances them and has
Dr. Laurience present his amazing findings to the Institute of London. There he is scoffed at by the Medical Society, which removes
his name from its roster.
The half-crazed doctor takes revenge on the publisher, whom

Donald Calthrop and Boris Karloff in <u>The Man Who Changed His Mind</u>
(1936).

he is convinced has double-crossed him. His plot involves exchang-
ing the man's mind with that of his assistant, and both men die.
Laurience then decides to share his work with his other assistant Dr.
Clare Wyatt (Anna Lee) but is distraught to note she is in love with
another, Dick Haslewood (John Loder). Laurience then commits a
murder and exchanges his mind with Dick's so that the latter will be
executed. This fails, however, and the doctor is shot trying to escape from the police. He gives Clare instructions to reverse the
process of minds and, this accomplished, he dies, making her promise
to destroy his equipment.
      The <u>New York Daily Mirror</u> commented: "... [The] settings
are on a grand scale and the players perform as melodramatically as
any California director could have demanded." The British publication
<u>Cinema</u> reported, "... the film is content to score on its strong story
values and wealth of melodramatic treatment."
      The film was released in the U.S. as <u>The Man Who Lived</u>
<u>Again</u>. It was reissued in the 1940s as <u>Dr. Maniac,</u> and it now plays
on TV as <u>The Brain Snatcher</u>. By any title, it is still the same story,
a very 1930s' concept of what psuedo-science was about and could
do.

Jane Baxter and Roland Young in The Man Who Could Work Miracles (1936).

THE MAN WHO COULD WORK MIRACLES (United Artists, 1936) 90 min.

Producer, Alexander Korda; director, Lothar Mendes; based on the short story by H. G. Wells; screenplay, Wells; music, Mischa Spoliansky; special effects, Ned Mann and Laurence Butler; special camera effects, E. Cohen; camera, Harold Rosson; editor, Philip Charlot Hornbeck.

Roland Young (George McWhirter Fotheringay); Joan Gardner (Ada Price); Ralph Richardson (Colonel Winstanley); Ernest Thesiger (Mr. Maydig); Robert Cochran (Bill Stoker); Lady Tree (Housekeeper); Wallace Lupino (P. C. Winch); Gertrude Musgrove (Effie Brickman); Edward Chapman (Major Grigsby); Sophie Stewart (Maggie Hooper); George Zucco (Moody); Bruce Winston (Landlord); Lawrence Hanray (Mr. Bampfyide); Bernard Nedell (Reporter); Wally Patch (Superintendent Smithells); Torin Thatcher, George Sanders, and Ivan Brandt (The Gods); Jane Baxter (Bit).

As a follow-up to his Things to Come (q. v.), H. G. Wells adapted his story "The Man Who Could Work Miracles" for the screen.

This offering was perhaps the better of the two British-made features, but it was not nearly so popular, perhaps because it was more whimsical fantasy than amazing futuristic fiction.

In the small village of Dewhinton, Essex, England, draper's clerk George McWhirter Fotheringay (Roland Young) receives superhuman powers from three Gods (Torin Thatcher, George Sanders, and Ivan Brandt) above. The Gods have been debating about the future of humanity and decide to bestow special powers to one Earthling, to observe how he copes with them.

At first, middle-aged Fotheringay enjoys his new capacity to do magical tricks: make things appear and disappear, or send an annoying policeman first "to blazes" and then to San Francisco. Next the man decides to use his powers for the betterment of the human race and decides to end wars. But big business powers pressure him to think otherwise. When he next determines to cure all the world's diseases, he is again advised that this would be catastrophic--it would put millions out of work. Fotheringay also learns that his strange powers have no effect on willing another to love him, as he finds to his disappointment when he romances shop girl Ada Price (Joan Gardner). Finally, a confused Fotheringay decides to make himself the ruler of the world and orders the planet to stand still. The Gods again intercede and the timid clerk is reduced back to his normal self. He now believes it was all a dream.

Mr. Wells' message is clear. The Earth is not ready for a Utopian existence, no matter how much we might wish it. Visually this rambunctious feature was more satisfying than in its slow-moving plotline. Author Wells would call the picture "a film of imaginative comedy," while the New York Herald-Tribune thought it "a first-rate film fantasy."

THE MAN WHO FELL TO EARTH (British Lion, 1976) C-140 min.

Executive producer, Si Litvinoff; producers, Michael Deeley and Barry Spikings; director, Nicholas Roeg; based on the novel by Walter Tevis; screenplay, Paul Mayersberg; music director, John Phillips; assistant director, Kip Gowans; sound, Robin Gregory; camera, Anthony Richmond; editor, Graeme Clifford.

David Bowie (Thomas Jerome Newton); Rip Torn (Nathan Bryce); Candy Clark (Mary-Lou); Buck Henry (Oliver Farnsworth); Bernie Casey (Peters); Jackson D. Kane (Professor Canutti); Rick Riccardo (Trevor); Tony Mascia (Arthur); Linda Hutton (Elaine); Hilary Holland (Jill); Adrienne Larussa (Helen); Lilybell Crawford (Jewelry Store Owner); Richard Breeding (Receptionist); Peter Prouse (Peter's Associate); Captain James Lovell (Himself).

"Though its cult future seems assured, its immediate chances will depend on audience reaction to its intriguingly offbeat appeal as a cerebral sci-fier, a sort of earthbound 2001: A Space Odyssey [q. v.] with Clockwork Orange [q. v.] undertones--though it remains a very different film indeed" (Variety).

An alien (David Bowie) descends to Earth from a drought-stricken planet to seek a water supply for his people. Assuming the

name Thomas Jerome Newton, the android finds patent attorney Oliver
Farnsworth (Buck Henry) and delivers to him some basic home-
brewed inventions from his outer space world. These are turned into money-generating patents by Farnsworth, who rises to run an in-
dustrial empire, with Newton his only superior. While waiting to
obtain the funds to build the space craft with which he can transport
his people back to Earth, Newton becomes enamored of a hotel clerk
named Mary-Lou (Candy Clark) and becomes involved with a relent-
less scientist, Nathan Bryce (Rip Torn). The latter betrays him to
the authorities. They in turn decide that one alien visitor is enough
for the Earth. A defeated man, Newton is forced to wander the
Earth, an oddity among odd mankind.

"The movie is pretty straightforward science fiction with a
gloss of social commentary thrown in.... What is compelling about
the film and what makes it still of interest is the burning immediacy
of the images: Newton skidding down a hill against a primordial New
Mexico landscape; crossing the blasted wastes of a distant planet;
Newton, finally without earthly disguise, standing as he really is before a terrified Mary-Lou or removing contact lenses from his hol-
low, glowing eyes" (Time).

For its U. S. release some twenty minutes were chopped from
the film. The box-office gimmick of having rock star David Bowie
in the lead (he does not sing here), teamed with Candy (American
Graffiti) Clark created interest in the film beyond its natural audience.
Without glitter, Bowie proved rather stalwart in the title role; but
Miss Clark as the oddball heroine was at acting odds with her co-
star.

THE MAN WHO LIVED AGAIN   see   THE MAN WHO CHANGED HIS
MIND

THE MAN WHO WANTED TO LIVE FOREVER (ABC-TV, 1970) C-88
min.

        Executive producers, Edgar J. Scherick and Henry Denker;
producer, Terence Dene; director, John Trent; screenplay, Denker;
art director, Jack McAdam; set decorator, Earl Fisset; music/mu-
sic director, Dolores Claman; assistant director, Al Simmonds;
sound, Russ Heise; sound editors, Ralph Brunjes and Ron Wisman;
camera, Marc Champion.
        Stuart Whitman (McCarter Purvis); Sandy Dennis (Enid); Burl
Ives (T. M. Trask); Tom Harvey (McBride); Robert Goodier (Morton); Jack Creley (Simmons); Ron Hartman (Emmett); Allan Doremus
(Bryant); Joseph Shaw (Heinemann); Kenneth James (Clinton); Clem
Harbourg (Pianist); and Harvey Fisher, Robert Warner, James Forrest, and Robert Mann.

        Presented as an episode of the ABC-TV "Movie of the Week,"
this entry was made in Canada. Despite a strong cast and sturdy
production values, it failed to impress American TV critics other
than containing a "very silly" (Judith Crist, TV Guide) story. On

the other hand, when it was released theatrically in England in 1971 as The Only Way Out is Dead, the British Monthly Film Bulletin complimented it on managing "to touch on the truly frightening potentialities of spare-part surgery, as well as polishing off routine suspense gimmicks with an entertaining flare."

Dr. McCarter Purvis (Stuart Whitman) is jobless after being dismissed for an unorthodox and unsuccessful organ transplant operation at his hospital. He accepts a post at T. M. Trask's (Burl Ives) Science City, located in a remote mountain hideaway. Another physician there, Enid (Sandy Dennis), informs Purvis that all the staff at Science City have the same blood and tissue type as the bed-ridden Trask. They later discover he plans to use his employees for heart transplant operations to keep himself alive. Purvis and Enid escape via the ski slopes and soon are out of Trask's domain. But the megalomaniacal Trask has already devised a scheme so that Purvis' story will not be believed by the outside world. For the meanwhile, he plans to use the heart of one of his helicopter pilots as the next transplant.

THE MAN WITH THE X-RAY EYES   see   X--THE MAN WITH THE X-RAY EYES

MANHUNT IN SPACE   see   BEYOND THE MOON

MAROONED (Columbia, 1969) C-133 min.

Producer, Mike J. Frankovich; associate producer, Frank Capra, Jr.; director, John Sturges; based on the novel by Martin Caidin; screenplay, Mayo Simon; second unit director, Ralph Black; assitant director, Daniel Caidin; production designer, Lyle R. Wheeler; set decorator, Frank Tuttle; costumes, Seth Banks; technical advisors, Martin Caidin and George Smith; sound, Les Fresholtz and Arthur Piantadosi; special visual effects, Lawrence W. Butler, Donald C. Glouner, and Robie Robinson; camera, Daniel Fapp; second unit camera, W. Wallace Kelley; aerial camera, Nelson Tyler; editor, Walter Thompson.

Gregory Peck (Charles Keith); Richard Crenna (Jim Pruett); David Janssen (Ted Dougherty); James Franciscus (Clayton Stone); Gene Hackman (Buzz Lloyd); Lee Grant (Celia Purett); Nancy Kovack (Teresa Stone); Mariette Hartley (Betty Lloyd); Scott Brady (Public Affairs Officer); Craig Huebing (Flight Director); John Carter (Flight Surgeon); George Gaynes (Mission Director); Tom Stewart (Houston Cape-Commander); Frank Marth (Space Systems Director); George Smith (Cape Weather Officer); Mauritz Hugo (Hardy); Bill Couch (Russian Cosmonaut); Mary-Linda Rapalye (Priscilla Keith).

Director John Sturges borrowed many of the plot elements of suspense from his 1953 melodrama Jeopardy and transferred them to the sci-fi genre for Marooned, the very possible story of astronauts caught in outer space and unable to return to Earth.

Astronauts Jim Pruett (Richard Crenna), Clayton Stone (James Franciscus), and Buzz Lloyd (Gene Hackman) have been launched in "Ironman One" to join up with an orbiting space lab. Their mission is to test man's capacity to function in outer space. After five months the men are fatigued and are ordered home by Charles Keith (Gregory Peck), the mission controller. Once back in "Ironman One" the astronauts discover that their re-entry rockets will not fire. Upon orders from the President a special rescue squad headed by Ted Dougherty (David Janssen) is launched. In the interim Pruett has given up his own life to leave his fellow astronauts adequate oxygen. Before Dougherty's rescue craft arrives, a Russian cosmonaut in his space capsule helps the floundering American space travelers. Also involved are the astronauts' frantic wives (Lee Grant, Mariette Hartley, and Nancy Kovack).

Nominated for three Academy Awards, Marooned, said Variety, was "timely ... [with] box office prospects strong though weakness inherent in contrivances of 'rescue'." Critic Judith Crist was harsher, dismissing the picture as "space travel soap opera ... a long lugubrious spectacle.... It has all the zip, zest and zing of a moon walk, and I suspect a computer-fed dictionary could come up with better dialogue...."

What struck most viewers about this film was not that it contained superior special effects, a striking backdrop, or a mediocre story, but that what they were seeing could come true. For space travel to date is truly a very fragile thing, based on vast research and work, but it requires only one mistake (or one misfire, as in Marooned) to end in disaster.

James Franciscus, Gene Hackman and Richard Crenna in Marooned (1969).

The very expensively-mounted Marooned did not live up to box-office expectations. Domestically it grossed only $4.35 million.

MARS ATTACKS THE WORLD see FLASH GORDON'S TRIP TO MARS

MASTER OF TERROR see THE 4-D MAN

MASTER OF THE WORLD (American International, 1961) C-104 min.

Executive producer, Samuel Z. Arkoff; producer, James H. Nicholson; director, William Witney; based on the novels Master of the World and Robur, the Conqueror by Jules Verne; screenplay, Richard Matheson; music composer/conductor, Les Baxter; song, Baxter and Lenny Addelson; orchestrator, Albert Harris; art director, Daniel Haller; set decorator, Harry Reif; makeup Fred Philipps; wardrobe, Marjorie Corso; assistant director, Robert Agnew; sound, Karl Zint, Bill Warmarth, Vinnie Vernon, and Jerry Alexander; special effects, Tim Barr, Wah Chang, and Gene Warren; special props and effects, Pat Dinga; camera effects, Ray Mercer; camera, Gil Warrenton; aerial camera, Kay Norton; editor, Anthony Carras.
Vincent Price (Robur); Charles Bronson (Strock); Henry Hull (Prudent); Mary Webster (Dorothy); David Frankham (Philip); Richard Harrison (Alistair); Vito Scotti (Topage); Wally Campo (Turner); Steve Masino (Weaver); Ken Terrell (Shanks); Peter Besbas (Wilson).

For one of its early excursions into the arena of high-budget filmmaking, American International selected a sure-fire box-office ingredient: works by Jules Verne. With a scenario by Richard Matheson, direction by old-time action serial expert William Witney, an excellent score (now a collector's item) by Les Baxter, and fine special effects, the film proved to be very popular and a delight for adventure fans. Perhaps the biggest financial draw of the film was the casting of Vincent Price as the title character, known as Robur.
In 1848, government agent Strock (Charles Bronson), accompanied by a munitions manufacturer, Prudent (Henry Hull), his daughter Dorothy (Mary Webster), and her fiancé Philip (David Frankham), investigates a number of strange eruptions in the vicinity of a Pennsylvania crater. Their balloon is shot down by Robur (Price) and they become his prisoners. It turns out that he is an inventor who has constructed a fabulous flying craft, "The Albatross," by means of which he intends to destroy all war instruments, bringing peace to the world. On their global path, Robur destroys the English naval yards, as well as the armies of Austria and Egpyt. Later, Strock manages to help the others escape while the craft is being repaired on a Mediterranean island. He plants explosives which cause "The Albatross" to sink to the bottom of the ocean, killing Robur and its crew.
"The featured player in effect is the flying craft, which as in most recent film derivations from 19th century Verne's conceptions,

Henry Hull, Mary Webster, Vincent Price, David Frankham and
Charles Bronson in Master of the World (1961).

combines the futuristic and the archaic, looks like a Zeppelin with an
oil refinery mounted on top, stained glass windows in the control cabin and various interior appurtenances mildly Victorian in style....
One can't help wondering if a younger generation that takes for granted the likely invasion of the moon will be suitably impressed by the
mechanical ingenuity or amused by the archaic decor" (New York
Herald-Tribune). The answer to the Tribune's query is yes.

MEMORIES OF THE FUTURE see CHARIOTS OF THE GODS?

MEN WITH STEEL FACES see THE PHANTOM EMPIRE

MENACE FROM OUTER SPACE see BEYOND THE MOON

METROPOLIS (Ufa, 1927) seventeen reels

        Producer, Erich Pommer; director, Fritz Lang; based on the
novel by Thea von Harbou; screenplay, Lang and von Harbou; art directors, Otto Hunte, Rich Kettelhut, and Karl Vollbrecht; costumes,

Alfred Abel and Rudolf Klein-Rogge in Metropolis (1927).

Anne Willkomm; music, Gottfried Happertz and Konrad Elfers; spe-
cial effects, Eugen Shuftan; camera, Karl Freund and Günther Rittau.
     Alfred Abel (Jon Fredersen); Gustav Fröhlich (Freder); Brigit-
te Helm (Maria); Rudolf Klein-Rogge (Rotwang); Fritz Rasp (Slim);
Theodor Loos (Josaphat); Erwin Biswanger (No. 11811); Heinrich
George (Foreman); Olaf Storm (Jan); Hanns Leo Reich (Marinus); and
Heinrich Gotho, Margarete Lanner, Max Dietze, Georg John, Walter
Kuhle, Arthur Rheinhard, Erwin Vater, Grete Berger, Olly Boheim,
Ellen Frey, Lisa Gray, Rose Lichtenstein, Helene Weigel, Beatrice
Garga, Anny Hintze, Helen von Munchhofen, Hilde Woitscheff, and
Fritz Alberti.

     In the year 2000 A.D. in the titanic title citadel there are
two district divisions in the classes: the labor force lives beneath
the city in slums and slaves in ten-hour shifts (turning the dials and
firing the furnaces which give Metropolis its power), while the upper
classes reside in luxury in the area above ground. Ruling over this
complex domain is Jon Fredersen (Alfred Abel), the master builder
and designer. His son Freder (Gustav Fröhlich), however, meets a
young girl, Maria (Brigitte Helm), and is sympathetic to the causes
of the masses. He goes below to take part in their gruelling work.

When the architect learns there are rumors of revolt among
the masses he visits a mad scientist, Rotwang (Rudolf Klein-Rogge),
hoping to learn the sources of the discontent. The man shows him
that it is Maria and he also unveils his newest invention, a mechanical robot. Fredersen orders him to make a robot in the exact image
of Maria so that this metal representation can foment chaos among
the workers. The robot tells the masses to destroy the dikes; they
do it, and soon their homes are flooded and many of their children
killed. Meanwhile Maria escapes from Rotwang and leads some of
the children to safety. Later Rotwang tries to kill Maria while the
masses burn the robot, thinking it is the troublesome girl. Subsequently Freder kills Rotwang. At the finale Fredersen and the leader of the revolting masses agree to work together to build a better
world. Freder and Maria can now embark on a life of happiness.
    In The Cinema of Fritz Lang (1969), Paul Jensen analyzes,
"Despite such occasional atmospheric success, Metropolis is simply
a compendium of Lang's theme with none sufficiently dramatised to
make it meaningful. There is mob violence, seduction, insanity,
duality of good and evil, the innocent hero, the threatening environment, the master-mind, opposing social forces, the virtues of love,
and even an attempt at science-mysticism-religion. But it is not for
any of these that the film will be remembered.
    "Aside from the atmosphere ... the chief merit of Metropolis
is its visual style. Most individual shots are carefully composed,
with the emphasis on a balanced arrangement of objects within the
frame. The organisation of shapes is formalised, but seldom as static as the picture's detractors claim. Many scenes require movement
for their effects, such as when the edge of the flood approaches the
fleeing children; in another case, only a few workers at the Tower
of Babel are standing in the foreground until a shift in position reveals thousands in the distance."
    A cold, stark film, Metropolis was a gigantic production for
Ufa, and it failed to pay off its enormous costs, leaving the studio
heavily in debt. When it was re-vamped for its American release
later in 1927, some seven reels were chopped from the film's original seventeen, with Channing Pollock, Julian Johnson, and Edward
Adams overseeing the revisions for the Paramount release. Unfortunately, this is the version which survives today, leaving the modern
viewer with only the muddled narrative of Lang's enormous expres-
sionistic conception.

MICROSCOPIA   see   FANTASTIC VOYAGE

MILCZACA GWITZADA   see   DER SCHWEIGENDE STERN

THE MIND BENDERS   see   QUATERMASS AND THE PIT

MISSILE MONSTERS   see   FLYING DISC MAN FROM MARS

MISSILE TO THE MOON (Astor, 1958) 78 min.

Producer, Marc Frederic; director, Richard Cunha; screenplay, H. E. Barrie and Vincent Fotre; music, Nicholas Carras; assistant director, Leonard J. Shapiro; makeup, Harry Thomas; set decorator, Harry Reif; costumes, Marjorie Corso; sound, Robert Post; sound effects, Harold Wooley; visual effects, Harold Banks; special effects, Ira Anderson; camera, Meredith Nicholson; editor, Everett Dodd.

Richard Travis (Arnold Dayton); Cathy Downs (June Saxton); K. T. Stevens (Queen Lido); Tommy Cook (Gary); Nina Bara (Alpha); Gary Clarke (Lon); Michael Whalen (Dirk Green); Laurie Mitchell (Lambda); Marjorie Hellen (Zeema); Lee Roberts (Henry Hunter); Sandra Wirth, Pat Mowry, Tania Velia, Sanita Pelkey, Lisa Simone, Marianne Gaba, Renta Hoy, and Mary Ford (Moon Women).

In 1958 Astor Pictures remade one of its earlier efforts, Cat-Women of the Moon (q. v.). The results were negligible. "None of Missile is very rewarding and it is so clumsily and unimaginatively done that the lack of conviction is staggering" (New York Herald-Tribune).

Space scientist Dirk Green (Michael Whalen), with the help of two reform school escapees (Tommy Cook and Gary Clarke), launches a missile to the moon. Green's associate Arnold Dayton (Richard Travis) and his fiancée (Cathy Downs) are unintentionally aboard the craft. En route they learn that Green is actually a moon man who had come to Earth to learn the ways of mankind. Green is killed when the ship passes through a missile field. On the moon the group is captured by Queen Lido (K. T. Stevens) and her moon women (cast from assorted beauty contest winners). Eventually they escape, are detained by the aggressive rock creatures, but thanks to the sacrifice of Gary, the survivors reach the safety of their space craft and plan to return to Earth.

Castle of Frankenstein magazine warned, that the film was "brimming with stock shots, laughable sets and 'special effects,' [and that the] grade-C space opera succeeds in one respect: it's worse than its forerunner."

MISSION MARS (Allied Artists, 1968) C-87 min.

Executive producer, Morton Fallick; producer, Everett Rosenthal; director, Nick Webster; story, Aubrey Wisberg; screenplay, Mike St. Clair; music, Berge Kalajian and Gus Pardalis; production designer, Hank Aldrich; assistant director, Sal Scoppa; costumes, Grover Cole; sound, Sanford Rackow; special effects, Haberstroh Studios; camera, Cliff Poland; supervising editor, Michael Calamari; editor, Paul Jordan.

Darren McGavin (Mike Blaiswick); Nick Adams (Nick Grant); George De Vries (Duncan); Heather Hewitt (Edith Blaiswick); Michael De Beausset (Cliff Lawson); Shirley Parker (Alice Grant); Bill Kelly (Russian Astronaut); Chuck Zink (Chuck the Radio Operator); Ralph Miller (Simpson); Art Barker (Doctor); Monroe Myers (Lawson's Aide).

Darren McGavin and Heather Hewitt in <u>Mission Mars</u> (1968).

"... an okay science-fictioner via a fairly original climactic
sequence which occurs once the film's team of future astronauts
reaches Mars. For, like <u>2001: A Space Odyssey</u> [q. v.], this film
sees monsters on distant planets as abstract rather than humanoid.
Unfortunately, the picture's final bit of ingenuity is preceded by an
hour of overwrought and cliched dramaturgy" (<u>Variety</u>). The project
was filmed entirely in Miami Beach.
    Mike Blaiswick (Darren McGavin), Nick Grant (Nick Adams),
and Duncan (George De Vries) are the first astronauts to make a
flight to Mars. Along the way they spot the frozen bodies of two
Russian cosmonauts who failed to reach Mars. Later they find another Soviet pathfinder frozen in the sub-zero atmosphere. He later
revives and helps Blaiswick and Grant (Duncan has been consumed
by an oversized ball-shaped object) combat the polarite enemy by re-
ducing its solar energy source. Grant dies in the effort, but Blaiswick and the Russian are able to return to Earth.

MISSION STARDUST   see   ORBITA MORTAL

MISTRESS OF ATLANTIS   see   L'ATLANTIDE (1932)

THE MOLTEN METEOR   see   THE BLOB

THE MONITORS (Commonwealth United, 1969) C-92 min.

Producer, Bernard Sahlins; director, Jack Shea; screenplay, Myron J. Gold; art director, Roy Henry; music, Fred Kaz; camera, William Zsigmond; editor, Patrick Kennedy.

Guy Stockwell (Harry); Susan Oliver (Barbara); Avery Schreiber (Max); Sherry Jackson (Mona); Shepperd Strudwick (Tersh); Keenan Wynn (General); Ed Begley (President); Larry Storch (Colonel Stutz); and Alan Arkin, Adam Arkin, Xavier Cugat, Stubby Kaye, Jackie Vernon, and Senator Everett Dirkson.

Filmed in Chicago by that metropolis' Second City cabaret troupe, this sought to be a preachment for human love and understanding. However, it emerged a dull mishmash of ideology, sci-fi, and bizarre cameo performances.

The Monitors are a super-intelligent race from another Universe who have invaded the Earth and taken control of the human race. They have regulated humans to being mere entities of existence, so that they cannot harm themselves or the Monitors. Finally a few Earthlings (Guy Stockwell, Susan Oliver, Avery Schreiber, et al.) form an underground resistance movement which overthrows the invaders, forcefully showing them that man is independent and wants to rule himself.

The film was "drowned by heavyhanded humor and undigested 'serious' moments," reported Variety. Perhaps the picture's funniest line occurred when cement-faced comic Jackie Vernon, doing a TV promotional spot for the invaders, announces, "The Monitors ... they're my kind of guys."

THE MONOLITH MONSTERS (Universal, 1957) 77 min.

Producer, Howard Christie; director, John Sherwood; story, Jack Arnold and Robert H. Fresco; screenplay, Norman Jolley and Fresco; makeup, Bud Westmore; art directors, Alexander Golitzen and Bob Smith; music supervisor, Joseph Gershenson; special camera effects, Clifford Stine; camera, Ellis W. Carter; editor, Patrick McCormack.

Grant Williams (Dave Miller); Lola Albright (Cathy Barrett); Les Tremayne (Martin Cochrane); Trevor Bardette (Professor Arthur Flanders); William Flaherty (Police Chief Dan Corey); Harry Jackson (Dr. Steve Hendricks); William Schallert (Weather Man); Linda Scheley (Ginny Simpson); Richard Cutting (Dr. Reynolds); Dean Cromer (Joe Higgins).

Jack Arnold co-wrote the original screen story for this appealing minor sci-fi thriller. The Monolith Monsters was one of the better of the tail-end films Universal turned out in the sci-fi cycle during the late Fifties.

The title monsters are actually meteor deposits from outer space which increase in size when touched by water. Also the monoliths absorb the silicone in humans, converting them into rocks. The stones grow in size until they are tumbling and mowing down most of

From The Monolith Monsters (1957).

the world.   Finally science finds out how to halt their advance--with salt.
        The Monolith Monsters was a different kind of entry in that the stratospheric invaders were not intelligent beings but works of nature, something that was plausible to the minds of filmgoers.   That the destructive abilities of these giant rocks was so admirably presented heightened the effect of their awesome power.

THE MONSTER FROM GREEN HELL (Distributors Corp. of America, 1958) 71 min.

        Producer, Al Zimbalist; director, Kenneth Crane; screenplay, Louis Vittes and Endre Bohen; special effects, Jess Davison; special camera effects, Jack Rabin and Louis DeWitt; camera, Ray Flin.
        Jim Davis (Quent Brady); Robert E. Griffin (Dan Morgan); Barbara Turner (Lorna Lorentz); Eduardo Ciannelli (Mahri); Vladimir Sokoloff (Dr. Lorentz); Joel Fleullen (Arobi); Tim Huntley (Territorial Agent); Frederic Potler (Radar Operator); LaVerne Jones (Kuana).

        An experimental space craft, filled with wasps, crashes in the African jungle.   Due to cosmic radiation the wasps enlarge in size, except for the wings, and they are thus unable to fly.   These abnormal insects terrorize the jungle and the natives.   An expedition of scientists fails to combat the peril.   Finally the mutant wasps are done in by a volcanic eruption.

Jim Davis in The Monster from Green Hell (1958).

This mediocre sci-fi chiller boasted a good cast (Jim Davis, Eduardo Ciannelli, Vladimir Sokoloff) which was unable to compensate for the silly dialogue and situations. The second-rate special effects left the film a very limp entry. Only its exploitable title gave the production any box-office push.

MONSTER OF TERROR   see   DIE, MONSTER, DIE

MONSTER ZERO   see   KAIJU DAISENSO

LOS MONSTRUOUS DEL TERROR   see   EL HOMBRE QUE VINE DEL UMMO

MOON PILOT (Buena Vista, 1962) C-98 min.

Producer, Walt Disney; co-producer, Bill Anderson; director, James Nielson; story, Robert Buckner; screenplay, Maurice Tombragel; music, Paul Smith; orchestrator, Joseph O. Roop; songs, Richard M.

and Robert B. Sherman; art directors, Carroll Clark and Marvin Aubrey
Davis; set decorators, Emile Kuri and William L. Stevens; assistant di-
rector, Joseph L. McEveety; costumes, Chuck Keehne and Gertrude
Casey; makeup, Pat McNalley; sound, Robert O. Cook and Harry M.
Lindgren; special effects, Eustace Lycett; camera, William Snyder; edi-
tor, Cotton Warburton.

Tom Tryon (Captain Richmond Talbot); Brian Keith (Major
General John Vanneman); Edmond O'Brien (McClosky); Dany Saval
(Lyrae); Tommy Kirk (Walter Talbot); Bob Sweeney (Senator Mc-
Guire); Kent Smith (Secretary of the Air Force); Simon Scott (Medical
Officer); Bert Remsen (Agent Brown); Sarah Selby (Mrs. Celia Tal-
bot); Dick Whittinghill (Colonel Briggs); Cheeta (Charlie the Chimp);
and Nancy Kulp, William Hudson, and Robert Brubaker.

There have been very few intentional science-fiction spoofs/
fantasies in recent years. This Walt Disney production, geared
strictly for young minds, appealed to both the public and the critics.
"Flippant fantasy.... Although such levity might seem out of keeping
with the general seriousness of the actual space program, the air of
fantasy surely divorces it sufficiently from reality to avert any such
charge" (New York Herald-Tribune). Time lauded, "a fairly steady
stream of healthy nonsense."

Charlie the Chimp has made a successful space flight and now
Captain Richmond Talbot (Tom Tryon) has been "volunteered" to join
the animal in another space orbit. On a leave home to visit his
mother, Talbot encounters a strange girl named Lyrae (Dany Saval).
He is convinced the girl is a spy and contacts his superiors. Later
she confesses that she is from the peaceful planet of Beta Lyrae and
that her mission is one of warning: technical advice on his forth-
coming space flight. He passes on the data to his commander and
when his craft is re-equipped, he is launched on his trip. Who should
appear in the space cabin but Lyrae. The couple decide to pay a
honeymoon visit to Beta Lyrae before making his moon landing.

MOON ZERO TWO (Warner-Pathé, 1969) C-100 min.

Producer, Michael Carreras; director, Roy Ward Baker; story,
Gavin Lyall, Frank Hardman, and Martin Davison; screenplay, Carreras; assistant director, Jack Martin; art director, Scott MacGregor;
music, Don Ellis; music supervisor, Philip Martell; costumes, Carl
Toms; sound, Claude Hitchcock; sound editor, Roy Hyde; sound re-
recorder, Len Abbott; special effects, Les Bowie; special camera
effects, Kit West and Nick Allder; camera, Paul Beeson; editor,
Spencer Reeve.

James Olson (Bill Kemp); Catherina von Schell (Clementine
Taplin); Warren Mitchell (J. J. Hubbard); Adrienne Corri (Liz Mur-
phy); Ori Levy (Karminski); Dudley Foster (Whitsun); Bernard Bress-
law (Harry); Neil McCallum (Space Captain); Joby Blanshard (Smith);
Michael Ripper and Robert Tayman (Card Players); Keith Bonnard
(Junior Customs Officer); Leo Britt (Senior Customs Officer); Carol
Cleveland (Hostess); Roy Evans (Workman); Tom Kempinski (Officer);
Chrissie Shrimpton (Boutique Attendant); Amber Dean Smith and

Simone Silvers (Hubbard's Girlfriends); and the Go-Jos.

Billed as the "first space-western," this motion picture was concocted by Hammer Films for approximately $2 million. Unfortunately the picture did not click with the public, because real space age adventures were more startling in concept and execution. "It's all just about bad enough to fill older audiences with nostalgia for the inspired innocence of Flash Gordon, or even the good old days of Abbott and Costello in outer space" (British Monthly Film Bulletin). In the year 2021 A.D., the moon has been colonized and Moon City is a reality. For many, the golden age of space exploration is a glory of the past. Bill Kemp (James Olson), once famous as the first man to land on Mars, is now a ferry ship pilot, using his craft "Moon Zero 2" to earn his livelihood. On Moon City, guns have been outlawed but the sixshooter is still employed to settle many a problem. A wealthy magnate, J. J. Hubbard (Warren Mitchell), plans to harness a six-thousand-ton asteroid made of sapphire to the far side of the moon and thereby gain control of the universe with its power. Kemp is hired for the mission and this leads him to the discovery that Hubbard and his henchmen have killed the brother of Clementine Taplin (Catherina von Schell), hoping to use his claim on the far side of the moon for landing the asteroid. Later, police chief Liz Murphy (Adrienne Corri) is killed by Hubbard's men, but Kemp emerges the victor. In the finale, Clementine is now owner of her brother's claim, including the asteroid (which Kemp had crashed onto the moon). It just happens to contain sufficient material needed for new outer space probes and Kemp can again be a pioneer.

One wonders how Gene Autry, Roy Rogers, or Hopalong Cassidy would act in such a setting?

MORTAL ORBIT   see   ORBITA MORTAL

MOTHRA (Toho, 1961) C-100 min.

Producer, Tomoyuki Tanaka; director, Inoshiro Honda; story, Shinichiro Nakamura, Takehiko Fukunaga, and Yoshie Hotta; screenplay, Sekizawa; music, Yuji Koseki; art directors, Takeo Kita and Kimei Abe; sound, Shoichi Fujinawa and Masanobo Miyazaki; special effects, Eiji Tsuburaya; camera, Hajime Koizumi.

English-language dubbed version: producer, David Horne; director, Lee Kresel; screenplay, Robert Myerson.

Franky Sakai (The Reporter); Hiroshi Koizumi (The Photographer); Kyoko Katawa (The Showman); The Itoh Sisters (The Twins).

As demonstrated here, man's incessant efforts to perfect war weapons and push into the future bring the past to haunt him.

On a Pacific isle, the site of an H-bomb test, inspectors find tiny twin women (the Itoh Sisters) guarding a huge, sacred egg. The women are brought back to civilization where they are exhibited to the masses. Meanwhile the egg hatches and a giant insect larva emerges and spins a cocoon which later produces the giant moth. It heads out to sea, in search of the two beautiful girls. Atomic weapons, which caused the creature to mutate, are useless against Mothra. Finally, in desperation, the government turns the twins over to the giant moth; the three return to their island.

Mothra marked the first time in a Japanese monster/sci-fi movie that a creature was permitted to live at the fade-out. The film also marked a decided comedown in the production values of the Toho studio; the models for Tokyo (from houses to cars) were all too obviously miniatures. It displayed none of the care exhibited in Godzilla (q. v.) and other such vehicles.

Despite its artistic problems, the film about the giant moth proved popular with Japanese filmgoers (and to a lesser extent in English-language countries). In 1964 Mothra returned to do battle with Godzilla in Godzilla vs. Mothra (Godzilla vs. The Thing) and in that contest the mighty being received his only celluloid defeat. In 1965, however, the two creatures, along with Rodan, teamed up to do battle with Ghidrah in Ghidorah, Sandai Kaiju Chikyu Saidai No Kessan (Ghidrah, the Three-Headed Monster) (q. v.), and in 1968 Mothra made yet another appearance. It was in Destroy All Monsters, a convention of Toho creatures.

MUTINY IN OUTER SPACE/AMMUTINAMENTO NELLO SPAZIO (Allied Artists, 1965) 85 min.

     Producers, Hugo Grimaldi and Arthur C. Pierce; director, Grimaldi; screenplay, Pierce; assistant director, Phil Cook; art director, Paul Sylos; music director/sound effects supervisor, Gordon Zahler; camera, Archie Dalzell; editor, George White.
     William Leslie (Towers); Dolores Faith (Faith Montaine); Pamela Curran (Connie); Richard Garland (Colonel Cromwell); James Dobson (Dr. Hoffman); Carl Crow (Webber); and Harold Lloyd, Jr., Ron Stokes, Robert Palmer, Gabriel Curtis, and Glenn Langan.
     A. k. a. Invasion from the Moon / Space Station X / Space Station X-14.

     An Italian/U. S. co-production, Mutiny in Outer Space tells of the exploration of planets centered around a traveling space station. A returning space craft carries with it a form of interplanetary fungus. Astronaut Webber (Carl Crow) dies from it, but the station physician, Dr. Hoffman (James Dobson), who contracts it, realizes that extreme cold will kill the fungus. The crew at the space station later mutinies when Colonel Cromwell (Richard Garland) refuses to contact Earth for help. The rebels refrigerate the station and call Earth for assistance. A rescue squad arrives and saturates the station with frozen particles, which kills the marauding fungus.
     A decidedly minor addition to the core of sci-fi pictures.

THE MYSTERIANS see CHIKYU BOEIGUN

THE MYSTERIOUS INVADER see THE ASTOUNDING SHE CREATURE

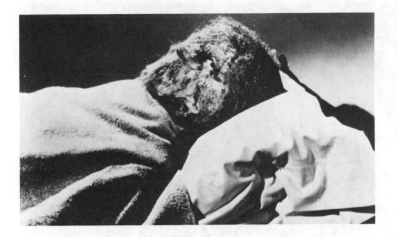

This sleeping beauty is from Mutiny in Outer Space (1965).

THE MYSTERIOUS ISLAND (MGM, 1929) C-9,569'

Directors, Lucien Hubbard, Maurice Tourneur, and Benjamin Christensen; based on the novel L'Ile mystérieuse by Jules Verne; screenplay, Hubbard; art director, Cedric Gibbons; music, Martin Broones and Arthur Lange; technical effects, James Basevi, Louis H. Tolhurst, and Irving Ries; sound, Douglas Shearer; camera, Percy Hilburn; editor, Carl L. Pierson.

Lionel Barrymore (Count Dakkar); Jane Daly (Sonia); Lloyd Hughes (Nikolai); Montagu Love (Falon); Harry Gribbon (Mikhail); Snitz Edwards (Anton); Gibson Gowland (Dmitry); Dolores Brinkman (Teresa).

MYSTERIOUS ISLAND (Children's Film Studio, 1941)

Director, E. Penzline and B. M. Chelintzev; based on the novel L'Ile mystérieuse by Jules Verne; screenplay, B. M. Chelintzev and M. P. Kalinine; special effects, M. F. Karukov; camera, M. B. Belskine.

With: M. V. Commisarov, A. S. Krasnopolski, P. I. Klansky, and R. Ross.

MYSTERIOUS ISLAND (Columbia, 1951) fifteen chapters

Producer, Sam Katzman; director, Spencer Gordon Bennet; based on the novel L'Ile mystérieuse by Jules Verne; screenplay, Lewis Clay, Royal K. Cole, and George H. Plympton; music, Mischa Bakaleinikoff; assistant director, R. M. Andrews; camera, Fayte

Browne; editor, Earl Turner.

Richard Crane (Captain Harding); Marshall Reed (Jack Pen-croft); Karen Randle (Rulu); Ralph Hodges (Bert Brown); Gene Roth (Captain Shard); Hugh Prosser (Gideon Spilett); Terry Frost (Ayrton); Rusty Wescoatt (Moley); Bernard Hamilton (Neb); Leonard Penn (Captain Nemo).

Chapters: 1) Lost in Space; 2) Sinister Savages; 3) Savage Justice; 4) Wild Man at Large; 5) Trail of the Mystery Man; 6) The Pirates Attack; 7) Menace of the Mercurians; 8) Between Two Fires; 9) Shrine of the Silver Bird; 10) Fighting Fury; 11) Desperate Chance; 12) Mystery of the Mine; 13) Jungle Downfall; 14) Men from Tomorrow; 15) The Last of Mysterious Island.

MYSTERIOUS ISLAND (Columbia, 1961) C-100 min.

Producer, Charles H. Schneer; director, Cy Enfield; based on the novel L'Ile mystérieuse by Jules Verne; screenplay, John Prebble, Daniel Ullman, and Crane Wilbur; art director, Bill Andrews; music Bernard Herrmann; special effects, Ray Harryhausen; underwater camera, Egil Woxholt; camera, Wilkie Cooper; editor, Frederick Wilson.

Michael Craig (Captain Cyrus Harding); Joan Greenwood (Lady Mary Fairchild); Michael Callan (Herbert Brown); Gary Merrill (Gideon Spilett); Herbert Lom (Captain Nemo); Beth Rogan (Elena); Percy Herbert (Sergeant Pencroft); Dan Jackson (Neb); Nigel Green (Tom).

THE MYSTERIOUS ISLAND / L'ILE MYSTERIEUSE (French/Spanish/ U.S., 1972) C-96

Producer, Jacques Bar; directors, Juan Antonio Bardem and Henri Colpi; based on the novel by Jules Verne; screenplay, Bardem and Jacques Champreux; assistant directors, Jean-Claude Garcia and Jose Puyol; music, Gianni Ferrio; designers, Cubero y Galicia and Philippe Ancellin; costumes, Leon Revuelta and Peris Hermanos; camera, Enzo Serafin, Guy Delecluze, and Juilo Ortaz; editors, Paul Cayatte, Aurore Camp, and Frederique Michaud.

Omar Sharif (Captain Nemo); Philippe Nicaud (Spilett); Gerald Tichy (Smith); Jess Hann (Pencroff); Rafael Bardem (Herbert); Ambroise M'Bia (Bit); Gabriele Tinti (Ayrton); Vidal Molina (Harvey); and Rick Bataglia (Finch).

A. k. a. The Mysterious Island of Captain Nemo.

No less than five full-length films have been derived from Jules Verne's 1870 novel, one of them a Russian production and another a serial cliffhanger.

In the late Twenties, MGM devoted three years and over a million dollars to filming The Mysterious Island, a version rarely seen today. The production was plagued by tremendous difficulties,

Opposite: top, Lloyd Hughes and Lionel Barrymore in the 1929 version of The Mysterious Island. Below, a scene from the 1961 remake.

including the destruction of its second unit when the feature was lensing near the Bahamas in 1927. By the time the tale was completed,
sound had become commercially feasible and several talking sequences had to be added to this early Technicolor production to make
it salable. With three directors involved (Maurice Tourneur, Benjamin Christiansen, and Lucien Hubbard--the latter shooting most of
the footage), the continuity of the resultant motion picture was sketchy
to say the least.
     The narrative tells of Count Dakkar (Lionel Barrymore), who
invents an underwater craft to investigate the ocean floor. He theorizes that another race, half-fish, half-human, dwells there. His
evidence consists of skeletons of a dwarfish creature which exists in
the briny deep. A Russian agent, however, wants to obtain the boat
for war purposes and attacks the count on his unique isle and tortures
him. Meanwhile Dakkar's associates are exploring the ocean floor in
the vessel. When they surface they are fired upon by the Russians
and the ship sinks to the depths. The men then explore further and
come across the unusual fish-men as well as large dragons and a huge
octopus. Eventually the men re-activate the ship and return to the
surface, where they find the count is dying.
     Photoplay judged the feature a "beautiful and thrilling all-color
production.... Entertaining fantasy." Other reviewers of the time
were equally responsive to the production which was visually imaginative, with excellent photography. Midgets were employed to play
the fish-men and they were supported by piano wires as they swam
about the studio "ocean" tank. In this cliffhanger-like narrative, the
character Captain Nemo does not appear.
     In the 1941 Russian version, Captain Nemo is a major figure
as he offers help to castaways in need.
     A decade later, portions of Verne's novel were adapted by
Columbia for a fifteen-chapter serial entitled Mysterious Island.
Here Confederate prisoners in 1865 make their escape under the
leadership of Captain Harding (Richard Crane). They drift in their
boat until they wash ashore on an uncharted island. Also on the isle
is an invader from Mercury, Rulu (Karen Randle), who seeks a radioactive metal with which she can destroy the Earth. The mysterious Captain Nemo (Leonard Penn) is on the island, too, and he
works with Harding and his men to stop the invader from Mercury.
Rulu is later responsible for detonating an explosion which destroys
the island, but the Confederates survive. "Although fantastic beyond
credibility, Mysterious Island actually contained more elements from
the original source than most such adaptations of the sound era"
(Jim Harmon and Donald F. Glut in The Great Movie Serials, 1972).
     The best-known version of Verne's work came in 1961 from
Columbia, highlighted by Ray Harryhausen's fine special effects and
Bernard Herrmann's apt score. Following closely the early portions
of the serial (rather than the novel), the film has a group of Confederate prisoners escaping in a balloon and being caught in a storm
and forced to land on a tropical isle. Two shipwrecked survivors
(Joan Greenwood and Beth Rogan) soon join the men and the group is
forced to battle such adversaries as a giant bird, deadly bees, land
crabs, and pirates. Much to their relief, the survivors discover
Captain Nemo (Herbert Lom), who has been living there in his

crippled submarine "Nautilus." He has been mutating animals, hoping that oversized creatures might be the answer to the world's food need. The captain agrees to get them off the island if they use their balloon to raise the hull of the sunken pirate ship. The plan works and all are saved from the impending volcano except Nemo, who is crushed beneath the outflow.

While the major critics were not impressed by the goings-on ("near the bottom of the Jules Verne barrel," stated the New York Herald-Tribune), action-minded audiences were appreciative.

In 1972 a French/Spanish/U.S. version was filmed in Africa. Based on the box-office appeal of the Jules Verne story and the nominal starring appearance of Omar Sharif, the entry was released in the U.S. in 1974 as The Mysterious Island of Captain Nemo. As the Independent Film Journal noted of this hastily-made effort, "This time the Spanish film-makers responsible seemed mainly content with putting down the basic roots of the story without giving much sense of adventure or intrigue to go along with it." The same journal observed, "... the one thing this version forgets is the spirit of Verne, his unquenchable interest in new machinery and ingenious inventions, his fascination with devising clever ways out of tricky situations." This film came and went very quickly on the double-bill circuit.

Perhaps the best delineation of the Nemo character who mans the fabulous "Nautilus" is Walt Disney's 20,000 Leagues Under the Sea (q.v.). There fantasy/fiction/entertainment abounds.

THE MYSTERIOUS ISLAND OF CAPTAIN NEMO see THE MYSTE-
RIOUS ISLAND

THE NEW ADVENTURES OF BATMAN AND ROBIN see BATMAN
AND ROBIN

THE NIGHT CALLER (Armitage, 1967) 84 min.

Executive producer, John Phillips; producer, Ronald Liles; director, John Gilling; based on the novel The Night Callers by Frank Crisp; screenplay, Jim O'Connolly; music composer/conductor, Johnny Gregory; title music, Joe Glenn, Larry Greene, and Bob Sande; art director, Harry White; assistant director, Ray Frift; sound, John Cox and Kevin Sutton; camera, Stephen Dade; editor, Philip Barnikel.

John Saxon (Jack Costain); Maurice Denham (Professor Morley); Patricia Haines (Ann Barlow); Alfred Burke (Detective Superintendent Hartley); John Carson (Major); Jack Watson (Sergeant Hawkins); Stanley Meadows (Grant); Warren Mitchell (Lilbum); Marianne Stone (Mrs. Lilbum); Aubrey Morris (Thorburn); Geoffrey Lumsden (Colonel Davy); Barbara French (Joyce Malone); Tom Gill (Police Commissioner's Secretary); John Sherlock (TV Newscaster); and Robert Crewdson (Medra).
A.k.a. Night Caller from Outer Space.

This literate sci-fi effort from Great Britain (made in 1965 but held up for two years before release) was saddled with a ludicrous title, Blood Beast from Outer Space, for U.S. playdates. It has now resurfaced on television where its display of both mystery and sanity in dealing with unearthly aliens has made it a popular item.

The film relates of the strange disappearance of several pretty young girls after they answer newspaper ads from a photography-modeling firm. Soon scientist Jack Costain (John Saxon) is on the trail of the lost beauties, all of whom had good moral reputations and were singularly noted as being rather shy. Eventually Costain deduces that a being from outer space is abducting the girls for his own purposes. A young woman is set up as a decoy and Costain is finally able to come to grips with the kidnapper, one Medra (Robert Crewdson), from the moon of Jupiter called Ganymede. He has been transmitting the girls back to his planet so that they might be used to repopulate his dying world. The alien informs Costain that the girls will not be harmed and then transmits himself back to Ganymede in an eerie finale.

Variety pinpointed the problem with The Night Caller: "it is simply too well-made for its own commercial good ... it eschews a standard action-adventure climax in favor of a 'philosophical' one."

NIGHT CALLER FROM OUTER SPACE   see   THE NIGHT CALLER

NIGHT OF THE BIG HEAT (Planet, 1967) C-94 min.

Producer, Tom Blakeley; associate producer, Ronald Liles; director, Terence Fisher; based on the novel by John Lymington; screenplay, Liles; additional scenes/dialogue, Pip and Jane Baker; art director, Alex Vetchinsky; music/music director, Malcolm Lockyer; sound, Norman A. Cole; camera, Reg Wyer; editor, Rod Keys.

Christopher Lee (Hanson); Peter Cushing (Dr. Stone); Patrick Allen (Jeff); Sarah Lawson (Frankie); Jane Merrow (Angela); William Lucas (Ken Stanley); Kenneth Cope (Tinker Mason); Jack Bligh (Ben Siddle); Thomas Heathcote (Bob Hayward); Sidney Bromley (Old Tramp) Percy Herbert (Gerald Foster); Anna Turner (Stella Haywood); Barry Halliday (Radar Operator).

On the island of Fara, off the British coast, it is winter, but the temperatures hover at the 100° mark. On Fara there have been several unexplained deaths and a mysterious scientist named Hanson (Christopher Lee) is performing secret experiments in a hotel run by Jeff (Patrick Allen). Kindly Dr. Stone (Peter Cushing), who has been investigating the deaths, is inexplicably burned to death, as were the other victims. Later, Hanson announces to the islanders that they have been invaded by aliens from a dying planet, and that these new arrivals require extreme heat to survive. Eventually the invaders (who look like large blobs of matter) appear to destroy the rest of the inhabitants. Hanson is done in, in his effort to combat the aliens. But a thunderstorm, caused by the heat-saturated atmosphere, decimates the invaders.

"John Lymington's novels are among the most cinematic of

Christopher Lee and Patrick Allen in Night of the Big Heat (1967).

science fiction works, but Night of the Big Heat is not one of his
best, and here is given conventional treatment ... though the appearance of the invaders is effectively deferred until the final sequence,
the plot is so cluttered up with irrelevancies ... that the atmosphere
created by the unseen threat is very soon dissipated" (British Monthly Film Bulletin).
          The box-office combination of Lee, Cushing, and director Ter-
ence Fisher helped the film to do decent business in its homeland.
The picture did not reach the U.S. until 1971, when it was retitled
Island of the Burning Damned. Almost immediately it was sold to
American TV as Island of the Burning Doomed.

NIGHT OF THE BLOOD BEAST (American International, 1958) 65 min.

          Executive producer, Roger Corman; producer, Gene Corman;
director, Bernard L. Kowalski; story, Gene Corman; screenplay,
Martin Varno; assistant director, Robert White; music supervisor,
Alexander Laszlo; art director, Dan Haller; sound, Herman Lewis;
camera, John Nicholaus, Jr.; editor, Dick Currier.
          Michael Emmet (Major John Corcoran); Angela Greene (Dr.
Julie Benson); John Baer (Steve Dunlap); Ed Nelson (Dave Randall);
Tyler McVey (Dr. Alex Wyman); Georgianna Carter (Donna Bixby);
Ross Sturlin (The Creature).

A. k. a. The Creature from Galaxy 27.

A manned space capsule, "X-100," blasts off into space with astronaut Major John Corcoran (Michael Emmet) aboard. Above the Earth's atmosphere the capsule explodes and a portion of it returns to Earth with Corcoran still alive. Unbeknown to the Major, his body has been impregnated with cells from an outer space creature whose world has been smashed by atomic explosions. (Once the cells are in his blood stream, Corcoran is capable of giving "birth" to other creatures.) Eventually Corcoran learns the ghastly truth and orders himself killed. As Corcoran dies, so does the creature. Only then is its mission revealed: to bring super-intelligence to Earth and save it from self-destruction. The dying creature promises that more of his kind will soon follow.

Variety announced, "It's finally happened--someone wrote a story about a pregnant man! Well, not exactly pregnant. Actually he breeds embryos of outer space creatures." The trade paper did admit that it was a "Respectfully suspenseful picture."

The production values were, at best, minimum.

NIGHT OF THE GHOULS see BRIDE OF THE MONSTER

NIGHT OF THE LIVING DEAD (Continental Distributing, 1968) 90 min.

Producer, Russell Streiner and Karl Hardman; director, George A. Romero; screenplay, John A. Russo; sound, Gary Streiner; special effects, Regis Survinski and Tony Pantanello; camera, Romero.
Judith O'Dea (Barbara); Russell Streiner (Johnny); Duane Jones (Ben); Karl Hardman (Harry); Keith Wayne (Tom); Judith Ridley (Judy); Marilyn Eastman (Helen); Kyra Schon (Karen).

Night of the Living Dead is one of the most controversial sci-fi/horror films of recent vintage. Made in Pittsburgh in the late Sixties on an under-$200,000 budget, the film was issued to rancid reviews. But it slowly began to build a cult following and by the early Seventies it was a very popular item, having grossed millions at the box-office. In the process it was analyzed endlessly in various fan journals and even denounced in large circulation publications such as Reader's Digest.

Plot-wise, the film resembles a partial remake of Plan 9 from Outer Space (q. v.). Recently dead corpses (here resurrected due to a radiation-saturated meteor falling in the area) crawl out of their graves and devour cannibalistically those humans who survived the meteor. Finally a group of survivors makes a stand at a farmhouse, fighting off the zombies. They hope to be able to live long enough for the authorities to appear on the scene. In the rather unnerving finish, only a black man (Russ Streiner) survives the attack of the corpses and as he runs out to greet the law he is shot. The police are convinced he is just another revived corpse out to attack them.

There is no doubt that the scenario and acting in Night of the Living Dead are abominable, and that the 90 minutes of black-and-

white storyline are crammed with gratuitous gore. One sequence
finds a little girl dying and coming back from the dead to stab her
mother to death and then she devours her. Variety pegged the film as
setting "a new low in box-office opportunism." But, as with other
exploitation items in this and other genres, it seems that the more
defiant the bad taste in production values, the better the young audiences enjoy it.

NIGHT SLAVES (ABC-TV, 1970) C-72 min.

     Producer, Everett Chambers; director, Ted Post; based on
the novel by Jerry Sohl; teleplay, Chambers and Robert Specht; art
director, Howard Hollander; music, Bernardo Segall; camera, Robert
Hauser; editor, Michael Kahn.
     James Franciscus (Clay Howard); Lee Grant (Marj Howard);

Tisha Sterling and James Franciscus in Night Slaves (1970).

Scott Marlowe (Matthew Russell); Andrew Prine (Fess Beany); Tisha
Sterling (Naillil); Leslie Nielsen (Sheriff Genshaw); Morris Buchanan
(Mr. Hale); John Kellogg (Mr. Fletcher); Virginia Vincent (Mrs.
Crawford); Cliff Carbell (Spencer); Victor Izacy (Jeff Pardee); Ray-
mond Mayo (Joe Landers); Russell Thorson (Dr. Smithers); Nancy
Valentine (Mary).

"What unearthly force is at work to enslave a whole town at
night?" asked the press blurbs from ABC-TV for Night Slaves, a
segment of its "Movie of the Week" series. This telefeature was one
of those quickly-constructed suspensers that involved the sci-fi motif
to attract viewers. Unfortunately its overall affect was neither pleasing nor very suspenseful.
     Clay Howard (James Franciscus) has had a metal plate inserted
in his skull following a serious car accident. He and his wife (Lee
Grant) stop overnight in a small town. In the middle of the evening
he awakens to find everyone but himself boarding trucks and leaving
the community. He traces the zombie-like group to their destination
and discovers they are being used to repair a disabled space ship. In
the morning, the townfolk remember nothing of their nocturnal manual
activities. Neither his wife nor the local sheriff (Leslie Nielsen) believes the hero's wild tale, but a young farm girl (Tisha Sterling)
appears convinced. As it develops, the plate in his head prevented
him from coming under the influence of the industrious aliens.
     Robert L. Jerome in Cinefantastique reported Night Slaves as
"an initially fascinating sci-fier which slipped into banality very
quickly."

THE NIGHT THAT PANICKED AMERICA (ABC-TV, 1975) C-75 min.

     Executive producer, Antony Wilson; producer/director, Joseph
Sargent; teleplay, Nicholas Meyer and Wilson; text of radio broadcast,
Howard Koch; production consultant, Paul Stewart.
     Vic Morrow (Hank Muldoon); Cliff De Young (Stefan Grubowski);
Michael Constantine (Jess Wingate); Walter McGinn (Paul Stewart);
Eileen Brennan (Ann Muldoon); Meredith Baxter (Linda Davis); Tom
Bosley (Norman Smith); Will Geer (Reverend Davis); Paul Shenar (Or-
son Welles); John Ritter (Walter Wingate); Granville Van Dusen (Tom);
Burton Gilliam (Tex); Joshua Bryant (Howard Koch); Ron Rifkin, Walk-
er Edminton, Casey Kasem, and Marcus J. Grapes (Radio Actors);
Liam Dunn (Charlie); Shelley Morrison (Toni); Art Hannes (Announcer).

     While not a true sci-fi film, The Night that Panicked Ameri-
ca was an excellent media example of the effect of the genre on the
unsuspecting. This telefilm was a recreation of the famous Orson
Welles War of the Worlds broadcast on Halloween (Monday, October
31), 1938. That historical airing caused millions of people throughout the country to panic, due its amazingly real approach to an outer
space invasion. As a telefilm, The Night that Panicked America is
divided into two contrasting segments: one detailing the actual broadcast, the other delving into the lives of those who heard the program
and believed it.

The most beguiling aspect of the TV movie was the presentation of the radio drama. Here the whole array of mechanical wonders used to simulate reality in a radio studio was displayed: the split-second timing, the varied sound effects, the assorted actors, and the staging of the H. G. Wells' work. Paul Shenar played Orson Welles, the star-director of "The Mercury Theatre of the Air," which presented the original broadcast. Paul Stewart, who had performed in the 1938 production, was a consultant for the telefeature.

The second aspect of the film detailed how various people were affected by the offbeat broadcast. One episode concerned a girl (Meredith Baxter) whose minister father (Will Geer) refuses to let her marry her lover (Cliff De Young), while another had an alienated father (Michael Constantine) and son (John Ritter) rushing out together to fight the Martians: a final episode depicted a separating husband (Vic Morrow) and wife (Eileen Brennan) reunited by fear of the invasion. As this brief synopsis indicates, the three tales were hokey and did not combine well with the re-creation of the actual broadcast.

1984 (Associated British Pictures, 1956) 91 min.

Producer, N. Peter Rathvon; director, Michael Anderson; based on the novel by George Orwell; screenplay, William P. Templeton and Ralph Gilbert Bettinson; art director, Terence Verity; music, Malcolm Arnold; special effects, B. Langley, G. Blackwell, and

Jan Sterling and Edmond O'Brien in 1984 (1956).

N. Warwick; camera, C. Pennington Richards; editor, Bill Lewthwaite.

Edmond O'Brien (Winston Smith); Jan Sterling (Julia); Michael
Redgrave (General O'Connor); David Kossoff (Charrington); Mervyn
Johns (Jones); Donald Pleasence (Parsons); Carol Wolveridge (Selina
Parsons); Ernest Clark (Announcer); Ronan O'Casey (Rutherford);
Kenneth Griffith (Prisoner).

George Orwell's novel 1984 was first published in 1949, a
year before the author's death. It is one of the most politically horrifying books ever penned, detailing a sterile society strictly run by
the state, "Big Brother," which oversees and manipulates every little
aspect of a person's life. Many feel that 1984 is a view of the possible future; others insist it is the reality of today.

In the 1950s, the type of society presented in Orwell's gripping novel was anametha to our values, and it is surprising that a
much better film version of the Orwell book was not made. For the
movie version of 1984 is relatively mundane and it pictures few of
the horrors of the Orwell state.

Winston Smith (Edmond O'Brien) works for the state in London
but is restless and unsatisfied with his existence. He wants a world
of more freedom. In the society of "Big Brother" where love is
forbidden he meets Julie (Jan Sterling) and they indulge in a clandestine love affair. Together they plan a revolt to overthrow "Big
Brother" and soon they encounter General O'Connor (Michael Redgrave), who agrees to aid their cause. But later the military leader
is revealed as a member of the "Big Brother" government and informs them of their folly in hoping to change the regime's life style.
In the finale, Winston screams "Down with Big Brother!" and he and
Julie are killed. (In the American release print, Winston is brainwashed so successfully that he denounces Julie for the love and protection of "Big Brother.")

NO BLADE OF GRASS (MGM, 1970) C-96 min.

Producer/director, Cornel Wilde; based on the novel Death of
Grass by John Christopher; screenplay, Sean Forestal and Jefferson
Pascal; art director, Elliott Scott; music director, Burnell Whibley;
songs, Louis Nelius and Charles Carroll; sound, Cyril Swern; special
effects, Terry Witherington; camera, H. A. R. Thompson; editors,
Frank Clarke and Eric Boyd-Perkins.

Nigel Davenport (John Custance); Jean Wallace (Ann Custance);
Patrick Holt (David Custance); Ruth Kettlewell (Fat Woman); M. J.
Matthews (George); Michael Percival (Police Constable); Tex Fuller
(Mr. Beaseley); Simon Merrick (TV Interviewer); Anthony Sharp (Sir
Charles Brenner); George Coulouris (Sturdevant); Anthony May (Pir-
rie); Wendy Richard (Clara); Max Hartnell (Lieutenant); Nigel Rath-
bone (Davey); Norman Atkyns (Dr. Cassop); Christopher Lofthouse
(Spooks); John Avison (Yorkshire Sergeant); Derek Keller (Scott);
Malcolm Toes (Sergeant Major).

After the critical and financial success of his The Naked Prey

(1966), producer/director/actor Cornel Wilde turned to the field of
ecology with this stark "message" picture about man's environment.
It is, in a way, a less entertaining, new version of Things to Come
(q. v.).

Set in the near future, No Blade of Grass tells of a virus that
attacks the world's food supply, causing famine and lawlessness
throughout the world. The narrative focuses on the Custance family
as they attempt to leave London, pass through hostile areas, and find
sanctuary at their relatives' farm. Along the way they are joined by
a ruthless killer (Anthony May) who has murdered his wife; they stave
off an attack by motorcycle hoods; and Mrs. Custance (Jean Wallace)
is raped but later kills her attacker. Eventually they reach the farm,
which is protected by a machine gun.

Pictorially No Blade of Grass is a fascinating effort, presenting an environment of death and decay. Cities and towns are shown
as devastated, with the corpses of humans and carcasses of animals
strewn over the terrain. The land is parched and rivers and streams
are polluted. All of this is a visual warning of the potential future if
ecology is not more balanced by our careless society.

Dan Scapperotti wrote in Cinefantastique, "Although the film is
science fiction ecologically oriented, it is best on a pure adventure
level. Although it shocks, it doesn't convince, and we'll have to wait
for the future crop of ecological doomsday films to make the point."

Comparing the film to Day of the Triffids (q. v.), David Pirie
wrote in A Heritage of Horror (1973), "No Blade of Grass has exactly the same quality of fumbling uncertainty as the earlier film: the
mood changes violently from one scene to another, the visual quality
and the color flash from shot to shot as though it has been photographed by different crews and the actors seem unsure of what kind
of fim they are supposed to be making."

This well-intentioned feature was a box-office disaster. Plans
to re-issue the feature in the mid-Seventies, complete with a new advertising campaign, never materialized.

NOT OF THIS EARTH (Allied Artists, 1956) 67 min.

Producer/director, Roger Corman; screenplay, Charles Grif-
fith and Mark Hanna; assistant director, Lou Place; music, Ronald
Stein; special effects, Paul Blaisdell; camera, John Mescall; editor,
Charles Gross.

Paul Birch (Paul Johnson); Beverly Garland (Nadine Storey);
Morgan Jones (Harry Sherbourne); Jonathan Haze (Jeremy Perrin);
Dick Miller (Joe Piper); Anne Carroll (Woman); Pat Flynn (Simmons);
Roy Engel (Sergeant Walton); Tamar Cooper (Joanne); Harold Fong
(Specimen).

In a period bombarded with bad B and C sci-fi features, Not
of This Earth stands out as one of genre's best in the Fifties. Made
by the prolific Roger Corman, the film embodies a decent storyline,
solid performances, and a sufficient budget to produce a suspenseful
blend of alien invasion and vampirism.

Paul Birch offers a very strong performance as an alien who

Morgan Jones and Beverly Garland in Not of this Earth (1956).

arrives on Earth in search of blood while a battle for survival rages
on his far-off planet. After killing a young girl for her blood, he
moves on to a hospital where he places a doctor under his power and
has a nurse (Beverly Garland) sent to his home to administer blood
transfusions. Her policeman boyfriend (Morgan Jones) is leery of
the stranger who, it develops, uses a form-transmission process to
transport hapless victims back to his planet, where their blood will
be drained. Later, a female citizen (Anne Carroll) from his world
arrives to say that the war is over and that chaos now reigns.
     The alien woman, who needs blood, is taken to the hospital
and there receives the blood of a rabid dog, which kills her. Thereafter, the plotline finds the alien being chased by the law; the sound
of the police car siren distracts the vampiric invader, and his car
crashes. It breaks the spell over the nurse and she can return to a
normal life. At the finish, a strange-looking man comes to visit the
alien's grave--he is another invader from the devastated planet.
     One amusing bit in this 67-minute feature occurs when Dick
Miller, as a vacuum salesman, comes to the alien's home and tries
to sell him a sweeper, only to come under the stranger's power and
be transported to another world.
     In Italy this film was titled Il Vampior del Planeta Rosso.

THE OMEGA MAN (Warner Bros., 1971) C-98 min.

Producer, Walter Seltzer; director, Boris Sagal; based on the novel I Am Legend by Richard Matheson; screenplay, John William Corrington and Joyce H. Corrington; action co-ordinator, Joe Canutt; art directors, Arthur Loel and Walter M. Simonds; set decorator, William L. Kuehl; costumes, Margo Baxley and Bucky Rous; make-up, Gordon Bau; assistant director, Bill Stern; music, Ron Granier; sound, Bob Martin; camera, Russell Metty; editor, William Ziegler.

Charlton Heston (Robert Neville); Anthony Zerbe (Matthias); Rosalind Cash (Lisa); Paul Koslo (Dutch); Lincoln Kilpatrick (Zachary); Eric Laneuville (Richie); Jill Giraldi (Little Girl); Anna Aries (Woman in Cemetery Crypt); DeVeren Bookwalter, John Dierkes, Monika Henreid, Linda Redfearn, and Forrest Wood (Family Members); Brian Tochi (Tommy).

Sci-fi fans had high hopes, when Warner Bros. announced a remake of Richard Matheson's novel I Am Legend, of which the first film version, Ultimo Nomo Della Terra (The Last Man on Earth) (q.v.) had been hopelessly mundane, a great disappointment. However, The Omega Man, as the new edition was labeled, betrayed its good budget and glossy scripting, and also provided an unsatisfactory exploration of Matheson's still-engrossing novel.

In 1977 scientist Robert Neville (Charlton Heston) is apparently the only plague-free human left on earth. Two years prior, a bacteriological war between China and Russia had killed most of the globe's population; the remaining victims were turned into albino-type mutants. (Neville had earlier immunized himself against the plague bacteria.) In his Los Angeles high-rise apartment he can look down on what is left of civilization--the living dead, vampires who want to destroy him but cannot reach him. They are headed by Matthias (Anthony Zerbe), a one-time newscaster who regards men of science as irresponsible and the direct cause of the world-wide disaster. Just when Matthias and his family have cornered Neville, he is rescued by a black woman, Lisa (Rosalind Cash), and by Dutch (Paul Koslo). They take him to the country hills where the scientist learns that there are some young people alive who are unaffected by the plague as yet. When they grow older they may develop the symptoms.

Neville develops a protective serum from his own blood which restores Lisa's brother Richie (Eric Laneuville) to normalcy. Later Lisa is infected and joins the family. When Neville attempts to escape--with Lisa in tow--he is killed by Matthias. Before he dies, he gives the last bottle of serum to Dutch. Dutch then escorts the youngsters to their hillside sanctuary where they hope to start a new civilization.

In reviewing this ambitious but faulty feature, the critics took occasion to compare it with other sci-fi pictures: "Omega Man's implausibilities are still somehow more pleasing than the glum and mundane semi-truths of The Andromeda Strain [q.v.]" (Washington Post).

Michael Kerbel in The Village Voice offered an essay on the species:

... From Fritz Lang's Metropolis [q.v.] to George Lucas'

THX 1138 [q. v.], sci-fi movies have regarded technology
as the major cause of man's eventual destruction: whether
through research, exploration or the atom bomb, cinema's
scientists have unleashed monsters, malicious machines,
and mass murder.
     ... Regarding The Omega Man, midway through the
film it becomes a conventional exercise in melodrama,
heroics, and suspense. Even these are undercut by in-
congruous, slick rock music in the Francis Lai tradition
and by campy, cynical dialogue that never creates the
genuine enjoyment of a film like Escape from the Planet
of the Apes [q. v.]. And except for one chilling shot (similar to the climax of Invasion of the Body Snatchers [q. v.])
in which we suddenly discover that the heroine has become a mutant, the film is never even as terrifying as
weighty-message apocalyptic films like On the Beach [q. v.].

     The San Francisco Chronicle's Paine Knickerbocker asked,
"Where, for instance, are the rats, or for that matter, the bugs of
The Hellstrom Chronicle [q. v.]? Where is the stink and putrefaction
of death?"
     Some critics were even jocular, retitling the Charlton Heston
feature, Moses Meets the Humanoids.

ON THE BEACH (United Artists, 1959) 134 min.

     Producer/director, Stanley Kramer; based on the novel by
Nevil Shute; screenplay, John Paxter; music, Ernest Gold; song, Ma-
rie Cowan and A. B. Paterson; art director, Fernando Carrere; costumes, Joe King; Miss Gardner's wardrobe, Fontana Sisters; makeup,
John O'Gorman and Frank Prehoda; technical advisor, Vice-Admiral
Charles A. Lockwood, USN (Ret.); assistant director, Ivan Volkman;
sound, Hans Wetzel; sound effects, Walter Elliott; special effects,
Lee Zavitz; camera, Giuseppe Rotunno; auto race camera, Daniel L.
Fapp; editor, Frederic Knudtson.
     Gregory Peck (Commander Dwight Towers); Ava Gardner (Moi-
ra Davidson); Fred Astaire (Julian Osborn); Anthony Perkins (Lieuten-
ant Peter Holmes); Donna Anderson (Mary Holmes); John Tate (Ad-
miral Bridie); Lola Brooks (Lieutenant Hosgood); Guy Doleman (Far-
rel); John Neillon (Swain); Harp McGuire (Sundstrom); Ken Wayne
(Benson); Richard Meikle (Davis); Joe McCormick (Ackerman); Lou
Vernon (Davidson); Basil Buller-Murphy (Froude); Paddy Moran (Port
Man); Grant Taylor (Morgan).

     It is nearing two decades since Stanley Kramer's haunting film,
On the Beach, was released. At the time it was promoted with the
catch phrase, "If you never see another motion picture, see On the
Beach." While the film was hardly this essential to the average
man's way of life, it did capture the gripping theme of Nevil Shute's
book: that man has programmed himself for extinction. The genius
of Kramer's craftsmanship (if one overlooks the compromise "name"
casting) is that the viewer is persuaded to care and almost believe

Ava Gardner and Gregory Peck in On the Beach (1959).

that what the film predicts could/will happen.
In 1964 the northern hemisphere is devastated by a huge nuclear war. Radioactivy-drenched clouds are making their inevitable
way southward, and scientists in Melbourne, Australia predict that
in another six months their doom will be complete. But there are
a few optimists. Commander Dwight Towers (Gregory Peck), an
American naval officer whose atomic submarine, "U.S.S. Sawfish,"
was in Australian waters at the time of the war, is dispatched northward. Among his passengers are scientist Julian Osborn (Fred Astaire), who drinks to forget, and Lieutenant Peter Holmes (Anthony
Perkins), whose mind is on his young wife and baby. The trip
proves futile; there is no life in the northern hemisphere.
        The "Sawfish" returns to Australian waters. Towers finds
momentary contentment with Moira Davidson (Ava Gardner), a reckless woman who only now realizes how foolish her life has been. As
the end approaches, Osborn participates in a death-seeking auto race
and wins--and then commits suicide; the Holmes family takes the "suicide pills" rather than suffer the agony of radiation death; the crew
of the "Sawfish" asks to head the craft northward to die at home.
Towers bids farewell to Moira and leaves with his ship.
        Not long afterward, the end comes. The only sign of move-
ment in Melbourne is a banner from an evangelists' meeting. It reads:
"THERE IS STILL TIME, BROTHER."
        The original running time of Kramer's picture was approximate-
ly three hours; but the distributor demanded that it be cut to 136
minutes. Although disjointed in spots, it still remains a powerful
indictment of mankind's folly. As the New York Times viewed it,
"The great merit of this picture, aside from its entertainment qualities, is the fact that it carries a passionate conviction that man is
worth saving, after all.... Mr. Kramer and his assistants have most
forcibly emphasized this point: life is a beautiful treasure and man
should do all he can to save it from annihilation, while there is still
time."
        Some sources found flaws in the production. Arthur Knight
(Saturday Review) wrote, "One wonders, for example, at the complete
absence of corpses, both in the periscope survey of San Francisco
and, later, in the exploration of a San Diego power plant.... And
although it is difficult to imagine just how ordinary folks would react
to the knowledge of certain death in the very near future, it is equally difficult to believe that they all would remain as calm and self-
possessed as the people seen here.... There is no looting, no licen-
tiousness, no desperate last-chance fling.... It all seems a bit too
perfect. But these are minor details in a film that aims at something big and emerges as something tremendous."
        A substantial contribution to the lingering, haunting tone of the
motion picture is the music score by Ernest Gold, which repeatedly
and effectively interweaves the Australian favorite, "Waltzing Matil-
da," into the soundtrack.
        On the Beach grossed $5 million in distributors' domestic
rentals.

ONE HOUR TO DOOMSDAY see CITY BENEATH THE SEA

ONE HUNDRED YEARS AFTER (Pathé, 1911) 780'

With: Tom Editt.

In the cinema's early years, science fiction was often played
for laughs and/or camera tricks. The French especially enjoyed this
type of cinema, beginning with the imaginative works of George Méliês.
One Hundred Years After was a rather typical French film which
poked fun at the genre, long before it became such an integral part
of world cinema.
   The two-reel film depicts a young scientist (Tom Editt) per-
fecting a means of suspending life. He puts himself to sleep for a
century. In the year 2011 he steps out of a safe deposit vault to find
a world run by women who wear knickerbockers and top hats, while
the males are in skirts. Taken to the female mayor, via radio-
pneumatic tube, the experimenter makes such lustful love (no wonder,
after a century!) to the lady that she is so satisfied, she gives back
the vote to men.
   This sexist comedy, running a scant 13 minutes, was one of
several such films of the time that projected life in the future.
Among others were: The Airship, or One Hundred Years Hence
(1908), Life in the Next Century (1909), Looking Forward (1910), In
the Year 2000 (1912), In the Year 2014 (1914) and Percy Pimpernickle,
Soubrette (1914).

THE ONLY WAY OUT IS DEAD   see   THE MAN WHO WANTED TO
LIVE FOREVER

OPERATION STARDUST   see   ORBITA MORTAL

ORBITA MORTAL (Aitor/P.E.A./Theumer, 1968) C-95 min.

   Director, Primo Zegli; based on the Perry Rhodan novels by
Clark Darlton [Walter Ernsting]; screen story, Karl H. Volgeman;
screenplay, Volgeman and Federico d'Urrutia; art director, Jaime
Perez Cubero; music, Antón Garcia Abril; camera, Manuel Merino.
Lang Jeffries (Major Perry Rand); Essy Persson (Thora);
Luis Davila (Captain Bull); and Daniel Martin, Gianni Rizzo, and
Joachin Hansen.
   A.k.a. 4,3,2,1, Muerte / Mortal Orbit / Operation Stardust.

   This well-done chiller was a Spanish/Italian/West German co-
production. It was released in the U.S. as Mission Stardust and was
promoted for its sci-fi angles rather than its literate concept and
script.
   A secret scientific expedition is launched to the Moon. As the
astronauts near the moon, a powerful magnetic field forces them to
land and they are met by a robot who escorts them to a huge space
craft where they are introduced to two aliens (Essy Persson and
John Karelson) who inform them they require the astronauts' help.

Although these strangers are far more advanced than the Earthlings, they are in desperate need: they are the last of a dying race from another galaxy, and are doomed unless a cure can be found for their blood disease.

The astronauts' leader (Lang Jeffries) agrees to aid the ailing creatures, but he must move slowly because of the secrecy of his mission. The two ships come to Earth and land in a secluded area to seek the help of a noted blood specialist. Powerful people, however, find out about the aliens and hope to ferret out their vast scientific knowledge. A battle then erupts between the astronauts and their fellow Earthmen who want to exploit the space visitors. Finally a cure is found for the patients. They leave Earth, their secrets untapped.

THE OUTER SPACE CONNECTION (Sun International, 1975) 94 min.

Producer, Alan and Sally Landsburg; director, Fred Warshofsky; based on the book by the Landsburgs; screenplay, Warshofsky. Rod Serling (Narrator).

"Startling Proof that We Are Not Alone in the Universe," claimed the ads for The Outer Space Connection, a film issued simultaneously with the paperback book by Alan and Sally Landsburg. Basically a follow-up to the Landsburgs' tepid TV special, In Search of Ancient Mysteries (1974), the film offered pictorial "evidence" that mankind has been visited frequently in the past by beings from outer space and that these "trespassers" may have altered the genetic makeup of humanity on Earth.

Narrated by Rod Serling, the picture presents actual footage of Unidentified Flying Objects (UFOs) as well as clips of various phenomena on the Earth such as the ancient pyramids of Egypt and South America. Also studied for the viewer's education are mummies, embryo transplants, cloning, communication with alien species, the nature of ancient surgery, suspended animation, and artifacts allegedly left behind by space visitors. Also included are interviews with astronauts James McDivitt and John Borman, both of whom reported witnessing UFOs during space flights.

As in Chariots of the Gods? (q.v.), the primary visual interest in this film occurs when ancient cities, monuments, pyramids, and other millenia-old remains are shown--structures so well constructed that their format cannot be duplicated today. (Among those examined are the Giza complex of pyramids in Egypt, Sillbury Hill in England, and the Pyramid of Magicians and the Nunnery at Uxmal, Mexico.) Also of startling interest is the discussion of the Mayan calendar, with its 5,000-year cycles. (The next cycle is to begin Christmas Eve, 2011, A.D., the date the authors' claim will be the outer space connection, when the aliens return to Earth.)

"More 'proof' that spacemen visited earth in the past and will do so again. As propaganda, not too convincing: as a film, not well structured. Some of the details, however, are fascinating," stated Frank Jackson in Cinefantastique. The Los Angeles Times was more enthusiastic, labeling it highly provacative and even persuasive documentary."

OUTLAWED PLANET see TERRORE NELLO SPAZIO

PANIC IN YEAR ZERO (American International, 1962) 92 min.

Executive producers, James H. Nicholson and Samuel Z. Arkoff; producers, Arnold Houghland and Lou Rusoff; director, Ray Milland; story, Jay Simms; screenplay, Simms and John Morton; art director/set decorator, Daniel Heller; makeup, Ted Cooley; wardrobe, Marjorie Corso; titles, Ray Mercer; assistant director, Jim Engle; sound, Steve Bass and Al Bird; special effects, Pat Dinga and Larry Butler; camera, Gil Karrenton; editor, William Austin.

Ray Milland (Harry Baldwin); Jean Hagen (Ann Baldwin); Frankie Avalon (Rick Baldwin); Mary Mitchel (Karen Baldwin); Joan Freeman (Marilyn Hayes); Richard Garland (Mr. Johnson); Richard Bakalyan (Carl); Rex Holman (Mickey); Neil Nephew (Andy); Willis Bouchey (Dr. Strong); O. Z. Whitehead (Hogan); Byron Morrow (Haenel); Shary Marshall (Mrs. Johnson); Hugh Sanders (Becker); Russ Bender (Harkness).

Shortly after the Baldwins leave their Los Angeles home for a fishing vacation, a nuclear attack devastates the metropolis. Harry Baldwin (Ray Milland) decides that the best thing is to continue onward. Their biggest problem is to keep away from the hordes of people thronging out of the city and the anarchy that ensues. They eventually reach their fishing retreat and begin a rather primitive

Ray Milland and Jean Hagen in Panic in Year Zero (1962).

existence in a cave. When the daughter Karen (Mary Mitchel) is raped, Harry and his son Rick (Frankie Avalon) shoot the violators. Later, another single girl (Joan Freeman) joins the group. Finally they hear on the radio that it is safe to return to Los Angeles. The survivors start the trip back, prepared to rebuild their lives and the city.

The title of the film derives from a United Nations decree about the day the bomb was dropped. The black-and-white feature concludes on an optimistic note: "There Must Be No End--Only a Beginning."

"A serious, sobering and engrossing film" was Variety's verdict, although the journal added, "The topic is unpleasant enough to repel one kind of customer, exploitable enough to attract another kind." Ray Milland, who both starred in and directed this thriller, was only regretful that the budget/production schedule prevented him from having a few more days of shooting to make the picture more complete.

In Science Fiction in the Cinema (1970) John Baxter appraised: "Panic in Year Zero might almost be a manual for the bomb-shelter generation, a styleless and documentary exercise in the transfer of information on how to get along after the attack."

The film would be re-issued in 1965 as End of the World.

PERCY PIMPERNICKLE, SOUBRETTE   see   ONE HUNDRED YEARS AFTER

PERIL FROM THE PLANET MONGO   see   FLASH GORDON'S TRIP TO MARS

THE PHANTOM EMPIRE (Mascot, 1935) twelve chapters

Supervisor, Armand Schaefer; directors, Otto Brower and B. Reeves Eason; screenplay, Wallace MacDonald, Gerald Geraghty, H. Freedman; sound, Terry Kellum; editors, Earl Turner and Wahlter Thompson.

Gene Autry (Gene Autry); Frankie Darro (Frankie); Betsy King Ross (Betsy); Dorothy Christy (Queen Tika); Wheeler Oakman (Argo); Charles R. French (Mal); Warner Richmond (Rab); Frank Glendon (Professor Beetson); Smiley Burnette (Oscar); William Moore (Pete); and Edward Pier, Sr. and Jack Carlyle.

This twelve-chapter Mascot cliffhanger successfully combined the genres of the Western and sci-fi into a competent juvenile action entry which launched the remarkable film career of radio entertainer/recording artist Gene Autry. (His only previous screen experience had been singing bits in two Ken Maynard sagebrush tales.)

Autry plays a dude rancher whose land is sought by crooks because it contains rich deposits of radium. Gene gives chase to the marauding outlaws. The former comes across the hidden entrance to the land of Murania, located 20,000 feet below the Earth's surface.

There a grasping Queen (Dorothy Christy) and her ambitious prime
minister Argo (Wheeler Oakman) evolve plans to rule the world with
their futuristic death ray and robots. Gene follows the crooks below
and is captured by the Muranians, as are his pals (Frankie Darro,
Betsy King Ross, and Smiley Burnette) who have tracked him to the
mysterious underground kingdom. All four are held prisoners by the
Muranians. However, a revolt breaks out and they escape and return
above-ground in the special surface elevator. Below, a war rages
and the civilization of Murania is destroyed when the killer ray is
loosed.

     Alan G. Barbour wrote in Days of Thrills and Adventure (1970),
"The exciting finale (of the serial) had a wildly gyrating ray-gun destroying the entire underground city, accompanied by the rousing
strains of 'Storm and War,' a thrilling piece of music often used in
Westerns and serials of the thirties. The 'destruction' of the city
was accomplished by printing a photo of it on a film with thick emulsion, then photographing it in slow motion while the print was heated;
the heat of course caused the emulsion to run. The same effect
was used in several later republic serials...."

     The oddball serial was also known as Gene Autry and the Phan-
tom Empire and in 1940 two feature versions of it were issued as Radio Ranch and Men with Steel Faces. Portions of the serial were
used as stock footage later in Captain Video (q. v.).

THE PHANTOM PLANET (American International, 1962) 82 min.

     Executive producer, Leo Handel; producer, Fred Gebhardt;

Francis X. Bushman, Al Jarvis, Anthony Dexter, Dean Fredericks,
Coleen Gray and Dolores Faith in The Phantom Planet (1962).

director, William Marshall; screenplay, Gebhardt; music, Hayes Pagel; art director, Bob Kinoshita; assistant directors, Maurice Vaccarino and Lindsley Parsons, Jr.; makeup, Dave Newall; costumes, Marla Craig; camera, Elwood J. Nicholson; editors, Hugo Grimaldi and Don Wolfe.

Dean Fredericks (Captain Frank Chapman); Coleen Gray (Liara); Anthony Dexter (Herron); Dolores Faith (Zetha); Francis X. Bushman (Seson); Richard Weber (Lieutenant Makonnen); Al Jarvis (Judge Eden); Dick Haynes (Colonel Lansfield); Earl McDaniel (Pilot Leonard); Michael Marshall (Lieutenant White); John Herrin (Captain Beecher); Mel Curtis (Lieutenant Cutler); Jimmy Weldon (Navigator Webb); Akemi Tani (Communications Officer); Lori Lyons (Radar Officer); Richard Kiel (Solarite).

A minor entry in the category, but one bolstered by the presence of a veteran cast.

Captain Frank Chapman (Dean Fredericks) and his ship are investigating the disappearance of a space ship in the outer reaches. After being forced to land on an uncharted asteroid, he discovers he has shrunk in size. Soon he is captured by the tiny people, but then another faction on the planet attacks and steals the mute girl Zetha (Dolores Faith). After saving her and the kingdom, Chapman puts on his space suit, returns to his normal size, and heads back to Earth. He is convinced no one will believe his adventure.

PHASE IV (Paramount, 1974) C-84 min.

Producer, Paul B. Radin; director, Saul Bass; screenplay, Mayo Simon; assistant director, Bill Cartlidge; art director, John Barry; music/music director, Brian Gascoigne; montage music, Yamash'ta; electronic music realized with David Vorhaus; sound, Norman Bolland; special effects, John Richardson; camera, Dick Bush; second unit camera, Jack Mills; special ant camera, Ken Middleham; editor, Willy Kemplen.

Nigel Davenport (Ernest Hubbs); Lynne Frederick (Kendra); Michael Murphy (James Lesko); Alan Gifford (Mr. Eldridge); Helen Horton (Mrs. Eldridge); Robert Henderson (Clete).

Planet of the Apes (q.v.) and many other recent features have examined the potential for mankind's destruction should nature's balance be shifted in favor of a subordinate creature. Here the possibility that ants, known to be amazingly organized, could take over man's civilization is examined. The British-made Phase IV had only a modest impact in its American release but won the Grand Prix at the 1975 International Festival of Science Fiction Films at Trieste, Italy. The special ant sequences were lensed by Ken Middleham, who did similar cinematography on The Hellstrom Chronicle (q.v.).

Following an astronomical phenomenon a surprising development occurs in the animal world. Species usually at war with one another ally to destroy their predators. In the Arizona desert a group of scientists sets up a laboratory to study a species of ants which has been bothersome to neighboring humans. Eventually the ants become

Nigel Davenport and Michael Murphy in Phase IV (1974).

so powerful that all but one family evacuate the area. When the scientists later blow up seven towers built by the insects, they retaliate by destroying the men's truck. The scientists then use sprays around the camp to kill many of the ants, but the persistent creatures develop an immunity to the poisoned gas. Ernest Hubbs (Nigel Davenport), head of the research group, remains in the experimental dome with Kendra (Lynne Frederick), the trauma-plagued survivor of one of the ants' rampages. At a later point Hubbs's associate, Lesko (Michael Murphy), manages to communicate with the ants and Kendra understands that the ants want her. Hubbs is driven out in the open, where he falls into a trench and is eaten by the insects. At the climax, Lesko and Kendra await being taken over by the ants, who require them for some unknown reason.

    "From its opening shot--the earth in orbit around the sun, accompanied by electronically devised 'celestial' voices--Saul Bass' first feature signals an almost abject reliance on various science fiction works that have preceded it: 2001 [q.v.] first and last, Orson Welles' War of the Worlds broadcast in the narration (begun by Hubbs, and after his death taken up by Lesko), the delimited use of enclosed space from The Thing [q.v.] in the experimental dome, and a trio of archaic stock figures (mad scientist, healthy romantic-lead sidekick, orphaned teenage girl) derived from some of the pulpier manifestations of the genre. Yet despite these embarrassing playbacks, and the stilted performances which make them even less tenable, Phase IV cannot be written off as a film lacking either originality or talent. ...

Bass imposes himself graphically even when he falters dramatically, and some isolated shots and sequences are impressive indeed" (British Monthly Film Bulletin).

THE PIER   see   LA JETEE

PLAN 9 FROM OUTER SPACE (Distributors Corporation of America, 1958) 79 min.

     Producer/director/screenplay, Edward D. Woods, Jr.; music, Gordon Zahler; camera, William Thompson; editor, Woods.
     Bela Lugosi (Ghoul Man); Vampira (Ghoul Girl); Lyle Talbot (General Roberts); Gregory Walcott (Jeff Trent); Mona McKinnon (Paula Trent); Duke Moore (Lieutenant Harper); Tom Keene (Colonel Edwards); Tor Johnson (Inspector Clay); Dudley Manlove (Eros); John Breckinridge (The Ruler); Joanna Lee (Tanna); Criswell (Narrator); Conrad Brook (Bit).

     Plan 9 from Outer Space is one of the more notorious items of the late Fifties' sci-fi quickies. The origins of the feature are

Tor Johnson and the double for Bela Lugosi in Plan 9 from Outer Space (1958).

not really known, but in 1958-59 it was given national release, with
Bela Lugosi billed as the star. Some sources claim Lugosi's sparse
footage was actually fimed for an unfinished project entitled The
Vampires' Tomb and was later salvaged and interpolated into Plan 9
for the late actor's posthumous box-office appeal. Whatever the origin, Lugosi appears on screen only for a few minutes and says not
a word of dialogue. In the graveyard sequences it is obvious that a
double has been employed behind a black cloak to simulate Lugosi's
presence.

Criswell narrated this tale of aliens who come from outer space
to conquer the Earth before Earthlings destroy the universe with their
nuclear testings. They land in a San Fernando graveyard and put Plan
9 (the other eight failed) into operation: the use of corpses revived
by a special ray to take over the world. The narrative reveals The
Ghoul Man (Lugosi) mourning over the death of his wife (Vampira),
and later he is killed in a car crash. The expired duo, however,
are revived by the ray and stalk the graveyard. The Ghoul Man
subsequently kills a police inspector (Tor Johnson) who has been
called in to check on mysterious happenings in the area. Finally the
army, led by a colonel (Tom Keene), learns of the aliens' plan.
Their flying saucer is set on fire and soon explodes, thus ending the
sinister Plan 9.

Joe Dante, Jr. wrote in Famous Monsters of Filmland magazine, "There is a distinct possibility it was the cheapest film ever
made. The entire cast was awful. Special effects were laughable
and even the old clips of Bela Lugosi were poor. The scene where
Tor Johnson rose from the grave was the only good five seconds in
the whole film."

The working and preview title was Grave Robbers from Outer
Space.

PLANET EARTH (ABC-TV, 1974) C-75 min.

Executive producer, Gene Roddenberry; producer, Robert H.
Justman; director, Marc Daniells; teleplay, Roddenberry and Juanita
Bartlett; camera, Arch M. Dalzell

John Saxon (Dylan Hunt); Janet Margolin (Harper-Smythe); Ted
Cassidy (Isiah); Christopher Carey (Baylok); Diana Muldaur (Marg);
Johanna DeWinter (Villar); Marjel Barrett (Yuloff); James D. Antonio,
Jr. (Dr. Jonathan Connor); Sally Kemp (Treece); Claire Brennen
(Delba); Corrine Camacho (Bronta); Sarah Chattin (Thetis); John Quade
(Kreeg Commandant); Raymond Sutton (Kreeg Captain); Rai Tasco
(R. Kimbridge); Aron Kincaid (Gorda); James Bacon (Bartha); Joan
Crosby (Kyla).

A sequel to the 1973 telefeature Genesis II (q.v.), produced
and co-scripted by Gene Roddenberry, the creator of TV's "Star
Trek" series.

Through a suspended animation experiment, an American astronaut named Dylan Hunt (John Saxon) has been thrust into the year
2133 and becomes a part of the enlightened community of Pax, a
well-knit organization devoted to the reclamation of Earth. (After

Jo DeWinter (standing) and John Saxon (directly in front of her) in
Planet Earth (1974).

a global contest, the world has been split into many competing, tribe-
like nations.) He is recruited to lead a team, including a communications expert (Janet Margolin), a nature and wildlife authority (Ted
Cassidy) and a medical diagnostician (Christopher Cary), in search
of an eminent physician, believed to be held captive by the Confederacy of Ruth. In the Confederacy, which is run by women, with men--
called "dinks"--as slaves, the astronaut is captured and sold to Marg
(Diana Muldaur). Hunt learns that the men are kept under control by
a drug in their food. Later he outwits Marg by drugging her and
freeing the men; the latter, however, fight for her possession against
a horde of outside invaders. Marg is so pleased with her slaves'
acts of loyalty that she sets them free. The missing scientist is
found and the party returns to the community of Pax.
          "This, Roddenberry's latest installment, is his most juvenile
and curiously, most satisfying as piece of escapist fiction," wrote
Robert L. Jerome in Cinefantastique.

PLANET OF BLOOD   see   QUEEN OF BLOOD; TERRORE NELLO
SPAZIO

PLANET OF THE APES (Twentieth Century-Fox, 1968) C-112 min.

Producer, Arthur P. Jacobs; associate producer, Mort Abrahams; director, Franklin J. Schaffner; based on the novel Monkey
Planet by Pierre Boulle; screenplay, Michael Wilson and Rod Serling;
music, Jerry Goldsmith; orchestrator, Arthur Morton; art directors,
Jack Martin Smith and William Creber; set decorators, Walter M.
Scott and Norman Rockett; special makeup design, John Chambers;
makeup, Ben Nye and Dan Strieple; costumes, Morton Haack; assis-
tant director, William Kissel; sound, Herman Lewis and David Dock-
endorf; special camera effects, L. B. Abbott, Art Cruickshank, and
Emil Kosa, Jr.; camera, Leon Shamroy; editor, Hugh S. Fowler.
Charlton Heston (George Taylor); Roddy McDowall (Cornelius);
Kim Hunter (Dr. Zira); Maurice Evans (Dr. Zaius); James Whitmore
(Assembly President); James Daly (Honorious); Linda Harrison (Nova);
Robert Gunner (Landon); Lou Wagner (Lucius); Woodrow Parfrey
(Maximus); Jeff Burton (Dodge); Buck Kartalian (Julius); Norman Bur-
ton (Hunt Leader); Wright King (Dr. Galen); Paul Lambert (Minister);
Dianne Stanley (Female Astronaut).

This superior screen adaptation of Pierre Bouille's novel is
one of the most engrossing sci-fi films of all time.   Producer Arthur
P. Jacobs provided a $1 million budget for the ape masks and cost-
umes alone, smartly used portions of Utah and Arizona National Park
for starkly effective location scenes, and cast a superior group of
performers for this action/morality drama.   The film proved to be
a milestone in the genre and produced four sequels (as well as a live
action and an animated TV series):   Beneath the Planet of the Apes,
Escape from the Planet of the Apes, Battle for the Planet of the
Apes, and Conquest of the Planet of the Apes (all q. v.).
Some 2000 years in the future, four astronauts crash-land on
an uncharted planet.   The only female of the group dies of unexplained sudden old age.   The survivors trek through miles of arid
desert and are later captured by a band of uniformed, horse-riding
gorillas.   One of the space travelers is killed, another is rendered
helpless by a frontal lobotomy, and the third, George Taylor (Charlton Heston), who has temporarily lost his speech, is chained with
other (sub)humans.   The latter are regarded as a bestial and threatening species by the cultured ape society which rules the planet.
Taylor later communicates with two simians, Dr. Zira (Kim Hunter),
and her archaelogoist beau Cornelius (Roddy McDowall), who take a
special interest in him.   But Dr. Zaius (Maurice Evans), the orangu-
tan state chief, insists that Taylor should be silenced via a lobotomy.
Thereafter Zira and Cornelius help Taylor--along with Nova (Linda
Harrison) one of the human captives--to escape to the Forbidden
Zone.   Dr. Zaius and his ape guard follow.   Taylor grabs hold of
Zaius and forces the militia to retreat to spare their leader's life.
Taylor and Nova continue into the Forbidden Zone, promising not

to return with proof of their once "superior" human culture.   Further
along the coastline Taylor finds his answer--there, half-submerged in
sand, is a remnant of the Statue of Liberty.   The shocked astronaut
cries out, "You finally did it ... You blew it up.... Damn you!
God damn you all to hell!"
        Most critics were unduly harsh on this epic thriller.   But
Variety was perceptive enough--before the box-office bonanza persuaded
reviewers to reconsider their earlier judgments--to note that this "is
an amazing film.   A political-sociological allegory cast in the mold
of futuristic science-fiction, the production is an intriguing blend of
chilling satire, a sometimes ludicrous juxtaposition of human and ape
mores, optimism and pessimism.... The totality of the film works
very well, leading to a surprise ending although, in hindsight, it
would have been deduced all along.   Yet, the suspense, and suspension of belief, engendered is one of the film's biggest assets."
        Planet of the Apes earned $15 million in distributors' domes-
tic rentals.

PLANET OF THE DAMNED   see   TERRORE NELLO SPAZIO

PLANET OF THE VAMPIRES   see   TERRORE NELLO SPAZIO

PLANET OUTLAWS   see   BUCK ROGERS

PLANETA BURG (COSMONAUTS ON VENUS / STORM PLANET)
(Leningrad Studio of Popular Science Films, 1962) 73 min.

        Director, Pavel Klushantsev; screenplay, Alexander Kazant-
sev, Klushantsev; camera, Arkady Klimov.
        With: Kyunna Ignatova, Gennadi Vernov, Vladimir Yemelianov,
Yurie Sarantsev, and Georgi Zhonov.

        This Russian-made sci-fi film was called Planeta Burg and
was issued in England as Cosmonauts on Venus.   Basically a gadgety,
scientific exercise, it told of two astronauts who crash-land on the
primitive world of Venus.   They are accompanied by an intelligent
robot and they must survive the hostile climate until a rescue team
finds them.   On the planet the astronauts battle slimy water creatures and seek shelter in a cave where the robot tends to their needs.
The members of the rescue team confront a pterodactyl and as a result fall to the waters below, where they eventually reconnoiter with
their stranded colleagues.   During their stay on the planet they have
heard a scream that sounds almost like a woman wailing a siren's
song.   But they are forced to take advantage of favorable flight condition and depart the new world.   Before they leave Venus they come
across a stone carving.   "They look like us," says one space ex-
plorer to another.
        "By comparison with the average American production, this
Russian space opera is saner, and has more genuine science fiction

attached to it than is usual, notably in the final speculation about intelligence. In general, the film is a curious blend of resourcefulness
and naivete. Its main weakness is the poverty of the acting..."
(British Monthly Film Bulletin).
    This Soviet film was never released in its original version in
the U.S. Roger Corman purchased the picture when he was still associated with American International Pictures and he turned the footage over to John Sebastian [Curtis Harrington] and Derek Thomas
[Peter Bogdanovich]. Sebastian wrote new material involving a scientist (Basil Rathbone) talking to the astronauts in a new dubbed soundtrack, with a newly-added female astronaut (Faith Domergue) waiting
for them in a space capsule above Venus. This pieced-together version was issued directly to TV as Voyage to a Prehistoric Planet
(1965). Derek Thomas's version, Voyage to the Planet of Prehistoric
Women (1968), however, contains much new footage of golden girls
on Venus (led by Mamie Van Doren) who attempt to fight the aliens
after they kill their god, the winged serpent. It proved to be an
eerie, hacked-up offering. It was narrated by Bogdanovich and issued
directly to television.

LA PLANETE SAUVAGE (FANTASTIC PLANET) Les Films Armorial/
Service de Recherche ORTF/Ceskoslovenksy Filmexport, 1973) C-71
min.

    Producers, Simon Damiani and André Valio-Cavaglione; direc-
tor, René Laloux; based on the novel Oms en série by Stefan Wul;
screenplay, Laloux and Roland Topor; original design, Topor; character animation, Josef Kabrt; background animation, Josef Vana;
chief animators, Jindrick Barta, Zdena Bartova, Bohumil Sedja,
Zdenek Sob, Karel Strebl, and Jiri Vokoum; drawings, Lidia Cardat,
Renata Celbova, Dana Drabova, Viktoria Kolarikova, Helena Najdrov-
ska, Alena Pokorna, Jarmila Rabanova, Helen Rohauerova, Marcela
Schneiderova, Marie Tomaskova, and Eva Udzalova; music, Alain
Goraguer; synchronisation adviser, Helene Tossy; sound, Jean Carrere
and Rene Renault; sound re-recording, Paul Bertault; sound effects,
Robert Pouret; sound background, Jean Guerin; camera, Lubomir
Rejthar and Borsi Baromykin; editors, Helene Arnal and Marta La-
tolova.
    Voices (English-language versions): Barry Bostwick, Cynthia
Alder, Mark Gruner, Nora Heflin, Marvin Miller, Monika Ramirez,
Hal Smith, Olan Soule, and Janet Waldo.

    In the U.S. this French/Czechoslovakian co-production was
issued by Roger Corman's New World Pictures. Director René Laloux and artist Roland Topor, in this their third collaboration, fashioned a powerful sci-film, one done in soft colors and hues, which
made an effective contrast to the harshness and violence of the Fantastic Planet. Given a Restricted (R) rating for its U.S. playdates,
the animated feature did contain quite a bit of nudity and direct violence. Yet it was largely a poetic re-telling of the story of David
and Goliath, the small vs. the large.
    On the distant planet of Ygam, the giant Draags keep tiny

From <u>La Planète Sauvage</u> / <u>Fantastic Planet</u> (1973).

Oms as pets. The Oms apparently are humans who long ago came
to this planet from their mother Earth. The Draags, a highly intellectual society, refuse to acknowledge that the short-living but prolific Oms have untapped mental capacities. Many of the Oms live in
the desolate and dangerous country outside the city of the Draags;
these renegades are forever being hunted by the large ones. One of
the young Oms, Terr, adopted by Tiwa, the Draags' High Magistrate's
daughter, accidentally benefits from his mistress' education. Thirst-
ing for more knowledge he escapes, carting the telephonic instruction
earphones with him. Terr is soon accepted by the renegade Oms.
Under his leadership they begin to expand their consciousness and
soon become a real threat to the Draags who, in turn, seek to annihilate them. Terr and some of the Oms later escape in a rebuilt
space ship and land on the Fantastic Planet. Here they learn the secret of the Draags: the Draags' souls come here to meditate. The
Oms destroy some of these Draags' souls, forcing the giants to sue
for peace. Eventually an uneasy peace is arranged.
      The most impressive aspect of the film is its captivating ani-
mation. "<u>Fantastic Planet</u> may not be a great trip for the mind,
but for the eyes, at least, it is a resplendent and strangely sensuous
journey" (David Bartholomew, <u>Cinefantastique</u>).

THE POWER (MGM, 1968) C-108 min.

      Producer, George Pal; director, Byron Haskin; based on the

George Hamilton and Suzanne Pleshette in The Power (1968).

novel by Frank M. Robinson; screenplay, John Gay; music composer/
conductor, Miklos Rozsa; art directors, George W. Davis and Merrill
Pye; set decorators, Henry Grace and Don Greenwood, Jr.; makeup,
William Tuttle; assistant director, E. Darrell Hallenbeck; sound,
Franklin Milton; special electronic sound effects, Lovell Norman;
special effects, J. McMillan Johnson, Gene Warren, and Wah Chang;
camera, Ellsworth Fredericks; editor, Thomas J. McCarthy.

George Hamilton (Jim Tanner); Suzanne Pleshette (Margery
Lansing); Michael Rennie (Arthur Nordlund); Nehemiah Persoff (Carl
Melniker); Earl Holliman (Talbot Scott); Arthur O'Connell (Henry Hall-
son); Aldo Ray (Bruce); Barbara Nichols (Flora); Yvonne De Carlo
(Sally Hallson); Richard Carlson (N.E. Van Zandt); Gary Merrill (Mark
Corlane); Ken Murray (Grover); Miiko Taka (Mrs. Van Zandt); Celia
Lovsky (Mrs. Hallson); Vaughn Taylor (Mr. Hallson); Lawrence Mon-
taigne (Briggs); Beverly Hills (Sylvia).

The Power is one of those ambitious projects that did not jell.
It had a more-than-competent script (by John Gay), a star-studded
and capable cast, excellent special effects, good pacing, and a well-
mounted production. "What started out as an ingenious, imaginative
sci-fi premise developed into a confusing maze of cloudy characters,
motivations and events in its development.... in the final wrap-up
the spectator will leave the theater with a dozen pertinent questions
and story points unanswered and wondering what it's all about..."
(Variety).

Shortly before he is murdered, Naval liaison officer Henry
Hallson (Arthur O'Connell) alerts his co-workers at a space laboratory that one of their number has a super-intelligence which can control and destroy through willpower. Biochemist Jim Tanner (George
Hamilton), the chief suspect in Hallson's murder, sets out to solve
the case himself. His only clue is the name "Adam Hart" written
near the corpse. From Hallson's widow Sally (Yvonne De Carlo),
Tanner learns that this is the name of a boyhood pal of the victim.
As time passes, more of the research team are murdered, and Tanner is almost pushed to suicide by The Power. In the outcome, it
is Arthur Hordlund (Michael Rennie) who is really Adam Hart and who
claims he intends to conquer the Earth for its own "good." In a battle of wills, Tanner overwhelms Nordlund. At the finale the hero
asks co-worker Margery Lansing (Suzanne Pleshette), "Must absolute
power corrupt absolutely?"

While most critics at the time of release were unfavorably in-
clined to The Power ("Heavy-handed," stated Saturday Review), the
film has gathered its adherents in subsequent years. John Baxter,
in Science Fiction in the Cinema (1970), claims "the film is one of
the finest of all sf films, a tightly wound thriller that comes close
on occasions to combining the optimism of science fiction with the
pragmatism of the cinema.... One admits the plot faults of this remarkable film without once denying its substantial status as fantasy
and cinema."

In the British release print and the version shown on American
TV, most of Yvonne De Carlo's scenes (about eight minutes) have
been deleted.

PREHISTORIC WORLD OUT OF THE DARKNESS   see   TEENAGE
CAVEMAN

PROJECT X (Paramount, 1968) C-97 min.

Producer/director, William Castle; based on the novels
The Artificial Man and Psychogeist by Leslie P. Davies; screenplay,
Edmund Morris; music, Van Cleave; art directors, Hal Pereira and
Walter Tyler; set decorators, Robert Benton and Joseph Stone; make-
up, Wally Westmore; assistant director, Michael Caffey;--special se-
quences: producers, William Hanna and Joseph Barbera, live action
director, Wally Burr; production designers, Carl Ubano and Alex
Toth; assistant director, William Kirkham; camera, Kenneth Peach;--
sound, Garry A. Harris and John Wilkinson; special camera effects,
Paul K. Lerpae; camera, Harold Stine; editor, Edwin H. Bryant.

Christopher George (Hagen Arnold); Greta Baldwin (Karen Sum-
mers); Henry Jones (Dr. Crowther); Monte Markham (Gregory Gallea);
Harold Gould (Colonel Holt); Phillip E. Pine (Lee Craig); Lee Delano
(Dr. Tony Verity); Ivan Bonar (Colonel Cowen); Robert Cleaves (Dr.
George Tarvin); Charles Irving (Major Tolley); Sheila Bartold (Sybil
Dennis); Patrick Wright (Stover); Maryesther Denver (Overseer); Keye
Luke (Sen Chiu); Ed Prentiss (Hicks).

Henry Jones (center) in Project X (1968).

In the year 2118, secret agent Hagen Arnold (Christopher George) returns from a mission to Sino-Asia with his memory obliterated, after having radioed a frantic message that the West would be destroyed in two weeks time. Scientists work to restore his memory. To do so, they freeze him and provide him with a new identity, that of a 1968 bank robber, and then proceed to materialize his dream images through holography. It develops that Arnold's id, released through these experiments, is capable of killing, even of murdering Arnold, the man of the future. Eventually the pieces of the puzzle fit together.

An agent, Gregory Gallea (Monte Markham), who had disappeared two years earlier, is actually a counter-operative, and he had implanted a bacterial culture of mammoth plague potential within Arnold's system. Within two weeks' time, Arnold would become a potent death force. Gallea is killed by Arnold's id and the scientists are able to save their subject, since he was frozen for part of the two weeks' time and his "death mechanism" is not yet operative. In the climax, the restored Arnold is given yet another new identity so that he can cope with his dual experiences, and he now finds himself wed to factory worker Karen Summers (Greta Baldwin).

The release of the ambling Project X was delayed for some time. During its production, producer/director William Castle remarked, "From the time we started working on Project X we had the future breathing down our necks and science stepping on our heels." By the date of release in 1968 many of the innovative story ideas and film techniques (including the special sequences by Hanna-Barbera using "liquid crystals," holograms, a lenseless photography process by laser beams, etc.) had become dated. And as Variety pointed out, "The cast is sorely hampered by crudely expository dialog and total absence of characterization."

THE PROJECTED MAN (Compton-Cameo, 1966) C-90 min.

Producers, John Croydon and Maurice Foster; associate producer, Pat Green; director, Ian Curteis; story, Fran Quattrocchi; screenplay, John C. Cooper and Peter Bryan; art director, Peter Mullins; music/music director, Kennet V. Jones; assistant directors, Derek Whitehurst and Tom Sachs; sound, S. G. Rider and Red Law; special effects, Flo Nordhoff, Robert Hedges, and Mike Hope; second unit camera, Brian Rhodes; camera, Stan Pavey; editor, Derek Holding.

Bryant Halliday (Professor Steiner); Mary Peach (Dr. Pat Hill); Norman Wooland (Dr. Blanchard); Ronald Allen (Christopher Mitchell); Derek Farr (Inspector Davis); Tracey Crisp (Sheila Anderson); Derrick de Marney (Latham); Gerard Heinz (Professor Lembach); Sam Kydd (Harry); Terry Scully (Steve); Norma West (Gloria); Frank Gatliff (Dr. Wilson).

Teleportation, the process by which matter is moved from one place to another by the breakdown of its molecules, has been employed for a variety of sci-fi films, including Four-Sided Triangle (q. v.) and The Fly (q. v.) film series. The premise was again

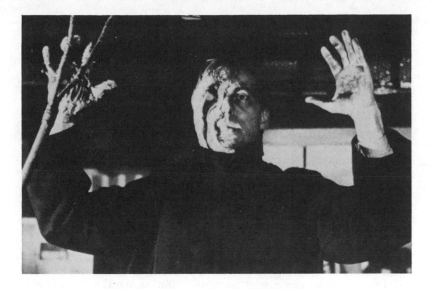

Bryant Halliday as The Projected Man (1966).

resurrected for this British-made production.
    At the Farber Research Lab. Professor Steiner (Bryant Halli-
day) and his assistant Christopher Mitchell (Ronald Allen) are experimenting with teleportation, much to the chagrin of their superior, Dr.
Blanchard (Norman Wooland). Finally they take their work out of the
laboratory and add a third scientist (Mary Peach) to their project.
Steiner is determined to prove that his theories are correct and that
if Dr. Blanchard had not sabotaged his equipment, he could have
vindicated his experiments. He decides to use himself as a human
guinea pig, projecting himself from one room to another. But Steiner is transformed into a disfigured monster who is electrically
charged. The rampaging victim later kills several people and in a
moment of desperation, destroys himself and his equipment.
    For its U.S. release, this Techniscope, color picture was
shorn to 77 minutes. Castle of Frankenstein noted, "Okay makeup
and abrupt climax add up to watchable but unstriking British programmer."

PURPLE DEATH FROM OUTER SPACE   see   FLASH GORDON CON-
QUERS THE UNIVERSE

THE PURPLE MONSTER STRIKES (Republic, 1945) fifteen chapters

Associate producer, Ronald Davidson; directors, Spencer Gordon Bennet and Fred Brannon; screenplay, Royal Cole, Albert DeMond, Basil Dickey, Lynn Perkins, Joseph Poland, and Barney Sarecky; music, Richard Cherwin; special effects, Howard and Theodore Lydecker; camera, Bud Thackery.

Dennis Moore (Craig Foster); Linda Stirling (Sheila Layton); Roy Barcroft (Purple Monster); James Craven (Dr. Cyrus Layton); Bud Geary (Garrett); Mary Moore (Marcia); John Davidson (Emperor of Mars); Joe Whitehead (Stewart); Emmett Vogan (Saunders); George Carleton (Meredith); Kenne Duncan (Mitchell); Rosemonde James (Helen); Monte Hale (Harvey); Wheaton Chambers (Benjamin); Frederick Howard (Crandall); Anthony Warde (Tony); Ken Terrell (Andy).

Chapters: 1) The Man in the Meteor; 2) The Time Trap; 3) Flaming Avalanche; 4) The Lethal Pit; 5) Death on the Beam; 6) The Demon Killer; 7) The Evil Eye; 8) Descending Doom; 9) The Living Dead; 10) House of Horror; 11) Menace from Mars; 12); Perilous Plunge; 13) Fiery Shroud; 14) The Fatal Trail; 15) Take-Off to Destruction.

Until the Fifties, the majority of sci-fi entries were confined to the world of serials, where, as any follower of chapterplays could tell you, anything was indeed possible. But no matter the genre of serial, it always followed the same formula: plenty of action, a cliffhanger finale for each episode, and the hero emerging victorious after numerous segments. Scientist Dr. Cyrus Layton (James Craven) has invented a fantastic new jet plane. On one occasion he notes an object zoom through the atmosphere and then land suddenly, not far from his laboratory. A strangely-garbed man (Roy Barcroft) emerges from the craft only moments before it explodes. A few seconds later the man, who identifies himself as the Purple Monster, is before Layton and tells him he is from Mars, the vanguard of an invasion of the Earth. He advises the scientist he will utilize the new jet for the conquest and then kills the inventor. Lawyer Craig Foster (Dennis Moore) surprises the alien after he has killed Layton, but he is overpowered. Meanwhile the Purple Monster takes over the scientist's body.

Thereafter Foster and Sheila (Linda Stirling), Layton's daughter, team to fight the monster, not knowing he has assumed her father's identity. The ruler of Mars (John Davidson) then sends Marcia (Mary Moore) from his planet to aid the Purple Monster, but she is killed on Earth. Eventually the hero realizes the space villain's ploy and places a camera in his laboratory to record the transformation. At the last moment the Purple Monster attempts an escape aboard the jet plane. But Foster employs the alien's own Annihilator and destroys the craft after take-off.

Although the plotline had large credibility gaps, The Purple Monster Strikes was certainly one of Republic's better-paced efforts. Thanks to Roy Barcroft and lovely Linda Stirling, the serial was a most pleasant diversion.

A sequel serial, Flying Disc Man from Mars (q.v.), used

much footage from this earlier production. In 1966 a feature version
of the serial was issued to TV as D-Day on Mars.

QUATERMASS AND THE PIT (Warner-Pathé, 1967) C-97 min.

Producer, Anthony Nelson Keyes; director, Roy Ward Baker;
based on the BBC television series by Nigel Kneale; story/screenplay,
Kneale; music, Tristram Cary; music supervisor, Philip Martell;
production designer, Bernard Robinson; art director, Ken Ryan; ward-
robe, Rosemary Burrows; makeup, Michael Morris; assistant director,
Bert Batt; sound, Sash Fisher and Roy Hyde; special effects, Bowie
Films; camera, Arthur Grant; editor, Spencer Reeve.
James Donald (Dr. Roney); Andrew Keir (Professor Quater-
mass); Barbara Shelley (Barbara Judd); Julian Glover (Colonel
Breen); Duncan Lamont (Sladden); Bryan Marshall (Captain Potter);
Peter Copley (Howell); Edwin Richfield (Minister); Grant Taylor
(Police Sergeant Ellis); Maurice Good (Sergeant Cleghorn); Ro-
bert Morris (Watson); Sheila Steafel (Journalist); Hugh Futcher (Sap-
per West); Hugh Morton (Elderly Journalist); Thomas Heathcote (Vic-
ar); Noel Howlett (Abbey Librarian); Keith Marsh (Johnson); Brian
Peck (Technical Officer); Charles Lamb (Newsvendor); John Graham
(Inspector).
A. k. a. The Mind Benders.

In the excavation for a London subway, workmen discover a
pit with the skulls and skeletons of prehistoric man. A doctor (James
Donald) from the Natural History Museum and his assistant (Barbara
Shelley) visit the site and soon the digging unearths a strangely-shaped
craft. Hearing of this discovery, Professor Quatermass (Andrew
Keir) and Colonel Breen (Julian Glover) rush to the spot. Quatermass
becomes convinced that the missile is of extraterrestrial origin.
When the object is opened, the dead bodies of locust-like creatures
are found; they turn out to be Martians. The opening of the craft
also unleashes the evil force of the creatures. Quatermass perceives
that at one time the warlike creatures, knowing they were doomed on
their dying planet, came to Earth and genetically changed sub-humans
into men and gave them war-like instincts. At the end the terrible
curse of the Martians is finally broken, but the uneasy knowledge of
mankind's origin remains.
"It is a pity that this, the most interesting of Nigel Kneale's
Quatermass parables, should prove the least satisfactory as a film.
The television version kept much of the nation on tenterhooks when
it first appeared, but the film version, though it keeps closely to the
original in outline, has been shortened and simplified and the story
now seems somewhat less adult then it did. Less detail has been
given to the development of rival theories and red herrings, and much
of the suspense and authenticity of the original has been lost" (British
Monthly Film Bulletin).
This film was the third in the Quatermass series. (The other
two were: Quatermass Xperiment [The Creeping Unknown] [q. v.] and
Quatermass II [Enemy from Space] [q. v.].) This time Roy Ward Baker replaced Val Guest as director. Also sorely missed was Brian

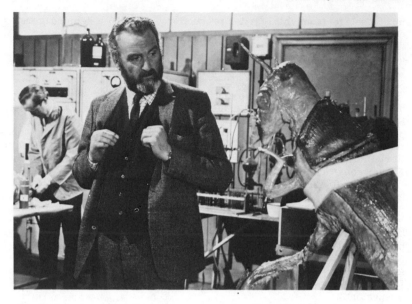

James Donald and Andrew Keir in Quatermass and the Pit (1967).

Donlevy as Professor Quatermass, although Andrew Keir proved competent in the focal role.
    The New York Times' Vincent Canby was not an enthusiast of the film (retitled Five Million Years to Earth) when it opened in America in the spring of 1968: "Unfortunately, all of its pseudo-scientific talk seemed to short-circuit the audience's interest...."

QUATERMASS II (Anglo-Amalgamated, 1957) 85 min.

    Executive producer, Michael Carreras; producer, Anthony Hinds; director, Val Guest; based on the BBC television serial by Nigel Kneale; screenplay, Kneale and Guest; art director, Bernard Robinson; music, James Bernard; camera, Gerald Gibbs; editor, James Needs.
    Brian Donlevy (Dr. Bernard Quatermass); Sidney James (Jimmy Hall); John Longden (Inspector Lomax); Bryan Forbes (Marsh); Vera Day (Sheila); William Franklyn (Brand); Charles Lloyd Pack (Dawson); Tom Chatto (Vincent Broadhead); John Van Eyssen (PRO); Percy Herbert (Gorman).

    In the U.S. Quatermass II was released as Enemy from Space, being Hammer Films' follow-up to their successful The Quatermass Xperiment (The Creeping Unknown) (q.v.) and the predecessor to Quatermass and the Pit (Five Million Years to Earth) (q.v.).

Brian Donlevy and Vera Day in Quatermass II (1957).

 Stocky Brian Donlevy again stars as Dr. Bernard Quatermass,
the head of Britain's space flight center. In this entry he is far
more the crux of action than in the initial feature. The story opens
with Quatermass driving home after a meeting with government officials in which he has been advised that the space project will no
longer be funded. A car nearly crashes into his and he soon finds
that the driver is infected with a rare type of fungus. The man had
been picnicking in an area called Wynerton Flats. Later the professor learns there have been strange sightings in the Wynerton Flats
area. He and his assistant (Bryan Forbes) go to trace the cause of
these occurrences. Once there Quatermass spots an installation
much like the one he devised for moon landings and settlement. He
soon becomes convinced that aliens have invaded Earth and have taken
over the bodies of most government and military officials. Later
he learns that the aliens, who can survive only in methane, want to
enslave the earth and reside there. Unable to obtain official sanction,
the professor instigates a riot among the workers at the installation
(which the "official" government claims is to make synthetic food for
the third world) and the aliens are destroyed when oxygen is pumped
into the area.
 Besides being sturdy science fiction, this number two entry
in the film series is highly political in its analogies. In addition to
a sterling performance by reliable Donlevy, the picture boasts ex-

quisite black-and-white cinematography by Gerald Gibbs. "In fact Gibbs' work is so good that, despite a number of weaknesses, the film is still a claimant [along with Losey's The Damned] for the title of England's most disturbingly expressionist movie" (David Pirie, A Heritage of Horror, 1973).

THE QUATERMASS XPERIMENT (Exclusive, 1958) 82 min.

Producer, Anthony Hinds; director, Val Guest; based on the teleplay The Quatermass Experiment by Nigel Kneale; screenplay, Richard Landau and Guest; art director, J. Elder Willis; special effects; Leslie Bowie; camera, Walter Harvey; editor, James Needs.
Brian Donlevy (Professor Bernard Quatermass); Jack Warner (Inspector Lomax); Margia Dean (Judith Carroon); Richard Wordsworth (Victor Carroon); David King Wood (Dr. Gordon Briscoe); Thora Hird (Rosie); Gordon Jackson (TV Producer); Harold Lang (Christie); Lionel Jeffries (Blake); Maurice Kaufmann (Marsh); Frank Phillips (BBC Announcer).

The Creeping Unknown was the U.S. release title of The Quatermass Xperiment (last word was changed from Experiment in order to tie in with the film's British X certificate), which was based on a BBC teleseries. The show ran from 1953 through 1960 and spawned three films--this one and two follow-ups, Quatermass II (Enemy from Space) and Quatermass and the Pit (Five Million Miles to Earth) (both q.v.).

The well-modulated feature opens with two lovers in a haystack being interrupted by the crash landing of a rocket. The craft is England's initial probe into space. Three astronauts have returned from the voyage, but only one of them (Richard Wordsworth) is alive. Professor Quatermass (Brian Donlevy), the chief of the operation, and his scientific team examine the man and find that he seems to be in an extreme state of flux. No one can figure out how or why his comrades in the space ship died. The doctors also note that the man is plagued by a strange growth on his hand. Eventually he becomes so terrified of his state of being that he escapes and roams the London slums, slowly degenerating as the alien force that controls him begins to absorb whatever life form it touches. Finally Quatermass and the military police corner the at-large astronaut in Westminister Cathedral during a TV program. He is accidentally electrocuted with high tension wires. At the film's finale, Quatermass prepares to launch another spaceship.
Although troubled by some inferior production values and substandard special effects (the rocket ship is especially shoddy), The Quatermass Xperiment does have a solid performance by Donlevy, excellent direction by Val Guest, and a terrifying portrayal of the astronaut-turned-monster by Richard Wordsworth.
As so often happens, films such as this suffer by comparison with more sophisticated later entries in the cycle.

QUEEN OF ATLANTIS   see   L'ATLANTIDE (1960)

QUEEN OF ATLANTIS   see   SIREN OF ATLANTIS

QUEEN OF BLOOD (American International, 1966) C-81 min.

Producer, George Edwards; associate producer, Stephanie Rothman; director/screenplay, Curtis Harrington; art director, Albert Locatelli; set decorator, Leon Smith; titles from the paintings of John Cline; music, Leonard Morand; sound, Harold Garver; camera, Vilis Lapeniks; editor, Leo Shreve.

John Saxon (Allan); Basil Rathbone (Dr. Farraday); Judi Meredith (Laura); Dennis Hopper (Paul); Florence Marly (Velena); and Robert Boon, Don Eitner, Virgil Frye, Robert Porter, Terry Lee, and Forrest Ackerman.

In 1990 Dr. Farraday (Basil Rathbone), the head of the U.S. space program, dispatches three astronauts--Allan (John Saxon), Paul (Dennis Hopper), and Laura (Judi Meredith)--to rendezvous with a space craft from another galaxy which has contacted the Earth for help.   No trace of the alien space ship is found on Mars, but on one of that planet's moons Allan locates the downed craft.   The sole survivor of the flight is the beautiful, green-tinted Velena (Florence

Judi Meredith, Robert Boon and Dennis Hopper in Queen of Blood (1966).

Marly). He brings the young woman to the main ship where, one by one, she kills the crew members, draining them of their blood. But in a struggle with Laura, Velena is scratched and, being a hemophiliac, she soon bleeds to death. Before Velena is wounded, she has produced several eggs, which Farraday, back on Earth, plans to study. He refuses to heed the astronauts' warning.

Queen of Blood is actually a patchwork, made up of footage from a Russian feature purchased by Roger Corman, and new material written and directed by Curtis Harrington for the sum of $50,000. The Soviet footage was employed for the scenes inside the alien space ship. In its dark, moody way, it was quite effective. The rest of the project was mediocre, although veteran Basil Rathbone gave his usual "strong" performance. (Rathbone, wearing the same outfit and working on the same set, was also used by producer Roger Corman for a lead role in the quickie, Voyage to a Prehistoric Planet, which was a potpourri of new scenes and integrated footage from another Soviet science-fiction movie, Planeta Burg (Storm Planet) (q.v.).

Queen of Blood was retitled Planet of Blood for TV. Its few reviews reflected its limited playdates and no one was more accurate than Variety, which said that the film had an "anemic future."

QUEEN OF OUTER SPACE (Allied Artists, 1958) C-80 min.

Producer, Ben Schwalb; director, Edward Bernds; story, Ben Hecht; screenplay, Charles Beaumont; art director, David Milton; set decorator, Joseph Kish; wardrobe supervisor, Irene Caine; Miss Gabor's wardrobe, Thomas Pierce; makeup, Emile LaVigne; assistant director, William Beaudine, Jr.; music, Marlin Skiles; sound, Joseph Lapis; camera, William Whitley; editor, William Austin.

Zsa Zsa Gabor (Talleah); Eric Fleming (Captain Neil Patterson); Laurie Mitchell (Yllana - Queen of Venus); Paul Birch (Professor Konrad); Barbara Darrow (Kaeel); Dave Willock (Lieutenant Michael Cruze); Lisa Davis (Motiya); Patrick Waltz (Lieutenant Larry Turner); Marilyn Buferd (Odeena); Marjorie Durant (Amazon Guard); Lynn Cartwright (Guard Leader); Gerry Gaylor (Friendly Guard); Mary Ford, Colleen Drake, Marya Stevens (Other Guards); Laura Mason, Tania Velia, and Kathy Marlowe (Councilors).

Proving that anything is possible in the world of sci-fi, the glamorous Zsa Zsa Gabor turned up in this CinemaScope, color entry. Obviously, story provider Ben Hecht and scripter Charles Beaumont intended this film to be a spoof outer space opera, but it fell flat. Variety reported, "Most of the female characters look like they would be more at home on a Minsky runway than the Cape Canaveral launching pad.... Predominantly feminine cast is attractively garbed in the brief raiment that appears to be customary on planets other than this one."

In 1985, three astronauts (Eric Fleming, Patrick Waltz, and Dave Willock) and a scientist, Professor Konrad (Paul Birch), are sent to a space station to check on the mysterious destruction of several space bases. As they leave the station it is blown up and an energy ray transports them to Venus where they crash-land. There the crew is taken prisoner by Queen Yllana's (Laurie Mitchell) Amazon

Paul Birch, Dave Willock, Laurie Mitchell, Zsa Zsa Gabor and Eric Fleming in Queen of Outer Space (1958).

guards. The chief astronaut, Captain Neil Patterson (Fleming) discovers that the masked Yllana (who has been badly disfigured) plans to kill the visitors, and later to destroy the Earth. But the gorgeous Talleah (Zsa Zsa Gabor) and some other female subjects are not about to allow these new males to be done away with. Talleah and her followers revolt, set the Earth men free, and prevent Yllana's Beta disintegrater from destroying the Earth. Before Patterson and his men depart, he promises Talleah he will return.

Queen of Outer Space should have been funny, but it was too silly and too pathetically dull. There just was not much outer space menace in this clinker.

THE QUESTOR TAPES (NBC-TV, 1974) C-75 mins.

Executive producer, Gene Roddenberry; producer, Howie Horowitz; director, Richard A. Colla; story, Roddenberry; teleplay, Roddenberry and Gene L. Coon; art director, Phil Barber; music, Gil Mellé; special camera effects, Albert Whitlock; camera, Michael Margulies; editorial supervisor, Richard Belding; editors, Robert L. Kimble and J. Terry Williams.

Robert Foxworth (Questor); Mike Farrell (Jerry Robinson); John Vernon (Darrow); Lew Ayres (Vaslovik); James Shigeta (Dr. Chan); Dana Wynter (Lady Helen Trimbal); Robert Douglas (Dr. Michaels); Ellen Weston (Allison Sample); Majel Barrett (Dr. Bradley);

Walter Koenig (Administrative Assistant); Fred Sadoff (Dr. Audret);
Reuben Singer (Dr. Gorlov); Gerald Sanderson Peters (Randolph);
Eydse Girard (Stewardess); Alan Caillou (Immigration Officer); Lal
Baum (Colonel Henderson); Patti Cubbison (Secretary).

    After the demise of his popular teleseries "Star Trek," pro-
ducer/writer Gene Roddenberry turned out a number of telefeatures
(Genesis II, Planet Earth, both q. v.) aimed as pilots for possible
series. None of them sold and neither did The Questor Tapes, a
TV movie about an android hero which was premiered on NBC-TV's
"Wednesday Night at the Movies."
    Robert Foxworth starred as Questor, an android (an ambula-
tory computer capable of all human functions) who is programmed by
scientists to locate his missing creator or face destruction. Scientists from five nations assemble in a Pasadena, California laboratory
to program Questor, who was created by a Nobel Prize-winning
Vaslovik (Lew Ayres). A micro-electronics engineer (Mike Farrell)
wants to use the scientist's tapes to program Questor, but his colleagues refuse; they use University tapes and fail. They then employ
Vaslovik's tapes but this only has a temporary effect on the android,
who is then left alone. He activates himself and escapes. Later,
Questor forces the engineer to help him construct a built-in compul-
sion to find his creator. The two become friends and eventually
track down the startling secret of Questor's origin.
    Kay Anderson wrote in Cinefantastique, "Production values are
surprisingly shoddy, performances often declamatory, and motivations
and plot twists murky in this off-hand-looking effort from Universal,
usually noted for its willingness to give a quality budget to quality
science fiction. Which perhaps tells the story."

RADAR MEN FROM THE MOON (Republic, 1952) twelve chapters

    Associate producer, Franklyn Adreon; director, Fred Brannon;
screenplay, Ronald Davidson; music, Stanley Wilson; special effects,
Howard and Theodore Lydecker; camera, John MacBurnie.
    George Wallace (Commando Cody); Aline Towne (Joan Gilbert);
Roy Barcroft (Retik); William Bakewell (Ted Richards); Clayton Moore
(Graber); Peter Brocco (Krog); Bob Stevenson (Daly); Don Walters
(Henderson); Tom Steele (Zerg); Dale Van Sickel (Alon); Wilson Wood
(Hank); Noel Cravat (Robal); Baynes Barron (Nasor); Paul McGuire
(Bream); Ted Thorpe (Bartender); Dick Cogan (Jones).
    Chapters: 1) Moon Rocket; 2) Molten Terror; 3) Bridge of
Death; 4) Flight to Destruction; 5) Murder Car; 6) Hills of Death; 7)
Human Targets; 8) The Enemy Planet; 9) Battle in the Stratosphere;
10) Mass Execution; 11) Planned Pursuit; 12) Take-off to Eternity.

    The major importance of this lower-case serial was that it
introduced the character of Jeff King (George Wallace), alias Commando Cody, Sky Marshal of the Universe. The athletic character
would inhabit another serial, Commando Cody (q. v.), and be the lead
figure of a teleseries.
    Borrowing much stock footage from The Purple Monster Strikes

(q. v.) and King of the Rocket Men, this cliffhanger tells of the United States' defenses being sabotaged. Commando Cody and his two allies (Aline Towne and William Bakewell) are called in by the government to investigate. The trio have invented a "flying suit" which Cody employs to travel on his missions. Subsequently he discovers two men about to destroy a train with an atomic gun. Cody learns they are using an unknown element from the moon. He and his two pals take a flight there and uncover a hidden city ruled over by Retik (Roy Barcroft). The latter intends to use a substance called "lunarium" to rule the universe. Realizing that without his super atomic weapon Retik would be powerless, the trio escapes back to Earth planning to warn global leaders of the invasion plans. Retik's henchmen (Clayton Moore and Bob Stevenson) follow in pursuit. In the finale Cody utilizes the atomic weapon to destroy Retik and his rocket ship.

This serial cast Roy Barcroft as the alien leader in order to utilize footage as well as his costume from the earlier The Purple Monster Strikes.

In 1966 a feature version of Radar Men from the Moon would be issued to TV as Retik, the Moon Menace.

RADIO RANCH see THE PHANTOM EMPIRE

RED PLANET MARS (United Artists, 1952) 87 min.

Producer, Anthony Veiller; director, Harry Horner; based on the play Red Planet by John L. Balderston and John Hoare; screenplay, Balderston and Veiller; art director, Charles D. Hall; music, David Chudnow; camera, Joseph Biroc; editor, Francis Lyon.

Peter Graves (Chris Cronyn); Andrea King (Linda Cronyn); Orley Lingdgren (Stewart Cronyn); Bayard Veiller (Roger Cronyn); Walter Sande (Admiral Carey); Herbert Berghof (Franz Calder); Marvin Miller (Arjenian); Willis Bouchey (President); Richard Powers (General Burdette); Morris Ankrum (Secretary Sparks); Lewis Martin (Dr. Mitchell); House Peters, Jr. (Dr. Boulting); Claude Dunkin (Peter Lewis); Gene Roth (UMW President); John Tops (Borodin); Bill Kennedy (Commentator); Vince Barnett (Man); Grace Leonard (Woman).

"In an era of A-bombs, B-pictures, cold wars and science-fiction, such items as Red Planet Mars ... would seem to be inevitable. But this excursion into the terrifying blue yonder--which, incidentally, never leaves California, the site of the experiment--switches from its pseudo-scientific exploration with such suddenness as to give even the most dedicated pulp fiction adventurer the megrims. In the midst of this tall tale the producers have seen fit to introduce a plea for a return to religion. It is a device that, in this case, is neither original nor convincing and serves only to make for loads of uninspired palaver about the comparative values of research and faith" (New York Times).

American scientists Chris and Linda Cronyn (Peter Graves and Andrea King) use the "hydrogen valve" system developed by

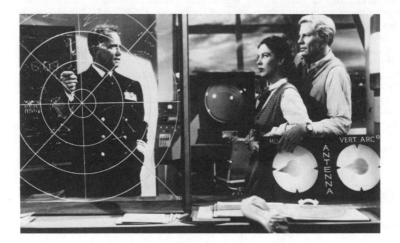

Walter Sands, Andrea King and Peter Graves in Red Planet Mars
(1952).

crazed Nazi scientist Franz Calder (Herbert Berghof). With this
television-like equipment they are able to contact a superior civilization on Mars. It develops that the inhabitants of the Red Planet have
a life-span of three hundred years, are working for peaceful uses of
the atom and are ruled by a Supreme Being (very similar to the Deity of
Christianity).

News of these events leaks out and the Russian government,
among others, is overthrown. A priest (!) is named as USSR ruler,
while religion takes hold in the U.S. and other parts of the world.
Finally, the Third Reich scientist comes out of his hiding place in
Tibet to downgrade the work accomplished by the Cronyns. The latter, rather than let his mad plan foster world anarchy, blow themselves up with the German and his pioneering equipment.

At the finale the U.S. President (Willis Bouchey) and the Supreme Being from Mars eulogize the late scientists for their bravery.

THE RENEGADE SATELLITE   see   BEYOND THE MOON

RETIK, THE MOON MENACE   see   RADAR MEN FROM THE MOON

RETURN OF CAPTAIN AMERICA   see   CAPTAIN AMERICA

RETURN OF CAPTAIN MARVEL   see   THE ADVENTURES OF CAP-
TAIN MARVEL

RETURN OF THE FIFTY FOOT WOMAN   see   ATTACK OF THE
FIFTY FOOT WOMAN

RETURN OF THE FLY (Twentieth Century-Fox, 1959) 78 min.

Producer, Bernard Glasser; director, Edward L. Bernds;
based on the story "The Fly" by George Langelaan; screenplay,
Bernds; art directors, Lyle R. Wheeler and John Mansbridge; set
decorators, Walter M. Scott and Joseph Kish; makeup, Hal Lierley;
music, Paul Sawtell; camera, Brydon Baker; editor, Richard C. Meyer.
Vincent Price (François Delambre); Brett Halsey (Philippe De-
lambre); David Frankham (Alan Hinds); John Sutton (Inspector Char-
as); Dan Seymour (Max Berthold); Danielle DeMetz (Cecile Bonnard);
Florence Strom (Nun); Janine Grandel (Mme. Bonnard); Richard Flato
(Sergeant Dubois); Pat O'Hara (Detective Evans); Barry Bernard
(Lieutenant Maclish); Jack Daly (Granville); Michael Mark (Gaston);
Francisco Villalobas (Priest); Joan Cotton (Nurse).

"A better sequel than you'd expect," said Films in Review.
Nevertheless this follow-up to the 1958 success, The Fly (q.v.) left
a good deal to be desired in the areas of plausibility and imagination.
Vincent Price was the only performer to be in both films, again playing François Delambre, the brother of the late experimenter. Here
his nephew Philippe (Brett Halsey) reassembles his father's disintegrating equipment which permits one to transfer matter and reinte-
grate it in another place. Unknown to Philippe, his assistant Alan
Hinds (David Frankham) is really an enemy operative. In an ensuing
scuffle Philippe suffers the same fate as his father, being transformed into a part-fly. But he is more fortunate, for François is
able to "reconstruct" Philippe as a normal human being again.
The third and final segment of this mini-series would be Curse
of the Fly (q.v.).

LA REVE D'UN ASTRONOME   see   THE ASTRONOMER'S DREAM

REVENGE OF THE CREATURE (Universal, 1954) 82 min.

Producer, William Alland; director, Jack Arnold; story, Alland; screenplay, Martin Berkelely; art directors, Alexander Golitzen
and Alfred Sweeney; makeup, Bud Westmore; music, Herman Stein;
music director, Joseph Gershenson; camera, Charles S. Welbourne;
editor, Paul Weatherwax.
John Agar (Clete Ferguson); Lori Nelson (Helen Dobson); John
Bromfield (Joe Hayes); Robert B. Williams (George Johnson); Nestor
Paiva (Lucas); Grandon Rhodes (Foster); Ricou Browing (The Gill Man);
and Dave Willock and Charles Crane.
Following the success of The Creature from the Black Lagoon
(q.v.), Universal and director Jack Arnold turned out a sequel, Revenge of the Creature, one of the last Fifties films to be issued in
3-D. This narrative picks up where the original ceased and manages

to develop a sensible storyline.

When the Gill Man (Ricou Browning) is captured in his black
lagoon in South America, he is drugged and taken to Oceanic Park,
Florida, where he is exhibited with other aquarian life. The creature makes a few abortive attempts to escape and finally does so in
order to abduct heroine Helen Dobson (Lori Nelson). She is later
found lying unconscious in a park, apparently having been raped by
the Gill Man. The creature is also in the park, but in its pool, for
it must return to the water every few hours to obtain oxygen. Subsequently the abnormal being is shot as it tries to find sanctuary in
the darker waters of the lake.

Director Jack Arnold infused the film with some verve. The
set-up of the heroine swimming in a pool with her fiancé (John Agar),
with the creature watching from below, is borrowed from the original. But this time the Gill Man reaches out and tries to steal the heroine from her love.

The film proved successful enough to revive the creature for
yet another go-round, The Creature Walks Among Us (q.v.).

One of the more (unintentionally) amusing scenes occurs when
the Gill Man stalks into a teenagers' jam session, causing the "cool"
youths to scatter to the winds.

RIDERS TO THE STARS (United Artists, 1954) C-82 min.

Producer, Ivan Tors; associate producers, Maxwell Smith and
Herbert L. Strock; director, Richard Carlson; screenplay, Curt Siodmak; art director, Jerome Pycha, Jr.; music, Harry Sukman; special
effects director, Harry Redmond, Jr.; special camera effects, Jack
R. Glass; camera, Stanley Cortez; editorial supervisor, H. L. Strock.

William Lundigan (Richard Stanton); Herbert Marshall (Dr.
Donald Stanton); Richard Carlson (Jerry Lockwood); Martha Hyer
(Jane Flynn); Robert Karnes (Walter Gordon); and Dawn Addams,
George Eldredge, King Donovan, Lawrence Dobkin, and James K.
Best.

George Pal and Ivan Tors were the two most prolific Hollywood producers of semi-documentary space operas in the early Fifties. This Tors production was directed by Richard Carlson, who
also played as astronaut in the film. Stanley Cortez's cinematography
was a distinct highlight of the project.

Dr. Donald Stanton (Herbert Marshall), the eminent space
scientist, heads a research team which tries to find out why steel
objects disintegrate in the Earth's atmosphere, but meteors do not.
He therefore directs a trio of astronauts (William Lundigan, Carlson,
and Robert Karnes) to man a space rocket. Their mission is to
"capture" a meteor and bring it back to Earth for proper study.
After many (documented) space adventures, a meteor is obtained.
Back on Earth it is learned that its shell of pure carbon and diamond dust protect it against atmospheric friction.

Seen today, Riders to the Stars is terribly dated and too low-
keyed. Most of the black-and-white story has long ago been acted
out in real life. Thus the film offers, for Seventies' viewers, no

William Lundigan and Martha Hyer in Riders to the Stars (1954).

more than a pictorial excursion into the pre-space flight days of the
mid-Fifties.

ROBINSON CRUSOE ON MARS (Paramount, 1964) C-110 min.

Producer, Aubrey Schenck; director, Byron Haskin; based on
the novel Robinson Crusoe by Daniel DeFoe; screenplay, Ib Melchior
and John C. Higgins; color consultant, Richard Mueller; art directors,
Hal Pereira and Arthur Lonergan; makeup, Wally Westmore and Bud
Bashaw; music, Van Cleve; technical advisor, Edward V. Ashburn;
sound, Harold Lewis; special camera effects, Lawrence Butler; cam-
era, Winton C. Hoch; editor, Terry Morse.
Paul Mantee (Commander Christopher Draper); Vic Lundin
(Friday); Adam West (Colonel Dan McReady); and Mona the Woolly
Monkey.

Daniel DeFoe's novel of 1719 has been frequently filmed but
here it was given an added twist. Director Byron Haskin, who made
Destination Moon (q. v.), returned to Death Valley for location sites
for this project. (John Sturges would also use the vicinity for

Paul Mantee in Robinson Crusoe on Mars (1964).

Marooned [q.v.]) This time around, the bleak, arid landscape of
Death Valley was employed to simulate the surface of the planet Mars
and it was accomplished so well that the landscape became a focal
part of the picture.
    Astronauts Christopher Draper (Paul Mantee) and Dan McReady
(Adam West) are drawn into the gravitational pull of Mars and are
forced to abandon their space ship via ejector capsules. McReady is
killed in the effort, but Draper--with his pet monkey Mona--lands
safely on Mars. Slowly the two learn to adapt to their new surround-
ings. Then a slave (Vic Lundin) escapes from a mysterious craft
from another planet and becomes Draper's companion on Mars.
Later the slave's former "owners" attempt to bombard Mars in order
to kill the refugee. Draper and his man "Friday" escape through
subterranean tunnels and emerge at the planet's ice cap. At the last
moment, they are rescued by a U.S. space ship.
    "Break out the ray guns, boys! Here comes a horde of little
green men? On the contrary, here comes a pleasant surprise: a
piece of science fiction based on valid speculation, a modest yet provocative attempt to imagine what might happen ... in the next decade
or so..." (Time). Other sources were equally enthusiastic about this

unpretentious venture: "Credit Byron Haskin, the experienced director, with the enjoyable result. His Mars has a genuine look to it,
and the space pilot's adventures have verisimilitude.... The film
manages to avoid the heavy literalness of less expert fantasies by
taking a calm approach" (New York Times).

THE ROBOT OF REGALIO see BEYOND THE MOON

ROCKET SHIP see FLASH GORDON

ROCKET TO THE MOON see CAT-WOMEN OF THE MOON

ROCKETSHIP X-M (Lippert, 1950) 78 min. (tinted sequences)

    Executive producer, Murray Lerner; producer/director/screen-
play, Kurt Neumann; art director, Thobold Holsopple; music, Ferde
Grofé; special effects, Jack Rabin and I. A. Block; camera, Karl
Struss; editor, Harry Gerstad.
    Lloyd Bridges (Floyd Oldham); Osa Massen (Lisa Van Horn);
John Emery (Karl Eckstrom); Noah Beery, Jr. (William Corrigan);
Hugh O'Brian (Harry Chamberlin); Morris Ankrum (Dr. Fleming); and
Patrick Ahern, Sherry Moreland, John Dutra, and Katherine Marlowe.

    About the time producer George Pal announced plans to film
Destination Moon (q.v.), producer/director/scripter Kurt Neumann
wrote and made Rocketship X-M, and the two films appeared in distribution at just about the same time. Whereas Pal's movie was
more or less a semi-documentary on space travel, this entry was
a definite space opera, involving a group of astronauts on Mars and
their assorted discoveries there. Despite a limited budget, Neumann's effort managed to entertain viewers far more than Destination
Moon. Its plot would serve as a basis for many space sci-fi pictures
that were to follow.
    A group of astronauts (Lloyd Bridges, Osa Massen, John
Emery, Noah Beery, Jr., and Hugh O'Brian) secretly blasts off to
the moon on an exploratory trip. Due to a craft malfunction they
end up crash-landing on Mars. There they find evidence of a once
powerful civilization that destroyed itself through atomic warfare.
The few human survivors there have reverted to savagery. Eventually only three of the party are able to escape from the Red Planet,
but due to a lack of fuel they crash and die on the return voyage.
Their ground chief (Morris Ankrum) is not discouraged. He announces, "the expedition was not a failure," for the crew was able
to relay valuable information before its demise.
    With its downbeat ending and its tinted scenes on Mars, the
film met with a very mixed critical reaction, although it enjoyed solid box-office response. Richard Hodgens wrote in Focus on the
Science Fiction Film, "Though Rocketship X-M seemed ludicrous, it
was level-headed and superb compared with what followed." Castle

Lloyd Bridges and Osa Massen in Rocketship X-M (1950).

of Frankenstein magazine would later note, "Frankly intended as a
rip-off of George Pal's Destination Moon, this low-budget space odyssey now stands up as far more imaginative and entertaining than its
sterile, science-bound model ... probably Kurt Neumann's best directing job."
    In Italy it was called Destinazione Luna.

ROLLERBALL (United Artists, 1975) C-129 min.

    Producer, Norman Jewison; associate producer, Patrick Pal-
mer; director, Jewison; based on the story by William Harrison;
screenplay, Harrison; assistant directors, Kip Gowans, Chris Kenny,
and Dietmar Siegert; second unit director, Max Kleven; production
designer, John Box; art director, Robert Laing; track architect, Herbert Schurmann; music/music director, André Previn; costumes, Julie Harris; makeup, Wally Schneiderman; sound, Derek Ball; sound
editor, Les Wiggins and Archie Ludski; sound re-recording Gordon
K. McCallum; stunt co-ordinator Max Kleven; skating co-ordinator,
Peter Hicks; special effects, Sass Bedig, John Richardson, and Joe
Fitt; camera, Douglas Slocombe; editor, Antony Gibbs.
    James Caan (Jonathan E); John Houseman (Bartholomew;) Maud

Adams (Ella); John Beck (Moonpie); Moses Gunn (Cletus); Pamela
Hensley (Mackie); Barbara Trentham (Daphne); Ralph Richardson (Li-
brarian); Shane Rimmer (Team Executive); Alfred Thomas (Team
Trainer); Burnell Tucker (Jonathan's Captain of Guard); Angus Mac-
Innes (Jonathan's Guard No. 1); Rick Le Parmentier (Bartholomew's
Aide); Burt Kwouk (Oriental Doctor); Robert Ito (Oriental Instructor);
Nancy Blair (Girl in Luxury Centre Library); Loftus Burton and Abi
Gouhad (Black Reporters); Stephen Boyum, Alan Hamane, Danny Wong,
and Bob Leon (Bikers); Craig Baxley, Tony Brunaker, Gary Epper,
Bob Minor, Jim Nickerson, Chuck Parkinson, Jr., Dar Robinson,
Roy Scammell, Walter Scott, Dick Warlock, and Jerry Wills (Stunt-
men).

Rollerball is not a film of tomorrow but an extention of today.
In the year 2018 there are no wars, no famine, no love, no wants, no
governments--only a corporate society and the rough sport of rollerball to keep the world's population amused. In this 1984-type thriller
producer/director Norman Jewison attempts to demonstrate on a lavish scale that the popular sports of today are only mind-controlling
pap used by governments to lull the population from thinking seriously about what its leaders really do.
Rollerball, the international sport, is a brutal combination of
hockey, football, motorcycle racing, and the roller derby. Jonathan
E (James Caan) has been a Houston Rollerball star for a decade.
Area Chief Executive Bartholomew (John Houseman) orders him to re-
tire, but he refuses. Jonathan E seeks advice from his trainer Cletus
(Moses Gunn) about just why they want to bench him, especially before
the important match with Tokyo. Cletus reasons that the corporation
is fearful that Jonathan E's continuing popularity is a threat to the
new philosophy of mass sameness, which the Rollerball game is supposed to demonstrate. Jonathan E does play in the Tokyo match, in
which his pal Moonpie (John Beck) is rendered permanently senseless.
In a later match, Houston vs. New York, all holds are loosened on
the rules in an effort to kill Jonathan E. The game evolves into a
bloody contest, with Jonathan E as a lonely survivor.
"All science-fiction can be roughly divided into two types of
nightmares. In the first the world has gone through a nuclear holocaust and civilization has reverted to a neo-Stone Age. In the second,
of which Rollerball is an elaborate and very silly example, all of mankind's problems have been solved but at the terrible price of individual freedom.
"... The only way science-fiction of this sort can make sense
is as a comment on the society for which it's intended, and the only
way Rollerball would have made sense is as satire of our national
preoccupation with television professional sports, particularly weekend
football" (New York Times).
The producers and distributors of Rollerball invested several
million dollars in this highly-touted science fiction thriller, but the
end results were more ludicrous and dreary than stimulating. It was
a big box-office disappointment. The main fault with the film is that
the supposed panacea game of Rollerball is not the brutally, dangerous
sport so talked about by all concerned in the plotline. It emerges as
a rather tame, boring, well-programed minor spectator sport. There

are very solemn performances by Caan and Houseman, and the obli-
gatory romantic diversion provided by Barbara Trentham (as Jonathan
E's wife) and Maud Adams (his mistress). However, it is the cameo
performance of Ralph Richardson, as the dotty librarian/keeper of
the giant computer Zero, which adds a delightful, zany note to the
lugubrious proceedings.

S.O.S. TIDAL WAVE (Republic, 1939) 60 min.

Associate producer, Armand Schaefer; director, John H. Auer;
story, James Webb; screenplay, Maxwell Shane and Gordon Kahn; art
director, Victor MacKay; music director, Cy Feuer; camera, Jack
Marta; editor, Ernest Nims.
Ralph Byrd (Jeff Shannon); George Barbier (Uncle Dan); Kay
Sutton (Laurel Shannon); Frank Jenks (Peaches Jackson); Marc Law-
rence (Sutter); Dorothy Lee (Mabel); Oscar O'Shea (Mike Halloran);
Mickey Kuhn (Buddy Shannon); Ferris Taylor (Farrow); Donald Barry
(Curley); Raymond Bailey (Roy Nixon).

This little tale of a mayoral race in a large city, complicated
by a crooked political candidate and a television reporter, was no
more than an excuse to use stock footage from Deluge (q.v.), which
Republic had purchased from RKO. Ralph Byrd starred as a "name"
for the action trade, but over-all the film was a very limp, second-
rate entry.
The finale shows the scenes of destruction as an earthquake
and tidal wave engulf the huge metropolis (New York City).

THE SATAN BUG (United Artists, 1965) C-114 min.

Producer/director, John Sturges; based on the novel by Ian
Stuart [Alistair MacLean]; screenplay, James Clavell and Edward An-
halt; assistant director, Jack Reddish; art director, Herman Blumenthal; set decorator, Chuck Vassar; music/music director, Jerry
Goldsmith; titles De Patie-Frelong; sound, Harold Lewis; special effects, Paul Pollard; camera, Robert Surtees; editor, Ferris Webster.
George Maharis (Lee Barrett); Richard Basehart (Dr. Hoffman); Anne Francis (Ann); Dana Andrews (The General); Edward Asner (Veretti); Frank Sutton (Donald); John Larkin (Michaelson); Richard Bull (Cavanaugh) Martin Blaine (Martin); John Anderson (Reagan);
Russ Bender (Mason); Simon Oakland (Tesserly); Hari Rhodes (Johnson); John Clarke (Raskin); Henry Beckman (Dr. Baxter); Harold
Gould (Dr. Ostrer); James Hong (Dr. Yang).

In a top-security research installation, Space Three, located
in the desert, scientists are studying a deadly virus called the Satan
Bug. It can cause instant death over great areas. Suddenly several
flasks of the potent liquid are stolen from the guarded laboratory.
The general in charge (Dana Andrews) works with Lee Barrett (George
Maharis), the government investigator on the case. Subsequently Barrett, who has been piecing together the mystery, and Ann (Anne

Richard Basehart, Anne Francis and Dana Andrews in The Satan Bug (1965).

Francis), the general's daughter, are captured by accomplices of Dr. Hoffman (Richard Basehart), a fanatic who is opposed to war and intends to blackmail the government into closing down the germ warfare installation. To prove his point the madman orders the germ infestation of a small Florida community, and announces that he has planted more deadly flasks in the Los Angeles area. Barrett later leads a helicopter chase which results in Hoffman falling to his death. The final deadly flask is recovered.
Everything seemed too pat in this sc-fi thriller. "Just harmless formula stuff, actually," reported Time. "The effects wear off before the film is half over." As the New York Times perceived, "... that old bane of the television drama, the tendency to gab, holds up whatever momentum and excitement The Satan Bug might have had."

SATAN'S SATELLITES   see   ZOMBIES OF THE STRATOSPHERE

SATAN'S TRIANGLE   see   THE DEVIL'S TRIANGLE

SATELLITE OF BLOOD   see   FIRST MAN INTO SPACE

DER SCHWEIGENDE STERN / MILCZACA GWIZADA / FIRST SPACE-
SHIP ON VENUS (East German/Polish, 1959) C-109 min.

Producer, Hugo Grimaldi; director, Kurt Mätzig; based on the
novel The Planet of Death [Astronauts] by Stanislaw Lem; screenplay,
J. Barckhausen, J. Fethke, W. Kohlaase, Mätzig, G. Reisch, G.
Rucker, and A. Steonbock-Fermor; art directors, Anatol Rabzinowciz
and Alfred Hirschmeier; music, Andrzej Markowski; special effects,
Ernst and Vera Kunstmann, Jan Olejniczak, and Helmut Grewald;
camera, Joachim Hasler; editor, Lena Neumann.
Yoko Tani (Sumiko Ogimura); Oldrich Lukes (Harringway);
Ignacy Machowski (Orloff) Julius Ongewe (Talua); Michail Postnikow
(Durand); Kurt Rackelmann (Sikarna); Güther Simon (Brinkman); Tang-
Hua-Ta (Tchen Yu); Lucina Winnicka (Joan Moran).

An East-German/Polish co-production, this feature sported an
international cast headed by Yoko Tani, the star of Twelve to the
Moon (q. v.). When released in the U.S. in 1963, it boasted an English-language-dubbed soundtrack.
A combine of international astronauts on the spaceship "Cosmostrator I" heads for Venus to solve its mysteries. Aboard ship,
they unravel a secret message found in a magnetic spool in the Gobi
desert. Later, after a turbulent trip to Venus, they link together
the clues in the spool with the devasted civilization they find. The
Venusians had destroyed themselves in their ambitious attempt to
launch a devastating attack on Earth. The surviving scientists reboard "Cosmostrator I" and return to Earth to report their findings.
"Colorful but shopworn," decided Variety, while Castle of
Frankenstein judged, "Spectacular but routine." Some of the comedy
relief, especially the chess-playing robot aboard "Cosmostrator I,"
could have been eschewed. The artistic concept of Venus as a destroyed civilization holds some genuine interest.

SEA MONSTER   see   THE GIANT BEHEMOTH

SECONDS (Paramount, 1966) 106 min.

Producer, Edward Lewis; director, John Frankenheimer; based
on the novel by David Ely; screenplay, Lewis John Carlino; music,
Jerry Goldsmith; songs, Johnny Mercer and Harold Arlen; Leo Robin
and Lewis E. Gensler; art director, Ted Haworth; set decorator, John
Austin; makeup, Jack Petty and Mark Reedall; assistant directors,
Francisco Day and Michael Glick; titles, Saul Bass; sound, Joe Ed-
mondson and John H. Wilkinson; camera, James Wong Howe; editors,
Ferris Webster and David Webster.
Rock Hudson (Antiochus "Tony" Wilson); Salome Jens (Nora
Marcus); John Randolph (Arthur Hamilton); Will Geer (The Old Man);
Jeff Corey (Mr. Ruby); Richard Anderson (Dr. Innes); Murray Ham-
ilton (Charlie Evans); Karl Swenson (Dr. Morris); Khigh Dhiegh (Da-
valo); Frances Reid (Emily Hamilton); Wesley Addy (John); John Law-
rence (Texan); Elisabeth Fraser (Plump Blonde); Dody Heath (Sue

Bushman); Robert Brubaker (Mayberry); Dorothy Morris (Mrs. Filter); Frank Campanella (Man in Station); De De Young (Nurse); Tina Scala (Young Girl); William Richard Wintersole (Doctor in Operating Room); Edgar Stehli (Tailor Shop Presser).

Middle-aged, bored, and restless, though financially successful, Arthur Hamilton (John Randolph) receives a phone call from Charlie (Murray Hamilton), a pal whom he thought had died. The telephone conversation leads Arthur Hamilton to a mysterious organization which agrees, for the sum of $32,000, to provide him with a new look, identity, and career. After he "dies" in a hotel fire, Hamilton undergoes the transformation, which alters everything from his facial structure to his handwriting to his mental attitudes. He emerges as painter Tony Wilson, who owns a California house and has an omnipresent manservant named John (Wesley Addy). A meeting with the offbeat Norma (Salome Jens) releases the extrovert in the "new" man and he throws a party. During the course of the free-wheeling evening he imbibes too much and reverts to his old self. The guests are shocked and only then does he learn that they all, including Norma are "seconds." Wilson/Hamilton panics and begs to be restructured back to his old self. Instead, the organization uses him as a corpse for the next customer who purchases a new "life."

It was a remarkable change-of-formula for romantic leading star Rock Hudson to accept the demanding focal role. Although the picture proved to be neither a commercial nor critical success, it remains his favorite film. (A decade later he would star--with embarrassing results--in another sci-fi "dramatic" entry, Embryo, q. v.) Ironically, now that Seconds has taken on a historical perspective, it has become a favorite TV late show item.

If anything diverted proper attention from the unique premise at hand, it was the unusual casting by director John Frankenheimer. As Judith Crist quipped in the New York World Journal Tribune, "Given a second chance at life, would you want to wind up Rock Hudson? This is the question confronting us, alas, midway through Seconds, and that's the pity of it because this new John Frankenheimer film starts out stunningly as a latter-day Faustian suspense story braced with science fiction."

At one point in this ambitious project, Hudson's character is told, "You've got what every middle-aged man in America would like to have--freedom, real freedom." This notion is as strong as the once-equally preposterous dream of reaching outer space and exploring undiscovered planets. The sober moral of the tale is that the revamped individual must be altered emotionally as well as physically and mentally, or the experiment will fail ultimately. The implicit message in this theme is that scientific advances have yet to conquer this stumbling block.

Director Frankenheimer told Gerald Pratley in The Cinema of John Frankenheimer (1969), "Your experience is what makes you the person you are. If you don't want to live with it, it's just too bad.... That's really what the film is about. It's also about all this nonsense in society that we must be forever young, this accent on youth in advertising and thinking which I'm very much opposed to. I wanted to make a matter-of-fact yet horrifying portrait of big business that

will do anything for anybody providing you are willing to pay for it--
an extension of the insurance company. It's a film that's very much
against 'The Dream, ' the belief that all you need to do in life is to
be financially successful. And of course, that's nonsense. "

SECRETS OF F. P. 1 see F. P. 1 ANTWORTET NICHT

SILENT RUNNING (Universal, 1972) C-90 min.

     Producer, Michael Gurskoff; director, Douglas Trumbull;
screenplay, Deric Washburn, Mike Cimino, and Steve Bochco; ·music
composer/conductor, Peter Schickele; songs, Schickele and Diane
Lampert; special designs, Wayne Smith, Richard Alexander, John
Baumbach, Leland McLemore, Bob Sheherd, Gary Richards, and Bill
Shourt; set decorator, Francisco Lombardo; drone units, James Down,
Paul Kraus, and Don Trumbull; titles consultant, Richard Foy; video
consultant, Tom Pishkura; wardrobe, Ann Vidor; makeup, Dick Daw-
son; assistant director, Brad Aronson; sound, John H. Newman,
Charles Knight, and Richard Portman; special lighting effects, Harry
Sunby; special camera effects, Douglas Trumbull, John Dykstra, and
Richard Yuricich; camera, Charles F. Wheeler; editor, Aaron Stell.
     Bruce Dern (Freeman Lowell); Cliff Potts (Wolf); Ron Rifkin
(Barker); Jesse Vint (Keenan); Mark Persons, Cheryl Sparks, Steven
Brown, and Larry Whisenhunt (Drones).

     Douglas Trumbull, one of the prime special-effects men on
2001: A Space Odyssey (q. v.), was the guiding force in this underrated venture. "... [It] is the most interesting science-fiction melodrama since Planet of the Apes [q. v.] and a new classic of the
genre.... the philosophic-mythic-religious dimensions of 2001 were
insupportably trite. I much prefer the scaled-down secular, humane
perspective expressed in Silent Running, but I'm afraid Trumbull's
avoidance of the grandiose may be used against him" (Washington
Post).
     Already in the early twenty-first century, nuclear pollution has
ruined all vegetation on earth. Botantist Freeman Lowell (Bruce
Dern) and three other astronauts supervise the remaining specimens
(of trees, plants, animals) in large dome protectors aboard the "Valley Forge, " a space freighter. Lowell, an eight-year veteran of his
space farm, hopes someday the Earth's atmosphere will again per-
mit foliation. When Lowell learns that the government has decided
to terminate the project and blow up the space forest, he kills his
three co-workers and heads toward the outer ring of Saturn, towing
one of the prize forests. Lowell survives the turbulent trip, aided
in functioning the machinery by three drones (small robots). Eventually Lowell realizes that his rebellion will be discovered: he
creates sufficient artificial sunlight to keep the forest alive, and with
one of the drones in charge, detaches the tow and sends it into a
sphere of darkness. Then to protect his actions from discovery,
Lowell blows up the "Valley Forge. "
     Some critics, instead of studying the film's import, took

Bruce Dern and director Douglas Trumbull on the set of Silent Running (1972).

occasion to throw potshots at Bruce Dern, long typecast as a celluloid psychotic. Newsday penned, "Dern's character is made to seem even more hysterical and immature than the schizophrenic computer Hal in 2001...." The inevitable comparisons to 2001 abounded and few cared to judge the production on its merits. "Trumbull probably had some noble intentions," insisted the Village Voice, "but I couldn't help feeling that he conceived his space odyssey primarily to show off some neat special effects, and that the story--developed secondarily and rather haphazardly--is therefore not especially effective. Since there is a fundamental fuzziness in his conception, the entire film seems more illogical than ecological."

Regardless of the critical slants, Silent Running is a very haunting screen study, a frightening forecast of what could occur. It is science fiction cinema in the grandest tradition.

THE SILENT STAR   see   DER SCHWEIGENDE STERN

SIREN OF ATLANTIS (United Artists, 1949) 75 min.

Producer, Seymour Nebenzal; associate producer, Roman I.

Pines; director, Gregg Tallas; based on the novel L'Atlantide by
Pierre Benoit; screenplay, Roland Leigh and Robert Lax; additional
dialogue, Thomas Job; music, Michel Michelet; music supervisor,
David Chudnow; music director, Heinz Roemheld; assistant director,
Milton Carter; makeup, Lee Greenway; choreography, Lester Horton;
production designer, Lionel Banks; set decorator, George Sawley;
costumes, Jean Schlumberger; sound, Corson Jowett; special effects,
Rocky Cline; camera, Karl Struss; editor, Tallas.
   Maria Montez (Antinea); Jean-Pierre Aumont (Andre St. Avit);
Dennis O'Keefe (Jean Morhange); Henry Daniell (Blades); Morris Car-
novsky (Le Mesge); Alexis Minotis (Cortot); Milada Mladova (Tanit
Zerga); Allan Nixon (Lindstrom); Russ Conklin (Eggali); Herman Bo-
den (Cegheir); Margaret Martin (Hand Maiden); Pierre Watkin (Col-
onel); Charles Wagenheim (Doctor); Jim Nolan (Major); Joseph Granby
(Expert).
   A. k. a. Atlantis/Queen of Atlantis.

   Futuristic societies need not always be in the reaches of outer
space. The legendary subterranean continent of Atlantis has fascinated the public for centuries. In the late Forties, producer Seymour
Nebenzal decided to remake his earlier version of the Pierre Benoit
novel, L'Atlantide (q. v.). The new edition was shot in Hollywood.
Almost from the beginning the project was saddled with production
problems: director Arthur Ripley quit and the sets for the sci-fi/
fantasy feature proved monstrously expensive.
   The storyline followed the other screen versions: two Foreign
Legionnaires (Dennis O'Keefe and Jean-Pierre Aumont) accidentally
stumble upon the lost world of Atlantis in the middle of the Sahara
Desert. They find this fabled underground kingdom dominated by a
ruthless but beautiful queen, Antinea (Maria Montez), who eventually
causes their destruction as well as that of her kingdom.
   Much more so than in the fantasy Lost Horizon (1937 and 1973
versions), the secret of Atlantis' advanced culture is the work of
science combined, to a lesser degree, with religious precepts. Unfortunately, in this United Artists release the focus is almost entirely on the She-like glamour of the vicious distaff ruler.
   After Siren of Atlantis was completed, the studio executives
realized it was overly long and just too dull. Director John Brahm
was hired to re-shoot some scenes which it was hoped would add life
to the project. Later, in disgust, he demanded that his name be re-
moved from the venture. Then editor Gregg Tallas (who was given
final directorial credit) was instructed to interpolate scenes from the
1932 G. W. Pabst (three-language) version, which had some engaging
desert sequences shot on location in the Sahara. Finally, the patchwork feature was issued a full two years after production began. It
was a box-office disaster. The New York Herald-Tribune labeled it
"the worst picture and the worst acting" of the year.

SLAUGHTERHOUSE--FIVE (Universal, 1972) C-104 min.

   Executive producer, Jennings Lang; producer, Paul Monash;
director, George Roy Hill; based on the novel Slaughterhouse-Five

or the Children's Crusade by Kurt Vonnegut, Jr.; screenplay, Stephen
Geller; music arranger/scorer/performer, Glenn Gould; production
designer, Henry Bumstead; art directors, Alexander Golitzen and
George Webb; set decorator, John McCarthy; makeup, Mark Reedall
and John Chambers; assistant director, Ray Gosnell; sound, Milan
Novotny, James Alexander, and Richard Vorisek; title and optical
effects, Universal Title; special camera consultant, Enzo Martinelli;
camera, Miroslav Ondricek; editor, Dede Allen.
    Michael Sachs (Billy Pilgrim); Ron Leibman (Paul Lazzaro);
Eugene Roche (Edgar Derby); Sharon Gans (Valencia); Valerie Perrine
(Montana Wildhack); Robert Blossom (Wild Bob Cody); Sorrell Brooke
(Lionel Merble); Kevin Conway (Weary); Gary Waynesmith (Stanley);
John Dehner (Rumford); Stan Gottlieb (Hobo); Perry King (Robert Pil-
grim); Nick Belle (Young German Guard); Henry Bumstead (Eliot
Rosewater); Lucille Benson (Billy's Mother); Holly Near (Barbara);
Tom Wood (The Englishman).

    Middle-aged optometrist Billy Pilgrim (Michael Sachs) resides
in Ilium, New York. He alerts the local newspaper that he has become "unstuck in time" and relates how his existence shifts randomly
between the past, present, and future. He recalls his terrifying experiences during World War II, especially at the bombing of Dresden,
his later mental breakdown, his marriage to plump Valencia (Sharon
Gans), and the birth/growth of his two children. There are also
jumps forward in his vision in which he is situated on the futuristic
world of Tralfamadore where he becomes involved with Hollwood sex-
ploitation starlet Montana Wildhack (Valerie Perrine). In the see-
sawing chronicle Billy, who has survived the Dresden bombings and
a plane crash, is later murdered by his former Army buddy Paul
Lazzaro (Ron Leibman).
    It is "a wild, noisy, sometimes very funny film that eventually
becomes as unstuck in its own exuberance as its hero" (New York
Times). The theme of the film is that mankind must accept the bad
things of life but try to focus on the good moments. This philosophy,
like so much of author Kurt Vonnegut, Jr.'s literary visions, has
been very fashionable with college audiences. Dressed up in the
guise of fantasy, science fiction, and visual intellectualization, it has
achieved a minor cult following over the years. As the Los Angeles
Times noted when the picture was issued, "... [it] is on its own
terms so marvelous, original, eccentric and satisfying a commentary
on our life and bedeviled times...."

SLEEPER (United Artists, 1973) C-88 min.

    Executive producer, Charles H. Joffe; producer, Jack Gross-
berg; associate producers, Marshall Brickman and Ralph Rosenblum;
director, Woody Allen; screenplay, Allen and Brickman; assistant director, Fred T. Gallo; production designer, Dale Hennesy; art director, Dianne Wager; set co-ordinator, Gary O. Martin; set decorator,
Gary Moreno; music, Allen; music supervisor, Felix Giglio; costumes,
Joel Schumacher; titles, Norman Gorbaty; sound, Jack Solomon; sound
effects, Jess Soraci and Norman Kasow; background projection, Bill

Hansard; special effects, A. D. Flowers; location special effects,
Gerald Endler; camera, David M. Walsh; editors, O. Nicholas Brown
and Trudy Ship.

Woody Allen (Miles Monroe); Diane Keaton (Luna Schlosser);
John Beck (Erno Windt); Mary Gregory (Dr. Melik); Don Keefer (Dr.
Tryon); Don McLiam (Dr. Agon); Bartlett Robinson (Dr. Orva); Chris
Forbes (Rainer Krebs); Marya Small (Dr. Nero); Peter Hobbs (Dr.
Dean); Susan Miller (Ellen Pogrebin); Lou Picetti (M.C.); Brian Avery
(Herald Cohen); Spencer Milligan (Jeb); Spencer Ross (Sears Wiggles);
and Jessica Rains.

Iconoclastic film star/filmmaker Woody Allen turned his comedic genius to a satirical look into the future with a storyline that
owes a nod of gratitude to H. G. Wells' When the Sleeper Awakes
(a vehicle once planned for Vincent Price in the mid-Sixties by
American International).

Health food store owner/jass musician Miles Monroe (Allen)
of Greenwich Village undergoes an ulcer operation. He awakes to
discover that he had been deep frozen due to a surgical complication,
and it is now 200 years into the future. The surgeons in this new
life want Miles to join in the crusade to overthrow the Leader. Instead he escapes (disguised as a domestic robot) and is delivered to
poetess Luna Schlosser (Diane Keaton), a wealthy dabbler. Later
Miles plots his escape and forces Luna to join him in fleeing from
the police. The two are caught; Miles is brainwashed, but Luna
manages to join the revolutionaries. Some time later, she is sent
to free Miles so that he can help ferret out the details of the Leader's Aires project. Using the Leader's nose (the only portion of his
body still alive) as a hostage, Miles and Luna escape the Establish-
ment headquarters.

To fully appreciate any Woody Allen screen exercise one must
be steeped in the monologue and one-line world of stand-up comedians,
Jewish humor, and the intellectual marriage of a high-order inferi-
ority complex and a deep reverence for anti-Establishment. Like
Alphaville (q.v.), Sleeper uses the format of science fiction to pro-
mulgate its own points: here satirical comedy is aimed at the middle class intellectual ethics of the Seventies.

In the course of the 88-minute color feature, there are jibes
at Norman Mailer ("he donated his ego to science"), MacDonald's
fast food eateries, death being preferable to sex on many counts,
e.g., at least one does not feel nauseous after the former), and most
of all at the absurd hero myths of contemporary mankind. Miles is
fully aware he is a twentieth-century schlepp and finds it absurd that
"I wake up two hundred years later and I'm Flash Gordon." One
British reviewing source took occasion to point out the tangible, in-
animate comedy of the sets ("the futuristic design overall rigged to
be a sort of toytown 2001").

Sleeper is not the most coherent of Woody Allen's madcap,
silent comedian-oriented features, but it is extremely delightful, and
perhaps needs more than one viewing to derive its full essence.

Scene from The Slime People (1963).

THE SLIME PEOPLE (Hansen Enterprises, 1963) 60 min.

    Producer, Joseph F. Robertson; director, Robert Hutton; screenplay, Vance Skarstedt; music, Lou Foman; special effects, Charles Duncan; camera, William Troiano; editor, Don Henderson and Lew Guinn.
    With: Robert Hutton, Les Tremayne, Robert Burton, Judee Morton, William Boyce, John Close, and Susan Hart.

    One-time Forties' heartthrob Robert Hutton directed and played the lead role in this sci-fi quickie about the invasion of Los Angeles by some ugly creatures unleashed from the bowels of the Earth. The title creatures in this cheapie look as if they had gotten that way from a ride on a garbage truck.
    A horde of blob-like scaly creatures from beneath the Earth's surface are disturbed by an atomic explosion. They surface through the sewer system (what else?) to take over Los Angeles. Only able to survive in extreme heat, the monsters set up a strong wall of fog around the city which retains the heat close to the ground. Hero Hutton and heroine Susan Hart battle these vicious creatures (the actors were so weighed down by their bulky costumes they could hardly attack the humans). Eventually Hutton devises a mean of forcing cold

air into the city。 The monsters are vanquished.

SOYLENT GREEN (MGM, 1973) C-97 min.

Producers, Walter Seltzer and Russell Thacher; director,
Richard Fleischer; based on the novel Make Room! Make Room! by
Harry Harrison; screenplay, Stanley R. Greenberg; art director, Ed-
ward C. Carfagno; set decorator, Robert Benton; music, Fred Mylow;
symphony music director, Gerald Fried; costumes, Pat Barto; tech-
nical consultant, Frank A. Bowerman; action scene co-ordinator, Joe
Canutt; sound, Charles M. Wilborn and Harry W. Tetrick; special ef-
fects, Robert R. Hoag and Matthew Yuricich; camera, Richard H。
Kline; editor, Samuel E. Beetley.
Charlton Heston (Detective Thorn); Leigh Taylor-Young (Shirl);
Edward G. Robinson (Sol Roth); Chuck Connors (Tab Fielding); Joseph
Cotten (William Simonson); Brock Peters (Hatcher); Paula Kelly (Mar-
tha); Stephen Young (Gilbert); Mike Henry (Kulozik); Lincoln Kilpatrick
(Priest); Roy Jenson (Donovan); Leonard Stone (Charles); Whit Bissell
(Governor Santini); Celia Lovsky (Exchange Leader); Dick Van Patten
(Usher); Morgan Farley, John Barclay, Belle Mitchell, and Cyril De-
levanti (Books); Forrest Wood and Faith Quabius (Attendants); Jane
Dulo (Mrs. Santini); John Dennis (Wagner); Carlos Romero (New Ten-
ant).

Charlton Heston, as in Planet of the Apes (q.v.) and The

Leigh Taylor-Young and Charlton Heston in Soylent Green (1973).

Omega Man (q. v.), is again the heroic Everyman in this science fiction entry. The artistic attempt to blend the genres of sci-fi, ecology, and mystery into one coherent package failed. But the results
are still very striking, especially in the performance of Edward G.
Robinson (who died before the film was released). The film grossed
over $3.5 million in distributors' domestic rentals.

In the year 2022, New York City has a population of over forty
million, most of whom are dependent on the synthetic foods produced
by the Soylent Company. The narrative focuses on Detective Thorn
(Heston) who shares his unique apartment with elderly Sol Roth (Robinson), a surviving scholar who has access to the city's few remaining books and helps Thorn with his cases. In tracing the killing of
a V.I.P., William Simonson (Joseph Cotten), the detective pieces together the clues of a massive corporate mystery. Meanwhile he conducts a romance with Shirl (Leigh Taylor-Young), Simonson's former
mistress.

Although Thorn is finally ordered to drop his investigation, he
refuses. Later Sol uncovers the secret which led Simonson to per-
mit his own assassination. Having left a message for Thorn, Roth
has himself admitted to a clinic where death is induced under uplift-
ing circumstances. Thorn arrives at the clinic and follows the truck-
loads of corpses to a Soylent plant where he discovers the bodies are
transformed into the company's newest product, Soylent Green. Government agents subsequently wound Thorn, but the injured man shouts
out his secret for any and all to hear.

More serious-minded viewers scoffed at the unelaborate efforts
to transform the MGM soundstage and backlot sets into futuristic sur-
roundings and the abundance of clichés that peppered the storyline.
Even the mass public--who liked the film's premise--were annoyed
by the glib emptiness of the production. However, beneath it all, the
shock ecology message was there, and in the performance of a few
(Robinson, Celia Lovsky) the theme surfaced.

SON OF BLOB   see   THE BLOB

SON OF FLUBBER   see   THE ABSENT-MINDED PROFESSOR

THE SPACE CHILDREN (Paramount, 1958) 69 min.

    Producer, William Alland; director, Jack Arnold; story, Tom
Filer; screenplay, Bernard C. Schoenfeld; art directors, Hal Pereira
and Roland Anderson; set decorators, Sam Comer and Frank McKelvy;
assistant director, Richard Caffey; makeup, Wally Westmore; music,
Van Cleave; "The Thing" created by Ivyl Burks; sound, Phillip Wisdom and Charles Grenzbach; special camera effects, John P. Fulton;
process camera, Farciot Edouart; camera, Ernest Laszlo; editor,
Terry Morse.
    Adam Williams (Dave Brewster); Peggy Webber (Anne Brew-
ster); Michel Ray (Bud Brewster); John Crawford (Ken Brewster);
Jackie Coogan (Hank Johnson); Sandy Descher (Eadie Johnson); Richard

Shannon (Lieutenant Colonel Manley); John Washrook (Tim Gable);
Russell Johnson (Joe Gamble); Raymond Bailey (Dr. Wahrman).

This picture was aimed at a children's audience, but the film
was so intellectually complex and involved in anti-war sentiment that
it was more suitable for adults. For the latter it may also have provided a good lesson, for the film dwelt on the alienation between
adults and children.
A group of children dwell with their parents in a hilltop trailer camp on the West Coast. The parents are part of a team working
on the launching of a new missile equipped with a nuclear warhead.
A few of the children wander along the beach and are drawn to a
nearby cave. There they encounter a glowing gelatinous mass sent
from outer space. "The Thing" wants to prevent the use of the hydrogen rocket and works with the children to sabotage the missile
project. The youths are given a peculiar power that renders their
adult families helpless. At one point the super-intelligent brain kills
a father who is savagely beating his child. Eventually the sabotage
plan is completed and the brain returns to outer space. Through
the children he sends a message of love, not war, to the world.
Director Arnold, long a specialist in the sci-fi field, considers
this production one of his favorite projects.

Sandy Descher and Michel Ray (center) in The Space Children (1958).

SPACE INVASION FROM LAPLAND see INVASION OF THE ANIMAL PEOPLE

SPACE SOLDIERS see FLASH GORDON

SPACE SOLDIERS CONQUER THE UNIVERSE see FLASH GORDON CONQUERS THE UNIVERSE

SPACE SOLDIERS' TRIP TO MARS see FLASH GORDON'S TRIP TO MARS

SPACE STATION X see MUTINY IN OUTER SPACE

SPACE STATION X-14 see MUTINY IN OUTER SPACE

SPACESHIP TO THE UNKNOWN see FLASH GORDON

SPACESHIP VENUS DOES NOT ANSWER see DER SCHWEIGENDE STERN

SPAZIALE K 1 see THE HUMAN DUPLICATORS

SPECIAL AGENT K 1 see THE HUMAN DUPLICATORS

STORM PLANET see PLENETA BURG

STRANGE JOURNEY see FANTASTIC VOYAGE

STRANGE NEW WORLD (ABC-TV, 1975) C-100 min.

　　　　Executive producers, Ronald F. Graham and Walter Green; producer, Robert E. Larson; director, Robert Butler; teleplay, Graham, Alvin Ramrus, and Green; music, Richard Clements and Elliott Kaplan; camera, Michael Margulies; editor, David Newhouse and Melvin Shapiro.
　　　　John Saxon (Captain Anthony Vico); Kathleen Miller (Dr. Allison Crowley); Keene Curtis (Dr. William Scott); James Olson (The Surgeon); Martine Beswick (Tania); Reb Brown (Sprang); Ford Rainey (Sirus); Bill McKinney (Badger); Gerrit Graham (Daniel); Cynthia Wood (Arana).

After a 180-year suspended animation aboard a space lab, three astronauts (John Saxon, Kathleen Miller, and Keene Curtis) return to Earth to discover that society has been strangely altered. They stop in Eterna, where The Surgeon (James Olson) controls the populace, who are actually the result of cloning, and thus capable of endless life. When the astronauts learn that The Surgeon wants to use the visitors' blood to nourish his people, they escape to the forest. There they encounter both a jungle-like tribe who abide by The Code of the United States Fish and Wildlife Service and their poacher adversaries.

It seemed the networks were oversatiating the public with scifiction telefeatures in the mid-Seventies. Their ploy seemed to be that the genre allowed for strange premises, and strange premises sufficed for entertainment values. No way.

STRANGE WORLD OF PLANET X (Eros, 1958) 75 min.

Producer, George Maynard; director, Gilbert Gunn; based on the novel by Rene Ray; screenplay, Paul Ryder; music, Robert Sharples; camera, Joe Amber; editor, Francis Brieber.

Forrest Tucker (Gil Graham); Gaby Andre (Michele Dupont); Martin Benson (Smith); Wyndham Goldie (Brigadier Cartwright); Alec Mango (Dr. Laird); Hugh Latimer (Jimmy Murray); Geoffrey Chater (Gerald Wilson); Patricia Sinclair (Helen Forsyth); Catherine Lancaster (Gillian Betts); Richard Warner (Inspector Burns); Hilda Fennemore (Mrs. Hale); Susan Redway (Jane Hale); Neil Wilson (P. C. Tidy).

A. k. a.   The Crawling Terror.

Far more than American moviemakers, the British film industry has often adapted TV works into cinema properties. In the scifi field, the trilogy of Quatermass films (The Creeping Unknown, Enemy from Space, Twenty Million Miles to Earth, all q. v.) is an example. However, not all these adaptations have been so sterling. One of the less fortunate was Strange World of Planet X, which was issued in the U.S. as Cosmic Monsters.

Alec Mango is the scientist whose experiments with metal magnetics causes a break in the Earth's magnetic field. While the world's population is going topsy-turvy and insects are mutating to enormous size, a visitor called Smith arrives on the scene, claiming he has been ordered from another planet to put an end to the doctor's mad ploys. Smith commands a waiting space ship to destroy the scientist and his lab. With his mission accomplished, Smith departs for his own planet.

To further hamper audience response, the picture was badly edited for its U.S. playdates, making the last half-hour of the film seem without logic.

Variety judged, "A singularly uninspired pot-boiler.... The dialog veers between desperately dull technical jargon and coy flippancy.... Camera work is not sufficiently distinguished to hide the phoniness of the studio-made insects, designed to provide a thrill which is more revolting than hair-raising. "

Gaby Andre in Strange World of Planet X (1958).

Emmett Vogan, Herbert Rawlinson and Kirk Alyn as Superman (1948).

SUPERMAN (Columbia, 1948) fifteen chapters

　　　　Producer, Sam Katzman; directors, Spencer Gordon Bennet and
Thomas Carr; based on the "Superman" adventure feature appearing in
Superman and Action comics, adapted from the "Superman" radio
program by George H. Plympton and Joseph F. Poland; screenplay,
Arthur Hoerl, Lewis Clay, and Royal Cole; assistant director, R. M.
Andrews; second unit director, Thomas Carr; music, Mischa Baka-
leinikoff; camera, Ira H. Morgan; editor, Earl Turner.
　　　　Kirk Alyn (Clark Kent [Superman]); Noel Neill (Lois Lane);
Tommy Bond (Jimmy Olsen); Carol Forman ("Spider Lady"); George
Meeker (Driller); Jack Ingram (Anton); Pierre Watkin (Perry White);
Terry Frost (Brock); Charles King (Conrad); Charles Quigley (Dr.
Hackett); Herbert Rawlinson (Dr. Graham); Forrest Taylor (Leeds);
Stephen Carr (Morgan); Rusty Westcoatt (Elton).
　　　　Chapters: 1) Superman Comes to Earth; 2) Depths of the
Earth; 3) The Reducer Ray; 4) Man of Steel; 5) A Job for Superman;
6) Superman in Danger; 7) Into the Electric Furnace; 8) Superman to
the Rescue; 9) Irresistible Force; 10) Between Two Fires; 11) Super-
man's Dilemma; 12) Blast in the Depths; 13) Hurled to Destruction;
14) Superman at Bay; 15) The Payoff.

　　　　Low-budget producer Sam Katzman acquired the film rights
for the comic strip "Superman" in the mid-Forties. Attempts to sell

the packaged idea to either Universal or Republic failed. Finally
Columbia agreed to make the cliffhanger and Kirk Alyn was hired to
portray the mighty man of steel. (It was a role that forever typecast the versatile performer. When he wrote and published his auto-
biography in 1971 he entitled it A Job for Superman.)
      The fifteen-chapter entry tells of a scientist on the distant
planet Krypton who brings his infant son to Earth as their homeland
explodes. A farmer finds the infant and raises him as his son.
When he grows up he tells him of his origin and that his superhuman
powers must be used only for the good of humanity. Disguised as
Clark Kent (Alyn) he wins a job as a reporter, and later encounters
the evil Spider Lady (Carol Forman), who wants to gain possession of
the reducer ray. In the meantime, a portion of Kryptonite, from the
long-deceased planet, reaches Earth. It is potent enough to render
the superman helpless; which it does periodically throughout the serial
when he falls into the hands of his adversaries. Eventually Superman
locates a neutralizer to Kryptonite, thwarts the Spider Lady's plans,
and restores law and order.
      In comparison to most late Forties' serial, Superman was well
made. It proved to be the highest-grossing serial of all time. It also introduced Noel Neill as Lois Lane, a role she would play in the
1950 chapterplay follow-up, Atom Man vs. Superman (q. v.) as well
as in the TV series with George Reeves.* An 88-minute feature
version of the Superman serial was issued after the initial run of the
cliffhanger.

SUPERMAN AND THE JUNGLE DEVIL   see   SUPERMAN

SUPERMAN AND SCOTLAND YARD   see   SUPERMAN

SUPERMAN AND THE MOLE MEN   see   SUPERMAN

SUPERMAN FLIES AGAIN   see   SUPERMAN

SUPERMAN IN EXILE   see   SUPERMAN

* In 1951 Reeves assumed the role of Clark Kent/Superman in the
low-budget Lippert entry, Superman and the Mole Men. The quickie
feature was used as a pilot for the subsequent TV series, "Adventures of Superman" and is now syndicated as Unknown People, episodes 25 and 26 of that enduring TV program.   Later, to features,
Superman in Peril and Superman Flies Again, would be pasted together from episodes of the teleseries. In 1954 Twentieth Century-
Fox would issue paste-up features from the teleseries. These theatrical releases were: Superman in Exile, Superman and Scotland
Yard, and Superman and the Jungle Devil. In 1973, Superman, also
made up of segments of the vintage teleseries, was issued to TV
only.

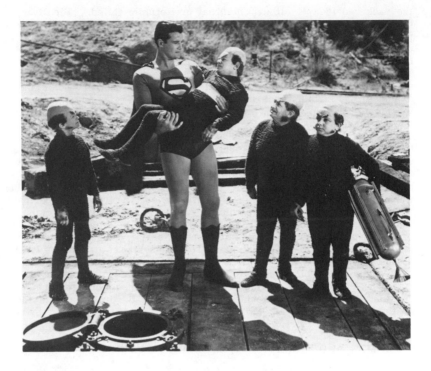

George Reeves in Superman and the Mole Men (1951).

SUPERMAN IN PERIL   see   SUPERMAN

TARANTULA (Universal, 1955) 80 min

    Producer, William Alland; director, Jack Arnold; based on the episode No Food for Thought by Robert M. Fresco from the teleseries "Science Fiction Theatre"; screenplay, Fresco and Martin Berkeley; makeup, Bud Westmore; art directors, Alexander Golitzen and Alfred Sweeney; music, Henry Mancini; special camera effects, Clifford Stine; camera, George Robinson; editor, William M. Morgan.
    With: John Agar, Mara Corday, Leo G. Carroll, Nestor Paiva, Ross Elliott, Ed Rand, Eddie Parker.

    Following the box-office success of It Came from Outer Space, Creature from the Black Lagoon, and Revenge of the Creature (all q.v.), Universal asked director Jack Arnold to prepare another vehicle in the same mold. He selected an episode from TV's "Science Fiction Theatre" as the basis for Tarantula. Once again Arnold

Advertisement for Tarantula (1955).

employed the desert as the background for this terror tale of natural experiments gone wrong. Perhaps the most gripping sequences are the ones near the finale when the giant title insect is on the prowl. Arnold later reported that some sixty photographable spiders were brought to the studio for the scenes and that jets of air were used to induce the insects to move in the proper direction. (No paper spiders or tacky animation for this perfectionist craftsman!)

In a small desert town a biochemist (Leo G. Carroll) is experimenting with nutrients in order to make crops grow larger and thus feed the world's hungry. He then concocts a serum which works on glandular activity, causing several laboratory animals to grow far larger than ordinary. When an assistant uses the serum on himself, it leads to cell deterioration and mutation; and later to insanity. The crazed man then forces serum into the doctor, turning him into a monster. Meanwhile a tarantula treated with the medication escapes from the lab. The local sheriff (Nestor Paiva) and the biochemist's friends (John Agar and Mara Corday) join in the hunt for the one-hundred-foot insect. The Air Force arrives and burns the creature to death with napalm.

In Science Fiction in the Cinema (1970), John Baxter says, "The result is one of his [Arnold's] most accomplished films." Of particular interest is that the arid setting for the picture is actually the cradle of civilization. At one point Agar tells Corday that everything that walked or crawled originated here and that one can still find sea shells on the desert floor.

Robert Vaughn in Teenage Caveman (1958).

TEENAGE CAVEMAN (American International, 1958) 65 min.

    Producer/director, Roger Corman; screenplay, R. Wright
Campbell; assistant director, Maurice Vaccarino; wardrobe, Marjorie
Corso; music, Albert Glasser; camera, Floyd Crosby; editor, Irene
Morra.
    Robert Vaughn (The Boy); Leslie Bradley (The Symbol Maker);
Darrah Marshall (The Maiden); Frank De Kova (The Villain); Joseph
Hamilton, Marshall Bradford, June Jocelyn, Jonathan Haze, Robert
Shayne, Beach Dickerson, and Charles P. Thompson (Tribe Members).

    The quality of producer/director Roger Corman's early fea-
tures varied greatly. This craftsman turned out dozens of B entries,
mostly horror and sci-fi, in the mid-to-late Fifties. One of the most
beguiling plotwise and poorest in production values was Teenage Caveman. It was a cheapie throughout, obviously made for the youth
market at drive-in theatres. The film's novelty is in its star, Robert Vaughn, who went on to TV fame as "The Man from U.N.C.L.E."
    It is forbidden to leave the rocky, barren land and travel to
lusher country beyond the great river. This is the law among the
primitive tribe. But The Boy (Vaughn) is curious to find out what

lies beyond the tribal domain. After gaining adulthood and marrying
the maiden (Darrah Marshall) he crosses the river. The tribe, with
murderous punishment on their minds, pursues him. Thereafter they
learn that the monster they so feared beyond the river is just another
human. It develops that these cavemen are actually the only survivors of atomic annihilation. Thus Teenage Caveman is a film of the
future not of the past.

   Variety generously reported, "Good exploitation item.... Also, somewhat surprisingly, a plea for international cooperation in
terms of the dangers of atomic radiation."

   In England it was released as Prehistoric World Out of the
Darkness.

THE TENTH VICTIM (LA DECIMA VITTIMA) (Embassy, 1965) C-92
min.

   Executive producer, Joseph E. Levine; producer, Carlo Ponti;
director, Elio Petri; based on the short story "The Seventh Victim"
by Robert Sheckley; screenplay, Tonino Guerra, Giorgio Salvioni, Ennio Flaiano, and Petri; art director, Giulio Coltellacci; assistant director, Berto Pelosso; music, Piero Piccioni; costumes, Giulio Coltellacci; sound, Ennio Sensi; camera, Gianni Di Venanzo; editor, Rug-
gero Mastroianni.

   Marcello Mastroianni (Marcello Polletti); Ursula Andress (Caroline Meredith); Elsa Martinelli (Olga); Massimo Serato (Lawyer);
Salvo Randone (The Professor); Luce Bonifassy (Lidia); Mickey Knox
(Chet); Richard Armstrong (Cole); Walter Williams (Martin); Evi Ri-
gano (Victim); Milo Quesada (Rudi); Anita Sanders (Relaxatorium Girl);

Ursula Andress and Marcello Mastroianni in The Tenth Victim (1965).

George Wang (Chinese Assailant).

In the twenty-first century, war is outlawed, but killing has been legalized and some persons are licensed to kill. After ten such murders the lucky individual wins international fame and a substantial fortune in money. The giant computer in Geneva selects at random Marcello Polletti (Marcello Mastroianni), who has just made his sixth kill, as the tenth victim of Caroline Meredith (Ursula Andress). Polletti is told he is again a target, but Caroline does not want this to be an ordinary kill. She has made a deal with a television company to make the keynote murder part of a video commercial. Thereafter follows a display of cunning as each tries to outwit and kill the other. At one point she plans to shoot the man in front of the Temple of Venus before the TV camera, but he is tipped off and the game of cat-and-mouse continues until one emerges the victor.

Variety judged this well-executed picture as a "wacky but frequently chilling glimpse at la dolce vita in the next century.... Crazy, but interesting." The British Monthly Film Bulletin confirmed, "On the whole the world of the Big Hunt is convincingly futuristic, maintaining a cunning balance between synthetic plastic sets ... and safely unchanged ancient monuments.... The cubist furniture appears impractically uncomfortable, but as the characters themselves are in a permanent state of uneasiness this is not without relevance; and there are pleasing, if predictable, touches like the library of such 'classics' as a first edition Flash Gordon and the 'antique' pin-table that is unobtrusively part of one room's decor."

From an entertainment standpoint, the charms of its stars compensated for some lapses: the non-heroic hero, the poor dubbing/editing (in the English-language version), and the overfamiliarity of the plotline premise.

In France this international co-production was issued as La Dixième Victime.

TERROR EN EL ESPACIO   see   TERRORE NELLO SPAZIO

TERROR FROM THE YEAR 5000 (American International, 1958) 74 min.

Executive producers, James H. Nicholson and Samuel Z. Arkoff; producer/director/screenplay, Robert J. Gurney, Jr.; art director, Beatrice Gurney; scenic design, William Hoffman; assistant director, Jack Diamond; sound, Robert Hathaway; camera, Arthur Florman; editor, Dede Allen.
Ward Costello (Robert Hedges); Joyce Holden (Claire Erling); John Stratton (Victor); Frederick Downs (Professor Howard Erling); Fred Herrick (Angelo); Beatrice Furdeaux (Miss Blake); Jack Diamond and Fred Taylor (Lab Technicians); Salome Jens (5,000 A.D. Woman).

Professor Howard Erling (Frederick Downs) has devised a time machine which can materialize people from future life spans.

A creature from Terror from the Year 5000 (1958).

Meanwhile his assistant Victor (John Stratton) is experimenting secretly
and creating highly radioactive subjects. When archaeologist Robert
Hedges (Ward Costello) arrives on the scene it is discovered that
Victor's experiments are bringing back to the present radioactive beings and things from a time when atomic destruction has contaminated
the world. In particular, Victor has materialized a disfigured woman (Salome Jens) from the year 5000. She seeks to draw Victor
into the future with her, to help start an uncontaminated colony. But
Professor Erling and Hedges manage to destroy the creature and to
save Erling's daughter Claire (Joyce Holden), who has been endan-
gered. Victor dies when the time vault is shortcircuited.
        This is a nicely made-little thriller but upon original release
it had the misfortune to share a double-bill with a horror clinker
called The Screaming Skull. Today the film has a minor cult following because of the presence of Salome Jens in her screen debut.
That fine actress was much better served by the genre in Seconds
(q. v.).
        In England the film was issued as Cage of Doom.

TERROR FROM THE SUN   see   HIDEOUS SUN DEMON

TERROR IN THE MIDNIGHT SUN   see   INVASION OF THE ANIMAL
PEOPLE

TERROR IS A MAN (Valiant Films, 1959) 89 min.

Producers, Kane Lyn and Eddie Romero; director, Gerry
De Leon; screenplay, Harry Paul Harber; music composer/conductor,
Ariston Auerlino; art director, Vicente Bonus; camera, Emmanuel I.
Rojas.
Francis Lederer (Dr. Girard); Greta Thyssen (Frances Gir-
ard); Richard Derr (Fitzgerald); Oscar Keesee (Walter); Lilia Duran
(Selene); Peyton Keesee (Tiago); Flory Carlos (The Man).

Inspired by H. G. Wells' novella, The Island of Dr. Moreau
(which was the basis of Island of Lost Souls, q.v.), this well-paced,
moody sci-fi thriller was shot entirely in the Philippines. Terror
Is a Man never obtained proper genre prominence, but it has been
in theatrical release almost continuously since it was first issued.
With touches of Frankenstein, the black-and-white feature tells
of a sailor (Richard Derr) who is shipwrecked on a small island off
the coast of Peru. On the isle is scientist Dr. Girard (Francis
Lederer) and his very attractive wife Frances (Greta Thyssen), plus
a drunken lab assistant (Oscar Keesee) and a few villagers. After
a gory murder, the villagers desert the island and the sailor finally
finds out why: the scientist is performing painful operations on a
panther, speeding up the process of evolution and turning it into a
man. The doctor's wife, however longs to leave the domain and begins an affair with the sailor. One night the creature escapes, kills the
assistant, and abducts Frances. The beast is tracked to the edge of
a cliff. There he drops the woman, charges after his creator/tor-
mentor and hurls him over the precipice. The badly-wounded beast
then stumbles down to the beach, where a native boy puts it in a
boat and directs the vessel out to sea. (It is much the same ending
as in the original Frankenstein novel.)
Highlighted by low-key lighting and mostly night shots, the
feature evokes both terror and sensuality. Continental Francis Lederer provided an inspired performance as the impotent Dr. Girard, and
Greta Thyssen was just right as the object of both the sailor's and the
creature's (Flory Carlos) lust. For most of the film's running time,
the creature was kept bandaged like a mummy, only his soulless eyes
and long panther claws being viewed.
The film would be re-issued in the mid-Sixties as Blood Creature.

THE TERROR STRIKES   see   WAR OF THE COLOSSAL BEAST

TERRORE NELLO SPAZIO / TERROR EN EL ESPACIO (Italian In-
ternational/Castilla Cinematografica, 1965) C-86 min.

Producer, Fulvio Lucisano; associate producer, Salvatore Bil-
litteri; director, Mario Bava; based on the story "One Night of 21
Hours" by Renato Pestriniero; screenplay, Callisto Cosulich, Antonio
Roman, Alberto Bevilacqua, Bava, and Rafael J. Salvia; assistant
director, Serena Canevari; art director, Giorgio Giovannini; music,

Barry Sullivan and Norma Bengell (at right) in Terrore Nello Spazio
(1965).

Gino Marinuzzi; costumes, Gabriele Mayer; sound, Mario Ronchetti;
camera, Antonio Rinaldi; editor, Antonio Gimeno.
     English-language version: Ib Melchior and Louis M. Heyward.
     Barry Sullivan (Captain Mark Markary); Norma Bengell (Sanya);
Angel Aranda (Wess); Evi Morandi (Tiona); Fernando Villena (Karan);
Franco Andrei (Garr); Massimo Righi (Nordeg); Alberto Cevenini (To-
by); Stelio Candelli (Mud); Mario Morales (Eldon); Ivan Rassimov
(Derry); Rico Boido (Key).
     A.k.a. Planet of Blood / Haunted Planet / Haunted World /
Outlawed Planet / Planet of the Damned.

     The space crafts "Argos" and "Galliot" are hovering near Aura,
a fog-shrouded world. The "Galliot" disappears but the "Argos" is
mysteriously drawn to the planet and lands. Once there, Captain
Mark Markary (Barry Sullivan) and his crew find the "Galliot" with
its crew gruesomely killed. Later Markary learns that the inhabitants
of Aura are disembodied beings, who hope to start a fresh race in a
new world by taking over the bodies of trapped astronauts and using
their space ships. Markary and two of his crew, Sanya (Norma Bengell) and Wess (Angel Aranda), eventually escape. Once aboard the
"Argos" Wess realizes his fellow crew members have been possessed,
and he is killed in a vain attempt to destroy the ship. Markary and
Sanya then make a sudden landing on an adjacent planet, which is

Earth. If all works well, they hope to have the remainder of their race follow them.

A very visual film, this was directed by ace cinematographer Mario Bava. There is excellent use of color to heighten the effect of the alien world and the mysteries of outer space. Restricted by a tight budget, Bava devised Aura as a planet enveloped in fog to save the expense of constructing a terrain for the orb.

This film has had many titles. In English-language countries it was called Planet of the Vampires (with one minute deleted from the dubbed footage); on U.S. TV it is known as The Demon Planet.

THE TERRORNAUTS (Embassy, 1967) C-75 min.

Producers, Max J. Rosenberg and Milton Subotsky; director, Montgomery Tully; based on the novel The Wailing Asteroid by Murray Leinster; screenplay, John Brunner; music, Elizabeth Lutyens; music conductor, Philip Martell; art director, Bill Constable; costumes, Eileen Welch; assistant director, Tom Wallis; sound, Laurie Clarkson; special effects, Bowie Films; camera, Geoffrey Faithful; editor, Peter Musgrave.

Simon Oates (Dr. Joe Burke); Zena Marshall (Sandy Lund); Charles Hawtrey (Joshua Yellowless); Patricia Hayes (Mrs. Jones); Stanley Meadows (Ben Keller); Max Adrian (Dr. Henry Shore); Frank Barry (Burke as a Child); Richard Carpenter (Danny); Leonard Cracknell (Nick); Robert Jewell (Robot Operator); Frank Forsyth (Uncle); Andre Maranne (Gendarme).

Zena Marshall in The Terrornauts (1967).

Of this British-made feature, Variety reported, "An inexpensive but tight little sci-fi programmer that holds the interest. " A
blend of comedy and action bolsters the proceedings.

Dr. Joe Burke (Simon Oates) is in charge of an English project trying to communicate with beings on other planets. Even though
he eventually makes slight contact with an uncharted planet, Burke's
superior, Dr. Henry Shore (Max Adrian), remains unconvinced and
places strictures on the group. Soon thereafter, the lab is sucked
up into an alien space ship and carted to a strange planet where a
very human robot tests the group's mentality. Later they are transported to yet another planet to witness the goings-on of green-tinted
savages. These humanoids, once civilized humans, plan to attack
Earth and reduce its population to their level. Burke and his associates are able to prevent this and they themselves maneuver to return to Earth.

THEM! (Warner Bros. , 1954) 93 min.

Producer, David Weisbart; director, Gordon Douglas; story,
George Worthing Yates; adaptor, Russell Hughes; screenplay, Ted
Sherdemann; art director, Stanley Fletcher; music, Bronislau Kaper;
special effects, Ralph Ayers; sound special effects, William Mueller
and Francis J. Scheid; camera, Sid Hickox; editor, Thomas Reilly.

James Whitmore (Sergeant Ben Peterson); Edmund Gwenn (Dr.
Harold Medford); Joan Weldon (Dr. Patricia Medford); James Arness
(Robert Graham); Onslow Stevens (Brigadier General O'Brien); Sean
McClory (Major Kibbee); Chris Drake (Ed Blackburn); Sandy Descher
(Little Girl); Mary Ann Hokanson (Mrs. Lodge); Don Shelton (Captain
of Troopers); Fess Parker (Crotty); Olin Howland (Jensen); Dub Tay-
lor, Leonard Nimoy, William Schallert, and Ann Doran (Bits).

The Fifties were jam-packed with giant bugs attacking from
near and far. For the most part these overgrown insect films were
exercises in poor special effects and even shoddier plot-lines. That
the genre could spawn a classic, however, is proven by Them!

A small girl (Sandy Descher) wanders in from the New Mexico
desert in a state of shock, able only to scream the word "them!"
Later a country general store is found nearly destroyed and its owner horribly mutilated. A policeman investigating the incident mysteriously disappears and an army sergeant named Ben Peterson (James
Whitmore) is called in to investigate the peculiar situation. He is
aided by entomologist Dr. Harold Medford (Edmund Gwenn), the
man's scientist daughter (Joan Weldon), and an F.B.I. agent (James
Arness). The latter two fall in love. While investigating catacombs
in the desert, the group discovers a bevy of enormous ants, their
huge size the result of radiation from atomic testing. The army is
alerted and they burn the insects with gas. They subsequently discover that the queen ant and her mate have not been killed, and soon
UFO reports reveal that the ants are proliferating again. Later a
freighter with a load of sugar, is mysteriously attacked at sea and
its crew killed. Thereafter a train carrying sugar is drained of its
contents near Chicago and two large ants are reported in the city

Scene from Them! (1954).

sewer system. Ben Peterson bravely rescues two trapped children,
but is killed by the recently-hatched new ants. The National Guard
then enters the sewer system and burns the ants to death with flame-
throwers.

Even the high brow New York Times was impressed by this
chiller with its eerie music signalling the approach of the giant ants.
The newspaper found "the proceedings tense, absorbing and, surprisingly enough, somewhat convincing. Perhaps it is the film's unadorned
and seemingly factual approach which is its top attribute.... Them!
is taut science-fiction."

Interestingly, when Them! was issued, Twentieth Century magazine denounced the Warner Bros. film as a vicious allegory calling
for the extermination, not of giant ants, but of communists.

THESE ARE THE DAMNED see THE DAMNED

THE THING (RKO, 1951) 86 min.

Producer, Howard Hawks; directors, Christian Nyby; and (uncredited) Hawks; based on the novelette Who Goes There? by Don

A. Stuart; screenplay, Charles Lederer; art directors, Albert D'Agostino and John J. Hughes; music, Dimitri Tiomkin; special effects, Donald Stewart; special camera effects, Linwood Dunn; camera, Russell Harlan; editor, Roland Gross.

Kenneth Tobey (Captain Patrick Hendry); Margaret Sheridan (Nikki Nicholson); Robert Cornthwaite (Carington); Douglas Spencer (Ned Scott); James Young (Lieutenant Eddie Dykes); Dewey Martin (Bob the Crew Chief); Robert Nichols (Lieutenant MacPherson); William Self (Sergeant Barnes); Eduard Franz (Dr. Stern); Sally Creighton (Mrs. Chapman); James Arness (The Thing); Tom Steele (Stunts).

The Thing is one of the all-time greats of the science fiction film category. It is a deliberate, well-paced thriller, that served as the focal point in the rejuvenation of the genre. Along with the previous year's Destination Moon (q. v.) it served to launch the type of speculative cinema still popular today. The film was supervised by producer Howard Hawks and (co-)directed by cutter Christian Nyby. Despite popular opinion, Orson Welles had absolutely nothing to do with the filming.

In the Arctic, a space ship is found embedded in the ice and in it is a being, obviously the pilot (James Arness). The strange object is taken to a nearby Army station by a scientist (Robert Cornthwaite) who hopes to communicate with it. When the creature thaws and comes to life, it escapes, eventually proving menacing to the base as it appears to be both cannabalistic and vampiristic. It also seems to be indestructible, as it is more vegetable than human and can regenerate any lost limbs (one scene has it losing an arm to a dog, but regrowing it). Eventually army captain Hendry (Kenneth Tobey) devises a plan whereby the monster is lured by the smell of human flesh into a room where it is trapped between electric charges and is cremated.

Set against the dark, Arctic night, the picture is shot largely in shadows. The monster is seen only as a distant figure or a shadowy substance until the very end, when it is glimpsed as it is incinerated.

The picture was apparently edited down to almost half its original length. The producer wisely eliminated all clear closeups of the creature in order to avoid making it seem common place and thus possibly undermining the fear and shock values.

The film concludes with a near hysterical narrative by the middle-aged newspaperman character, Ned Scott (Douglas Spencer):

> One of the world's greatest battles was fought and won today by the human race. Here on top of the world, a handful of American soldiers met the first invasion from another planet.... Now, before I bring you the details of the battle, I bring you a warning ... to every one of you listening to the sound of my voice. Tell the world ... tell this to everyone wherever they are ... watch the skies ... watch everywhere ... keep on looking.... Watch the skies!

In their book Cinema of the Fantastic (1972), Chris Steinbrunner and Burt Goldblatt wrote: " ... The Thing is curiously anti-science. Over and over again the scientists are portrayed as men of weak and ineffectual ideas, while the soldiers are men of action.... The film also contains curious propaganda for the actual possibility of extraterrestrial invasion. At a time when many parts of the nation were already near hysteria over flying saucer sightings ... the ending of The Thing ... seriously exploited this national anxiety. "

The film proved to be extremely successful at the box-office and remains an enduringly popular item. The movie was issued with the subtitle, here and abroad, as The Thing from Another World. RKO would re-issue it in the U.S. in 1954 and Buddy Rogers Films did the same in 1957.

THE THING FROM ANOTHER WORLD see THE THING

THE THING WITH TWO HEADS (American International, 1972) C-93 min.

Executive producer, John Lawrence; producer, Wes Bishop; director, Lee Frost; story, Frost and Bishop; screenplay, Bishop, Frost, and James Gordon White; songs, Porter Jordan and the Mike Curb Congregation.

Ray Milland (Dr. Max Kirshner); Rosey Grier (Jack Moss); Don Marshall (Dr. Fred Williams); Roger Perry (Dr. Philip Desmond); Kathy Baumann (Nurse Patricia); Chelsea Brown (Lila); John Dullaghan (Thomas); John Bliss (Dr. Donald Smith); Rich Baker (Gorilla); Lee Frost (Sergeant Hacker); Dick Whittington (TV Newscaster); William Smith (Hysterical Condemned Man); Tommy Cook (Chaplain); Jerry Butler, George E. Carey, and Albert Zugsmith (Guest Performers).

This shoddy, but fun, exploitationer deals with two men who are about to die from an unorthodox experiment which saved their lives but unleashed a monster upon civilization. The chief (Ray Milland) of a hospital and transplant foundation is confined to a wheelchair due to arthritis and he is dying of cancer. A convicted (but innocent) black criminal (Rosey Grier), who is about to be electrocuted, is brought to the hospital. The bigoted doctor's co-workers then perform a clandestine operation in which the doctor's head is attached to the criminal's pudgy body. The white bigot and the black convict are then forced to fight each other for mental control of their mutual body.

"One of those rarities that's so bad it's good" (Castle of Frankenstein). The film was competently made and acted and more than satisfied the action crowds for which it was intended. It certainly was an improvement over the studio's ludicrous The Incredible Two-Headed Transplant (q.v.).

THINGS TO COME (United Artists, 1936) 130 min.

Producer, Alexander Korda; director, William Cameron

Margaretta Scott and Raymond Massey in Things to Come (1936).

Menzies; based on the book The Shape of Things to Come by H. G. Wells; screenplay, Wells and Lajos Biro; art director, Vincent Korda; costumes, John Armstrong, René Hubert, and the Marchioness of Queensberry; music, Arthur Bliss; special effects, Ned Mann; special camera effects, Edward Cohen and Harry Zech; camera, George Perinal; editor, Charles Crichton.

Raymond Massey (John Cabal/Oswald Cabal); Cedric Hardwicke (Theotocopulos); Margaretta Scott (Roxana); Ralph Richardson (The Boss); Edward Chapman (Pippa Passworthy/Raymond); Maurice Barddell (Dr. Harding); Sophie Stewart (Mrs. Cabal); Derrick de Marney (Richard Gordon); Ann Todd (Mary Gordon); Pearl Argyle (Katherine Cabal); Kenneth Villiers (Maurice Passworthy); Ivan Brandt (Mitani); Anthony Holles (Simon Burton); Allan Jeayes (Mr. Cabal); John Clements (Airman); Pickles Livingston (Horrie Passworthy); Patricia Hilliard (Janet Gordon); George Sanders (Pilot).

H. G. Wells' book The Shape of Things to Come, published in 1933, was a philosophical exploration of what the future might

hold for mankind. Three years later a quasi-adaptation of the work
was made for the screen, detailing what the next one hundred years
would be like. Since Wells was a firm believer that conflict and
struggle were part of man's destiny, his account focused on this aspect of life.

Set in the city of Everytown, the film commences on Christmas Eve, 1940 and the beginning of World War II. By 1966 the
world is devastated and "wandering sickness" is plaguing the land.
Into the battered city comes scientist John Cabal (Raymond Massey).
Alighting from his plane he tells the Boss (Ralph Richardson), who
is waging a war with the hill tribes, that he is from the Airmen base
at Basra and that he and his colleagues intend to rebuild civilization.
The narrative then jumps to the year 2036 and the community is now
a futuristic city, overseen by Cabal's descendant, Oswald Cabal (Massey). In this peaceful, prosperous and sterile city trouble brews.
A noted sculptor, Theotocopulos (Cedric Hardwicke), tries to lead a
revolt, hoping to return society to the more humanistic ways of yes-
teryear. Cabal, however, stops the revolt and instigates the launching of a space ship to the moon. Passengers in the space craft are the
Cabal's son and the sculptor's daughter. Perhaps on the new land
there may be a more compassionate way of life.

Made on a huge scale, Things to Come is at its most impressive when totally visual: the scenes of devastation after the final war,
when cities are shambles and the survivors have regressed back to
near savagery; and the city of the future, with its clear spirals and
swift flying machines. The major drawback of the production is its
overemphasis on polemics and its failure to give dimensions to the
characters. These aspects are responsible for the film's financial
failure. As the New York Herald-Tribune complained, "... [it] hints
of great things in the cinema rather than provides them."

In Cinema of the Fantastic (1972), Chris Steinbrunner and Burt
Goldblatt note, "Things to Come stands unique. No other film has
been made that quite attempts its chronology, or provides in such
stirring detail the sweep of its hundred-year look into the future.
Even though its heroes are somewhat cardboard and its brave new
world somewhat placid, Things to Come's singular vision makes it
a film still very viewable today ... and perhaps a film not too far
out of date when we catch up with it in the year 2036."

THIS ISLAND EARTH (Universal, 1955) C-86 min.

Producer, William Alland; director, Joseph Newman; based on
the novel by Raymond F. Jones; screenplay, Franklin Coen and Edward
G. O'Callaghan; art directors, Alexander Golitzen and Richard H.
Riedel; makeup, Bud Westmore; music, Herman Stein; music director,
Joseph Gershenson; special camera effects, Clifford Stine and Stanley
Horsley; camera, Stine; editor, Virgil Vogel.

Rex Reason (Cal Meacham); Faith Domergue (Ruth Adams);
Jeff Morrow (Exeter); Lance Fuller (Brack); Russell Johnson (Steve
Carlson); Eddie Parker (Mutant); and Robert Nichols, Karl Lindt,
Douglas Spencer, and Regis Barton.

A young scientist, Cal Meacham (Rex Reason), and a college
colleague, Ruth Adams (Faith Domergue), are hired by a mysterious
white-haired scientist named Exeter (Jeff Morrow) and his "family. "
At his Georgia retreat they find out that the man is actually from the
dying planet of Metaluna and he is here trying to uncover enough uranium to keep his planet's force field from collapsing; in turn per-
mitting enemy invasion. The two Earthlings are taken by force to
the planet to aid in the project and there they find that the strange
world is indeed decaying both physically and politically. The ruler
(Douglas Spencer) hopes to conquer the Earth and use it as an evac-
uation post for his people. A short time thereafter the force field
collapses, as predicted, and the giant insect-like mutants who serve
the people revolt. Exeter, badly ravaged by one of the monsters, is
able to set Meacham and Ruth free and they board a flying saucer,
set the controls for Earth and depart, just as the planet of Metaluna
explodes.
     Universal's publicity said that this Technicolor effort was some
two years in the making. (Actually the project was in preparation
for about six months, with a four-week shooting schedule.) The technical staff did make good use of the color and the special effects (especially in the brief but stunning glimpses of Metaluna). The huge
mutant was constructed around actor Eddie Parker at a cost of
$24,000, and showed makeup expert Bud Westmore at his most im-
aginative.
     Fantastic Monsters magazine appraised, "This Island Earth
remains a landfall of spectacular action in a universe of super-
science that grows even closer to us Earthlings as we travel further
into the future each day of our lives. "

THOSE FANTASTIC FLYING FOOLS   see   FROM THE EARTH TO
THE MOON

THX 1138 (Warner Bros. , 1971) C-88 min.

     Executive producer, Francis Ford Coppola; producer, Law-
rence Sturhahn; director/story, George Lucas; screenplay, Lucas and
Walter Murch; music composer/conductor, Lalo Schifrin; art direct-
or, Michael Haller; titles/animation, Hal Barwood; stunts arranged
by Jon Ward and Duffy Hamilton; costumes, Donald Longhurst; sound
montages, Murch; location sound, Lou Yates and Jim Manson; camera, Dave Meyers and Albert Kihn; editor, Lucas.
     Robert Duvall (THX 1138); Donald Pleasence (SEN 5241); Don
Pedro Colley (SRT); Maggie McOmie (LUH 3417); Ian Wolfe (PTO);
Marshall Effron (TWA); Sid Haig (NCH); John Pearce (DWY); Irene
Forrest (IMMO); Gary Alan Marsh (CAM); John Seaton (OUE); Raymond J. Walsh (TRG); Eugene I. Sullivan (JOT); Johnny Weissmuller,
Jr. and Robert Ferro (Chrome Robots); Henry Jacobs (Mark 8 Stu-
dent); Gary Austin (Man in Yellow); Mello Alexander and Barbara J.
Artis (Dancers).

     While a cinema student at the University of California at Los

Maggie McOmie and Robert Duvall in THX 1138 (1971).

Angeles, George Lucas turned out a twenty-minute experimental short
called THX 2238 4EB (or Electronic Labyrinth) which showed a good
deal of visual promise. The film was basically a long chase sequence, set in the future, with the "hero" running from an oppressive
totalitarian government. After viewing this short, Francis Ford Coppola was so impressed that he chose it for the first project of his
San Francisco-based American Zoetrope film producing unit. The
feature is thus an embellishment upon the original short.
        In the computer-run, subterranean world of the future, humans
are so drug-induced that they are, at best, conditioned automatons.
Children are conceived in test tubes, sex is forbidden, everyone
dresses the same (white robes, shaved heads), and order is maintained by mechanical robots. THX 1138 (Robert Duvall) and LUH 3417
(Maggie McOmie) have reduced their drug intake, which stimulates
their sex drive; they engage in fornication and she conceives a child.
Later they are separated and he is jailed for several society viola-
tions; his arch enemy proves to be SEN 5241 (Donald Pleasence). Still
later, THX learns that LUH is dead and that one of the bottled embryos in the lab is the fetus of his unborn child. THX and another
seek to escape, and the latter is killed. But THX is finally free of
his pursuers when the computer determines that stopping his flight is

more costly than the budget permits. THX climbs up a steel ladder
and makes his way out onto the Earth's surface. He encounters sunlight and a bird flying overhead.
"THX 1138 is not so much a vision of the future as a grim
extension of the present.... His subterranean city of tomorrow, reminiscent in its hermetic horror of the proposed underground subur-
ban cities a few years back, is ruled by a tyranny of computers,"
said Newsweek. The magazine added that there was a flaw to the
plot premise: "Lucas has set up a system so tightly structured that
we cannot accept on the simple level of adventure the possibility of
Duvall's escape. But this is a small reservation about an extremely
professional first film." The Los Angeles Times commented, "the
real excitement of THX 1138 is not really the message but the me-
dium--the use of film not to tell a story so much as to convey an
experience, a credible impression of a fantastic and scary dictatorship of tomorrow. Anyone fascinated with the potentials of film must
catch THX 1138."
        Sadly, Warner Bros. had no faith in the film and the promo-
tion and distribution of the project were negligible. It is a picture
well worth studying in conjunction with 1984 (q.v.) and other visionary
looks at the future of mankind. As always, the prediction of life in
later centuries is sterile, computerized, dour.

THE TIGER MAN   see   THE LADY AND THE MONSTER

THE TIME MACHINE (MGM, 1960) C-103 min.

        Producer/director, George Pal; based on the novel by H. G.
Wells; screenplay, David Duncan; art directors, George W. Davis
and William Ferrari; set decorators, Henry Grace and Keogh Gleason;
assistant director, William Shanks; makeup, William Tuttle; music,
Russell Garcia; sound, Franklin Milton; special camera effects, Gene
Warren and Wah Chang; camera, Paul C. Vogel; editor, George
Tomasini.
        Rod Taylor (George the Time Traveler); Alan Young (David
Filby/James Filby); Yvette Mimieux (Weena); Sebastian Cabot (Dr.
Hillyer); Tom Helmore (Anthony Bridewell); Whit Bissell (Walter
Kemp); Doris Lloyd (Mrs. Watchell); Paul Frees (Voice of the His-
tory Machine).

        Producer/director George Pal derived this colorful production
from H. G. Wells' well-remembered 1895 novel. A posh mounting,
adequate performances, and a fairly faithful adaptation of the book
make this a top-flight entertainment. It is probably Pal's best genre
film.
        In 1899 London, George (Rod Taylor) constructs a time ma-
chine which can project a person into the future. As the first pas-
senger he travels forward in time, through World War I and II and
to the final atomic war in 1966. He speeds onward, stopping in the
year 802,701 A.D. where he encounters a rich, green Earth.
        Exploring this new world he finds the Eloi, a peaceful race

of blond, beautiful people, who are rather dense. They are the willing slaves of the Morlocks. George fights off the oppressors (who
are afraid of fire) and manages to save some members of the Eloi,
especially Weena (Yvette Mimieux). Thereafter he returns via his
time machine to 1900 to meet with his amazed friends. Still later
he again journeys forward to the land of the Eloi, determined to
help them make a new world. He has taken three books with him
to the future, but just which three texts they are his Victorian
friends cannot determine.

Unlike the novel, in which Weena is killed and the time traveler plunges on into the future until the end of time, the film concludes
on an upbeat note and with a possible sequel in mind. Though no
follow-up from Pal's unit evolved, several films dealing with time
travel did emerge. In general, these successors (The Time Travelers, Journey to the Center of Time [both q.v.], etc. were inferior.)

The critics, like the public, were enchanted with this glossy
entry. "The social comment of the original has been historically re-
fined to encompass such plausible eventualities as the physical mani-
festation of atomic war weapons. But the basic spirit of Wells' work
has not been lost.... Pal's direction can be faulted only for its
pace..." (Variety). Time enthused, "The Time Machine deserves a
place on the very short list of good science fiction films, partly because its hokum is entrancing, its special effects expertly rigged and
its monsters sufficiently monstrous." The New York Herald-Tribune
summed it up: "Lots of fun."

THE TIME TRAVELERS (American International, 1964) C-84 min.

Producer, William Redlin; associate producer, Don Levy; di-
rector, Ib Melchior; story, Melchior and David Hewitt; screenplay,
Melchior; art director, Ray Storey; music, Richard LaSalle; special
effects, Hewitt; camera, William Zsigmond; editor, Hal Dennis.
Preston Foster (Dr. Erk von Steiner); Philip Carey (Steve
Connors); Merry Anders (Carol White); Joan Woodbury (Gadra); Do-
lores Wells (Reena); Stephen Franken (Danny McKee); Gloria Leslie
(Councilwoman); Peter Strudwick (The Deviant); Margaret Seldeen
(Technician); Forrest J. Ackerman (Third Technician).

Following the popularity of The Time Machine (q.v.), a number of sequel projects were discussed but discarded. But in 1964
director Ib Melchior and special effects artist David L. Hewitt wrote
the scenario for The Time Travelers, which had the same type of
theme as the H. G. Wells novel. Here, however, the time journey-
ers are from the present day. They work their way into the future,
and then have a bit of a problem getting back.

Four scientists (Preston Foster, Philip Carey, Merry Anders,
and Stephen Franken) are working with the theory of time travel and
accidentally evoke a Time Portal in their laboratory. They pass
through this door into a world 107 years in the future, and there they
find a war-ravaged land with humans and their faithful robot servants
being attacked behind their enclosed cities by a gang of mutants, the
latter also survivors of the atomic wars.

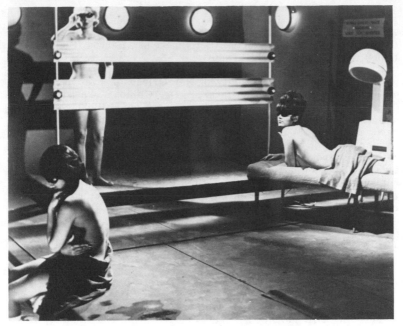

Scene from The Time Travelers (1964).

The scientists, who have lost the location of their Time Portal, are forced to remain in this "new" world and aid the inhabitants in constructing a space ship to transport the survivors to another planet before the mutants overrun the city. The ship, with a few of the inhabitants, does take off, but the mutants win the battle for the Earth. Three of the scientists escape back to the present via the portal but, having misjudged their time span, must project themselves again into the future, into a regenerated Earth period. The other member of the party is trapped in a perpetual time circle.

The British Monthly Film Bulletin complimented this feature for its ending--"bold and not without irony." Variety was more practical: "Good idea, so-so acting and other values. Okay for intended market."

TIME TRAVELERS (ABC-TV, 1976) C-76 min.

Producer, Irwin Allen; director, Alex Singer; based on the story by Rod Serling; teleplay, Jackson Gillis; music, Morton Stevens; camera, Fred Jachman; editor, William Brame.

Sam Groom (Dr. Clinton Earnshaw); Tom Hallick (Jeff Adams); Richard Basehart (Dr. Henderson); Trish Stewart (Jane Henderson);

Francine York (Dr. Lene Sanders); Booth Colman (Dr. Cummings); Walter Burke (Dr. Stafford); Dort Clark (Sharkey); Kathleen Bracken (Irish Girl); Victoria Meyerink (Betty); Baynes Barron (Chief Williams); Albert Cole (News Vendor).

In the year 1976 the city of New Orleans is overwhelmed by a deadly epidemic of "woods fever." Dr. Clinton Earnshaw (Sam Groom) and research scientist Jeff Adams (Tom Hallick) embark via a time machine back to 1871, where Dr. Henderson (Richard Basehart) had found a cure. They have just one day to learn the experimenter's secret cure before the Chicago fire destroys his files.

Yet another series pilot that never gelled beyond the telefeature stage. "Painted in strokes broad enough to coat a barn, telefilm has all the earmarks of a child's delight since it plays with sci-fi, pretty much avoids the mush, and works up some lab stuff, including computer hardware, to dazzle young eyes" (Daily Variety).

TRICK FOR TRICK see CHANDU THE MAGICIAN

A TRIP TO MARS see LE VOYAGE DANS LA LUNE

A TRIP TO THE MOON see THE ASTRONOMER'S DREAM; LE VOYAGE DANS LA LUNE

THE TROLLENBERG TERROR (Eros, 1958) 85 min.

Producers, Robert S. Baker and Monty Berman; director, Quentin Lawrence; based on the British teleseries by Peter Key; screenplay, Jimmy Sangster; music, Stanley Black; camera, Berman; editor, Henry Richardson.

Forrest Tucker (Alan Brooks); Laurence Payne (Philip Truscott); Jennifer Jayne (Sarah Pilgrim); Janet Munro (Anne Pilgrim); Warren Mitchell (Crevett); Frederick Schiller (Klein); Stuart Saunders (Dewhurst); Andrew Faulds (Brett); Colin Douglas (Hans); Derek Sydney (Wilde); Garard Green (Pilot); Leslie Heritage (Carl); Theodore Wilhelm (Fritz); Richard Golding, George Herbert, and Anne Sharp (Villagers); Jeremy Longhurst and Anthony Parker (Student Climbers).

A. k. a. The Flying Eye / Creatures from Another World / The Creeping Eye.

Like so many English sci-fi films, this entry was based on a television serial.

In the mountainous ski resort of Trollenberg, a number of mysterious activities have occurred. Eventually scientist Alan Brooks (Forrest Tucker) deduces that the problem is with an alien from outer space, a giant eye with long tentacles which is shrouded in a heavy radioactive fog. The monster has the ability to take mental control of many of the villagers. But Brooks finds that Anne Pilgrim (Janet Munro) can be used as a medium to communicate with the deadly creature. Finally the evil monster attacks the village. But U.N. planes arrive and bomb the fiend to destruction, thus saving the populace.

The Trollenberg Terror was retitled The Crawling Eye for U.S. distribution and was exhibited on a double bill with Strange World of Planet X (Cosmic Monsters) (q.v.), also a Forrest Tucker feature from England. The Trollenberg Terror, fortunately, was many times better than the inferior Strange World of Planet X. 'It shows real skill in quick development of a sense of threat and mystery and manages to hold this in suspense while concentrating on character and atmosphere" (New York Herald-Tribune). One scene in which Tucker saves a little girl, who has been caught by one of the monster's tentacles, is especially well-staged. Also the monster is smartly kept under wraps during most of the chronicle. Its ugliness is quite a shock to viewers when it finally makes a full appearance.

12 TO THE MOON (Columbia, 1960) 74 min.

   Producer, Fred Gebhardt; director, David Bradley; story, Gebhardt; screenplay, DeWitt Bodeen; music composer/conductor, Michael Andersen; art director, Rudi Feld; set decorator, John Burton; assistant director, Gilbert Mandelike; sound, Herman Lewis; special effects, Howard A. Anderson and E. Nicholson; camera, John Alton; editor, Edward Mann.

   Ken Clark (Captain John Anderson); Anthony Dexter (Dr. Luis

Moonscape from 12 to the Moon (1960).

Vargas); Robert Montgomery, Jr. (Roddy Murdoch); Tom Conway (Dr.
Feodor Orloff); John Wengraf (Dr. Erik Heinrich); Cory Devlin (Dr.
Asmara Makonen); Tema Bey (Dr. Selim Hamid); Anna-Lisa (Dr.
Sigrid Bromark); Michi Kobi (Dr. Hideko Murata); Roger Til (Dr.
Etienne Martel); Richard Weber (Dr. David Ruskin); Phillip Baird
(Dr. Rochester); Francis X. Bushman (Narrator).

The underlying message of this low-budget affair was brother-
ly love, as a group of international astronauts flies to the moon for
peaceful exploration in the craft "Lunar Eagle One." Upon landing
they explore the planet but eventually find that under Menelaus, where
they set down, exists the Great Coordinator, the ruler of the moon,
who is hostile to the astronauts. In revenge for disturbing his world
the ruler envelopes the Earth in a white cloud that drains off heat,
in an attempt to freeze the Earth into oblivion. The Earthlings return to The Earth's atmosphere and two of the group sacrifice their
lives in dropping an atom bomb into a Mexican crater (hoping to
bring about a temperature thaw). The plan fails but the moon people
are impressed by the acts of the humans and decide to allow the
Earth a reprieve.
       "Timely, but crude and cliché-ridden..." was Variety's ver-
dict.

20 MILLION MILES TO EARTH   (Columbia, 1957) C-82 min.

       Producer, Charles H. Schneer; director, Nathan Juran; story,
Charlotte Knight and Ray Harryhausen; screenplay, Bob Williams and
Christopher Knopf; assistant directors, Eddie Saeta and Octavio Oppo;
art director, Cary Odell; music, Mischa Bakaleinikoff; special effects,
Harryhausen; camera, Irving Lippman and Carlos Ventigmillia; editor,
Edwin Bryant.
       With: William Hopper, Joan Taylor, Frank Puglia, John Za-
remba, Thomas B. Henry, Tito Vuolo, Jan Arvan, Arthur Space,
Bart Bradley, George Peling, George Khoury, Don Orlando, Rollin
Mortyama.

       A space craft returns from the initial manned flight to Venus
and crash-lands off the coast of Italy. One of the astronauts (William Hopper) is found alive. However, a carton with an egg from
the planet is missing. It has been found by a young boy and sold to
a scientist. The mass turns into a small lizard-type creature called
Ymir. It begins to grow at an alarming rate. When it reaches the
size of a house the Army is called in to capture the creature, and
does so with the aid of electrical anesthesia. The alien Ymir is then
put on display at the Rome Zoo, where it still continues to expand in
size. When a fuse blows at the zoo lab, the creature escapes and
does battle with an elephant; the latter is vanquished. Ymir bounds
through Rome causing havoc, destruction and death. Finally it goes
to the ruins of the Coliseum, where the Army again closes in and
this time liquidates the creature with bazookas.
       The best asset of this minor entry was Harryhausen's animated
Venusian monster.

Peter Lorre, Kirk Douglas and Paul Lukas in 20,000 Leagues under the Sea (1954).

20,000 LEAGUES UNDER THE SEA (Universal, 1916) 105 min.

Director, Stuart Paton; based on the novels Deux Cent Mille Lieues sous les Mers and L'Ile Mystérieuse by Jules Verne; screenplay, Paton; underwater supervisors, J. Ernest Williamson and George M. Williamson; camera, Eugene Gaudio.

Allen Hollubar (Captain Nemo); June Gail (A Child of Nature); Matt Moore (Lieutenant Bond - U.S. Army); William Welsh (Charles Denver); Lois Alexander (Prince Dasker's Daughter); June Gail (Princess Daaker); Dan Hamlon (Professor Aronnax); Edna Pendleton (His Daughter); Curtis Benton (Ned Land); Howard Crampton (Cyrus Harding); Wallace Clark (Pencroft); Martin Murphy (Herbert Brown); Leviticus Jones (Neb).

20,000 LEAGUES UNDER THE SEA (Buena Vista, 1954) C-127 min.

Producer, Walt Disney; director, Richard Fleischer; based on the novel Deux Cent Mille Lieues sous les Mers by Jules Verne; screenplay, Earl Fenton; art director, John Meehan; set decorator, Emile Kuri; costumes, Norman Martien; music, Paul J. Smith; orchestrator, Joseph S. Dubin; song, Richard and Robert Sherman; assistant directors, Tom Connors, Jr. and Russ Haverick; second unit director, James Havens; diving master, Fred Zendar; Techni-

color consultant, Morgan Padleford; matte artists, Peter Ellenshow;
sketch artist, Bruce Bushman; sound, C. O. Slyfield; special effects,
John Hench, Josh Meador, and Ub Iwerks; special camera effects,
Ralph Hammeras; underwater camera, Till Gabbani; camera, Franz
Planer; editor, Elmo Williams.

Kirk Douglas (Ned Land); James Mason (Captain Nemo); Paul
Lukas (Professor Pierre Arronnax); Peter Lorre (Conseil); Robert
J. Wilkie (First Mate on "Nautilus"); Carleton Young (John Howard);
Ted de Corsia (Captain Farragut); Percy Helton (Diver); Ted Cooper
(Mate on "Lincoln"); Edward Marr (Shipping Agent); Fred Graham
(Casey Moore); Harry Harvey (Shipping Clerk); J. M. Kerrigan (Bil-
ly); Herb Vigran (Reporter).

At least three screen versions have appeared of Jules Verne's
1870 classic adventure novel. The first, Deux Cent Mille Lieues
sous Les Mers (q.v.), was made in 1907 in Paris by the master of
fantasy cinema, Georges Méliès. Although a short film it was hand-
colored and filled with imaginative props. In 1916 Universal filmed
a lengthy (105-minute) version of the tale, which utilized the basic
novel plus Verne's L'Ile Mysterieuse and incorporated into the plotline a girl located on a deserted island, as well as explaining Nemo's beginnings as an Indian prince. Unfortunately this version has
not survived in popularity. In fact the studio was led to make a
spoof of it the following year, entitled The Cross-Eyed Submarine.

The definitive screen version came in 1954 from Walt Disney.
James Mason starred as the unfathomable Captain Nemo, the skipper
of the futuristic submarine, "The Nautilus," who vows revenge on all
slavers and slave ships after the death of his wife and child at their
hands. Set in the year 1868, it has Nemo rescuing a party of
stranded seafarers. Among the party are a harpoonist (Kirk Douglas), a humanitarian scientist (Paul Lukas) and his valet (Peter
Lorre). Captain Nemo eventually informs the captives of his plans
for slaves. The scientist eventually persuades him to trade the
submarine to neutral world powers in return for the abolition of sla-
very. He agrees, but when they surface a group of war ships is
awaiting them, having been informed of the sub's location by notes
in a bottle from one of the party. The "Nautilus" is sunk and Nemo
killed.

Walt Disney was so enthusiastic about this project that he la-
vished a heavy budget on the production, from location shooting in
the Bahamas to constructing a 200'-long submarine, geared to the
specifications as detailed in Verne's novel. As Leonard Maltin
pointed out in The Disney Films (1973), "20,000 Leagues Under the
Sea is fantasy at its best, with the Disney production team making
the unbelievable come to life, in order to project a convincing tale
against real-life backgrounds. The sumptuous mounting and careful
attention to detail contribute immeasurably to the overall effect."

Not only was the cast ideal, from Mason as the misguided
genius to Douglas as the jaunty sailor (who sings the song "A Whale
of a Tale"), but there were also Oscar-Winner Lukas and comic
relief Lorre. John Meehan and Emile Kuri would win Oscars for
their art direction and set decorations for the film, which has
grossed over $9 million domestically and is periodically re-issued

to theatres. (A 60-minute documentary on the making of the film, entitled Operation Undersea, was shown on the TV series, "The Wonderful World of Disney," and won an Emmy that year.)

As for the mad genius Captain Nemo, he would reappear in other features, such as Captain Nemo and the Underwater City (q.v.) with Robert Ryan in the lead role.

2001: A SPACE ODYSSEY (MGM, 1968) C-160 min.

Producer, Stanley Kubrick; associate producer, Victor Lyndon; director, Kubrick; based on the story "The Sentinel" by Arthur C. Clarke; screenplay, Kubrick and Clarke; production designers, Tony Masters, Harry Lange, and Ernie Archer; art director, John Hoesli; assistant director, Derek Cracknell; costumes, Hardy Amies; make-up, Stuart Freeborn; sound, Winston Ryder; special camera effects designed and directed by Kubrick; special effects, supervisors, Wally Veevers, Douglas Trumbull, Con Pederson, and Tom Howard; camera, Geoffrey Unsworth; additional camera, John Alcott; editor, Ray Lovejoy.

Keir Dullea (David Bowman); Gary Lockwood (Frank Poole); Douglas Rain (The Voice of Hal); William Sylvester (Dr. Heywood Floyd); Leonard Rossiter (Smyslov); Robert Beatty (Halvorsen); Frank Miller (Mission Controller); Penny Brahms and Edwina Carroll (Stewardesses); Daniel Richter (Moonwatcher); Margaret Tyzack (Elena); Jean Sullivan (Michaels); Alan Gifford (Poole's Father); and Edward Bishop, Mike Lovell, Peter Delman, Danny Grover, Brian Hawley, and Glenn Beck.

"Big, beautiful, but plodding and confusing..." (Variety). Despite all its intellectual pretentiousness, 2001: A Space Odyssey

Scene from 2001: A Space Odyssey (1968).

is a stupendous visual experience and remains one of the greatest of
all science fiction space films.

Opening at the dawn of mankind, the astounding feature depicts
aliens genetically changing the dying race of sub-humans into thinking,
aggressive beings capable of charting their own destiny for thousands
of years. The narrative then switches to the year 2001, where a
monolithic slab (like the one discovered by early man) is located
on the moon beneath its surface. When the sun strikes the huge
stone it emits a piercing beam toward Jupiter. The U.S. dispatches
the space ship "The Discovery" on a nine-month mission to investigate the situation on Jupiter. Aboard the craft are astronauts David
Bowman (Keir Dullea), Frank Polle (Gary Lockwood), three other
space men in deep-freeze sleep, and the all-knowing computer nick-
named HAL. The latter, fearing man's contrariness, plots his take-
over craftily. Poole is sent out in a space pod to replace a defective
piece of ship's mechanism and his life line is cut. Later, while
Bowman leaves the craft to investigate, HAL stops the functioning of
the hibernating astronauts. Subsequently Bowman forces his re-entry
into "The Discovery," makes his way to HAL's control center and
turns off the computer. He continues the voyage outward beyond
Jupiter and finds a third monolith among that planet's moons.

Thereafter Bowman is whisked through a blazing dimension of
space and time, where he is shown the marvels of the ages. Unseen
aliens provide him with the comforts of home for the rest of his life.
From his death is born a new and more intelligent human, who returns to Earth to face a new age.

"I don't want to spell out a verbal road map for 2001 that
every viewer will feel obligated to pursue or else fear he's missed
the point," said filmmaker Kubrick. "I think that if 2001 succeeds
at all, it is in reaching a wide spectrum of people who would not
often give a thought to man's destiny, his role in the cosmos and his
relationship to higher forms of life...."

2001 was filmed in England at a cost of $10.5 million over
a four-year period. Shortly after its U.S. film debut, some nineteen
minutes were excised by Kubrick from the release print. (Earlier
the voice of HAL, originally performed by Martin Balsam was re-
dubbed with the voice of Douglas Rain.) The MGM release grossed
$14.5 in its U.S./Canadian domestic rentals, and earned another $5.4
million in its 1972 domestic re-issue. It debuted on TV in early 1977.

Like the public, many critics were baffled, annoyed, and dis-
turbed by Kubrick's masterpiece. "Has he gone to all this trouble
... to tell us that life goes on from tomb to womb, that there's
something, or someone, out there who's going to outlast us all, and
that there's a star up in heaven for every baby born? And even if
this were not too banal to bear repetition, should its repetition be
in technical terms all-too-familiar to watchers of a number of television series, with techniques more effectively used in various Expo
films?" (Judith Crist, New York magazine).

While many of the older generation carped at the juxtaposition
of classical/popular music selections as the basis of the soundtrack,
the younger set--especially those into the drug scene--were entranced
by the visual special effects which provide (almost on their own) a
self-induced high.

In The Cinema of Stanley Kubrick (1972), Norman Kagan offers his own interpretation of the meaning of 2001: "... Kubrick's evolution of consciousness operates like a canal with locks, linking two bodies of water at different heights. To get from the lower to the higher body, a species moves into the first and lowest lock. The monolith closes the doors to the outside, and the species (by pumping in water) raises itself to the level of the second lock. Then the monolith opens the doors linking the first and second lock, and the species sails into the second lock. The monolith closes the first-lock-second-lock doors, and the species begins raising itself to the third level. Substitute 'consciousness' or 'intelligence' for water, 'instinct' for the lower water body, 'rationality' or 'toolmaking' for the first lock, 'super-rationality' or 'transcendence' for the second lock (or possibly the upper body), 'refining techniques' for pumping, and you have an essentially complete interpretation of what happens in A Space Odyssey."

Whatever the intellectual conclusions about 2001, it established a visual and intellectual standard by which all science fiction thereafter must be judged. Kubrick, who had directed the biting satirical, futuristic political drama/comedy Dr. Strangelove (1964), would later make Clockwork Orange (q.v.), itself another frightening glimpse into the potentials of the future.

U. F. O.   see   UNIDENTIFIED FLYING OBJECTS

THE UFO INCIDENT (NBC-TV, 1975) C-100 min.

Producers, Richard Colla and Joe L. Cramer; director, Colla; based on the book The Interrupted Journey by John G. Fuller; teleplay, S. Lee Pogostin and Hesper Anderson; music, Billy Goldenberg; camera, Rexford Metz; editor, Dick Bracken.

James Earl Jones (Barney Hill); Estelle Parsons (Betty Hill); Barnard Hughes (Dr. Benjamin Simon); Beeson Carroll (Lieutenant Colonel John MacRainey); Dick O'Neill (General Davidson); Terrence O'Connor (Lisa MacRainey).

In 1966 John G. Fuller's book The Interrupted Journey was a a sensation. It revealed that a married couple, Betty and Barney Hill of Portsmouth, New Hampshire, had both undergone hypnosis and in these sessions had revealed that they had been abducted and examined by aliens aboard a UFO. This NBC-TV entry for "Monday Night at the Movies" was an adaptation of the book, but the force of the written work was lessened by sloppy production values, indifferent performances and an unnecessary emphasis on the racial issue. (Mr. Hill is a black postal worker; his wife, a white social worker.) In the autumn of 1961, Betty (Estelle Parsons) and Barney Hill (James Earl Jones) are driving to their New Hampshire home near midnight along country roads when they spot a light following them. After a lapse of several hours they arrive home full of anxieties that remain with them for months until they are put under hypnosis by a psychiatrist (Barnard Hughes). Under the separate hypnotic

James Earl Jones and aliens in The UFO Incident (1975).

sessions they each reveal that they were abducted by humanoid creatures, taken aboard a UFO, and intensively examined separately.
After the experiences are re-lived under hypnosis, the Hills are re-
lieved of some of their traumas and have a better understanding of
their adventures.
      The production had its moments of suspense, but there were
too many long periods of uninteresting psychological discussion between the couple and probing scenes with the psychiatrist. The producers of this TV movie chose to reveal the aliens rather than having
them in shadow or fuzzy focus. The creatures, unfortunately, looked
like refugees from a Halloween party.
      James Earl Jones, who had purchased the screen rights to the
Hill story in 1973 and finally sold it to NBC-TV when he could not
finance a theatrical film version, stated, "I am convinced that something of the sort really happened. There is too much corroborating
physical evidence to dismiss it. There were marks on the terrain
that might have been made by a laser beam. The man's warts, which
he said came from something thrown over his head, were real. The
wife's description of a map she saw in the craft was one that scientists agreed was valid if one considered it from the viewpoint of a
visitor from afar. "

ULTIMO UOMO DELLA TERRA (THE LAST MAN ON EARTH) (American International, 1964) 86 min.

Producer, Robert L. Lippert; associate producer, Harold E. Knox; directors, Ubaldo Ragona and Sidney Salkow; based on the novel I Am Legend by Richard Matheson; screenplay, Logan Swanson and William P. Leicester; art director, Giorgio Giovannini; music, Paul Sawtell and Bert Shefter; camera, Franco Delli Colli; editor, Gene Ruggiero.

Vincent Price (Robert Morgan); Franca Bettoia (Ruth); Emma Danieli (Virginia); Giacomo Rossi Stuart (Ben Cortman); and Umberto Rau, Tony Corevi, Christi Courtland, and Hector Ribotta.

Richard Matheson's striking novel I Am Legend was the basis for this Italian/American co-production. Ubaldo Ragona directed the European version while Sidney Salkow helmed the English language edition. Vincent Price starred as scientist Robert Morgan, the last man left on Earth after a wide-sweeping plague has destroyed the human race, leaving only a few vampires as survivors. Morgan isolates himself from the blood drinkers who seek to make him one of their own. Later he meets Ruth (Franca Bettoia), who is among those who claim to have found an antidote to the plague. After he had given her a transfusion of his normal blood she is freed of any possible plague reinfection. But her comrades, whom Morgan had been hunting (thinking they too were vampires), kill him. The last male on earth is dead.

The poor production values and the slapdash scripting detracted greatly from the box-office potential of the combination of horror film star Price and a well-regarded book property. It was all a victim of "crude effects, erratic editing and silly dialogue" (British Monthly Film Bulletin).

A much more lavish version of I Am Legend, entitled The Omega Man (q.v.), would be produced by American International Pictures in 1971 with Charlton Heston in the lead.

EL ULTIMO VARON SOBRE LA TIERRA see THE LAST MAN ON EARTH

THE UNDERSEAS KINGDOM (Republic, 1936) twelve chapters

Supervisor, Barney Sarecky; directors, B. Reeves Eason and Joseph Kane; story, John Rathmell and Tracy Knight; screenplay, Rathmell, Maurice Geraghty, and Oliver Drake; music, Harry Grey; camera, William Nobles and Edgar Lyons.

Ray "Crash" Corrigan (Crash Corrigan); Lois Wilde (Diane); Monte Blue (Khan); William Farnum (Sharad); Boothe Howard (Ditmar); C. Montague Shaw (Professor Norton); Lee Van Atta (Billy Norton); Smiley Burnette (Briny); Frankie Marvin (Salty); Lon Chaney, Jr. (Hakur); Lane Chandler (Darius); Jack Mulhall (Lieutenant Andrews); John Bradford (Joe); Ralph Holmes (Martos); Ernie Smith (Gourck); Lloyd Whitlock (Captain Clinton); David Horsley (Naval

Vincent Price in <u>Ultimo Uomo della Terra</u> (1964).

Sentry); Kenneth Lawton (Naval Doctor); Raymond Hatton (Gasspon);
Rube Schaeffer (Magna).
    Chapters: 1) Beneath the Ocean Floor; 2) Undersea City;
3) Arena of Death; 4) Revenge of the Volkites; 5) Prisoners of Atlantis; 6) The Juggernaut Strikes; 7) The Submarine Trap; 8) Into the
Metal Tower; 9) Death in the Air; 10) Atlantis Destroyed; 11) Flaming Death; 12) Ascent to the Upperworld.

    Professor Norton (C. Montague Shaw) speculates that some
subterranean force is the cause of a series of earthquakes that
threaten to destroy the North American continent. The scholar, his
son Billy (Lee Van Atta), naval officer Crash Corrigan (Ray Corrigan) and reporter Diane Compton (Lois Wilde) descend to the ocean
floor in a special underwater submarine. There they locate the lost
world of Atlantis, which is at war. Sharad (William Farnum) is the
leader of the White Robes. He is the high priest and rightful ruler
of Atlantis, but he is competing with Khan (Monte Blue), the chief
of the Black Robes and the new dictator of the walled city. With
his disintegrating ray machine Khan intends to rule the world but he
is opposed by Corrigan and friends, who ally themselves with Sharad
and his soldiers. Eventually the ray machine is used to unleash a
war on Atlantis. Khan and his sinister cohorts are killed. Now
Crash and Diane can plan to marry.
    The Underseas Kingdom is a brisk entry that never lacks for
action, imagination, or entertainment value (something that cannot be
said for many sci-fi pictures). It is a strange conglomeration of the
old (chariots, bows and arrows, spears, armored soldiers) and futuristic (submarines, ray guns, robots, advanced flying craft). The
blend, together with the comedy relief (Smiley Burnette and Frankie
Marvin) and vicious villain (Monte Blue, with Lon Chaney as his chief
henchman), adds greatly to the serial's impact. The excellent cinematography and rousing film score were exceptions rather than a
rule in the field of serials, especially those made outside of Republic
Studios.
    In 1966 a condensed feature version was issued to TV as Sha-
rad of Atlantis.

THE UNEARTHLY (Republic, 1957) 73 min.

    Producer/director, Brooke L. Peters; story, Jane Mann;
screenplay, Geoffrey Dennis and Mann; art director, Dan Hall; music,
Henry Vars and Michael Terr; camera, Merle Connell; editor, Rich-
ard Currier.
    John Carradine (Professor Charles Conway); Allison Hayes
(Grace Thomas); Myron Healey (Mark Houston); Sally Todd (Natalie);
Marilyn Buferd (Dr. Gilchrist); Arthur Batanides (Danny Green); Tor
Johnson (Lobo); Harry Fleer (Jedrow); and: Roy Gordon, Guy Pres-
cott, and Paul MacWilliams.

    An uneven mixture of sci-fi and horror ingredients.
    In his remote Georgia mansion a mad scientist, Professor
Charles Conway (John Carradine), and his sexy assistant (Marilyn

John Carradine in The Unearthly (1957).

Buferd) experiment with gland transplants in order to obtain immortality. Unfortunately, most of the doctor's experiments to date have been unsuccessful, although one victim, Lobo (Tor Johnson), a moronic giant, serves as his butler. Chancing onto this macabre scene are escaped convict Mark Houston (Myron Healey) and mental patient Grace Thomas (Allison Hayes), sent to the mansion-hospital by an unscrupulous doctor in Conway's pay. Later Houston falls in love with Grace and fears for her safety after another female (Sally Todd) on the premises is horribly mutilated in an operation. When all seems lost, Lobo turns on his master and allows the two to escape. The police arrive to find Professor Conway, his assistant and Lobo dead. They discover a cellar-full of horribly scarred mutants. In the film's best moment, one policeman looks at the other and questions, "What if they do live forever?"

THE UNEARTHLY STRANGER (Anglo Amalgamated, 1963) 75 min.

Producer, Albert Fennell; director, John Krish; screenplay, Rex Carlton; art director, Harry Pottle; music, Edward Williams; music director, Marcus Dods; camera, Reg Wyer; editor, Tom Priestley.

Gabriella Licudi and John Neville in The Unearthly Stranger (1963).

John Neville (Dr. Mark Davidson); Gabriella Licudi (Julie);
Philip Stone (Professor John Lancaster); Patrick Newell (Major
Clarke); Jean Marsh (Miss Ballard); Warren Mitchell (Dr. Munro).

In this British-made thriller, Dr. Mark Davidson (John Neville) meets and falls in love with a beautiful, desirable girl (Gabriella Licudi). Their courtship is brief and they soon wed. But
the man's marital bliss is soon darkened by minor suspicions about
the girl. He finds she sleeps with her eyes open, has no pulse, and
her actions are not always human or rational. Later, it becomes
clear that Julie (Licudi) is involved in the death of several of the research team who are working on the time projection project that
Davidson is researching at the government lab. She admits she is
an alien from another world and that she is one of many such visitors sent in female form to take over the planet.
Davidson joins with others in trying to wipe out the invaders,
despite the fact that he loves Julie and that she has admitted she
cares for him in her own way. This is not permitted in her world
and she dies in his arms, disintegrating before him. Later a secretary, Miss Ballard (Jean Marsh), at the Research Institute proves to
be an alien, and in her escape she falls from a window. On the
pavement below, all that remains of her is a heap of clothing.
This is a surprisingly well-made film, successfully combining

drama with a love story theme. It is not shackled by any of the ill-
effects of the sci-fi species (i. e. , ludicrous monsters, scientific
mumbo jumbo, or far-fetched gadgets). The fact that the lovely girl
is an alien from another solar system is told rather than seen.
(Ironically, most filmgoers will find the heroine-alien more ingratiating than the rather bland Earthlings.) One interesting scene has
Julie crying, with the tears burning her face like acid.

UNIDENTIFIED FLYING OBJECTS (U. F. O.) (United Artists, 1956)
92 min. (color sequences)

    Producer, Clarence Greene; associate producer, Fernando
Carrere; screenplay, Francis Martin; music, Ernest Gold; camera,
Howard Anderson, Ed Fitzgerald, and Bert Spielvogel; editor, Chest-
er Schaeffer.
    Tom Powers (Albert M. Chop/Narrator).

    This documentary was two years in the making and combined
footage of Unidentified Flying Objects, commonly called flying saucers,
from all over the world. The compilation contained sitings made
since 1947 and both black-and-white and previously classified color
footage of UFOs. It proved to be a very thought-provoking study.
    The film was based on the unusual experiences of Los Angeles
newsman Albert M. Chop (Tom Powers), chief of the press section
of the Air Materiel Command in Washington, D. C. Among the footage of verified UFO sightings included were those in Montana in 1950
and the spottings in both Utah and Washington, D. C. in 1952. The
film study revealed that about fifteen per cent of UFO sightings are
officially designated as inexplicable. There were some tedious spots
in the presentation, but the finale, with footage of jet planes trying
to intercept a UFO, was gripping.
    The New York Times concluded: "The fact that truth can be
more engrossing than fiction is quietly and effectively demonstrated
in Unidentified Flying Objects.... [It] is not as startling as an imaginary invasion by tiny, green men with pointed heads, it does,
however, leave an impression that is instructive and sobering."

UNKNOWN PEOPLE see SUPERMAN

UNNATURAL see ALRAUNE (1952)

IL VAMPIOR DEL PLANETA ROSSO see NOT OF THIS EARTH

VAMPIRE MEN OF THE LOST PLANET see HORROR OF THE
BLOOD MONSTERS

VARAN THE UNBELIEVABLE see DAIKAIJU BARAN

VENGEANCE (BLC/British Lion/Garrick, 1963) 83 min.

Producer, Raymond Stross; director, Freddie Francis; based on the novel Donovan's Brain by Curt Siodmak; screenplay, Robert Stewart and Philip Mackie; art director, Arthur Lawson; music/music director, Ken Jones; sound, Stephen Dalby and William Bulkley; camera, Bob Huke; editor, Oswald Hafenrichter.

Anne Heywood (Anna); Peter Van Eyck (Corrie); Cecil Parker (Stevenson); Bernard Lee (Frank); Ellen Schwiers (Ella); Maxine Audley (Marion); Jeremy Spenser (Martin); Siegfried Lowitz (Walters); Hans Nielsen (Immerman); Miles Malleson (Dr. Miller); Jack Mac-Gowran (Furber); George A. Cooper (Gabler); Irene Richmond (Mrs. Gabler); Ann Sears (Secretary); Frank Forsythe (Francis); Allan Cuthbertson (Dr. Silva); John Watson (Priest); Bryan Pringle (Master of Ceremonies).

"This preposterous mixture of crime, horror and science fiction, with a dash or two of neurosis, art and medical ethics stirred in, comes off unexpectedly well. . . . But pointless implausibilities in the story--brain-baths apart--will jar on the observant spectator. And it's a bit much having apparently two alcoholics in one picture" (British Monthly Film Bulletin).

Curt Siodmak's sturdy novel Donovan's Brain has been the official source for no less than three sci-fi films, one each during the Forties, Fifties, and Sixties. In the World War II years, Republic Pictures produced a version entitled The Lady and the Monster (q.v.), and in the early 1950s, United Artists released Donovan's Brain (q.v.). This latest addition was a German-British co-production.

Peter Van Eyck is young Dr. Corrie, who saves the living brain of a man killed in an airplane crash. The organ, however, belonged to a most evil industrialist. Very slowly, as it gains strength, it takes over the thought patterns of the physician through mental telepathy. The reason for the brain's activities is to get revenge on the person who planted the accident-causing explosives on the aircraft. The culprit turns out to be the dead man's lovely daughter (Anne Heywood), who murdered her ruthless father in order to gain control of the release of a valued drug. Eventually both the brain and the equally-sinister young woman are thwarted. (Having the daughter as the murderess was a twist in this newest rendition of Donovan's Brain.)

Here the story is given a rather somber touch. If Van Eyck's removal of the living brain is a bit gory, it is still educational. The remainder of the picture maintains interest, especially after attractive Miss Heywood is announced as the murderess and the doctor has developed a romantic eye for her.

VILLAGE OF THE DAMNED (MGM, 1960) C-78 min.

Producer, Ronald Kinnoch; director, Wolf Rilla; based on the novel The Midwich Cuckoos by John Wyndham; screenplay, Sterling Silliphant, Rilla, and George Barclay; art director, Ivan King; assistant director, David Middlemas; makeup, Eric Aylott; wardrobe,

Eileen Sullivan; music, Ron Goodwin; sound, A. W. Watkins; camera
effects, Tom Howard; camera, Geoffrey Faithfull; editor, Gordon
Hales.

George Sanders (Dr. Gordon Zellaby); Barbara Shelley (Anthea
Zellaby); Michael Gwynne (Major Alan Bernard); Martin Stephens (David); Laurence Naismith (Dr. Willera); John Phillips (General Leigh-
ton); Richard Vernon (Sir Edgar Hargraves); Jenny Laird (Mrs. Harrington); Richard Warner (Mr. Harrington); Thomas Heathcote (James
Pawle); Charlotte Mitchell (Janet Palwe); Rosamund Greenwood (Miss
Ogle); Peter Vaughan (Constable Gobbey); Sarah Long (Evelyn Harrington); Robert Marks (Paul Norman); Billy Lawrence (John Bush).

"One of the trimmest, most original and serenely unnerving
little chillers in a long time.... The picture will get you, we guar-
antee, and anyone coming upon it cold, will exit colder" (New York
Times).

In the small English community of Midwich a dozen females,
some unmarried, are impregnated suddenly on a single day during
which the entire town is rendered insensible. The children (six boys,
six girls) who are born from these mysterious circumstances all appear alike: blond hair, strange piercing eyes, and telepathic powers.
A physicist Dr. Gordon Zellaby (George Sanders), whose wife (Barbara Shelley) has given birth to one of these superior children, decides to offer the youngsters a superior education. By the time the
children are nine years old, there is no doubt that they are mental
giants. Zellaby theorizes that these "freaks" are the vanguard of
an invasion from outer space. He predicts that by the time they are
fully grown, they will have the capacity to control the world. The
children, including Zellaby's "son" David, realize the physicist is
aware of their gambit. They match him in a game of wits. In a
final desperate ploy, he plants dynamite in their schoolhouse and
blows them and himself to bits.

With location scenes shot at Letchmore Heath, England, this
black-and-white, widescreen feature was shot for less than $300,000.
It was the sleeper of the year and grossed $1.5 million in the U.S.
and Canada alone. It was so popular that it infused new life into the
seemingly dying sci-fi film genre. It did so well that it was re-
issued in the U.S. in 1966 on a double-bill with These Are the
Damned (q.v.). It also fostered a sequel, the less gripping Children
of the Damned (1963).

Contemporary critics were at variance over the impact of this
feature. Variety passed it off as "mediocre," explaining that it is
"A rather tired and sick film which starts off very promisingly but
soon nosedives." Time countered, "Village is one of the neatest
little horror pictures produced since Peter Lorre went straight."
The New York Herald-Tribune enthused, "Rilla directed with a canny
feel for the uncanny that shows him to have a fine, wry taste for the
plausible implausible," and concluded, "Far and away the neatest,
cleverest and most believable of that unbelievable genre called sometimes 'horror' and sometimes pseudo-science films."

Young Martin Stephens offers a most eerie performance, almost diverting attention from wry, dry George Sanders.

Joan Blackman and Jerry Lewis in Visit to a Small Planet (1960).

VISIT TO A SMALL PLANET (Paramount, 1960) 85 min.

Producer, Hal B. Wallis; director, Norman Taurog; based on
the play by Gore Vidal; screenplay, Edmund Beloin and Henry Garson;
art directors, Hal Pereira and Walter Tyler; set decorators, Sam
Comer and Arthur Krams; costumes, Edith Head; makeup, Wally
Westmore; assistant director, D. Michael Moore; music, Leigh Har-
line; choreography, Miriam Nelson; sound, Gene Merritt and Charles
Grenzbach; special camera effects, John P. Fulton; camera, Loyal
Griggs; editors, Warren Low and Frank Bracht.

Jerry Lewis (Kreton); Joan Blackman (Ellen Spelding); Earl
Holliman (Conrad); Fred Clark (Roger Putnam Spelding); Lee Patrick
(Rheba Spelding); Gale Gordon (Bob Mayberry); Jerome Cowan (George
Abercrombie); John Williams (Delton); Barbara Lawson (Beatnik Dan-
cer).

When this literate hit farce by Gore Vidal was produced on
Broadway in February, 1957, it was directed by and starred Cyril
Ritchard. Its underlying theme was that war was foolhardy no matter how justified the original cause. As transformed to the screen,
it became much more of a knockabout affair for the special talents
of Jerry Lewis. "A watered-down film version ... whoever dictated

the changes, gave neither the screenplay nor the star a fair shake"
(Variety).
     Kreton (Lewis), a fun-loving inhabitant of outer space, has
long studied the Earth and decides to pay it a visit. He lands in
Virginia and attends a costume ball being given by over-opinionated
TV commentator Roger Putnam Spelding (Fred Clark), a man who
has long scoffed at the public's fascination with flying saucers. Later Kreton convinces Spelding that he is actually from another world
and the newsman insists he remain as his house guest. It is not
long before Kreton falls in love with Spelding's daughter Ellen (Joan
Blackman) and seeks to disillusion her about her dull-witted beau,
Conrad (Earl Holliman). Meanwhile Delton (John Williams), Kreton's
celestial boss, seeks to teach his wayward underling a lesson. He
transforms him into a mortal and as such Kreton speaks his piece.
Just as it seems the state guard will capture this creature from outer space, Kreton is allowed to return to his home planet.
     With Lewis at the creative helm, the storyline becomes "about
as subtle as a meat cleaver" (New York Times). The gimmick that
an alien visitor could be much smarter than Earthlings was nearly
lost in the shuffle. One bright sequence--overdone, of course--has
Kreton doing a group of beatniks one better in performing a nonsen-
sical ballad and then launching into a frenetic dance (with lively Barbara Lawson).

VOICE FROM THE SKY (G.Y.P. Productions, 1930) ten chapters

     Producer/director, Ben Wilson.
     With: Wally Wales and Jean Delores.
     Chapters: 1) Doomed; 2) The Cave of Horror; 3) The Man
from Nowhere; 4) Danger Ahead; 5) Desperate Deeds; 6) Trail of Vengeance; 7) The Scarlet Scourge; 8) Trapped by Fire; 9) The Pit of
Peril; 10) Hearts of Steel.

     Voice from the Sky was the first independent sound serial
made in Hollywood; it was turned out by producer/director Ben Wilson, a one-time serial star, and was distributed on a states rights
basis by G. Y. P. Productions. Minor league Western star Wally
Wales (later Hal Taliaferro) was starred, along with Jean Delores.
     Issued in ten chapters, the cliffhanger told of a mad inventor
who develops a secret formula that could destroy the world by suspending all energy in the atmosphere. The scientist develops a
transmitter to throw his voice into the air so that an entire city can
hear his threats to destroy the metropolis if the citizens and public
officials do not meet his demands. Eventually the madman is stopped.
     Voice from the Sky is a rare item; no known prints survive.
Even the film's star, Hal Taliaferro, recently stated that he was unaware the serial had even been issued.

VOYAGE AU CENTRE DE LA TERRE (Pathé, 1909) 540'

     Director, Segundo de Chomon; based on the novel by Jules

Verne.
See: Journey to the Center of the Earth.

LE VOYAGE DANS LA LUNE (A TRIP TO THE MOON) (French,
1902) 845'

     Producer/director, Georges Méliès; suggested by the novels
From the Earth to the Moon and A Trip Around It by Jules Verne
and The First Men in the Moon by H. G. Wells; screenplay/costumes/
sets, Méliès; camera, Lucien Tainguy.
     Georges Méliès (Leader of Expedition); Bluette Bernon (Lady
in the Moon); and Victor André, Delpierre and Farjaux-Kelm-Brunnet,
and Ballet Girls of the Théâtre du Chatelet.

     A pathfinding venture for all the space adventure movies to
come.   Although only two reels long, the silent picture captivated
its awe-struck audiences.
     Several scientists are launched to the moon in a space craft
fired from a huge cannon.   Follies girls provide the boys with their
sendoff and soon they have set down on the lunar surface, after having landed in the eye of the man in the moon.   They sleep on the
surface for the night and are covered with lunar dust.   They awake
to explore the new world, going into a cave where they find giant
mushrooms and soil so fertile that even their planted umbrellas take
root.   Soon they meet a moon being, but he disappears when he is
tapped with an umbrella.   The Earthlings are later captured and
taken to the ruler of the moon, who is protected by his lobster guard.
They later make their escape and return to Earth, where they land
in the ocean and are picked up by a passing ship.
     The Lubin Company in the U.S. would pirate and release the
film in America as A Trip to Mars.   The motion picture would years
later be included in The Great Méliès and as a prologue for Around
the World in 80 Days.
     Méliès had made an earlier version of A Trip to the Moon,
a variation of the same subject.

VOYAGE TO A PREHISTORIC PLANET   see   PLANETA BURG;
QUEEN OF BLOOD

VOYAGE TO THE BOTTOM OF THE SEA (Twentieth Century-Fox,
1961) C-105 min.

     Producer/director/story, Irwin Allen; screenplay, Allen and
Charles Bennett; music, Paul Sawtell and Bert Shefter; title song,
Russell Faith; orchestrator, Max Reese; art directors, Jack Martin
Smith and Herman A. Blumenthal; set decorators, Walter M. Scott
and John Sturtevant; assistant director, Ad Schaumer; makeup, Ben
Nye; costumes, Paul Zastupnevich; sound, Alfred Bruzlin and Warren
B. Delaplain; special camera effects, L. B. Abbott; underwater cam-
era, John Lamb; camera, Winton Hoch; editor, George Boemler.

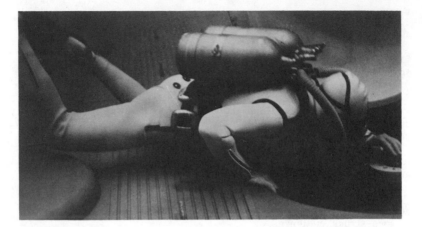

Scene from Voyage to the Bottom of the Sea (1961).

    Walter Pidgeon (Admiral Harriman Nelson); Joan Fontaine
(Dr. Susan Hiller); Barbara Eden (Cathy Connors); Peter Lorre
(Commodore Lucius Emery); Robert Sterling (Captain Lee Crane);
Michael Ansara (Miguel Alvarez); Frankie Avalon (Chip Romano);
Regis Toomey (Dr. Jamieson); John Litel (Admiral Crawford); How-
ard McNear (Congressman Parker); Henry Daniell (Dr. Zucco); Char-
les Tannen (Gleason); Mark Slade (Smith); Robert Easton (Sparks);
Larry Gray (Dr. Newmar); Skip Ward and Michael Ford (Crew Mem-
bers).

    Irwin Allen wrote, produced and directed and poured over $3
million into this rather humdrum sci-fi saga which was at its best
when demonstrating L. B. Abbott's special effects. A superior cast
was forced to mouth rather mediocre dialogue.
    On a trial run of the U.S.D.S. "Seaview," a giant glassnosed
experimental atomic submarine built by the U.S. Department of
Science, the craft travels under the polar cap. There a bombardment
of huge rocks signals a great explosion on the Earth's surface. When
the submarine surfaces, the sky is afire, with the Van Allen radiation belt circling the atmosphere and the temperature a very hot 135°.
Unable to contact Washington, the ship's commander (Walter Pidgeon)
takes the vessel to the Marianas to fire a Polaris missile into the
flames, which he hopes will cause the radiation belt to explode outward into space. Among those opposed to his wild plan is Dr. Susan
Hiller (Joan Fontaine), who initiates sabotage aboard the "Seaview"
before she meets a gruesome demise. The plan is eventually put into operation and proves successful. The world is saved.
    Time chortled, "Voyage rates poorly in science fiction's Foam-
Rubber Monster and Magnified Chameleon category; its only people
eaters are a shamefully lethargic giant squid, an octopus and a

shark.... Voyage, however, does creditably in Wires, Dials, and
Doodads; there is an atomic submarine almost as gorgeous as a producer's Cadillac, with a control room like a Parisian pinball machine. But it is in the often neglected Professor's Daughter and
Beautiful Lady Scientist department that the film excels. Joan Fontaine plays a World-Renowed Psychiatrist with fierce disregard for
tradition: she is snappish and mean to Walter Pidgeon, the World's
Greatest Scientist. Balance is provided by blonde Barbara Eden ...
she plays Pidgeon's secretary, not his daughter."

The film was successful enough in the action market to en-
gender a long-lived teleseries (1964-1968) of 110 segments.

VOYAGE TO THE END OF THE UNIVERSE   see IKARIE XB-1

VOYAGE TO THE PLANET OF PREHISTORIC WOMEN   see PLANE-
TA BURG

VYNALEZ ZKAZY (WEAPONS OF DESTRUCTION) (Czechoslovakian,
1958) 83 min.

Director, Karel Zeman; based on novels (including The Deadly
Invention) by Jules Verne; screenplay, Zeman and Frantisek Hrubin;
music, Zdenek Liska; camera, Jiri Tarantik.

A Jules Verne submarine in Vynalez Zkazy (1958).

Lubor Tokos (Simon Hart); Arnost Navratil (Professor Roche);
Miloslav Holub (Artigas); Jana Zatloukalova (Jana); Vaclav Kyzlink
(Serke); English-language prologue: Hugh Downs (Narrator).

"This is one picture for children adults can enjoy.... I don't
think its innovations are a major contribution to filmmaking but they
are a novelty that is well worth seeing. Carl [Karel] Zeman studied
the illustrations drawn for the Verne books in the 19th century and
decided their naive style was just the thing to use in a film to disguise the fact that Verne's science fiction is now very obsolete indeed.... Turning his camera on the original illustration, he suddenly made it come to life by switching the camera to his live actors
in the positions of the characters in the drawings" (Films in Review).
Professor Roche (Arnost Navratil), a nineteenth-century scientist, and his assistant, Simon Hart (Lubor Tokos), are whisked away
by pirates to a remote island in the Atlantic. The kidnappers' leader, Artigas (Miloslav Holub), wants to use Roche's improved explosive to conquer the world. Hart manages to dispatch a message for
help via a balloon. The assistant later escapes and returns with a
French submarine, but it is too late. The disillusioned Roche detonates the explosives, killing the pirates and himself, and destroying
the island.
At the 1958 Brussels Film Festival, this entry won the Best
Picture Award.
Variety enthused, "Certainly the oddest and essentially the
most artistically authentic translation of Verne's works to the screen."
But, pondered the New York Herald-Tribune, "... one can't help wondering if children of the space age can respond with any suitable awe
to forecasts long since surpassed by reality." They did.
For its U. S. release in 1961, the film was dubbed into English
and the title changed to The Fabulous World of Jules Verne.

THE WALKING DEAD (Warner Bros. , 1936) 66 min.

Producer, Lou Edelman; director, Michael Curtiz; story,
Ewart Adamson and Joseph Fields; screenplay, Adamson, Peter
Milne, Robert Andrews, and Lillie Hayward; makeup, Perc Westmore;
camera, Hal Mohr; editor, Tommy Pratt.
Boris Karloff (John Ellman); Ricardo Cortez (Nolan); Warren
Hull (Jimmy); Robert Strange (Merritt); Joseph King (Judge Shaw);
Edmund Gwenn (Dr. Beaumont); Marguerite Churchill (Nancy); Barton
MacLane (Loder); Henry O'Neill (Warner); Paul Harvey (Blackstone);
Joseph Sawyer (Trigger); Eddie Acuff (Betcha); Ruth Robinson (Mrs.
Shaw); Addison Richards (Prison Warden); Kenneth Harlan (Stephen
Martin); Miki Morita (Sako); Adrian Rosley (Florist).

A judge is murdered by big-time racketeers, led by Nolan
(Ricardo Cortez), a crooked lawyer. To avoid suspicion, the gang
frames an ex-convict, John Ellman (Boris Karloff), and Nolan acts as
his attorney. Naturally, Ellman is found guilty and sentenced to be
electrocuted. After the execution, scientist Dr. Beaumont (Edmund
Gwenn) asks to operate on the dead man to try to revive him. The

Ricardo Cortez, Marguerite Churchill, Boris Karloff, Henry O'Neill, Barton Machane, and Warren Hull in The Walking Dead (1936).

operation works but the patient seems more like a half-human robot than a living person. Later the executed man tracks down those responsible for his false conviction and frightens each of them into a violent demise. Surviving members of the gang, however, track Ellman to a deserted cemetery where they shoot him; as they speed off they run into a utility pole and are electrocuted. The end has the dying man telling Dr. Beaumont to let the dead rest, and expiring before he can answer the doctor's query, "What is death? Tell me-- you must!" (The patient breathes his last before he can reveal the mysteries of the afterlife.)

In the late Thirties and early Forties Karloff would frequently play a falsely-accused man who returns from legal execution to punish the real wrongdoers. These plotlines were in a way derivative of the actor's greatest screen triumph, the role of the monster in Frankenstein (q. v.).

Here we have a blend of science fiction/medical fiction/horror fiction. Michael Curtiz' slick direction, Perc Westmore's excellent makeup job, Hal Mohr's low-keyed cinematography, and a diverting cast add up to very possible entertainment.

WAR-GODS OF THE DEEP (American International, 1965) C-83 min.

Executive producer, George Willoughby; producer, Daniel

Vincent Price in War-Gods of the Deep (1965).

Haller; director, Jacques Tourneur; based on the poem by Edgar Al-
lan Poe; screenplay, Charles Bennett and Louis M. Heyward; addi-
tional dialogue, David Whittaker; music, Stanley Black; underwater
camera director, John Lamb; special effects, Frank George and Lee
Boure; camera, Stephen Dade; editor, Jordan Hales.
    Vincent Price (The Captain); Tab Hunter (Ben Harris); David
Tomlinson (Harold Tufuell Jones); Susan Hart (Jill Tegellis); John Le
Mesurier (Reverend Jonathan Ives); Henry Oscar (Mumford); Derek
Newark (Dan); Roy Patrick (Simon); Anthony Selby (George); Michael
Heyland (Bill); Steven Brooke (Ted); William Hurondell (Tom); Jim
Spearman (Jack); Dennis Blake (Harry); Arthur Hewlett, Walter Spar-
row, and John Barrett (Fishermen); Herbert (The Rooster); George
Ricarde (Bart Allison); Hilda Campbell and Barbara Bruce (Guests).
    A.k.a. City in the Sea (British title) / City under the Sea /
War-Lords of the Deep.

    Beautiful young Jill Tegellis (Susan Hart) is kidnapped from her
Cornish Coast home and two of her friends, engineer Ben Harris (Tab
Hunter) and a crazy artist named Harold Tufuell Jones (David Tomlinson), along with his pet rooster, go to her rescue. Their search
leads them through secret doorways and subterranean passages to a

strange city under the sea inhabited by sailors and fishermen who are centuries old. The city is ruled by an eternally young king (Vincent Price) who heats the metropolis from a nearby volcano and obtains air through hoses connected to the surface. The ruler believes the young woman is a reincarnation of his beloved late wife.

Later the volcano's activity threatens the underwater city and the Captain tries to use Harris to aid him in protecting his town. But when the volcano erupts, Harris, Jones, and Jill make their escape and start a long swim to the surface, being chased by the Captain's scaly serpent men who are armed with long bows. The volcanic action, however, catches the pursuers off guard and destroys them and the city. The fleeing trio makes it to the surface and safety.

This adventure/sci-fi tale was supposedly based on two Edgar Allan Poe short stories but it resembled ill-adapted Jules Verne. Some of the underwater settings were appealing, but the magical ingredient of imagination was missing. As Films and Filming noted, "[Director Jacques] Tourneur describes it as an adventure film and the feeble comic element doesn't go against this; but there ought to be some sense of tension and uncertainty about straying into a strange and hostile world, even if horror and suspense aren't to be part of the recipe."

WAR OF THE COLOSSAL BEAST (American International, 1958) 68 min. (Final scene in color)

Executive producers, James H. Nicholson and Samuel Z. Arkoff; producer/director/story, Bert I. Gordon; screenplay, George Worthing Yates; assistant directors, H. E. Mendelson and John W. Rogers; music composer/conductor, Albert Glasser; sound, Josef von Stroheim; special effects, Gordon; camera, Jack Marta; editor, Ronald Sinclair.

Sally Fraser (Joyce Manning); Dean Parkin (Colonel Glenn Manning); Roger Pace (Major Baird); Russ Bender (Dr. Carmichael); Charles Stewart (Captain Harris); George Becwar (Swanson); Robert Hernandez (Miguel); Rico Alaniz (Sergeant Luis Murillo); George Alexander (Army Officer); George Navarro (Mexican Doctor); John McNamara (Neurologist); Bob Garnet (Pentagon Correspondent); Roy Gordon (Major); Bill Giorgio (Bus Driver); Loretta Nicholson (Joan); June Jocelyn (Mother); Stan Chambers (TV Announcer).

Bert I. Gordon completed his Cyclops trilogy (The Amazing Colossal Man and The Cyclops [both q. v.] were the other two) on an even weaker note. Without Glenn Langan to play the role of Colonel Manning, who is sixty feet tall after exposure to plutonium, this follow-up lacked what little charm the original had. Variety observed, "Gordon has interpolated a film clip from the early film into this one, as a dream sequence, and unfortunately it is more exciting than anything in the current version...."

The film picks up the storyline where the first entry left off, with Colonel Manning falling from Boulder Dam. The fall does not kill the giant, but it does destroy one of his eyes, scars his head,

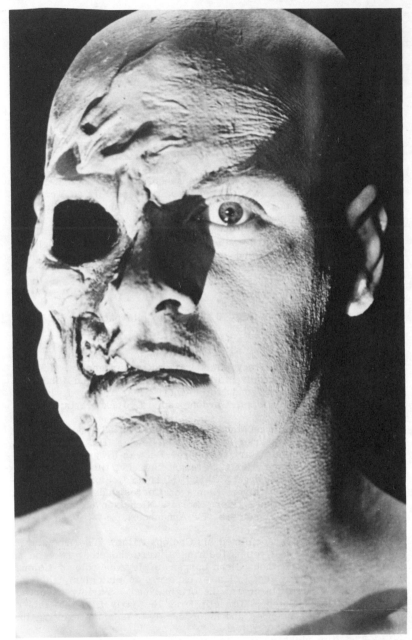

Dean Parkin in War of the Colossal Beast (1958).

and turns him into an oversized, rampaging maniac. The Army manages to corral the creature but he escapes and embarks on a terror spree, destroying everything in his path. Finally the titan is doomed when he deliberately walks into high voltage power lines, ending his bizarre existence.

The low-grade production values, synonymous with Gordon's output, are not even forgivable.

British release title: The Terror Strikes.

WAR OF THE WORLDS (Paramount, 1953) C-85 min.

Producer, George Pal; director, Byron Haskin; based on the novel by H. G. Wells; screenplay, Barré Lyndon; art directors, Albert Nozaki and Hal Pereira; music, Leith Stevens; astronomical art, Chesley Bonestell; special effects, Gordon Jennings, Wallace Kelley, Paul Lerpae, Ivyl Burks, Jan Domela, and Irmin Roberts; sound effects, Gene Garvin; camera, George Barnes; editor, Everett Douglas.

Gene Barry (Dr. Clayton Forrester); Ann Robinson (Sylvia Van Buren); Les Tremayne (General Mann); Bob Cornthwaite (Dr. Pryor); Sandro Giglio (Dr. Bilderbeck); Lewis Martin (Pastor Collins); Ann Codee (Dr. DuPrey); Walter Sande (Sheriff); Houseley Stevenson, Jr. (Aide to General Mana); Paul Frees (Radio Announcer); Vernon Rich (Colonel Heffner); Bill Phipps (Wash Perry); Paul Birch (Alonzo Hogue); Jack Kruschen (Salvatore); Robert Rockwell (Ranger); Sir Cedric Hardwicke (Narrator).

This adaptation of H. G. Wells' 1898 novel is best remembered for its fabulous special effects, for which Gordon Jennings won, posthumously, an Academy Award. Producer Pal's decision to modernize the book and switch its setting from England to California robbed the film of atmosphere and feeling.

A small California town is suddenly invaded by a space craft. The townspeople gather around the ship and a clergyman (Lewis Martin) approaches the ship with a cross, a bible, and a message of peace. He is promptly killed by a Martian death ray, and the war of the worlds is on. An atomic physicist named Dr. Clayton Forrester (Gene Barry) witnesses the event. Later he and Sylvia Van Buren (Ann Robinson), like the rest of the population, try to flee from the bellicose Martians who are now swamping the world, bent on destroying the planet. All the weapons known to mankind, including the atomic bomb, are useless against the super-intelligent alien marauders with the death-dealing heat guns. Finally Forrester, Sylvia, and a group of refugees huddle in a church, seeking salvation and awaiting the horrible end of their world. Suddenly the metallic clinking noise of the Martian ships stops. The war has ended; the Martians are dead. It develops that common Earth germs did in the invaders; their systems were not able to combat them.

The battle scenes are excellently staged in this color feature. Especially memorable is the sequence in which the long, tenacled spider-like arm of a Martian reaches for Sylvia and Forrester lopes off the alien's head. Sir Cedric Hardwicke's stately narration at the opening and closing of the film provide a properly eerie, mood and lends tone to the production.

John Baxter judged the film from a historical perspective in Science Fiction in the Cinema (1970): "Squarely in the tradition of the American sf film, where all attempts are bent to creating a literal depiction of the fantastic rather than evoking a mood; all but two of the film's sequences are shot indoors, and model work is extensively used. Despite Haskin's energetic visual style, the film has the smooth unreality of a comic strip."

While the film was popular at the box-office, it had nowhere near the traumatic effects of Orson Welles' historical 1938 broadcast of Wells' tale on "Mercury Theatre on the Air."

In mid-1976, Richard Burton narrated a rock adaptation of the H. G. Wells' work. The LP album boasts the guest singing of rock star David Essex, theme music by Jeff Wayne, and spoken roles scripted by Britisher Doreen Juggler. The album was packaged in London, with Burton recording his segments in Hollywood. The English rock band, The Fighting Machine, provided the basic rock music sections.

WEAPONS OF DESTRUCTION see VYNALEZ ZKAZY

WESTWORLD (MGM, 1973) C-89 min.

Producer, Paul N. Lazarus III; associate producer, Michael I. Rachmil; director/screenplay, Michael Crichton; assistant director, Claude Binyon, Jr.; visual effects co-ordinator, Brent Sellstrom; automated image processing, John Whitney, Jr. and Information International Inc.; art director, Herman Blumenthal; set decorator, John Austin; makeup, Frank Griffin and Irving Pringle; action scenes co-ordinator, Dick Ziker; sound, Richard Church and Harry W. Tetrick; special effects, Charles Schulthies; camera, Gene Polito; editor, David Bretherton.

Yul Brynner (Gunslinger); Richard Benjamin (Peter Martin); James Brolin (John Blane); Norman Bartold (Medieval Knight); Alan Oppenheimer (Chief Supervisor); Victoria Shaw (Medieval Queen); Dick Van Patten (Banker); Linda Scott (Arlette); Steve Franklin (Technician); Michael Mikler (Black Knight); Terry Wilson (Sheriff); Majel Barrett (Miss Carrie); Anna Randall (Servant Girl); Julie Marcus (Girl in Dungeon); Sharyn Wynters (Apache Girl); Anne Bellamy (Middle-Aged Woman); Chris Holter (Stewardess); Charles Seel (Bellhop); Wade Crosby (Bartender); Lin Henson (Ticket Girl); Nora Marlowe (Hostess).

This frightening tale of a futuristic Disneyland gone haywire involves two young Chicago businessmen, Peter Martin (Richard Benjamin) and John Blane (James Brolin), who take a paid vacation at Delos, a fantasy world utilizing space age technology to recreate periods of the past in life-like detail. The two men choose to reside in Westworld, a recreation of the American West of the 1880s in which the main inhabitants are human-looking robots. The contemporary duo enjoy wearing Western garb, visiting an atmospheric

saloon where Martin shoots a black-garbed robot-gunfighter (Yul
Brynner), and sampling the pleasures of the automated saloon girls
(who are also equipped for the bedroom).   But the vacation goes
awry when malfunctions in the robots cause them to deviate from
their programmed roles and to kill or maim the tourists.   The gunslinger (Brynner) in Westworld becomes the deadliest menace.   He
kills Blane and hunts Martin through the various destroyed worlds of
Delos.   Finally Martin causes the robot to short-circuit and eventually burn, ending the horrible experience.

    Michael Crichton, who wrote the novel The Andromeda Strain
(q. v.), turned scripter/director.   On the whole he performed com-
mendably in his assignment, turning out a generally creditable sci-
fi film.   The various backgrounds for Westworld were: Mojave Desert landscapes, the gardens of the Harold Lloyd estate, and a variety
of recreated sets on several MGM sound stages.   Special contact
lenses were designed to distinguish the robots from the humans, and
computer filmmaking was utilized to give an accurate display of the
robot's vision.   The premise of the film, that sophisticated man-
conceived machinery can go amuck (rebel?), has long intrigued scientists and sci-fi writers.   This concept is neatly packaged with the
common man's delight in reliving rough-and-tumble myths from the
past ("when a man was a man").

    The film grossed a healthy $3.4 million in U.S. and Canadian
domestic rentals, the last such big grosser before MGM dissolved its
releasing company.   In 1975 the movie was re-issued with ten minutes

Yul Brynner and James Brolin in Westworld (1973).

deleted from the footage to allow for a PG rating (instead of the
original R, Restricted, rating).   In 1976, American International produced a sequel to Westworld, entitled Futureworld filmed
largely in Houston and again starring Yul Brynner.

WHEN WORLDS COLLIDE (Paramount, 1951) C-93 min.

     Producer, George Pal; director, Rudolph Maté; based on the
novel by Edwin Balmer and Philip Wylie; screenplay, Sydney Boehm;
art directors, Hal Pereira and Al Nozaki; technical advisor, Chesley
Bonestell; music, Leith Stevens; special effects, Gordon Jennings and
Harry Barndollar; process camera, Farciot Edouart; camera, John
F. Seitz and W. Howard Greene.
     Richard Derr (Dave Randall); Barbara Rush (Joyce); Peter
Hanson (Tony); John Hoyt (Stanton); Larry Keating (Dr. Hendron); Ju-
dith Ames (Julie Cummings); Stephen Chase (Dean Frey); Frank Cady
(Harold Ferris); Hayden Rorke (Dr. Bronson); Sandro Giglio (Ottinger);
Mary Murphy (Student); Laura Elliot (Stewardess).

     When Worlds Collide is a lushly-photographed George Pal fea-
ture, adapted from a work written in the Twenties.   Cecil B. DeMille
had planned to film the project in 1934, but it was seventeen years
until George Pal engineered this worthwhile production.   While hardly

Rocket ship in When World Collide (1951).

a top-flight classic, it is technically sound enough to be properly considered one of Pal's better ventures into the sci-fi genre.

Pilot Dave Randall (Richard Derr) is assigned to fly top-secret photographs from a South American observatory to the United States. When he arrives the pilot ingratiates himself with a scientist and is advised that the Earth is about to collide with a dying star called Bellus, which is roaming through the solar system. The scientist also tells him that the only hope for humanity is the colonization of Bellus' satellite Zyra, which appears to have an atmosphere similar to the Earth's.

A rocketship is prepared, built from funds provided by a billionaire who decides to go along on the voyage. Randall falls in love with Joyce (Barbara Rush), the scientist's daughter, but he has a rival among the ship's crew. Also the scientist and the benefactor have a falling out; the former causes himself and the billionaire to be killed so as to leave the journey to Zyra to a younger group of people. The space craft blasts off to Zyra in time as Bellus storms into the Earth's gravitational pull, causing the mass destruction of cities and the end of the two heavenly bodies. When the rocket lands, the target planet appears to be a lush, green world--a new Eden.

Paramount's special effects department won an Academy Award for its efforts on the picture, which enjoyed visually stunning scenes (e. g. , the construction of the rocket, its takeoff, and the final destruction of Earth).

Arthur C. Clarke wrote in the Journal of British Interplanetary Society in 1952, "On balance, When Worlds Collide certainly contains enough interesting material to make it worth a visit. Whether any producer of lesser genius than D. W. Griffith could have handled this theme properly is a subject on which everyone will have his own opinion."

As an offshoot of the giant disaster film cycle, Paramount is planning a remake of When Worlds Collide as a 1977 release.

WHERE HAVE ALL THE PEOPLE GONE (NBC-TV, 1974) C-73 min.

Producer, Jerry Isenberg; director, John Llwellyn Moxey; based on the story by Lewis John Carlino; teleplay, Carlino and Sandor Stern.
With: Peter Graves, Verna Bloom, Ken Sanson, George O'-Hanlon, Jr. , Kathleen Quinlan, Michael-James Wixted.

A man (Peter Graves) is on a camping trip with his son and daughter when a solar flare hits the Earth. The three were in a cave during the incident. When they emerge they discover that their radio is dead and their car ignition will not work. Soon they find that several people have literally disintegrated. Panicked, they start a hurried trek home to find the mother of the family. Along the way they find more dead, deserted homes and towns, packs of wild dogs, and a frightened girl. Eventually they are joined by several other people on their journey. When they reach home, they are sickened to find that the mother has also disintegrated from the effects of the

solar flare which has killed off most of the world's population.   The
survivors decide to head for the mountains to start a new life and
world.   (The ending appeared to be the opening set-up for a series,
but this pilot telefeature did not generate a continuing show.)
        One of the highlights of this made-for-TV movie was its fo-
cus on the effects of crisis on varying individuals.   It made the rather hackneyed premise acceptable.   Peter Graves as the staunch father figure was especially suitable for the proceedings.

THE WISHING MACHINE (AUTONAT NA PRANI) (Xerox Films, 1971)
C-75 min.

        Director/screenplay, Josef Pinkava; adaptor, Jiri Blazek; mu-
sic, William Bukovy; scenic designer, Zdenek Rozkopal; camera,
Jiri Kolin.
        English-language version: executive producer, Robert Braver-
man; additional music, Arthur De Cenzo; lyrics, Robert Braverman.

        Few sci-fi films are produced especially for children, although
many have either a juvenile quality or plotlines intended to appeal to
undemanding audiences.   Genre films for children would be deemed
risky box-office in this country, but in Europe--especially Eastern
Europe--pictures are often geared directly to young audiences.   A
case in point was The Wishing Machine, English-adapted/dubbed from
the Czech-French co-production, Autonat Na Prani (1967).

Two young boys on a trip to the moon, in The Wishing Machine (1971).

Women of the Prehistoric Planet   361

The film is about the imagination of children and how they
may come to have a greater appreciation and understanding of the
real world by comparing the things they imagine to reality.   Here
two boys attend a carnival and view a wishing machine.   They are
so impressed by it that they try to build one of their own.   Thanks
to their contraption, they almost make it to the Moon.   For their
troubles they are reprimanded by the military and they learn that
dreams and reality do not always mix.
"... the tone of the picture is briskly gentle and never sticky.
Best of all, the entire enterprise is geared to the viewpoint of the
capering youngsters, minus cutesie-piece condescension" (New York
Times).

WOMEN OF THE PREHISTORIC PLANET (Realart, 1966) C-87 min.

Producer, George Edwards; director/screenplay, Arthur
Pierce; art director, Paul Sylos; assistant director, Jack Voglin;
camera, Archie Dalzell; editor, George White.
Wendell Corey (Admiral King); Keith Larsen (Commander
Scott); John Agar (Doctor); Irene Tsu (Linda); and Paul Gilbert, Mer-
ry Anders, and Suzie Kaye.

This film marked the re-emergence of Jack Broder's Realart
Pictures, a company which made many a B film in the early Fifties.
As this entry demonstrated, the quality of its product had not improved
in the interim.
En route home from a planet in the Centaurus star system,
a space ship with its crew and captives crash-lands on an unexplored
new planet.   Three months later, Admiral King (Wendell Corey) commands a craft exploration trip to find survivors.   Due to a time
warp, eighteen years have passed on the landing site and the sole survivor, a Centaurian child has grown to adulthood.   He is attracted
immediately to Linda (Irene Tsu) from the rescue ship and takes her
prisoner.   By the time she convinces him to return her to Admiral
King, that ship has been forced to leave due to a volcanic eruption.
From his orbiting position, Admiral King decides to name the unknown planet "Earth."
Even with the presence of such screen veterans as Wendell
Corey, Keith Larsen and John Agar, this was a "minor entry on
cosmic flight" (Variety).   Production values were negligible.

WORLD WITHOUT END (Allied Artists, 1956) C-80 min.

Producer, Richard Heermance; director/screenplay, Edward
Bernds; art director, David Milton; music, Leith Stevens; special
effects, Milton Rice; camera, Ellsworth Fredericks; editor, Eda
Warren.
With: Hugh Marlowe, Nancy Gates, Rod Taylor, Lisa Mon-
tell, Nelson Leigh, Shawn Smith, Paul Brinegar.

Four astronauts return to Earth after orbiting Mars in a test

Shawn Smith in World without End (1956).

space flight.   They belatedly discover they have been caught in a time
warp and have landed on the Earth of the twenty-sixth century.   By
this point the planet's population has been decimated by a nuclear war.
On the globe's surface live one-eyed mutants, ugly, once human, survivors of the holocaust.   Below the terrain exist the hostile survivors
of the human race.   After a spell, one of the astronauts (Hugh Marlowe) falls in love with one of the underground people and they unite
to rid the surface of the killer mutants and a giant spider.   The astronauts realize they will never be able to return to the Earth they
once knew.   Thus they agree to remain and help build a new civilization and a fresh future.
        Decent acting and a pliable storyline made this an entertain-
ing entry.   Time, unfortunately, has not been especially kind to this
picture.   Its story was dated even when the film was issued and the
plot ploy has been re-used frequently in many versions and styles.

X--THE MAN WITH THE X-RAY EYES (American International, 1963)
C-80 min.

        Executive producers, James H. Nicholson and Samuel Z.

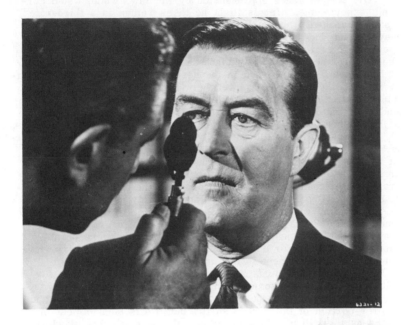

Harold J. Stone and Ray Milland in X--The Man with the X-Ray Eyes (1963).

Arkoff; producer/director, Roger Corman; story, Ray Russell; screenplay, Robert Dillon and Russell; music, Les Baxter; art director, Daniel Haller; costumes, Marjorie Corso; makeup, Ted Coodley; assistant director, Jack Bohrer; camera, Floyd Crosby; editor, Anthony Carras.

    Ray Milland (Dr. James Xavier); Diana Van Der Vlis (Dr. Diane Fairfax); Harold J. Stone (Dr. Sam Brant); John Hoyt (Dr. Willard Benson); Don Rickles (Crane); John Dierkes (Preacher); Lorie Summers (Party Dancer); Vicki Lee (Young Girl Patient); Kathryn Hart (Mrs. Mart); Carol Irey (Woman Patient).

    A.k.a. The Man with the X-Ray Eyes.

    Dr. James Xavier (Ray Milland), working for the betterment of mankind through experiments with the human eyes, develops a serum which increases the power of sight. He experiments on himself with the serum and finds that he is able to see various objects. (At a party he is voyeuristically amused at being able to see through women's clothing.) Dr. Xavier's girlfriend (Diana Van Der Vlis) and his friend/assistant Dr. Sam Brant (Harold J. Stone) oppose his working in this uncharted field. In an ensuing argument Brant is accidentally pushed out a window to his death.

Dr. Xavier fears apprehension by the law, which would curtail his experiments. In his flight he takes refuge in a third-rate sideshow managed by con artist Crane (Don Rickles). By this point the eye serum has become addictive and so powerful that the scientist cannot tolerate light of any kind and must exist in perpetual darkness, swathed under heavy black cloth to avoid dreadful eye pain. Still later, while being chased in the desert, Dr. Xavier stumbles onto a revivalist camp where a preacher (John Dierkes) asks him what troubles him. The scientist replies that his eyes do. "If thine eye offend thee, pluck it out!" the revivalist extorts. Xavier does just that; but by now his eyes have degenerated into nothing but blackness.

Cinematographer Floyd Crosby filmed this picture in "Specterama," a new optical effect in which an arrangement of prisms and light images are bent and colors change. Resulting distortions appear as eerie color paintings in actual motion. This effect, plus an overall mysteriousness, gives the production the proper offbeat feeling, heightened by Oscar-winner Milland's sturdy performance.

The film, which was voted best picture in 1963 at the Trieste Science Fiction Film Festival, even pleased--to a degree--the hard-to-woo New York Times: "... it shapes up as a modern parable about a dedicated doctor done in by humanity after he tampers with the unknown. The concept is original and the tone is thoughtful." The Times summed it up as an "an odd little movie that aims for sensible novelty and to some extent succeeds."

Granted, many of the characterizations are stereotypes and the latter portion of the film is shrill, but it was such offbeat productions as these that helped to solidify Roger Corman's standing in his craft.

YEAR 2889 see THE DAY THE WORLD ENDED

ZARDOZ (Twentieth Century-Fox, 1974) C-105 min.

Producer, John Boorman; associate producer, Charles Orme; director/screenplay, Boorman; story associate, Bill Stair; production designer, Anthony Pratt; design associate, Stair; set decorators, John Hoesli and Martin Atkinson; music, David Munrow; costumes, Christel Kruse Boorman; assistant director, Simon Relph; makeup, Basil Newall; sound, Liam Saurin; sound re-recording, Doug Turner; special effects, Gerry Johnston; camera, Geoffrey Unsworth; editor, John Merritt.

Sean Connery (Zed); Charlotte Rampling (Consuella); Sara Kestelman (May); Sally Anne Newton (Avalow); John Alderton (Friend); Niall Buggy (Arthur Frayn); Bosco Hogan (George Saden); Jessica Swift (Apathetic); Bairbre Dowling (Star); Christopher Casson (Old Scientist); Reginald Jarman (Death).

In the year 2293 Earth's society is split into two distinct groups: the Eternals, who dwell in the Vortex and the tribes of Brutals who exist in the Outlands. The Vortex is an Eden-like existence where death does not exist and the birth rate is nil. Imprisoned within the Vortex are the Renegades, a group of non-conformists, and the Apathetics, who live in catatonia because they cannot cope with eternal life. In the Vortex communication is done through telepathy as well as the usual means; sleep is non-existent, as is sex. The Eternals utilize a group called the Exterminators to control the Brutals in the Outlands, largely to govern their population growth. The Exterminators worship a god called Zardoz, a giant stone head which floats through the air and rains bullets on the Brutals.

In this complex setting, an Exterminator named Zed (Sean Connery) discovers that Zardoz is a false god, only a machine controlled by a man. He kills the latter. Zed follows the God-machine back to the Vortex and is captured. Geneticist May (Sara Kestelman) conducts experiments and determines that he is both mentally and physically superior to those in the Vortex. Later, Zed impregnates May and arouses the ire of another female scientist, Consuella (Charlotte Rampling). Knowing he will be killed and has nothing to lose, Zed determines to free the Brutals from their slave status. With the help of May he finds a flaw in the Tabernacle crystals that control the fate of the Vortex. His plan causes time to turn backward briefly, and the Exterminators enter the area and slaughter the three groups within the Vortex. Zed escapes with Consuella. The finale finds them having children, growing old and dying together.

To say the least, "Zardoz eventually tailspins into a philosophical labyrinth from which the spectator, unlike the persistent hero, has little chance of escaping into lucid enlightenment" (British Monthly Film Bulletin). Yet, despite its overcomplex plotline and posturing, Zardoz is a captivating intrigue. Certainly the superior mounting and solid acting, especially by Connery (who replaced a previously-signed Burt Reynolds), make for a thoughtful presentation. One can almost forgive filmmaker's Boorman's attempt to turn out his own variation of 2001: A Space Odyssey (q. v.) in a highly different posture and format. Frank Jackson wrote in Cinefantastique, "The value of Boorman's messages can be debated, but that he has created a well-integrated vision of the present/future cannot be denied."

Twentieth Century-Fox did its best to market the film to a wide audience and in the process of promoting it as a successor to its Planet of the Apes (q. v.) series, drove away many intellectuals. The expensively-produced film only grossed $1.5 million in its initial U.S./Canadian release; it was re-issued in 1975.

ZEX   see   ESCAPEMENT

ZOMBIES OF THE STRATOSPHERE (Republic, 1952) twelve chapters

Associate producer, Franklin Adreon; director, Fred C. Brannon; screenplay, Ronald Davidson; music, Stanley Wilson; special effects, Howard and Theodore Lydecker; camera, John MacBurnie.
Judd Holdren (Larry Martin); Aline Towne (Sue Davis); Wilson Wood (Bob Wilson); Lane Bradford (Marex); John Crawford (Roth); Craig Kelly (Mr. Steele); Ray Boyle (Shane); Leonard Nimoy (Narab);

Tom Steele (Truck Driver); Dale Van Sickel (Telegraph Operator);
Roy Engel (Lawson); Jack Harden (Kerr); Paul Stader (Fisherman);
Gayle Kellogg (Dick); Jack Shea (Policeman); Robert Garabedian (Elah).
    Chapters: 1) The Zombies Vanguard; 2) Battle of the Rock-
ets; 3) Undersea Agent; 4) Contraband Cargo; 5) The Iron Executioner; 5) Murder Mine; 7) Death on the Waterfront; 8) Hostage for Murder; 9) The Human Torpedo; 10) Flying Gas Chamber; 11) Man vs.
Monster; 12) Tomb of the Traitors.

    Long before the advent of the "Star Trek" teleseries, this
serial offered Leonard Nimoy in the role of an alien.
    A rocket ship lands on earth from another planet. Its passen-
gers, Marex (Lane Bradford) and Narab (Nimoy), ally themselves
with two Earthlings: Roth (John Crawford) and Shane (Ray Boyle).
Their plan is to blow the Earth out of its orbit so that their own
planet can be brought into the cycle of the Earth's present atmoshere/
climate. The quartet inducts a reluctant doctor (Stanley Waxman)
into their scheme to construct a hydrogen bomb for their sinister
plan.
    However, the aliens are opposed by Larry Martin (Judd Hold-
ren) of the Inter-Planetary Patrol, a universal policing organization.
He and his two assistants (Aline Towne and Wilson Wood) eventually
are successful in quashing this threat to the world's existence.
    This low-quality follow-up to Radar Men from the Moon (q. v.)
had the hero utilizing the same flying suit employed in King of the
Rocket Men and Radar Men, so that stock footage could be more
easily employed.
    In 1957 Republic issued a feature version of the uninspired
chapterplay, called Satan's Satellites.

ZONTAR: THE THING FROM VENUS see IT CONQUERED THE
WORLD

SCIENCE FICTION SHOWS ON RADIO AND TELEVISION

Compiled by Vincent Terrace

RADIO

Arch Oboler's Plays (a. k. a. Arch Oboler Presents) (Syndicated 1945).

Astounding Science Fiction (Syndicated - date unknown).

The Avenger. With: James Monks, Helen Adamson, Allyn Edwards (Syndicated 1946).

B. B. C. Science Fiction (British; Syndicated 1950s).

Beyond Tomorrow (CBS 1950).

The Black Book. With: Paul Frees, John Dehner (CBS 1952).

The Black Castle. With: Don Douglas (Syndicated 1940s).

Buck Rogers in the 25th Century. With: Matt Crowley, Adele Ronson, Alaine Melchior (Syndicated 1931, 1939).

Captain Midnight. With: Ed Prentiss, Angeline Orr, Bill Rose, Art Hern (Mutual 1940).

Chandu, The Magician. With: Jason Robards, Sr. , Gayne Whitman, Tom Collins (Blue Network 1932).

Creeps by Night. With: Boris Karloff (Host) (Blue Network 1944).

Dark Fantasy (NBC 1941).

Destination Space (NBC 1949).

Dimension X (a. k. a. X Minus One). With: Norman Rose (Host) (NBC 1950).

Escape. With: William Conrad, Paul Frees (Narrators) (CBS 1947).

Exploring the Unknown. With guest performers: Walter Huston, Orson Welles (Mutual 1945).

Exploring Tomorrow (Mutual 1940s).

Flash Gordon. With: Gale Gordon, Maurice Franklin, Bruno Wick (Mutual 1935).

The Halls of Fantasy. With: Jim Ameche (Host) (NBC 1953).

Inner Sanctum (a. k. a. Inner Sanctum Mysteries). With: Raymond Edward Johnson, Paul McGrath, House Jameson (Hosts) (Blue Network 1941; CBS 1942).

Into the Future with Biff Baker (No credits given) (Mutual 1942).

Lights Out. With guest performers: Ted Maxwell, Betty Winkler, Sidney Ellstrom, Vincent Price (NBC, CBS 1942).

The Mysterious Traveler. With: Maurice Tarplin (Mutual 1943).

Mystery House. With: Nanette Sargeant, Forrest Lewis (Syndicated 1946).

The Phantom (Syndicated c. mid-1930s).

The Planet Man (Syndicated - date unknown).

Quiet Please. With: Ernest Chappell (Host) (ABC 1948).

S. F. '68 (British; Syndicated 1968).

Satin's Waitin'. With: Frank Graham (CBS 1950).

The Sealed Book (Mutual 1945).

The Shadow. With: Orson Welles, Brett Morrison, Bill Johnstone, Agnes Moorehead, Lesley Woods, Santos Ortega (Mutual 1936).

The Space Adventures of Super Noodle. With: Charles Flynn, Robert Englund (CBS 1952).

Space Patrol. With: Ed Kemmer (ABC 1950).

Starr of Space. With: John Larch, Jane Harlan (ABC 1953).

The Strange Dr. Karnac. With: James Van Dyke, Jean Ellen (Blue Network 1943).

The Strange Dr. Weird. With: Maurice Tarplin, Dick Willard (Mutual 1944).

Superman. With: Clayton "Bud" Collyer, Joan Alexander, Jackie Kelk (Mutual 1943).

Superstition. With: Ralph Bell (The Voice of Superstition) (ABC 1948).

Tom Corbett, Space Cadet. With: Frankie Thomas, Al Markhim
(NBC 1950).

2000 Plus (NBC 1950).

Weird Circle (Syndicated 1940s).

The Witch's Tale. With: Adelaide Fitz-Allan, Martha Wentworth
(Mutual 1934).

TELEVISION

The Adventures of Superman. With: George Reeves, Noel Neill,
Phyllis Coates, John Hamilton, Jack Larson, Robert Shayne (Syndicated 1953).

The Amazing Three (Animated Cartoon) (Japanese; Syndicated 1967).

Aquaman (Animated Cartoon). With the voices of: Marvin Miller (Syndicated 1970).

The Atom Squad. With: Bob Hastings, Bob Courtleigh (NBC 1953).

Batman. With: Adam West, Burt Ward, Yvonne Craig, Neil Hamilton (ABC 1966).

The Bionic Woman. With: Lindsay Wagner, Richard Anderson (ABC
1976).

Buck Rogers in the 25th Century. With: Kem Dibbs, Lou Prentiss,
Harry Sothern (ABC 1950).

Captain Midnight (a. k. a. Jet Jackson, Flying Commando). With:
Richard Webb, Sid Melton (CBS 1954).

Captain Scarlet and the Mysterons (Marionette Adventure). With the
voices of: Francis Matthews, Donald Gray, Ed Bishop, Sylvia
Anderson (Syndicated 1967).

Captain Video and His Video Rangers. With: Richard Coogan, Al
Hodge, Don Hastings (DuMont 1949).

Captain Z-ro. With: Roy Steffins, Bobby Trumbull (Syndicated 1955).

Colonel Bleep (Animated Cartoon) (Syndicated 1957).

Commando Cody. With: Judd Holdren, Aline Towne, William Schallert (NBC 1955).

Cyborg Big "X" (Animated Cartoon) (Syndicated 1965).

Dark Shadows. With: Joan Bennett, Alexandra Moltke, Jonathan
    Frid, Nancy Barrett, Louis Edmonds (ABC 1966).

Dr. Who. With: Peter Cushing, Jon Pertwee, Jennie Linden (Bri-
    tish; Syndicated 1966).

The 8th Man (Animated Cartoon) (Japanese; Syndicated 1965).

Evil Touch. With: Anthony Quayle (Host) (Syndicated 1973).

The Fantastic Four (Animated Cartoon). With the voices of: Gerald
    Mohr, Jo Anne Pflug, Paul Frees (ABC 1967).

Fantastic Voyage (Animated Cartoon). With the voices of: Marvin
    Miller, Jane Webb (ABC 1968).

Far Out Space Nuts. With: Bob Denver, Chuck McCann (CBS 1975).

Fireball XL-5 (Marionette Adventure). With the voices of: Paul
    Maxwell, Sylvia Anderson, John Bluthal (NBC 1963).

Flash Gordon. With: Steve Holland, Irene Champlin, Joseph Nash
    (Syndicated 1953).

Frankenstein Jr. and the Impossibles (Animated Cartoon). With the
    voices of: Ted Cassidy, Paul Frees, Don Messick (CBS 1966).

Ghost Story (a. k. a. Circle of Fear). With: Sebastian Cabot (Host)
    (NBC 1972).

The Gemini Man. With: Ben Murphy, Katherine Crawford (NBC
    1976).

The Ghost Busters. With: Forrest Tucker, Larry Storch, Bob
    Burns (CBS 1975).

Gigantor (Animated Cartoon) (Japanese; Syndicated 1966).

Goober and the Ghost Chasers (Animated Cartoon). With the voices
    of: Paul Winchell, Jerry Dexter, Jo Anne Harris, Ronnie Schell
    (ABC 1973).

Great Ghost Tales. With guest performers: Lee Grant, Kevin Mc-
    Carthy, Peter Brandon, Richard Thomas (NBC 1961).

The Herculoids (Animated Cartoon). With the voices of: Mike Road,
    Don Messick, Virginia Gregg (CBS 1967).

High Tension (Syndicated 1953).

In Search of ... With: Leonard Nimoy (Host) (Syndicated 1976).

The Invaders. With: Roy Thinnes (ABC 1967).

The Invisible Man. With: Lisa Daniely, Deborah Walting, Ernest Clark (British; Syndicated 1958).

The Invisible Man. With: David McCallum, Melinda Fee, Craig Stevens (NBC 1975).

Isis (a. k. a. The Shazam! -Isis Hour). With: JoAnna Cameron, Brian Cutler, Joanna Pang (CBS 1975).

Johnny Cypher in Dimension Zero (Animated Cartoon) (Syndicated 1967).

Johnny Jupiter. With: Vaughn Taylor, Wright King, Cliff Hall (Du-Mont 1953).

Johnny Sokko and His Flying Robot. With: Milsundbu Kanko, Akjo Ito (Japanese; Syndicated 1968).

Josie and the Pussycats in Outer Space (Animated Cartoon). With the voices of: Janet Waldo, Jackie Joseph, Barbara Pariot, Jerry Dexter (CBS 1972).

Journey to the Center of the Earth (Animated Cartoon). With the voices of: Pat Harrington, Jr. , Ted Knight, Jane Webb (ABC 1968).

Journey to the Unknown. With guest performers: Patty Duke, Vera Miles, Michael Callen, Carol Lynley (ABC 1968).

King Kong (Animated Cartoon) (ABC 1966).

Land of the Giants. With: Gary Conway, Don Marshall, Heather Young, Deanna Lund (ABC 1968).

Land of the Lost. With: Wesley Eure, Kathy Coleman, Spencer Milligan (NBC 1974).

Lights Out. With: Frank Gallop (Host) (NBC 1949).

Lost in Space. With: Guy Williams, June Lockhart, Jonathan Harris, Angela Cartwright, Billy Mumy (CBS 1965).

Lost Saucer. With: Jim Nabors, Ruth Buzzi, Alice Playten (ABC 1975).

Men into Space. With: William Lundigan, Joyce Taylor (CBS 1959).

My Favorite Martian. With: Ray Walston, Bill Bixby, Pamela Britton (CBS 1963).

My Favorite Martians (Animated Cartoon). With the voices of: Jonathan Harris, Edward Morris, Jane Webb (CBS 1973).

The New, Original Wonder Woman. With: Lynda Carter, Lyle Waggoner (ABC 1976).

Night Gallery (Part of Four-in-One Series). With: Rod Serling (Host) (NBC 1970).

The Night Stalker (a. k. a. Kolchak: The Night Stalker). With: Darren McGavin, Simon Oakland (ABC 1974).

One Step Beyond. With: John Newland (Host) (Syndicated 1962).

Operation Neptune. With: Tod Griffin, Humphrey Davis, Margaret Stewart (NBC 1953).

Out There (CBS 1951).

The Outer Limits. With guest performers: Nancy Malone, Jacqueline Scott, Cliff Robertson, Nick Adams, Eddie Albert (ABC 1963).

Planet of the Apes. With: Roddy McDowall, Ron Harper, James Naughton (CBS 1974).

Planet Patrol (Marionette Adventure) (Syndicated 1963).

Prince Planet (Animated Cartoon) (Japanese; Syndicated 1963).

Quiet Please. With Ernest Chappell (Host) (ABC 1949).

Return to the Planet of the Apes (Animated Cartoon). With the voices of: Austen Stoker, Henry Corden, Edwin Miles (NBC 1975).

Rocky Jones, Space Ranger. With: Richard Crane, Sally Mansfield, Scott Beckett (Syndicated 1954).

Rod Brown of the Rocket Rangers. With: Cliff Robertson, Bruce Hall (CBS 1953).

Science Fiction Theatre. With: Truman Bradley (Host) (NBC 1955).

Shazam! (a. k. a. The Shazam! -Isis Hour). With: Michael Gray, Les Tremayne, Jackson Bostwick (CBS 1974).

Shazzan (Animated Cartoon). With the voices of: Barney Phillips, Janet Waldo, Jerry Dexter (CBS 1967).

The Six Million Dollar Man. With: Lee Majors, Richard Anderson (ABC 1973).

Scooby Doo, Where Are You? (Animated Cartoon). With the voices of: Don Messick, Frank Welker, Heather North (CBS 1971).

Space Angel (Animated Cartoon) (Syndicated 1959).

James Naughton, Ron Harper (bottom) and Roddy McDowall in <u>Planet of the Apes</u> (CBS-TV, 1974).

Space Ghost (Animated Cartoon). With the voices of: Gary Owens, Ginny Tyler, Johnny Carson (CBS 1966).

Space Giants (Japanese; Syndicated 1969).

Space Kidettes (Animated Cartoon). With the voices of: Chris Allen, Don Messick, Lucille Bliss, Jane Webb (NBC 1966).

Space: 1999. With: Barbara Bain, Martin Landau, Barry Morse (Syndicated 1975).

Space Patrol. With: Ed Kemmer, Lyn Osborn, Jack Narz, Virginia Hewitt (ABC 1950).

Spider-Man (Animated Cartoon). With the voices of: Bernard Cowan, Peg Dixon, Paul Sols (ABC 1967).

Star Trek. With: William Shatner, Leonard Nimoy, De Forest Kelly, Nichelle Nichols, Grace Lee Whitney, Majel Barrett, James Doohan (NBC 1966).

Star Trek (Animated Cartoon). With the voices of: William Shatner, Leonard Nimoy, Nichelle Nichols, James Doohan, Majel Barrett (NBC 1973).

The Starlost. With: Keir Dullea, Gay Rowin, Robin Ward (Canadian; Syndicated 1973).

Stingray (Marionette Adventure). With the voices of: David Graham, Sylvia Anderson, Ray Barrett (Syndicated 1965).

Strange Paradise. With: Colin Fox, Sylvia Feigel, Tudi Wiggins, Dawn Greenhalgh (Canadian; Syndicated 1969).

Superfriends (Animated Cartoon). With the voices of: Sherry Alberoni, Denny Clark, Casey Kaseem, Ted Knight (ABC 1973).

Thriller. With: Boris Karloff (Host) (NBC 1960).

Thriller. With guest performers: Linda Thorson, Polly Bergen, Barbara Feldon, Paul Burke (British; Shown in the United States via The ABC Wide World of Entertainment 1973).

Thunderbirds (Marionette Adventure). With the voices of: Sylvia Anderson, David Graham, Ray Barrett, Matt Zimmerman (Syndicated 1968).

The Time Tunnel. With: James Darren, Robert Colbert, Lee Meriwether, Whit Bissel (ABC 1966).

Tom Corbett, Space Cadet. With: Frankie Thomas, Jan Merlin, Al Markhim (NBC 1950).

DeForest Kelly, William Shatner and Leonard Nimoy in <u>Star Trek</u>
(NBC-TV, 1966).

The Twilight Zone.   With Rod Serling (Host) (CBS 1959).

U. F. O.   With: Ed Bishop, George Sewell, Gabrielle Drake, Michael
    Billington (British; Syndicated 1973).

Ultraman (Live-action Adventure; Japanese; Syndicated 1967).

Valley of the Dinosaurs (Animated Cartoon).   With the voices of:
    Melanie Baker, Shannon Farnon, Joan Gerber, Mike Road (CBS
    1974).

Voyage to the Bottom of the Sea.   With: Richard Basehart, David
    Hedison (ABC 1964).

Way Out.   With: Ronald Dahl (Host) (CBS 1961).

The World of Giants.   With: Marshall Thompson, Arthur Franz
    (Syndicated 1961).

Yuusha Raideen (The Brave Raideen) (Animated Cartoon.   Shown in
    Japanese with English sub-titles) (Syndicated 1975).

A SELECT BIBLIOGRAPHY OF SCIENCE FICTION BIBLIOGRAPHIES, INDEXES, AND CHECKLISTS

by Stephen Calvert

Barron, Neil. Anatomy of Wonder: Science Fiction: A Bibliographic Guide for Contemporary Collections. New York: Bowker, 1976. 290p.

Bleiler, Everett F. The Checklist of Fantastic Literature: A Bibliography of Fantasy, Weird and Science Fiction Books Published in the English Language. Reprint of 1968 ed., Naperville, Ill.: Fax, 1972. xvii, 455p. [new ed., rev. & enl. in preparation.]

Briney, Robert E., and Wood, Edward. SF Bibliographies: An Annotated Bibliography of Bibliographical Works on Science Fiction and Fantasy Fiction. Chicago: Advent, 1972. ix, 49p. [2d ed., rev. & enl., in preparation.]

Burger, Joanne. SF Published in [year]. Annual vol., 1968- . Available from the compiler, 55 Blue Bonnet Court, Lake Jackson, TX. 77566. paper.

Clareson, Thomas D. Science Fiction Criticism: An Annotated Checklist. Kent: Kent State University Press, 1972. x, 274p.

Clarke, Ignatius F. The Tale of the Future from the Beginning to the Present Day: An Annotated Bibliography.... 2d ed. London: Library Association, 1972; dist. by Gale Research, Detroit. 196p.

Cockroft, T. G. L. Index to the Weird Fiction Magazines. Reprint of 1962-1964 ed., New York: Arno, 1975. 2 vol. in 1.

Cole, Walter R. A Checklist of Science-Fiction Anthologies. Reprint of 1964 ed., New York: Arno, 1975. xvi, 374p.

Day, Bradford M. The Checklist of Fantastic Literature in Paperbound Books. Reprint of 1965 ed., New York: Arno, 1975. 128p.

_____. The Complete Checklist of Science-Fiction Magazines. Woodhaven, N.Y.: Science-Fiction & Fantasy Publications, 1961. 63p. paper.

_____. Index to the Science Fiction Magazines, 1926-1950. Portland, OR.: Perri Press, 1952. xv, 184p.

_____. The Supplemental Checklist of Fantastic Literature. Reprint of 1963 ed., New York: Arno, 1975. 155p.

Franson, Donald, and DeVore, Howard. A History of the Hugo, Nebula and International Fantasy Awards. 1975. Available from Howard DeVore, 4705 Weddel St., Dearborn, MI. 48125. paper.

Gove, Philip B. The Imaginary Voyage in Prose Fiction: A History of Its Criticism and a Guide for Its Study with an Annotated Check List of 215 Imaginary Voyages from 1700 to 1800. Reprint of 1941 ed., New York: Arno, 1975.

Hall, Holbert W. Science Fiction Book Review Index, 1923-1973. Detroit: Gale Research, 1975. xviii, 438p.

Halpern, Frank M. International Classified Directory of Dealers in Science Fiction and Fantasy Books and Related Materials. Philadelphia: Haddonfield House, 1974.

Index to British Science Fiction Magazines, 1934-53. Canberra: Australian Science Fiction Association, 1968. 3 vols. 9 [174] p. paper.

Lee, Walt. Reference Guide to Fantastic Films: Science Fiction, Fantasy, and Horror. Los Angeles: Chelsea-Lee Books, 1972-1974. 3 vols. (Vol. 1: A-F; vol. 2: G-O; vol. 3: P-Z). 559p. paper.

Lewis, Anthony R. Index to the Science Fiction Magazines, 1966-1970. Cambridge: New England Science Fiction Association, 1971. ix, 82p.

Locke, George. Voyage in Space: A Bibliography of Inter planetary Fiction, 1801-1914. Ferret Fantasy, 1975; dist. by Donald M. Grant.

McGhan, Barry. An Index to the Science Fiction Book Reviews in Astounding/Analog, 1949-69, Fantasy and Science Fiction, 1949-1969, Galaxy, 1950-1969. College Station, TX: Science Fiction Research Association, 1973; available from SFRA, Box 3186, College of Wooster, OH. 44691.

_____. Science Fiction and Fantasy Pseudonyms. Rev. ed., 1973. Available from Howard DeVore, 4705 Weddel St., Dearborn, MI. 48125. 34, 21p. paper.

Metcalf, Norman. The Index of Science Fiction Magazines, 1951-1965. El Cerrito, CA.: J. Ben Stark, 1968. xi, 253p. paper.

_____. The NESFA Index: Science Fiction and Original Antholo-

gies, 1971-1972. Cambridge: New England Science Fiction Association, 1973. 42p.

_____ . The NESFA Index to the Science Fiction Magazines and
Original Anthologies, 1973. Cambridge: New England Science
Fiction Association, 1974. 30p.

_____ . The NESFA Index to the Science Fiction Magazines, 1974.
Cambridge: New England Science Fiction Association, 1975.
[new annual eds. in preparation.]

Owings, Mark, and Chalker, Jack L. The Index to the Science-Fan-
tasy Publishers: A Bibliography of the Science Fiction and Fantasy Specialty Houses. Baltimore: Mirage, 1966. ix, 75p. paper.

Perkins, Shirley. Science Fiction: A Bibliography. Regina, Sask.:
Provincial Library, Bibliographic Services Division, 1973. 33p.

Pfeiffer, John R. Fantasy and Science Fiction: A Critical Guide.
Filter Press, 1971. 64p. cloth and paper.

Reginald, Robert. The Contemporary Science Fiction Authors. Rev.
reprint of Stella Nova: The Contemporary Science Fiction Authors, 1970. New York: Arno, 1975. [365]p.

_____ and Menville, Douglas. Science Fiction and Fantasy Literature: A Checklist, from Earliest Times to 1974, with Contemporary Science Fiction Authors II. Detroit: Gale Research,
1976.

Siemon, Frederick. Science Fiction Story Index, 1950-1968. Chicago:
American Library Association, 1971. x, 274p. paper.

Stone, Graham. Australian Science Fiction Index, 1925-1967. Canberra: Australian Science Fiction Association, 1968. vi, 158p.
paper.

Strauss, Erwin S. The MIT Science Fiction Society's Index to the
S-F Magazines, 1951-1965. Cambridge: MIT Science Fiction
Fiction Society, 1966. 207p.

Suvin, Darko. Russian Science Fiction Literature and Criticism,
1956-1970: A Bibliography. Toronto: Secondary Universe 4
Conference, 1971. 35p. paper [rev. ed. in preparation.]

Sween, Roger D. Fan Publishing Record: A Current Awareness
Listing of the Contents of Non-commercial Science Fiction and
Fantasy Publications. Available from the compiler, Box 408,
Platteville, WI. 53818.

Tuck, Donald H. The Encyclopedia of Science Fiction and Fantasy
through 1968. [3d ed.] Chicago: Advent, 1974- . 3 vols.
Vol. 1: Who's Who and Works, A-L. 1974. 298p. -Vol. 2:

Who's Who and Works, M-Z. [in preparation] - Vol. 3: Paper-
backs and Miscellaneous [in preparation]

Tymn, Marshall B. The Checklist of Fantastic Literature II, Naperville, IL.: Fax, 1976.

Versins, Pierre. Encyclopédie de l'Utopie, des Voyages Extraor-
dinaires, et de la Science Fiction. Lausanne: 1972.

Viggiano, Michael, and Franson, Donald. [Science Fiction] Title
Change Index. 2d ed., 1967. Available from National Fantasy
Fan Federation, Rte 1, Box 364, Heiskell, TN. 37754.

Whyte, Andrew A. Index to SF Books, 1974. Paratime Press, 1974.
42p.

Willis, Donald C. Horror and Science Fiction Films: A Checklist.
Metuchen, N.J.: Scarecrow, 1972. 612p.

ABOUT THE AUTHORS AND STAFF

JAMES ROBERT PARISH, New York-based freelance writer, was born in Cambridge, Massachusetts. He attended the University of Pennsylvania College and Law School. As president of Entertainment Copyright Research Co., Inc. he headed a major researching facility for the film and television industries. Later he was a film reviewer/interviewer for entertainment trade papers. He has been responsible for such reference volumes as The American Movies Reference Book: The Sound Era; The Emmy Awards: A Pictorial History; and Actors Television Credits. He has co-authored The MGM Stock Company, Vincent Price Unmasked, Hollywood Players: The Thirties, among others, and has authored such volumes as The RKO Gals and The Jeanette MacDonald Story. With Michael R. Pitts he prepared The Great Spy Pictures, The Great Gangster Pictures, Film Directors: A Guide to Their American Pictures, and The Great Western Pictures.

MICHAEL R. PITTS is an Indiana-based freelance writer who, with Mr. Parish, has written such books as The Great Spy Pictures, Film Directors: A Guide to Their American Films, The Great Gangster Pictures, and The Great Western Pictures. He is a graduate of Ball State University in Muncie, Indiana; he has a Bachelor of Science degree in history and a master of Arts degree in journalism. Formerly in public education and the newspaper field, Mr. Pitts currently is a researcher for the Madison County Council of Governments, a planning and advisory agency; editor of Anderson Newspapers' weekly Televisit tabloid; and is film reviewer for Channel 7 in Anderson, Indiana, where he resides with his wife Carolyn. Mr. Pitts has been published in cinema journals both here and abroad and is the author of two other entertainment-oriented books: Radio Soundtracks: A Reference Guide and Hollywood on Record: The Film Stars' Discography.

STEPHEN CALVERT attended Oberlin College, is a graduate of the University of Wisconsin-Madison, and is currently completing his master's degree at the Pratt Graduate School of Library & Information Science in New York City. He has been the head of the circulation department for the American Institute of Aeronautics and Astronautics, reference librarian for the Engineering Societies Library, assistant librarian for Computer Usage Education, assistant editor of IBID: International Bibliography, Information, Documentation, and

an assistant editor of Books in Print, Weekly Record, and American
Book Publishing Record.   Mr. Calvert is now a freelance editor/in-
dexer/bibliographer.

JOHN ROBERT COCCHI has been viewing and collating data on motion pictures since an early age.   He is now regarded as one of
America's most thorough film researchers.   He is the New York
editor of Boxoffice Magazine.   He was research associate on The
American Movies Reference Book: The Sound Era, The Paramount
Pretties, The Hollywood Dependables, The Best of MGM, and many
other books.   He has written cinema history articles for such jour-
nals as Film Fan Monthly and Screen Facts and is the author of The
Westerns: A Picture Quiz Book.   He is the co-founder of one of
Manhattan's leading film societies.

New York-born FLORENCE SOLOMON attended Hunter College and
then joined Ligon Johnson's copyright research office.   Later she
was appointed director of research at Entertainment Copyright Research Co., Inc. and is currently a reference supervisor at ASCAP's
Index Division in New York City.   Ms. Solomon has collaborated on
such works as TV Movies, Film Actors Guide: Western Europe and
The Indestructibles.   She is the niece of the noted sculptor, the late
Sir Jacob Epstein.

VINCENT TERRACE, a native New Yorker, is a graduate of the New
York Institute of Technology, possessing a Baccalaureate Degree in
Fine Arts.   He is author of The Complete Encyclopedia of Television
Programs: 1947-1976, and is completing volumes on Charlie Chan:
A Definitive Study and The Complete Encyclopedia of Radio Programs:
1920-1960.   He previously assisted Mr. Parish and Mr. Pitts with
media information on The Great Spy Pictures, The Great Gangster
Pictures, and The Great Western Pictures.